The Plural Self

The Plural Self

Multiplicity in Everyday Life

edited by
John Rowan and Mick Cooper

SAGE Publications
London • Thousand Oaks • New Delhi

First published 1999

SAGE Publications Ltd
6 Bonhill Street
London EC2A 4PU

SAGE Publications Inc
2455 Teller Road
Thousand Oaks, California 91320

SAGE Publications India Pvt Ltd
32, M-Block Market
Greater Kailash – I
New Delhi 110 048

British Library Cataloguing in Publication data

A catalogue record for this book is available from
the British Library

ISBN 0 7619 6075 9
ISBN 0 7619 6076 7 (pbk)

Library of Congress catalog record available

Typeset by Photoprint, Torquay, Devon
Printed in Great Britain by Athenaeum Press, Gateshead

CONTENTS

NOTES ON CONTRIBUTORS

John Altrocchi, Ph.D., is a Professor of Behavioral Sciences in the Department of Psychiatry and Behavioral Sciences, at the University of Nevada School of Medicine. In 1950, he was awarded a BA from Harvard University, and in 1957 a doctorate from the University of California, Berkeley. He is author of a textbook on abnormal psychology, and specializes clinically in couple therapy and dissociative identity disorders.

Steve R. Baumgardner received his doctorate in social psychology at Kansas State University and is now Professor of Psychology at the University of Wisconsin Eau Claire. He is co-author of a textbook in social psychology, author of *College and Jobs: Conversations with Recent Graduates*, and currently studying impacts of culture change on the self.

George D. Boone obtained his Ph.D. at Kansas State University in 1995, where he began empirical studies of polypsychism. He is currently assistant professor at Sul Ross State University, Rio Grande College, where he is helping to establish a new department of Psychology.

Mick Cooper is a senior lecturer in counselling at Brighton University and an existential psychotherapist and counsellor. His research interests include self-plurality, the psychology of masks, and men and masculinity. He is co-author of *The MANual: The Complete Man's Guide to Life* (Thorsons, 1996).

Helen Cruthers is a trainer for the Women's Refuge Project and an integrative arts psychotherapist in private practice. She specializes in the use of creative therapy techniques as a means of self-expression and self-exploration.

James S. Grotstein is Clinical Professor of Psychiatry at UCLA School of Medicine and Training and supervising analyst at The Los Angeles Psychoanalytic Society/Institute and The Psychoanalytic Center of California, LA. He is the author of *Splitting and Projective Identification* (1981), *Through the Unknown Remembered Gate* (in press), and *Psychic Presences* (in press). He has published over two hundred contributions to the literature. He is in private practice in West Los Angeles.

Ruth-Inge Heinze has been Research Associate at the Center for Southeast Asia Studies, University of California, Berkeley, since 1974. She began her studies at the University of Berlin (Germany, 1967) and received her BA in anthropology (1969) as well as her MA (1970) and her Ph.D. in Asian Studies (1974) from the University of California, Berkeley. She is the founder and National Director of Independent Scholars of Asia and on the board of other professional organizations. Having explored different states of consciousness and alternative modes of healing in Asia, Europe, and the USA for the last 39 years, she has published 4 books, edited or contributed to 18 other books and has contributed over 100 essays to professional journals.

Hubert J.M. Hermans is professor of personality psychology at the University of Nijmegen, the Netherlands. His early work was on achievement motivation and fear of failure. Partly as a reaction, he later developed a valuation theory, together with a self-confrontation method. He is the chairman of a Foundation which has developed national and international training programs for this theory and method. He is the first international associate of the Society for Personology.

Brian Lancaster is Principal Lecturer in Psychology at Liverpool John Moores University, where he leads postgraduate courses in Consciousness and Transpersonal Psychology. He is also Honorary Research Fellow in Manchester University's Centre for Jewish Studies. His interests include research into brain function and analysis of mystical literature. He is the author of the award-winning *Mind, Brain and Human Potential* and *Elements of Judaism*.

Alvin R. Mahrer, Ph.D., is Professor Emeritus, University of Ottawa, Canada, author of 11 books and approximately two hundred publications. Recipient of the 1997 American Psychological Association Division of Psychotherapy's Distinguished Psychologist Award, he is probably best known for his experiential psychotherapy, for the experiential conceptualization of personality, for his discovery-oriented approach to psychotherapy research, and for his alternative philosophical foundation of the field of psychotherapy.

Leon Rappoport completed doctoral work in personality-social psychology at the University of Colorado in 1963, and is Professor of psychology at Kansas State University. He is the author of *Personality Development: the Chronology of Experience*, and co-author with George Kren of *The Holocaust and the Crisis of Human Behavior*.

Colin A. Ross is a Past President of the International Society for the Study of Dissociation. He is the author of over a hundred peer-reviewed papers and a number of books including *The Osiris Complex: Case Studies in Multiple Personality Disorder* (1994) and *Dissociative Identity Disorder: Diagnosis, Clinical Features, and Treatment of Multiple Personality*, Second Edition (1997).

John Rowan is a Fellow of the British Psychological Society. He is the author of *Subpersonalities*, and has been researching, speaking, writing and leading workshops in that area since 1973. His book *The Transpersonal: Psychotherapy and Counselling* was the first general text to be published in the UK in that field. A psychotherapist (primal integration) in private practice, he also teaches at the Minster Centre, London.

Richard Schwartz, Ph.D., formerly an associate professor in the Department of Psychiatry at the University of Illinois College of Medicine, is now on the faculty of the Family Institute at Northwestern University. He has authored over forty articles and book chapters on a variety of topics related to psychotherapy and has authored or co-authored 5 books: *Internal Family Systems Therapy*; *Mosaic Mind: Empowering the Tormented Selves of Child Sexual Abuse Survivors*; *Family Therapy: Concepts and Methods*; *Metaframeworks: Transcending the Models of Family Therapy*; and *The Handbook of Family Therapy Training and Supervision*. He is on the editorial board of 5 professional journals.

John Shotter is a professor of interpersonal relations in the Department of Communication, University of New Hampshire. His long-term interest is in the social conditions conducive to people having a voice in the development of participatory democracies and civil societies. He is the author of *Images of Man in Psychological Research* (Methuen, 1975), *Human Action and Psychological Investigation* (with Alan Gauld, Routledge, 1977), *Social Accountability and Selfhood* (Blackwell, 1984), *Cultural Politics of Everyday Life: Social Constructionism, Rhetoric, and Knowing of the Third Kind* (Open University, 1993), and *Conversational Realities: the Construction of Life through Language* (Sage, 1993). He is also a co-editor with Kenneth J. Gergen and Sue Widdicombe of the series *Inquiries in Social Construction* (Sage). In 1997 he was an Overseas Fellow at Churchill College, Cambridge and a Visiting Professor at The Swedish Institute of Work Life Research, Stockholm, Sweden.

Mary Watkins, Ph.D., is the Chair of the Ph.D. Program in Depth Psychology and coordinator of community/ecological fieldwork projects at Pacifica Graduate Institute, Santa Barbara, California. She is the author of *Waking Dreams* and *Invisible Guests: The Development of Imaginal Dialogues*; co-author of *Talking With Young Children About Adoption*; co-editor of *Psychology and the Promotion of Peace*.

INTRODUCTION: SELF-PLURALITY – THE ONE AND THE MANY

Mick Cooper and John Rowan

The self is fragmented!

'Things fall apart; the centre cannot hold; Mere anarchy is loosed upon the world' – as Yeats (1921/1992, p. 76) prophesied, the late twentieth century has witnessed a mass sociocultural fragmentation. (Post)modern individuals no longer devote themselves to one job in one workplace but rush, blur-like, from office to study to other-office, to office to home; they no longer read one book, but hyperlink from website to website to home page, with just a few minutes in between to scroll through their e-mail. The postmodern woman is no longer a mother and a housewife, but a post-feminist mother-lover-friend-colleague-partner; and the postmodern man is no longer a husband and worker, but a post-new man father-friend-confidant-lover-lad. In some cases, even the he who is 'he' and the she who is 'she' begins to fragment. 'Gender-deviants' and 'trans-genderists' blur the very boundaries of what it means to be male or female. Everywhere, plurality and incon-sistency seems to transcend unity and consistency: multi-screened cinemas blare out a plurality of male and female icons, from Bruce Willis to Beavis and Butthead, Mia Farrow to Madonna; 'lifestyle' magazines bombard us with a multiplicity of contradictory injunctions – 'Be yourself!'/'Wear this!', 'Don't care what others think about you!'/'Get to the top!', 'Make the most of out of life!'/'Don't take things too seriously!', 'Just do it!'/'Just be!'. Even food fragments and multiplies: what was once a hamburger is now a multi-coloured, multi-layered 'Big Mac', 'Whopper', or 'Quarter Pounder'.

Good point

As the postmodern individual turns and turns to face the onslaughts of an ever-fragmenting social world, so the notion of a unified, monolithic self appears increasingly untenable. Within a modernist world, characterized by 'one man, one job' – along with such 'grand narratives' as linear develop-ment, progress, and the scientific search for truth – the notion of an auto-nomous, singular self moving towards its ownmost future seems deeply credible, to the point of being transparent. But in a world characterized by multi-fragmented social positionings and the deconstruction of absolute truths, the notion of a unified self begins to stand out like a relic from a bygone era.

In its stead, postmodern thinking has heralded the 'death of the subject': swallowed up by the 'blank and pitiless' forces of language games, dis-courses and texts. From this perspective, subjectivity is no longer the writer

self

but the written; no longer the signified but a signifier in a two-dimensional world of free-floating, interconnected signifiers. '[W]e no longer exist as play-wrights or actors but as terminals of multiple networks', writes Baudrillard (quoted in Gergen, 1991: 157). What began the century as master of its domain has thus been reduced to little more than a website in cyberspace, a momentary resting place for multiple narratives as they weave their way through the fabric of social relationships.

It is one thing, however, to deconstruct subjectivity from the rarefied atmosphere of an academic institution, quite another to encounter it face-to-face in the personalized intimacy of a therapeutic relationship. Here, one finds a subjectivity that is anything but dead: human beings racked by intense emotional anguish and pain; human beings floundering against the meaninglessness or hopelessness of their existence; human beings who cannot trivialize or annihilate them-selves however much they may wish for a submergence into a me-free world. And, indeed, it is often the very sense of self-fragmentation that is the most painful and 'real' of the difficulties that these human beings face. As Glass (1993) argues, the postmodern celebra-tion of 'subjectivity in slippage' displays a radical insensitivity to the feel-ings of abandonment, terror and implosion that can accompany such a process of personal fragmentation.

A major challenge for today's psychologists, psychotherapists and coun-sellors, therefore, is to find a way of embracing contemporary critical think-ing without losing the human being in the process: to find a path between a modernist monism and a postmodernism which, in its consistent refusal to think in such terms as 'subjectivity', 'origins', 'truth', and 'authenticity', is in danger of being as monist as the monism it critiques (Calinescu, 1991). In between these two monoliths, Calinescu proposes a path of 'authentic pluralism' – characterized by an openness towards multiple irreducible principles, multiple worlds, and dialogue – and it is along this road that a self-pluralistic perspective treads.

The essence of a self-pluralistic approach is the proposition that an individual can be conceptualized as a plurality of qualitatively distinct selves as well as a one: an interpenetrative, dialogical constellation of 'subselves' (Martindale, 1980; Shapiro, 1976), 'subpersonalities' (Assagioli, 1965; Rowan, 1990; Stone and Winkelman, 1989), 'ego states' (Berne, 1961; Watkins and Watkins, 1979–80), 'voices' (Hermans et al., 1993), 'parts' (Schwartz, 1995), 'roles' (Landy, 1993), 'alter egos' (Grotstein, 1997), 'potentials' (Mahrer, 1996), or 'selves' and 'others' (Shotter, 1997). In this respect, a self-pluralistic perspective moves on from modernism's unified self, but it does not go so far as to kill off that subjectivity entirely. Rather, it postulates an individual who encounters his or her world from a plurality of positions, through a plurality of voices, in relation to a plurality of self-concepts, yet who still retains a meaningful coherence, both at the level of the constituent pluralities and at the level of the total system. While a self-pluralistic perspective proposes, therefore, that a person may not always be one person, nor the same person from moment to moment, the individual is always seen as encountering their world in the mode of personhood, and these personhoods together are seen as forming a meaningful whole. In this respect, a self-pluralistic perspective acknowledges that the self may have fallen apart, that the centre may not have held, but it does not go so far as entirely to anarchize our view of the self. Rather, it sees the self as a meaningful, integrative and fundamentally *human* being woven into the fabric of a multi-dimensional universe.

Historically, the notion of self-plurality is by no means new. Plato (1988) spoke of three parts to the psyche, while early psychologists such as Janet (1889), James (1890/1981) and Prince (1906) all posited the existence of plural selves. What is new, however, is the degree of interest in self-plurality that has emerged over recent years – a 'pluralistic renaissance' (Calinescu, 1991). Since 1980, a pluralistic conception of the self has been proposed by psychotherapists (Capacchione, 1991; Ferruci, 1982; Grotstein, 1997; Landy, 1993; Mahrer, 1996; Rowan, 1990, 1993; Schwartz, 1995; Sliker, 1992; Stone and Winkelman, 1989; Watkins, 1990; Watkins and Watkins, 1979–80), cognitive psychologists (Martindale, 1980), neuropsychologists (Gazzaniga, 1985), social psychologists (Gergen, 1991; Hermans et al., 1993; Rosenberg and Gara, 1985), personality psychologists (Gregg, 1995; Lester, 1992), and humanistic psychologists (Larsen, 1990) – and these are but a few. The aim of this edited volume, then, is to bring together some of the key contemporary writers in this field for the first time, and to develop a greater understanding of the self from a pluralistic perspective.

As befits a book on self-pluralism, the chapters in this volume present a plurality of pluralistic perspective. There are chapters which advocate an intrapsychic model of self-plurality (e.g., Grotstein, Chapter 2; Lancaster, Chapter 7; Rowan, Chapter 1), those that advocate an experiential model (e.g., Cooper, Chapter 3; Mahrer, Chapter 12), and those that advocate an intersubjective model (e.g., Hermans, Chapter 6; Shotter, Chapter 4; Watkins, Chapter 14). There are chapters which tend towards associating self-plurality with maladjustment (e.g., Altrocchi, Chapter 9), those that tend towards associating it with adjustment (e.g., Rappoport, Baumgardner and Boone, Chapter 5), and those that associate it with both maladjustment and adjustment, depending on the type of self-plurality (e.g., Cooper, Chapter 3; Ross, Chapter 10). There are chapters which emphasize the universality of self-pluralism (e.g., Ross, Chapter 10), and those that emphasize individual differences (e.g., Altrocchi, Chapter 9). There are chapters which view self-plurality as a product of postmodernity (e.g., Rappoport et al., Chapter 5), and those that also view it as a product of modernity (e.g., Cooper, Chapter 3). There are chapters which emphasize the role of a 'centre' to coordinate the different selves (e.g., Schwartz, Chapter 13), and those that see the selves in a more leaderless light (for example, Lancaster, Chapter 7). There are chapters which view self-plurality on a continuum with dissociated identity disorder (formerly known as multiple personality disorder) (e.g., Altrocchi, Chapter 9; Grotstein, Chapter 2), and one chapter which very much challenges this viewpoint (Ross, Chapter 10). In accord with much self-pluralistic thinking, then, what is presented in this volume is neither a homogeneous monologue on self-plurality nor its definitive exposition, but a mosaic of interpenetrative arguments: an ongoing dialogue between constituent voices which together create an integrated whole.

The Plural Self is divided into three, entirely interrelated, parts: theory, research and practice. Part I, the theoretical part, begins with John Rowan's discussion of the primal development of subpersonalities (Chapter 1). Rowan proposes that the infant's initial state of 'OK-ness', a 'primordial paradise', is shattered through the experience of trauma and abuse. Faced with what feels like a very real threat of extinction, Rowan argues that the young infant defends itself by splitting – turning away from its original OK-self and putting in its place a 'not-OK-me' – a tactic which it then adopts again and again as a means of surviving potentially annihilating experiences.

Chapter 2, by James Grotstein, also looks at the development of self-plurality in the early stages of an individual's life: specifically the acquisition of an eerie, uncanny sense of having a 'second self' – a stranger, phantom, demon, doppelgänger or 'rogue subject' – within. Grotstein terms this the 'alter ego phenomenon': a mysterious double which surfaces in the denizens of our dreams, in imaginary friends, in therapeutic transference, in the phenomenon of déjà vu, and in such literary works as Stevenson's *The Strange Case of Dr Jekyll and Mr Hyde*, Conrad's *The Heart of Darkness*, and, of course, Dostoevsky's *The Double*. In contrast to Rowan, Grotstein describes the development of these second selves primarily in psycho-analytical terms, but argues that they are more than just internal 'objects'. Rather, as the internalization of an externality onto which the subject has projected their own *subjectivity*, he suggests that they are internal 'subjects': with an autonomy, volition and sense of 'I-ness' of their own; and with the potential to hound the projecting subject and 'demand repatriation'.

The strange case of Dr Jekyll and Mr Hyde once more surfaces in Mick Cooper's existential-phenomenological exploration of self-plurality (Chapter 3). In contrast to Rowan and Grotstein, Cooper moves away from an intrapsychic perspective and looks at the development of plural 'modes' of Being-in-the-world: each of which, he argues, is constellated around a particular concept of self. How the existent human being constructs a plurality of self-concepts is a central concern of Cooper's chapter. Among other ways, he suggests that the development of a rigid, narrow, restrictive self-concept – a self-concept which excludes much of the individual's actual lived-experiences – may necessitate the development of an alter self-concept to compensate. As the title of his chapter proposes: 'If you can't be Jekyll, be Hyde'.

Drawing on the work of Bakhtin and Volosinov, John Shotter (Chapter 4) takes this self-plurality one step further away from the 'psyche'. For Shotter, self-plurality does not emerge from the 'within' but from the 'between': the back-and-forth dialogue that unfolds in the meeting between two human freedoms and which precedes any internal 'mind'. In this respect, Shotter argues that the human being is not a Cartesian, self-contained unity, but one side of a two-sided act in which an other is always implicit – albeit invisibly. For Shotter, therefore, the internal, internalized world is not a monological voice, but a dialogical polyphony: a meeting of multiple voices and speech genres.

Instead of resorting to empirical research (with all its own taken-for-granted assumptions) Shotter suggests that poetic methods are needed if we are to study this area successfully. It is not so much a question of studying people from the outside, but rather of entering into their lives in a human way. We have to do justice to the way in which we encounter each other through dialogue and interaction, not as separate divisible entities, but as co-constituing that dialogue, that interaction. It is an activity which is distributed between us; it is joint action. And Shotter goes on further, to argue that it is partly the context which constitutes the interaction – it is not even just the parties involved. We are what we are inside a world, and that world also co-constitutes us. No wonder we are complex and multi-voiced. We are called forth by our actions and our interactions.

Like Shotter (Chapter 4), Rappoport, Baumgardner and Boone (Chapter 5) adopt a distinctly postmodern perspective. In contrast to previous authors, however, they locate the development of self-plurality within a specific socio-historical context. Rappoport and his colleagues argue that a pluralistic sense of self is all but a requirement of a postmodern society: first, because rapid social change necessitates a readiness to access alternate views of the self (what the authors refer to as 'adaptive pluralism'); second, because 'leading edge' academic thinking – from philosophy to physics – increasingly encourages pluralistic epistemologies; and third, because, in a culture where Madonna and Michael Jackson reinvent their identities as swiftly as Bill Clinton and Tony Blair reinvent their politics, transformation, flux and plurality have become the celebrated values of our time. In this respect, the portrait of the pluralist postmodern individual that Rappoport and colleagues paint has little of the Jekyll and Hyde qualities suggested by Grotstein and Cooper. Rather, he or she has 'the multiple, flowing qualities of early Picasso cubism', with an ability to tolerate complexity and uncertainty and a taste for diversity in living.

Rappoport and his colleagues also question the whole idea of being finally right about how exactly the divided self is divided. Not only is there multiplicity in the personality, there is also multiplicity in the ways of conceiving this multiplicity. For example, it was all right in modern discourse to talk about serial pluralism – the way in which people could move through different apparent personalities as they moved through life. People could be changed by age, by the influence of other cultures, by shattering life experiences, by marriage and so forth. But in postmodern discourse we can also talk about simultaneous pluralism – the way in which a person can maintain a dynamic portfolio of alternative self concepts as they move through the world. It is quite common to talk about different periods in the work of a writer or painter, where quite different styles can be seen (although it has to be said that personality theorists and researchers are the worst offenders in not doing justice even to that), but we are now going further and saying that at any given time there are several co-existing modes of experience and behaviour which are often compatible, but sometimes not even that.

Part II of this book explores self-plurality from a more empirical stand-point. In Chapter 6, Hubert Hermans presents an experimental investigation of the polyphonic, Bakhtinian self. To demonstrate the existence of multiple, relatively autonomous 'I' positions, Hermans invited participants to 'valu-ate' them-selves both from their familiar position and from the position of their imaginal other. His idiographic findings illustrate the way in which an individual can develop multiple self-narratives, and demonstrates the differ-ence between a functional and dysfunctional orchestration of a multi-voiced self.

Like Cooper, Brian Lancaster (Chapter 7) explores the paradox of a plurality that experiences itself as a unity. Lancaster asks the question as to what sort of a brain we would have to have to make this plurality possible. After all, if the brain is such that it can only operate as a whole, the idea of multiplicity in the psyche would have to be rejected as pure fiction. However, through a review of the research in brain functioning, what he finds is that the brain is arranged in such a way that such a multiplicity is not only possible, it is perhaps inevitable. He also suggests, in his notion of the 'I-tag', the exact way in which this idea could make sense.

In Chapter 8, Ruth-Inge Heinze uses her 39 years of cross-cultural fieldwork – primarily in South-east Asia – to question the modernist, occidental assumption of a unified self. Through case-examples of spirit mediumship, glossolalia, channelling, automatic writing, possession trances, and dramatic performance, she demonstrates that the self-plurality which still tends to be considered abnormal and pathological in Western cultures may be considered quite acceptable – and frequently valuable – in other cultural contexts.

John Altrocchi (Chapter 9) significantly develops the debate on self-plurality by arguing that some individuals may have a more plural concept of self than others. To demonstrate these individual differences, Altrocchi's chapter presents findings from the administration of a self-pluralism scale, along with findings from the administration of related, individual difference measures: self-complexity, self-concept differentiation, and self-concept clarity. To complicate matters further, Altrocchi goes on to suggest that an individual's degree of self-plurality may vary over time, such that we can neither say that individuals have a unified self-concept, nor that they have a plural self-concept, nor that some individuals have a unified self-concept and some a plural self-concept; we can say only that some people have a plural conception of self some of the time.

This research part of *The Plural Self* concludes with an intriguing and challenging chapter by Colin Ross (Chapter 10), one of the world's leading psychiatric authorities on dissociated identity disorder (formerly known as multiple personality disorder). Since the time of Janet, writers on self-plurality have tended to assume the existence of a 'dissociation continuum', with clinically diagnosed dissociative identity disorder at one extreme and everyday multiplicity at the other. Ross, however, fundamentally challenges this assumption by presenting research evidence which suggests a clear, qualitative distinction between the clinical and everyday forms of self-plurality. Just as you cannot be a little pregnant, argues Ross, so you cannot have a little bit of dissociative identity disorder. Furthermore, Ross argues that individuals with dissociated identity disorder are no more – or no less – self-pluralistic than anyone else. To resolve the many intriguing paradoxes in his chapter, Ross proposes a reconfigured continuum with 'normal polypsychism' at one end, 'psychiatric polypsychism' at the other, and a state of 'abnormal polypsychism' in the middle – or what Ross refers to as the statistically 'normal' state of 'pathological pseudounity'.

The final part of the book, Part III, examines clinical and non-clinical applications of self-pluralistic thinking. Chapter 11, by Mick Cooper and Helen Cruthers, presents a detailed review of the numerous descriptive, projective and experiential techniques that can be used to facilitate the expression of subpersonalities: e.g. the evening review, the 'Who am I?' exercise, guided visualizations, sand-play, chair-work and written dialogues. The authors illustrate each of these techniques with clinical case-examples and go on to discuss the underlying psychological principles on which these techniques are based.

In contrast, Al Mahrer (Chapter 12) focuses on one very specific and very intense means of accessing the 'deeper potentials for experiencing'. Mahrer calls this precious doorway down into the unknown inner world the 'instant of peak feeling' in 'the scene of strong feeling': that tiny moment, perhaps only a second or two, when the individual experiences an intensely powerful sense of sheer unbounded energy, force, and spontaneous excitement. Using case-examples, Mahrer describes how clients can be helped to penetrate down through these instances of peak feelings, such that they can discover their deepest and most powerful potentialities for experiencing.

While Cooper and Cruthers (Chapter 11) and Mahrer (Chapter 12) focus on specific techniques, Richard Schwartz (Chapter 13) offers a more integrative perspective on working psychotherapeutically with subpersonalities. Coming from a family therapy background, Schwartz's 'internal family systems model' applies systemic thinking to the client's inner world: tracking the interrelationships between different parts, emphasizing the importance of clear boundaries and direct communication, and acknowledging that 'good' parts may end up in 'bad' or extreme roles. Schwartz discusses the application of family therapy techniques to this internal system, and goes on to look at the means by which a therapist can help their clients to identify the 'Self' – an untarnished, accepting, compassionate core – a part of the person which can lead the client's own process of self-healing.

The final chapter of *The Plural Self*, by Mary Watkins (Chapter 14), completes the journey from intra-psyche to inter-psyche. For Watkins, the development of a tolerant, empathetic, constructive dialogue between the imaginal figures of the inner world cannot take place without an equivalent development in the interpersonal world of political and pedagogical dialogues. Where there is prejudice between persons, she argues, so the internal world will be characterized by prejudicial relationships. Equally, where there is autocracy and a silencing of alternative voices in the external world, so the internal world will be characterized by the dominance of one voice over others. With this in mind, Watkins discusses recent attempts at enhancing interpersonal and social dialogue – for example, Freire's work on the voicing of the oppressed – and examines the intrapersonal implications of this work.

Despite the plurality of perspectives in this book, Watkins's chapter highlights an essential thread that runs through each of these contributions: the importance of dialogue, both 'within' the person and between persons. Through open and fluid communication, selves can come to know each other, come to understand each other, and come to work together without sacrificing their individual boundaries. In this respect, all of the contributors – each in a different way – make the point that the functionality of self-plurality is fundamentally related to the level of dialogue between the different selves. Where there is a lack of communication, where selves disown each other or where one self dominates to the exclusion of all others, then the result tends toward a cacophony of monologues – a discordant wail which will always be less than the sum of the individual parts. But where selves talk to selves, where there is an acceptance and understanding between the different voices and an appreciation of diversity and difference, then there is the potential for working together and co-operation – an interwoven harmony of voices which may transcend the sum of the parts alone.

References

Assagioli, R. (1965) *Psychosynthesis: A Manual of Principles and Techniques.* London: Aquarian/Thorsons.

Beahrs, J.O. (1982) *Unity and Multiplicity.* New York: Brunner/Mazel.

Berne, E. (1961) *Transactional Analysis in Psychotherapy.* New York: Grove Press.

Calinescu, M. (1991) 'From the one to the many: pluralism in today's thought', in I. Hoesterey (ed.), *Zeitgeist in Babel: The Postmodern Controversy.* Indianapolis: Indiana University Press.

Capacchione, L. (1991) *Recovery of your Inner Child.* London: Simon and Schuster.

Ferrucci, P. (1982) *What We May Be.* London: Aquarian.

Gazzaniga, M. (1985) *The Social Brain.* New York: Basic Books.

Gergen, K.J. (1991) *The Saturated Self: Dilemmas of Identity in Contemporary Life.* London: Basic Books.

Glass, J.M. (1993) *Shattered Selves: Multiple Personality in a Postmodern World.* London: Cornell University Press.

Gregg, G.S. (1995) 'Multiple identities and the integration of personality', *Journal of Personality*, 63 (3): 617–41.

Grotstein (1997) ' "Internal objects" or "chimerical monsters?": the demonic "third forms" of the internal world', *The Journal of Analytical Psychology*, 42: 47–80.

Hermans, H.J.M., Rijks, T.I. and Kempen, H.J.G. (1993) 'Imaginal dialogues in the self: theory and method', *Journal of Personality*, 61 (2): 207–36.

James, W. (1890/1981) *The Principles of Psychology*. London: Harvard University Press.

Janet, P. (1889) *L'Automatisme Psychologique*. Paris: Alcan.

Landy, R. (1993) *Persona and Performance*. London: Jessica Kingsley Publishers.

Larsen, S. (1990) 'Our inner cast of characters', *Humanistic Psychologist*, 18 (2): 176–87.

Lester, D. (1992) 'The disunity of self', *Personality and Individual Differences*, 13 (8): 947–8.

Mahrer, A.R. (1996) *The Complete Guide to Experiential Psychotherapy*. New York: Wiley.

Martindale, C. (1980) 'Subselves: the internal representations of situational and personal dispositions', in L. Wheeler (ed.), *Review of Personality and Social Psychology*, vol. 1. Beverly Hills, CA: Sage.

Ornstein, R. (1986) *MultiMinds*. Boston, MA: Houghton Mifflin.

Plato (1988) *Phaedrus*. Warminster: Aris and Phillips.

Prince, M. (1906) *The Dissociation of a Personality*. London: Longman's Green and Co.

Rosenberg, S. and Gara, M.A. (1985) 'The multiplicity of personal identity', in P. Shaver (ed.), *Self, Situations, and Social Behaviour: Review of Personality and Social Psychology*, vol. 6. Beverly Hills, CA: Sage.

Rowan, J. (1990) *Subpersonalities: The People Inside Us*. London: Routledge.

Rowan, J. (1993) *Discover your Subpersonalities*. London: Routledge.

Ryle, A. (1990) *Cognitive-analytic Therapy*. Chichester: John Wiley.

Schwartz, R. (1995) *The Internal Family Systems Therapy*. New York: Guilford.

Shapiro, S.B. (1976) *The Selves Inside You*. Berkeley, CA: Explorations Institute.

Shotter, J. (1997) 'Dialogical realities: the ordinary, the everyday, and other strange new worlds', *Journal for the Theory of Social Behaviour*, 27: 345–57.

Sliker, G. (1992) *Multiple Mind*. Boston: Shambhala.

Stewart, I. and Joines, V. (1987) *TA Today: A New Introduction to Transactional Analysis*. Nottingham: Lifespace Publishing.

Stone, H. and Winkelman, S. (1989) *Embracing Ourselves: The Voice Dialogue Manual*. Mill Valley, CA: Nataraj Publishing.

Watkins, J.G. and Watkins, H.H. (1979–80) 'Ego states and hidden observers', *Journal of Altered States of Consciousness*, 5 (1): 3–18.

Watkins, M. (1990) *Invisible Guests*. Boston, MA: Sigo Press.

Yeats, W.B. (1921/1992) *Selected Poems*. London: Bloomsbury Poetry Classics.

PART I

THEORY

1 THE NORMAL DEVELOPMENT OF SUBPERSONALITIES

John Rowan

In my previous work (Rowan 1990) it became clear that there are such things as subpersonalities. They are to be found as one of the positions on a continuum of dissociation:

ASCs > moods > subpersonalities > possession > multiple personality

At one end of this continuum (Beahrs, 1982) we have altered states of consciousness (ASCs) such as dreams, drunken states, drugged states, hypnagogic states, hypnotic states and so forth, which are quite transient and wear off quite predictably. Quite close to these we find moods, defined as states of mind which we cannot shake off at will, but which go away quite unpredictably after a while. Then come subpersonalities – defined as *semi-permanent and semi-autonomous regions of the personality capable of acting as a person* – some of which seem to be universal and which again are quite normal. Then comes possession, defined (Crabtree, 1988) as states of mind where we seem to be taken over by another person or other being, voluntarily or involuntarily. In the final position on the continuum is multiple personality, where one person inside us does not know anything about at least one person, who is leading quite a different life and who takes over quite unpredictably, causing a real psychiatric problem. (See Chapter 10 by Colin Ross, this volume.)

The left-hand end of this continuum is quite normal and everyday; the right-hand end is more of a psychiatric problem, which may be quite hard to treat and which has been recounted in books such as *The Three Faces of Eve*, *Sybil*, *The Minds of Billy Milligan*, *When Rabbit Howls*, and so on.

Subpersonalities, which are mostly quite normal, can at times become a problem, and this is most likely to occur when we hotly deny that we have any such thing. Repression, splitting and denial are likely to cause trouble. Subpersonalities have to be taken at times as solid characters, but they are really in process and may split into two, merge into one, appear or disappear.

There are twenty-five (at least) synonyms for subpersonalities, such as ego states, subselves, subidentities, identity states, alter-personalities, deeper potentials and so on. They are common in everyday life and are often mentioned in literature and the media generally. It is important to emphasize that there is not just one origin for subpersonalities. There are at least six: roles, internal conflicts, fantasy images, the personal unconscious, the cultural unconscious, and the collective unconscious.

Roles   Different roles bring out different subpersonalities, as William James urged long ago; so do different social frames, as Erving Goffman (1974) has outlined. Even children can play different roles at home and at school, for example. McCall and Simmons (1966), in the field of sociology, show how role-identities can cluster into sub-patterns and that 'these clusters may themselves be linked more or less closely with other clusters or may be quite rigidly "compartmentalized" or dissociated from others.' Certain roles are notorious for the creation of subpersonalities: mother, teacher and social worker are examples.

Internal conflicts   Two or more sides arguing within us ('on the one hand I want to – but on the other hand . . .') may become repetitive enough, frequent enough and vivid enough to require an identity each before they can be worked out. Gestalt therapy and psychodrama are full of this. Also under this heading come those times when our bodies, or parts of our bodies, seem to act as if they were our antagonists. They, too, can be regarded as subpersonalities with motives of their own. Mahrer (1989) has a very full discussion of this sort of thing, emphasizing the positive or negative relationships between the subpersonalities.

Fantasy images   We may identify with a hero or heroine, or with an admired group, and take on their characteristics. Orrin Klapp (1969) has an excellent discussion of how celebrities are used in a search for identity. These fantasy images may come from the past, as well as from the present. John Watkins (1978) has shown how the psychotherapist can deliberately set up within him or herself a fantasy image of the client, so as to be better able to tune in to the client. Alvin Mahrer (1989) suggests something similar. Actors of the 'method' school work in this way. It is easy to see how therapists could create fresh subpersonalities, and this would be a good example of an iatrogenic affliction. Therapists, beware of suggestion!

The personal unconscious   The complexes described by Jung can be worked with through the Jungian technique of 'active imagination', as has been well described by Robert Johnson (1986). The internal objects of the object relations school can come out as subpersonalities, though this is very rarely taken seriously by psychoanalysts. On the other hand, the ego states described in Transactional Analysis (Clarkson 1992) as 'Parent', 'Adult' and 'Child' are very frequently used and referred to. Fritz Perls (1969) introduced the idea of splits within the person, and the use of the empty chair to work with such entities. The 'voice dialogue' approach of Stone and Winkelman (1985) has taken this further. All these seem to derive from early experiences in the family and, as Grof (1992), Lake (1980) and Laing (1982) have pointed out, some of the traumas which can lead to the violent defence of splitting can happen at or before birth. Janov and Holden (1977) have tried to give a theoretical account of this linked to physiology.

The cultural unconscious This is where the patripsych comes from – what Southgate and Randall (1989) have described as the 'internal constellation of patriarchal patterns'. This is similar to what Claude Steiner and his co-workers (1975) have called the 'Pig Parent' – an internalized form of cultural oppression. It is the self-hater – the voice of domination within us that says hierarchy is the only right way of organizing and patriarchy the truest form of hierarchy (Starhawk, 1982).

The collective unconscious If Jung is right, this is where the archetypes come from, and the Shadow often seems to emerge as one of the subpersonalities. Anima figures are also quite common. So it seems that we should allow this as one of the sources. Another important group who have worked in this area have been the practitioners of psychosynthesis, from whom I first heard of the idea of subpersonalities. There is much more on this in my book on the transpersonal (Rowan, 1993).

In this chapter I propose to look at only one of these origins of subpersonalities: the personal unconscious. This is the unconscious as formed through our biographical experiences. In discussing this particular source, it seems useful to look at it developmentally. There is a theory of child development, which has been put together by those working with very early experience, that seems to make sense of a number of puzzling phenomena. Some of the material which follows is along the same lines as my earlier text on subpersonalities (Rowan, 1990), but the emphasis there was on psychotherapy and the part it can play, whereas here there is a much more technical emphasis on the process itself. Let us start, then, at the beginning.

Stage 1

At this stage the person is, and feels, OK. (I use the term 'OK' to mean 'without negative qualities'; thus it does not mean 'good', it is just that there is nothing negative to be said about it.) It seems quite possible to regard this stage as a myth, in the sense of an unverifiable story which somehow makes sense of things. In other words, some people may have an actual state like this which they can get back to in their experience of this life, but others may not – they may have to go back further, into previous lives (Netherton and Schiffrin, 1979; Woolger, 1990) or into the great archetypes of the human race (Jung, 1968), before they can find anything as positive as this.

The essential thing is that this is a state before trauma. Somehow we all seem to have memories of such a state, and the sense of it has regularly been projected in the form of myths of a Golden Age, the Garden of Eden, the Primordial Paradise, and so on (Neumann, 1973). I only postulate it because none of the rest seems to make sense unless we do start here.

At this stage there is nothing wrong. Whatever is needed is given, without the need to ask. The self is OK, and the world is OK, and there is no need to differentiate between the two. The world understands me in a very intimate way, so that I do not need to be able to communicate my needs. Freud (1991: 466) calls this a state of 'total narcissism'. It is peaceful and quiet (who ever heard of a noisy Utopia?) and when I do become aware of lights or sounds, they are filtered and muffled before they get to me. There is one sound which may become symbolic of this whole state of being – my mother's heartbeat (Verny, 1982). My body is relaxed and energy can easily flow in and flow out again. Energy is not trapped – I am open to the world (Boadella, 1987). But this also indicates that I have no protection against harsh events which may occur. I assume that I am free, and even perhaps omnipotent (Fenichel, 1945). I am totally identified with myself. I am whole. This stage may be very far back, because the foetus is a very active creature; and for some people, apparently, their first trauma was implantation (Laing, 1976, 1982) or even conception (Peerbolte, 1975).

It is important to see even this very early form of being as rational. Development is not just a question of energy flow; it is also a question of levels of rationality. At this level, rationality is trapped in a kind of naive subjectivity which is all-pervasive and very open to the subjectivity of others (Hegel, 1971: 20). I am totally in touch with my own body and my own feelings.

But we now go on to a second phase within the primary level (first stage). Hegel says that there is a very important *feeling* phase here too; and this feeling phase is all about experiencing things *directly*, without any kind of mediation or interpretation. This we do in relation to our internal states: my own feeling of pain, rage or fear is not something I have to infer or judge, and my bodily reactions of screaming or pounding or shaking are not events which I have to construct or interpret. Hegel actually calls this a *magical* relationship: 'the magic which is devoid of any mediation whatever is that which the individual mind exercises over its own bodily nature' (1971: 97). We do not have to work out how to lift our arm – we just do it. And this direct knowledge is not only magical in this sense – it is also extremely accurate. A baby is in no doubt as to whether it feels miserable or not, and in no doubt about how to scream if it does – and it is *right* about these things.

This, by the way, is the answer to those writers and researchers who say that emotions like anger are mediated by cognitive factors. A baby does not have anything like the same cognitive apparatus which is conferred later by entry into the symbolic world and through the acquisition of language; but anyone who says that babies cannot be angry has little acquaintance with babies. And it is not just anger: Bradley (1989) says babies have a 'basic propensity for misery' which shows itself as early as the first three months of life. For more light on these points, see the massive volume edited by Fedor-Freyburgh and Vogel (1988).

Ken Wilber (1980) calls the first phase in this first stage the 'Pleroma stage', and points out how important it is not to confuse it with the later, more developed, stages. It is possible to confuse it with mystical states described in religious literature as have many people, including Freud (1985: 259–60), Rank (1929), and others. Such lack of distinction Wilber (1983) calls the 'Pre/Trans Fallacy', because it confuses what is pre-personal with what is transpersonal.

There have been some attempts in recent years to challenge this account, on the grounds that the early life of infants is not like that. Daniel Stern, in particular, has been influential in putting forward the view that there is no symbiosis and no confusion of baby with mother (Stern, 1985) and others, for example Firman and Gila (1997), have taken up this idea very firmly. But they are all talking about life after birth whereas I am talking about prenatal life, for the most part. So is Grof, when he says of the pre-birth period: 'It is an "oceanic" state without any boundaries between ourselves and the maternal organism or ourselves and the external world.' (Grof, 1992: 38). This comes from someone who has studied and researched this period perhaps more than anyone else in the world.

Stage 2

At some point – maybe pre-birth, maybe during birth, maybe some while after birth – an event happens which indicates that I am not in control of my world. My assumption of freedom – and perhaps of omnipotence – is contradicted, and my total identification with myself is split (see Freud, 1938; Klein, 1948; Winnicott, 1965; Balint, 1968; Janov, 1970; Grof, 1975; Lake, 1980; Moss, 1987; Beahrs, 1982; Levine, 1997).

What is meant, exactly, by splitting? It has been studied at great length by the Kleinian school, who are very good in the field of the pre-Oedipal consciousness. We all know, and probably accept, that the very young baby splits things into good and bad. What we often do not accept or understand is that, as Melanie Klein says, 'the ego is incapable of splitting the object without a corresponding splitting taking place within the ego' (Klein, 1948: 6). The clearest account I have seen of this comes from Donald Winnicott whose diagram (1975: 224) shows the way in which – given a sufficiently traumatic experience – the ego can split into a false self, built on a compliance basis, and a secret inner life, which he later calls the true self. He says that after a trauma where splitting takes place:

> The infant gets seduced into compliance, and a compliant False Self reacts to environmental demands and the infant seems to accept them . . . The False Self

has one positive and very important function: to hide the True Self, which it does by compliance with environmental demands.

So the split is a defence against the annihilation of the experiencing subject. We shall encounter this extreme word – annihilation – again and again in this area; each time it appears it reminds us that we are dealing here with matters which have all the appearance of life and death to the experiencing subject.

Trauma

The event which happens must be one which produces panic. I seem to be invaded by some aggressive force. It could, objectively, be said that I am being abused. But the way I take it – whether as foetus, neonate, infant or child – generally seems to amount to a belief that I am wrong, and am being punished. How could I be hurt if I were perfect? But I am being hurt. Therefore, I am not perfect. In a state of panic, I resort to some kind of defensive tactic. At this stage I have no resources for dealing with trauma. As Levine (1997: 48–50) has said, the effects of a traumatic experience depend on:

- The event itself;
- The context of a person's life at the time of the traumatising event;
- Physical characteristics of the individual;
- A person's learned capabilities; and
- The individual's experienced sense of his or her capacity to meet danger.

At a sufficiently early age, all of these aspects are problematic. I cannot cobble together any complicated defence. It seems as if I am faced with extinction, annihilation. Firman and Gila (1997) put it even more strongly: it may seem to me, they say, that I am faced with the loss of my Self, and this means ceasing to exist altogether. In desperation, I split into two. I turn my back on my original OK self, and put in its place a self which has lost the notion of being perfect and whole. So now there is an OK-me (distanced and disowned) and a not-OK-me (fostered and put forward as the answer to the insult). This is the basic split; and, of course, splitting is a much more drastic defence than repression (Guntrip, 1961, 1977; Grotstein, 1981).

> The fundamental schizoid phenomenon is the presence of splits in the ego; and it would take a bold man to claim that his ego was so perfectly integrated as to be incapable of revealing any evidence of splitting at the deepest levels, or that such evidence of splitting of the ego would in no circumstances declare itself at more superficial levels, even under conditions of extreme suffering or hardship or deprivation. (Fairbairn, 1952: 8)

But Firman and Gila make it clear that it is not so much a split in the ego as a split between the 'non-OK' ego and the Self; 'And this disruption is, of course, the primal wound' (1997: 48). This contribution by Firman and Gila seems to me to be extremely important and to throw a new and highly relevant light on this whole phenomenon of the primal split. What exactly do they mean by the Self? Words like this are notoriously difficult to use, but it seems to me that Ken Wilber provides a useful framework for discussing this question.

The Self

Wilber (1980) states that the notion of the self changes at various stages in psychospiritual development. After going through a number of developmental phases, the person normally arrives at the stage Wilber labels as the 'Mental Ego'. This is the normal definition of the self we use in our culture. At this stage we see ourselves as people capable of playing various social roles more or less successfully; and as being capable of handling language, logic, mathematics and so on. The next stage we may reach in our development (I say may reach because there is nothing inevitable about this, and the evidence from people like Kohlberg [1984] and Loevinger [1976] is that only a minority do so) Wilber calls the 'Centaur'. This represents a version of the self which has been variously labelled as the existential self (Spinelli, 1989), the actualized self (Maslow 1987), the fully functioning person (Rogers, 1961), the self as opposed to the self-image (Perls 1969), the 'I' as opposed to the subpersonalities on the one hand and the higher self on the other (Assagioli, 1975), the real self (Sartre, 1950), the real or true self (Laing, 1965), and so on. In all these cases this is contrasted with a false or unreal self of some kind, of which terms such as 'persona', 'imaginary self', 'public relations self' or 'guiding fiction' are used.

If we then continue on our psychospiritual way, says Wilber, we take on a new version of the self again, which he calls the 'Psychic/Subtle'. I join these two in this way because in some of his writings he separates them, but in others he combines them. My own preference is to merge them and to call this whole level the subtle, mainly because the word psychic arouses so many irrelevant and even misleading associations. The subtle self is what Assagioli (1975) calls the higher self, what Hillman (1989) calls the soul, what Whitmont (1987) calls the guidance self, what Starhawk (1982) calls the deep self, and what I have called the transpersonal self (Rowan, 1993). This is a self which questions the boundaries between me and others, and has a much more ecological sense of the world. It is essentially multiple and polytheistic in its orientation, and it glories in symbols and images, ritual and romance. It is very happy to entertain such notions as the collective unconscious. Jung was very much at home with this level and actually did not want to go any further (Coward, 1985).

If we then continue on the path, we arrive at the causal self. This again is quite different and new. It is very much oriented towards the One, and has abandoned all need for symbols and images. We are now in the deep water of spirituality, of mysticism; we are in the territory of Western mystics like Meister Eckhart (Blakney, 1941) and Eastern mystics like Sri Ramana

Maharshi (Ramana, 1972), as Wilber (1995) has explained at length. This is a state of consciousness which is generally only reached by meditative or contemplative practices, but when we do that the results do seem to be strikingly uniform, no matter where in the world we live.

If we continue still further on our psychospiritual path, we come to the most paradoxical stage of all – one which Wilber (1995) calls the 'Nondual' – where there is really no self at all, merely a state sometimes labelled inadequately as the 'Void'. If we now go back to our starting point – the split which can often take place in the human mind – we can picture the situation as a series of concentric circles. Inside the real self, now split off from the false self, there is the subtle self; inside that the causal self; and inside that the nondual. When Firman and Gila talk about the self, then, it is either the subtle or the causal self they are talking about. Since they do not make that distinction, it does not matter to them which it is and so need not matter to us. Either way, it connects us with the divine, the mystical.

It is one of the most disappointing features of our conventional culture, located for the most part at the level of the mental ego, that it always thinks of mysticism as something vague and uncertain. But since about 1979 there has been a proliferation of map-making in this area, such that it is now crystal clear that mysticism is simply the way of working favoured by people who want to experience the divine for themselves, rather than getting it from books or teachers. John Bradshaw has also argued that it is the loss of the true inner self that is the real trauma, which has endless results throughout life (Bradshaw, 1988b). Thus we have here not only a psychological wound, but also a spiritual one. The stakes are higher than we thought.

Let us get back to our story.

Birth as trauma

The non-OK-me, in order to repair itself and feel better about itself, may instantly adopt something salient from the invading and punishing entity, and incorporate it. After all, that is where the power is, and power is what the non-OK-me needs or lacks. So we often get identification with the aggressor. We also get guilt (Freud, 1985: 325) and toxic shame (Bradshaw, 1988a), all based upon this basic split. It is sometimes objected, in relation to this account, that something as early as the birth trauma cannot possibly be remembered, never mind events even earlier. The answer to this was discovered a long time ago, and stated quite clearly by Fodor (1949), who says:

> [When the patient relives the shock of birth, he] invariably apologises and assures the analyst that he was not making up a story. This is the very reaction we should expect. At his birth emotions have never been verbalised, in putting them into words the patient is making up a story. It is a true story, in spite of the fact that it is not based on memories registered by consciousness but rests on organismic

impressions. The imprints of the latter may be just as real and vivid as the rings in a cross-section of a tree showing its physical growth.

In more recent years, of course, this has been verified many times, and Janov (1977) has published photographs showing how bruises made in pre-verbal experiences may actually come to the surface as visible marks during psychotherapy. I have seen a video made with a heat camera by a Gestalt therapist which shows very clearly the marks of early trauma becoming visible as the client relives the experience. The many papers and the book published by David Chamberlain (1988) show very clearly that many people can remember their own birth. This is not now something which can be denied. It seems clear from all the evidence that we have to accept the possibility of muscular memory and cellular memory as well as the more common kinds of memory using the cerebral cortex (Ridgway, 1987; Buchheimer, 1987). This means that it is possible to suffer from even earlier traumas, such as the trauma of abortion:

> Phoebe is renowned in our state as being what you people call a 'polar bear'. We call them 'icebergs'. They swim in cold pools in the winter. Phoebe, being a very powerful physical person, can swim miles and miles, and does daily; but she never gets out of the pool feeling she has swum far enough. She never feels completed. Her mother admitted, 'Yes, I did try and abort you . . . I had four girls and I had twins, and I thought, My God if it's another two girls I just can't cope. So I tried to kill you and I did it by jumping into a ice-cold pool and swimming and swimming and swimming.' (Farrant, unpublished)

The work of Graham Farrant in Australia is particularly important, but his papers have not as yet been published. One of the points he makes is that remembering an event is different from reliving an event. What happens in psychotherapy involving regression – and most forms of therapy do, sooner or later, whether they intend to or not – is that events are relived. The person goes through them again and many details come back which had been completely forgotten or never put into words before. This is quite different from remembering an event, and all the research on memory is quite irrelevant to the phenomenon of reliving. There are several research papers bearing on this in Blum (1993).

Now this experience of trauma and splitting is a particularly powerful one, because it is only in this experience that I first become conscious that there is a 'me' at all, as distinguished from the world. My very first experience of being me is tied in with the first experience of being not-OK. We do not fully understand yet how this can happen with the foetus or with very young babies – it becomes more obvious at about the three-year-old stage (Duval and Wicklund, 1972) – but somehow it does seem to occur. There may be a whole chain of such events, one of which may be more dramatic than the rest and may come to symbolize the rest: Grof (1975) has been clearer about this than most, as has Arthur Janov, who says:

> In the maturation of the brain each new trauma is represented and then re-represented holographically on higher and higher levels of the brain neuraxis. In

this way a Primal chain is developed, with later traumas reactivating related first-line Pains. What this means is that at each stage of brain development an imprint of the trauma occurs, and as the brain develops each imprint joins other related imprints of traumas, the early imprints becoming connected to the later ones. This fusion and representation continues to occur and becomes more elaborate and complex as maturation goes on. (Janov and Holden, 1977: 88)

I want to make it clear that some birth processes are quite all right and may well induce a feeling of triumph at having made it into the world, overcoming all obstacles (Grof, 1975; Janov, 1983). It is not at all suggested that birth is always a trauma, but rather that there is always some kind of a trauma which starts this process going. Michael Balint is also very clear about this:

> One possible theoretical explanation of these differences uses the idea of trauma. According to it the individual has developed more or less normally up to the point where he was struck by a trauma. From that point on his further development has been fundamentally influenced by the method he developed at the time for coping with the effects of that particular trauma – his basic fault. (Balint, 1968: 82)

Frank Lake (1980) has been very specific about different levels of trauma and exactly how that makes a difference to how the trauma is taken and experienced. He argued that there are four levels of trauma, and what happens inside the individual depends very much on exactly what level of trauma is involved. He made no distinction between sexual and any other type of trauma. The first level is pain-free and is the resting state. The second level has to do with coping, and is where the stimulation is bearable and even perhaps strengthening, because it evokes effective and mostly non-neurotic defences. The third level involves opposition to the pain, but it is so strong that it cannot be coped with, and repression takes place. If the trauma happens in infancy or earlier, the defence will be splitting rather than repression. The fourth level Lake calls 'transmarginal stress', and it is so powerful or so early – or both – that the person cuts off completely and may even turn against the self, wanting to die. Some recent work by Southgate and others suggests that many child accidents are in fact unconscious attempts at suicide, based on this fourth level of trauma. And if the trauma was actually a case of sexual or other abuse, and if the abuse is repeated or recreated somehow in later life, a real adult suicide may result – again possibly disguised as an accident. This has been coming up recently in a number of cases. Arthur Janov has said:

> It is the terrible hopelessness of never being loved that causes the split. The child must deny the realisation that his needs will never be filled no matter what he does. He cannot live knowing that he is despised or that no one is really interested in him. It is intolerable for him to know that there is no way to make his father less critical or his mother kind. The only way he has of defending himself is by developing substitute needs, which are neurotic. (Janov, 1970: 26)

Grof (1985) is very clear that early trauma can be very real and very important, and relates it particularly to the process of birth. He distinguishes four stages of birth and says that adult neurosis is very frequently based upon traumas suffered at one or other of these stages. Lake (1980), in one of his charts, brings out the way in which his four levels of trauma can be related to Grof's four stages of birth to make a matrix of sixteen cells which account between them for many of the origins of a large number of the neuroses. Again, of course, many of the drastic things which happen in the lives of adults may result from repetitions of the original trauma in some direct or disguised form. Partly it is a matter of how the mother and the other close and important figures react to various situations – and the very young infant seems to be able to pick up emotional reactions very quickly. Few of the writers in this area do real justice to the dialectical nature of the process: the non-OK self is the negation of the OK-self. It sees itself as the answer to the problem of the OK-self; and it devalues the real self. This is the first and most dramatic instance of something which will happen again and again throughout life – the move into objectivity and away from subjectivity. The non-OK self is, or wants to be, objective, right, or on the side of those who are right. The OK self feels itself to be defined as wrong – subjectivity is wrong – it is wrong to see things my way. Once this split has been established, it has effects which continue long afterwards. The psychoanalyst Leo Rangell has expressed this well:

> Reflecting on the subject of psychic trauma, I suggest that the trauma an analyst is pitted against is often no longer the trauma of childhood but the cumulative traumata of a lifetime of psychic repetition of the original in an attempt to master it. . . . If the trauma is repeated indefinitely and mastery fails to evolve, it is like a series of reinoculations which come to exceed the original dose and restore the original disease in chronic and even more virulent forms. (Rangell, 1973)

This links with the work of Alice Miller (1987), which has underlined the importance of early trauma and the way in which many analysts in the past have downplayed it and failed to do it justice. But if it is important, it must continue to be important, because the way of dealing with this first split will set the pattern for the way in which the person deals with the next trauma – and the next, and the next.

It would not be right to leave this stage without commenting on the question of memory. Many psychologists, including some of the most prestigious, deny the possibility of memories going back before the age of about three years. The reason is that they are making use of research designs which are not designed in such a way as to enable early memories to emerge. What we find in psychotherapy is that new clients very often start off with the belief that their childhood cannot be remembered but was doubtless 'happy'. As they begin, however, to build up a rapport with the therapist and a sense of trust, memories of their childhood begin to return. In other words, early memories need an atmosphere of trust and permission and acceptance before they will emerge. With this in mind, let us look at a passage by Sheingold and Tenney (1982), reprinted in a standard text used in under-graduate courses. The section is headed 'Childhood Amnesia'.

In an experiment on childhood amnesia, college-age subjects were asked 20 questions about the events surrounding the birth of a younger sibling. The average number of questions answered is plotted as a function of the subject's age when the sibling was born. If the birth occurred before the fourth year of life, no subject could recall a thing about it; if the birth occurred after that, recall increased with age at the time of the event. (Sheingold and Tenney, in Atkinson et al., 1993: 312–13)

It is quite clear that none of the required conditions are fulfilled. A relationship of trust has not been achieved or even attempted, no attempt has been made to create an atmosphere of relaxation and acceptance – the rational human is in charge! We might add that people tend to come into therapy at the age of thirty or more, when they are relatively well adjusted to the adult world and prepared to look at their own lives. At the age of twenty or so, people are still 'putting away childish things' and trying to become adults; it is, therefore, even less likely that they will be open to their childhood experiences.

This absurd attitude to research is still continuing as I write; there is a website where people are being asked about their earliest memories, in exactly the same way as in the above passage, clearly assuming that rational conscious responses elicited at a computer keyboard are going to be enough to answer all the research questions. It seems hard for the ordinary academic researcher to admit that their empirical quantitative methods might not be suitable for all purposes. All the way through our discussion of this stage we have seen that it is a stage of heightened emotion and vivid images. It is not the field of rational and supposedly detached scientists; it cannot be reached by people in white coats asking questions from their clipboards.

Stage 3

Once the non-OK region has been established, it starts to become populated by somewhat separated subregions (Lewin, 1936). This happens by the same process as the original split – in a situation of panic some defence is thrown up, and this defence is then used in other, similar situations. It is important to recognize that the events we are talking about here may be insignificant and unimportant to the adults yet very important to the baby. Donald Winnicott is very precise about how this can happen:

The feeling of the mother's existence lasts x minutes. If the mother is away more than x minutes, then the imago fades, and along with this the baby's capacity to use the symbol of the union ceases. The baby is distressed, but this distress is soon mended, because the mother returns in x + y minutes. In x + y minutes the baby has not become altered. But in x + y + z minutes the baby has become traumatized. In x + y + z minutes the mother's return does not mend the baby's altered state. Trauma implies that the baby has experienced a break in life's continuity, so that primitive defences now become organized to defend against a repetition of 'unthinkable anxiety' or a return of the acute confusional state that belongs to disintegration of nascent ego structure. (Winnicott, 1971: 114)

So if we are right that the primitive defence which Winnicott is talking about may very often be splitting, we can see how not only in the very first experience of trauma but also in the later experiences of trauma, this defence can result in the setting up of more and more subregions within the person.

Each of these subregions is contained within the not-OK region, so that even those which seem to function well are only marginally 'OK' – they are easily shaken and easily questioned. This leads to the phenomenon, often seen in group therapy, which I have called the 'Samurai-and-Slob' pattern: the person comes forward with great confidence and confronts another person, but if this other person fights back in any way, the first person collapses. The internal objects mentioned by the object relations school are set up in the following way:

> The figures with whom we have relationships in our phantasies are called appropriately, by Melanie Klein, 'internal objects' because we behave with respect to them, emotionally and impulsively, in the same ways as we do towards externally real persons, though in more violent degrees of intensity than would be socially permissible. The formation of this inner world of internal objects and situations proceeds from the very beginnings of life. (Guntrip, 1961: 226)

Each subregion that is set up represents a decision – 'this is the way to lead my life' – often made in a hurry and on inadequate evidence. Some of them are complete introjects – someone else's way of being is swallowed whole. Hinshelwood (1989) has a very thorough discussion of the whole question of internal objects in the Kleinian tradition.

Stanislav Grof casts a flood of light on this whole area by his notion of the 'COEX system' (system of condensed experience). He shows how the trauma can be represented again and again in the life of the person by successive experiences in which the original feelings are re-invoked:

> A COEX system can be defined as a specific constellation of memories consisting of condensed experiences (and related fantasies) from different life periods of the individual. The memories belonging to a particular COEX system have a similar basic theme or contain similar elements and are associated with a strong emotional charge of the same quality. The deepest layers of this system are represented by vivid and colourful memories of experiences from infancy and early childhood. More superficial layers of such a system involve memories of similar experiences from later periods, up to the present life situation. Each COEX system has a basic theme that permeates all its layers and represents their common denominator. (Grof, 1975: 46–7)

If we personify a COEX system, it comes to life as a subpersonality. It may also remind us of Goffman's (1974) idea of a frame – except that this is an internal frame which we carry around inside us. It may also remind us of Hegel's abstract systems, inadequate because one-sided; and it may also remind us of Freud's idea of a core problem.

The central OK self is often called the 'real self', or the 'true self' or the Self, and it tries to come out from time to time, giving and receiving love, but is often countered again and goes back behind a barrier – a barrier which is then further strengthened. This is a painful process and helps us to understand why there is so much childhood amnesia, extending in some cases well into the teenage years. As Alvin Mahrer says, 'Little wonder that some adults have practically no memory of huge slabs of their childhood: they were engaged in responding to parents, in carrying out what parents got them to do, in never owning their own behaviour.' (Mahrer, 1989: 730). So all the way through childhood the OK-me is retreating further and further. Reality is given away to the outside world, so that all the power seems to be out there and none (or very little) of it seems to be within – in here with me. And when I do try to use my personal power, I may be put down or punished for it: so it, too, gets defined as not-OK. This may happen in very ambiguous, 'double-bind' kinds of ways (Laing and Esterson, 1970).

One of the earliest subregions to become well defined is the sex-role one – 'I am a boy or girl' – which later becomes the ego and the patripsych (Southgate and Randall, 1989). In recent years we have become much more conscious of how problematic is the question of gender and Judith Lorber (1994), among others, has been influential in opening up the whole area. She has pointed out that there are many femininities, many masculinities. The whole idea of masculinity and femininity can be deconstructed. This leaves the way open to the possibility that we have within us not just an internal contrasex person, as Jung (1991) has suggested, but many subpersonalities of different sexes. These have been introjected at different times in our lives. The introjects start off by 'riding herd' on one of the subregions, telling it what to and what not to do. Then they move inside the subregion and become a part of it. This can then lead to a topdog/underdog split inside the subregion affected. Freud's superego is formed in just this way; he actually writes:

> A portion of the external world has, at least partially, been abandoned as an object and has instead, by identification, been taken into the ego and thus become an integral part of the internal world. This new psychical agency continues to carry on the functions which have hitherto been performed by people in the external world. (Freud, 1938: 203)

This is one of the clearest statements, and one of the earliest, about one way in which subpersonalities can come into being.

The negating and devaluing of the subjective level is going on apace here. Each success in 'getting by' leads to an inflation of one or more of the subpersonalities which are incipient. This leads to the 'puffing up' and 'selfishness' which children often display at this time. 'Being good' means denying the subjective level. All the things we accept are called 'objective' or 'true', and all the things we reject are called 'subjective' or 'false'. This is a continuous social process which goes on for years.

At this stage the body is very important, and things are seen very much in terms of the body, as Wilber (1980) emphasizes.

In my book on the whole subject of subpersonalities (Rowan, 1990), the story is continued through five more stages, but the main point of this chapter was to expand and deepen the very important stage: Stage 2. It is here that the basic tactic is usually laid down. Once this has been done, the rest follows very naturally. Once we know how to create subpersonalities, the same defence can be used again and again, with the results found elsewhere in this book.

References

Assagioli, R. (1975) *Psychosynthesis.* Wellingborough: Turnstone Press.

Atkinson, R.L., Atkinson, R.C., Smith, E.E. and Bem, D.J. (1993) *Introduction to Psychology.* (11th edn) Fort Worth: Harcourt Brace Jovanovich.

Balint, M. (1968) *The Basic Fault: Therapeutic Aspects of Regression.* London: Tavistock.

Beahrs, J.O. (1982) *Unity and Multiplicity.* New York: Brunner/Mazel.

Blakney, R.B. (1941) *Meister Eckhart: A Modern Translation.* New York: Harper & Row.

Blum, Thomas (ed.) (1993) *Prenatal Perception, Learning and Bonding.* Berlin: Leonardo Publishers.

Boadella, D. (1987) *Lifestreams: An Introduction to Biosynthesis.* London: Routledge.

Bradley, B.S. (1989) *Visions of Infancy.* Cambridge: Polity Press.

Bradshaw, J. (1988a) *Healing the Shame that Binds You.* Deerfield Beach: Health Communications.

Bradshaw, J. (1988b) *Bradshaw on the Family.* Deerfield Beach: Health Communications.

Buchheimer, A. (1987) 'Memory – preverbal and verbal', in T.R. Verny (ed.), *Pre- and Peri-Natal Psychology: An Introduction.* New York: Human Sciences Press.

Chamberlain, D. (1988) *Babies Remember Birth.* New York: Ballantine.

Clarkson, P. (1992) *Transactional Analysis Psychotherapy: An Integrated Approach.* London: Routledge.

Coward, H. (1985) *Jung and Eastern Thought.* Albany, NY: SUNY Press.

Crabtree, T. (1988) *Multiple Man: Explorations in Possession and Multiple Personality.* London: Grafton Books.

Duval, S. and Wicklund, R.A. (1972) *A Theory of Objective Self-Awareness.* New York: Academic Press.

Fairbairn, W.R.D. (1952) *Psychoanalytic Studies of the Personality.* London: Tavistock.

Fedor-Freybergh, P.G. and Vogel, M.I.V. (1988) *Prenatal and Perinatal Psychology and Medicine.* Carnforth: Parthenon.

Fenichel, O. (1945) *Psychoanalytic Theory of Neurosis.* New York: W.W. Norton.

Firman, J. and Gila, A. (1997) *The Primal Wound.* Albany, NY: SUNY Press.

Fodor, N. (1949) *The Search for the Beloved.* New York: University Books.

Freud, S. (1938) 'Splitting of the ego in the process of defence', *Standard Edition*, vol. 23. London: Hogarth Press.

Freud, S. (1985) *Civilization, Society and Religion.* Harmondsworth: Penguin.

Freud, S. (1991) *Introductory Lectures on Psychoanalysis.* London: Penguin.

Goffman, E. (1974) *Frame Analysis.* New York: Harper & Row.

Grof, S. (1975) *Realms of the Human Unconscious.* New York: Viking Press.

Grof, S. (1985) *Beyond the Brain.* Albany, NY: SUNY Press.

Grof, S. (1992) *The Holotropic Mind.* San Francisco: Harper.

Grotstein, J.S. (1981) *Splitting and Projective Identification*. New York: Jason Aronson.

Guntrip, H. (1961) *Personality Structure and Human Interaction*. London: Hogarth.

Guntrip, H. (1977) *Psychoanalytic Theory, Therapy and the Self*. London: Maresfield Reprints.

Hegel, G.W.F. (1971) *The Philosophy of Mind*. Oxford: Clarendon Press.

Hillman, J. (1989) *The Essential James Hillman*. (Intro. and ed. Thomas Moore.) London: Routledge.

Hinshelwood, R.D. (1989) *A Dictionary of Kleinian Thought*. London: Free Association Books.

Janov, A. (1970) *The Primal Scream*. New York: Putnam.

Janov, A. (1977) *The Feeling Child*. London: Abacus.

Janov, A. (1983) *Imprints: The Lifelong Effects of the Birth Experience*. New York: Coward-McCann.

Janov, A. and Holden, E.M. (1977) *Primal Man: The New Consciousness*. London: Abacus.

Johnson, R. (1986) *Inner Work: Using Dreams and Active Imagination for Personal Growth*. San Francisco: Harper & Row.

Jung, C.G. (1968) 'Archetypes of the collective unconscious', in *Collected Works*, vol. 9, part 1. (2nd edn) London: Routledge.

Jung, C.G. (1991) *Psychological Types*. London: Routledge.

Klapp, O. (1969) *Collective Search for Identity*. New York: Holt, Rinehart & Winston.

Klein, M. (1948) *Contributions to Psychoanalysis*. London: Hogarth Press.

Kohlberg, L. (1984) *The Psychology of Moral Development*. San Francisco: Harper & Row.

Laing, R.D. (1965) *The Divided Self*. Harmondsworth: Penguin.

Laing, R.D. (1976) *The Facts of Life*. Harmondsworth: Penguin.

Laing, R.D. (1982) *The Voice of Experience*. Harmondsworth; Penguin.

Laing, R.D. and Esterson, A. (1970) *Sanity, Madness and the Family*. Harmondsworth, Penguin.

Lake, F. (1980) *Studies in Constricted Confusion*. Oxford: Clinical Theology Association.

Levine, P.A. (1997) *Waking the Tiger: Healing Trauma*. Berkeley, CA: North Atlantic Books.

Lewin, K. (1936) *Topological Psychology*. New York: McGraw-Hill.

Loevinger, J. (1976) *Ego Development*. San Francisco: Jossey-Bass.

Lorber, J. (1994) *Paradoxes of Gender*. New Haven: Yale University Press.

McCall, G.J. and Simmons, J.L. (1966) *Identities and Interactions*. New York: Free Press.

Mahrer, A.R. (1989) *Experiencing*. Ottawa: University of Ottawa Press.

Maslow, A.H. (1987) *Motivation and Personality*. (3rd edn) New York: Harper & Row.

Miller, A. (1987) *For Your Own Good: The Roots of Violence in Child-Rearing*. London: Virago Press.

Moss, R.C.S. (1987) 'Frank Lake's maternal-fetal distress syndrome: Clinical and theoretical considerations', in T.R. Verny (ed.) *Pre- and Peri-natal Psychology: An Introduction*. New York: Human Sciences Press.

Netherton, M. and Shiffrin, N. (1979) *Past Lives Therapy*. New York: Ace Books.

Neumann, E. (1973) *The Origins and History of Consciousness*. Princeton, NJ: Princeton University Press.

Peerbolte, L. (1975) *Psychic Energy in Prenatal Dynamics*. Wassenaar: Servire Press.

Perls, F.S. (1969) *Gestalt Therapy Verbatim*. Moab: Real People Press.

Ramana Maharshi, Sri (1972) *The Collected Works*. London: Rider.
Rangell, L. (1973) 'On the cacophony of human relations', *Psychoanalytic Quarterly*, 42: 333–4.
Rank, O. (1929) *The Trauma of Birth*. New York: Harcourt Brace.
Ridgway, R. (1987) *The Unborn Child*. Aldershot: Wildwood House.
Rogers, C.R. (1961) *On Becoming a Person*. London: Constable.
Rowan, J. (1990) *Subpersonalities: The people inside us*. London: Routledge.
Rowan, J. (1993) *The Transpersonal: In Psychotherapy and Counselling*. London: Routledge.
Sartre, J.-P. (1950) *Psychology of Imagination*. London: Rider.
Sheingold, K. and Tenney, Y.J. (1982) 'Memory for a salient childhood event', in U. Neisser (ed.), *Memory Observed: Memory in Natural Contexts*. San Francisco: Freeman.
Southgate, J. and Randall, R. (1989) *The Barefoot Psychoanalyst*. (3rd edn) Loughton: Gale Centre Publications.
Spinelli, E. (1989) *The Interpreted World*. London: Sage.
Starhawk (1982) *Dreaming the Dark*. Boston, MA: Beacon
Steiner, C., Wyckoff, H., Goldstine, D., Lariviere. P., Schwebel, R., Marcus, J. and members of the Radical Psychiatry Centre (1975) *Readings in Radical Psychiatry*. New York: Grove Press.
Stern, D.N. (1985) *The Interpersonal World of the Infant*. New York: Basic Books.
Stone, H. and Winkelman, S. (1985) *Embracing Our Selves*. Marina del Ray, CA: Devorss & Co.
Verny, T. (1982) *The Secret Life of the Unborn Child*. London: Sphere.
Watkins, J. (1978) *The Therapeutic Self*. New York: Human Sciences Press.
Whitmont, E. (1987) 'Archetypal and personal interaction in the clinical process', in N. Schwartz-Salant and M. Stein (eds), *Archetypal Processes in Psychotherapy*. Wilmette: Chiron.
Wilber, K. (1980) *The Atman Project*. Wheaton, IL: Quest.
Wilber, K. (1983) *Eye to Eye*. New York: Anchor/Doubleday.
Wilber, K. (1995) *Sex, Ecology, Spirituality*. Boston, MA: Shambhala.
Winnicott, D.W. (1965) *The Maturational Process and the Facilitating Environment*. London: Hogarth Press.
Winnicott, D.W. (1971) *Playing and Reality*. Harmondsworth: Penguin.
Winnicott, D.W. (1975) *Collected Papers*. London: Karnac Books.
Woolger, R.J. (1990) *Other Lives, Other Selves: A Jungian Psychotherapist Discovers Past Lives*. Wellingborough: Crucible.

2 THE ALTER EGO AND DÉJÀ VU PHENOMENA: NOTES AND REFLECTIONS

James S. Grotstein

> There is someone who is living my life, and I know nothing about him!
>
> (Pirandello, 1995)

> I thus drew steadily nearer to the truth, by whose partial discovery I have been doomed to such dreadful shipwreck: that man is not truly one, but truly two. I say two, because the state of my knowledge does not pass beyond that point. Others will follow, others will outstrip me on the same lines; and I hazard the guess that man will ultimately be known for a polity of multifarious, incongruous and independent denizens.
>
> (Stevenson, 1886/1992)

> I cannot understand the mystery, but I am always conscious of myself as two.
>
> (Whitman, 1921/1932)

The alter ego or 'second self' phenomenon, the experience of a strange yet familiar second self or doppelgänger, has had an unappreciated role in the history and development of psychoanalysis. I will contend that it is a concept that seems to have become 'bleached out' in the current Zeitgeist of excessive sensory stimulation which jeopardizes our awareness of imaginary mental life. In the past alter egos were experienced as 'phantoms', 'ghosts', 'spirits', 'demons', 'werewolves', and the pleomorphic transformations of demoniacal possession. The analytic term 'internal object' or 'object representation' does not convey the sense of the paradoxical and eerie strange familiarity, the déjà vu experience, in which once familiar aspects of one self ostracized through projective identification have become 'misrecognized demons'. In recent contributions I have called these by such names as 'monsters', 'demons', 'phantoms', 'chimerae' (Grotstein, 1997) and 'rogue subjects' (Grotstein, in press).

I propose that the alter ego phenomenon has had a significant role in the development of psychoanalysis, that it has a clinical and phenomenological immediacy superior to other conceptualizations, and that it offers bridges between psychology, sociology, and neurobiology. I understand Freud's concept of thinking as 'trial action' and as describing the mediative and communicative interaction of alter egos representing thoughts and phantasies in experimental rehearsals awaiting externalization into and/or onto external persons in order to be expressed and known. The concept of the alter ego allows us to reinterpret imaginary (pre-symbolic and symbolic) mental life as a dance of archetypes. These images undergo projective alteration, transformation, and justification through the splitting and projective identification of aspects of our affects and senses, and are modified by the impact of external objects upon our senses – all in montage.

Alter egos constitute our inventory of phantom actualities and possibilities. The term designates the presence of one or more other selves (subpersonalities) within the overall personality and assigns the status of personification or separate subjective personhood (an autonomous 'I' function) to areas of the overall personality otherwise termed 'impulses', 'affects', etc. Frank dissociation of personalities – such as occurs in multiple personality, temporal lobe epilepsy, and post-traumatic stress disorders – represents the pathological extreme of a normal phenomenon. One can conceive of the alter ego phenomenon as a 'Siamese twinship' (Grotstein, 1981) or a 'dyadic subjectivity' (Ogden, 1986); there are two separate heads but one body, allowing for separateness and togetherness at the same time. The figure of 'Siamese-twinship' (or the 'Medusa') describes the unique simultaneity of separate individuality *and* merged coexistence (originally termed 'symbiosis') with another self, alone or in identification with an object. The connection between the 'twin selves' is like that of a Möbius strip, a paradoxically discontinuous/continuous ribbon and an image analogous to sleep/wakefulness, conscious/unconscious, right hemisphere/left hemisphere, etc.

The structure of the psychic apparatus can be considered as containing alter egos in the form of the instinctual self (id), the realistic self (ego), and the ideal self (superego). The psychoanalytic theory of psychical conflict can be reinterpreted as conflicts between seemingly sovereign subselves which exist either in temporary or permanent opposition to one another. The concept of psychical conflict is more alive (and I believe more accurately described phenomenologically) when it is thought of as a contention between two or more selves or subselves. The value of this distinction lies partly in the understanding that each conflicting self, rather than merely a transient impulse, is a separate subjectivity ('I'), with its own volition (sense of agency), understanding, narcissism, sensitivity, world-view, etc. Such concepts as the 'internal saboteur' (Fairbairn, 1952), 'pathological organizations' (Rosenfeld, 1987), or 'psychic retreats' (Steiner, 1993) are easily considered as alter egos. Alter egos need not be, necessarily, conflictual. Their dispositions may be normally concordant, complementary, oppositional, and commensal (not yet interactive). Pathologically, alter egos may relate in oppositional (discordant or conflictual) or parasitic ways.

The phenomenon of mirroring described by Lacan, Winnicott, and Kohut – like that of the myth of Narcissus – includes the paradox of the uncannily strange familiarity when we encounter our second selves. Many of our personal object choices of deep intimacy and friendship are based upon a balance between this concordance and complementarity. The experience of the alter ego is uncanny, as is that of déjà vu, which I consider to be the temporal counterpart to the former. The alter ego mystique can be observed from another point of view – in the universal human fascination about having a mysterious double, contemplating another self in the real world who is one's duplicate. This phenomenon is concretized in the real experience of identical twins, who have had a fascinating and uncanny status from earliest times since they evoke the unsettling yet fascinating fantasy that there may be a duplicate of ourselves somewhere else in the world.

All the denizens of our dreams are alter egos from our autobiographical dream smithy, and their links to external objects are of less importance than their links to ourselves. The alter ego phenomenon is fundamentally involved in aspects of transference and in the formation of internal objects and self and object representations through the assignment of personal meaningfulness to the objects of one's experiences, a phenomenon hitherto known as the attribution of 'cathexis' ('investment', to which I should add the term 'personal'). As psychoanalytic theory and practice has shifted from an id analysis orientation and moved toward ego psychology, and more lately towards a two-person intersubjective approach, the alter ego phenomenon has been eclipsed. Analysts emphasize those aspects of the manifest content that reveal the analysand's own *cathexis* (attribution of personal importance) of the object, not the object *per se* as a separate entity. In other words, how the analysand *personally feels* about the object conveys '*alter ego-ness*' to the perception of the object, that is, transference. Transference, in its purest essence, especially from the Kleinian point of view as projective identification, is fundamentally an alter ego phenomenon.

Transference in analysis and confusions of personalities outside analysis are Möbius strip encounters in which we experience ourselves living on various levels of mind, contacting archetypes, and revisiting images of important personages in our early lives; and experience uncanny déjà vu recollections of selves and others – all adding to the beauty, complexity, and puzzlement of our experiences. Nowhere more than in dreams do we encounter these concordant, complementary, opposing, and commensal alter egos and alter imagos, as the following dream from a borderline patient attests:

> I'm telling people about how to perform a certain medical procedure. A person right next to me is mocking me while I'm doing this. He looks Oriental. Either another doctor, a female, or my wife is going over a list of candidates who were accepted for medical school. The name of the man next to me was not on this list.

The patient's associations were, first of all, to the fact that he looked more oriental when he was younger. Secondly, he believed that he had been lucky to get into medical school and always felt that there was a part of him that did not really make it. The female doctor represents his anima (female counterpart in the Jungian sense), as does his wife. The anxiety of the dream represents the growing disparity, as he makes progress in the analysis, between his progressing self and his lost twin: the one who never made it, the one who feels disoriented from his progressing self.

Background

In the primeval dawn of human existence our forebears attempted to comprehend and organize the natural forces which confronted them. They created cosmologies in the form of personifications of these natural forces; that is, everything outside them was seen in terms of references to the familiar (for example, as extensions of the self). Following this initial technique of familiarization through personification and/or of animism, those larger-than-life aspects of themselves – particularly disturbing affects such as anger, grandiosity, and so on – were split off, and a world of gods and demons was created by positive and negative idealization and projective identification. These projected attributes were then recalled and reintroduced to explain extremes of nature within human beings (for example, enthusiasm, anger, pride, inspiration, hubris, etc.). Someone who was artistically and creatively inspired was inhabited by muses; if reckless, he or she was possessed by the goddess Ate (Dodds, 1951). These 'divine' elements seemed to be the return of those attributes which testify to the human being's 'generosity' to their gods, and this process is partially responsible for the myths of the quasi-human, quasi-divine origin of ancestors found in virtually all cultures. This vitalistic notion of human nature persisted into medieval times and, according to Jung (1953), seems to have found its way into the thinking of alchemists, which held that we are composed of myriads of little homunculi and are inhabited by gods or by demons, depending upon fate and the portion (moira) delivered to us.

The alter ego phenomenon and related phenomena such as heautoscopy or autoscopy[1] have been described since Aristotle and Heraclitus. Plato's myth of the Androgyne represents the complementarity of alter egos between men and women. Ovid's version of the myth of Narcissus is another example, in which the alter ego phenomenon is doubly represented. Narcissus, forswearing the love of Echo (his first authentic alter ego), fell in love with his own image in the mirror reflection in the water of the River Styx. In Ovid's version of this myth the mirror reflection is understood as his other self, the one he can never possess (his second alter ego). The concept of the alter ego perfused medieval and Renaissance thinking in the ecclesiastical belief in the soul: that aspect of the self which had an existence separate from the body. Whereas the soul was the sublime form of one's spiritual being, its decomposition or degradation devolved into the sinister phenomenon of the ghost. One can also see the phenomenon of the alter ego in the philosophy of vitalism and in demoniacal possession, in which an innocent soul becomes corrupted, possessed, and transformed into an altered self.

The darker side of the soul has hovered in the penumbra of evil, where one's soul could be possessed by the intrusive power of the devil – who can also be thought of as our alter ego. Frazer (1922) describes how primitive tribes are afraid of shadows, twins, water reflections of self, mirror images, and so on because of the fear of losing their soul. I have suggested (Grotstein, 1979a, 1979b) that the devil is, on one level, the alter ego of Christ and, on another level, the alter ego of everyone, formed initially as the split-off 'scapegoat' self into which all our shame and guilt is projectively identified. These then return to 'bedevil' us, to steal our shadows, to take possession of our souls, etc. – in proportion to the way we cruelly exiled and ostracized the devil. Throughout the Middle Ages and the Renaissance, the concept of the devil and his infiltrating activity (via succubi and incubi) dominated the content of the religious obsessions of Europeans. The devil's power was also associated with clairvoyance and extrasensory perception. Reversals in particular were thought to be the devil's work – thus their connection with the reversals in mirror images.

Dualism first appeared as a philosophical concept in Western culture in the work of Descartes, who separated the observing or spiritual self (*res cogitans*) from its objective contemplation (*res extensa*). This separation of the observing self from the objects observed, which pertains to self-reflection as well as to mind-body separation, has dominated Western cultural and scientific thinking. It has been the basis of our cosmology and understanding of the relationship of vital as well as non-vital objects until challenged by the newer physics ushered in with Einstein's theory of relativity, the uncertainty principle of Heisenberg, and Heisenberg and Bohr's principle of complementarity. The discovery of the laws of sub-atomic particles challenges Cartesian-Newtonian laws of physical nature by introducing the concept of stochastic randomness (unpredictability of location and vector direction of movement of particles) and the notion of the inescapable interrelationship between the observer and the observed. This aspect of subatomic physics has been applied as a metaphor to newer psycho-analytic thinking, particularly interactionalism and intersubjectivity. These ideas challenge the concept that the individual person comprises a single entity alone.

A revival of interest in the double nature of humans seems to have taken place in the eighteenth century, particularly beginning with the Mesmerists, or animal magnetists. In English poetry there was a special preoccupation with the 'stranger within thee', a notion of the subjective self beyond the grasp of the self's reflection in its sensibility and sympathy. Rogers (1970) and Cox (1980) note that eighteenth- and nineteenth-century fiction was replete with the phenomenon of the alter ego or doppelgänger. Cox, in his book *The Stranger Within Thee: Concepts of the Self in Late-Eighteenth-Century Literature*, analyses the work of Samuel Richardson, Thomas Gray, Thomas Chatterton, William Cowper, and William Blake and finds that these authors and many of their contemporaries were preoccupied with the elusiveness of the true (inner) self. Eighteenth-century thinkers believed that a person could glimpse their truer nature via their relationship with others, in terms of their capacity to experience and to reveal sympathy (which we would today call empathy) and sensibility (sensitiveness). Nevertheless, the true self was always felt as a 'stranger within thee', not to be grasped, only to be reflected.

In nineteenth-century literature the awareness of the 'stranger within' came even more to the fore, and many literary themes around the 'double' emerged. The subjective 'I' differed from its 'self', which it could regard in the mirror of experience. Whereas the self as an object seemed to be clearer, subjective 'I' always remained a mystery. Subjective 'I'-ness also seemed to emerge when hidden, uncanny, lost parts of the self would return in the form of personifications as strangers.

Literary doubles took the form of either concordant or complementary twinships: the former designating exact duplicates, the latter dialectical aspects of oneself. Generally, the double seemed to connote one's darker, more sensuous, and less socially consonant self. The following works demonstrate the doppelgänger phenomenon: von Chamisso *The Wondersome Tale of Peter Schlemhyl*, who was haunted by having sold his shadow to the devil; E.T.A. Hoffmann 'The Story of the Lost Reflection', 'The Doubles'; Melville (1949) *Pierre*, and (1977) *Bartleby The Scrivener*; Dickens *The Mystery of Edwin Drood* and *A Christmas Carol* (the transformations of Scrooge); Dostoyevsky (1958) *The Double*,[2] (1955) *The Idiot*, (1956) *Crime and Punishment*, (1936) *The Possessed*, (1943) *The Brothers Karamozov*; Edgar Allen Poe 'The Story of William Wilson'; Robert Louis Stevenson (1886) *'The Strange Case of Dr Jekyll and Mr Hyde'*; de Maupassant (1903) *La Horla*; Henry James (1948) *The Jolly Corner*; Balzac (1888) *Peau de Chagrin*; Goethe (1870) *Faust*; de Musset (1906) *La Nuit Venitienne*; Mary Shelley (1918) *Frankenstein*; Oscar Wilde (1905) *The Picture of Dorian Gray*; Steinbeck (1946) *The Long Valley*; and Joseph Conrad (1960) *The Heart of Darkness* and (1929) *The Secret Sharer*. The tradition of doppelgänger fiction continued into the twentieth century with Thomas Mann's *Dr Faustus*; Kafka's (1964) *The Trial*; O'Connor's *The Violent Bear*; William Faulkner's (1932) *Sartoris*, (1942) *Go Down Moses*, and (1936) *Absalom Absalom!*; Vladimir Nabokov's *Pale Fire*; Jorge Luis Borges' (1964) 'The Other' and (1960) 'Borges and I'; and many others. Faulkner himself seems to have experienced an alter ego of himself, according to Joseph Lichtenberg (personal communication). Apparently his original name was spelled without the 'u' (Falkner) and represented the designation of a different self. For further literary studies on the double, the reader is advised to consult Guerard (1967), Rosenfield (1967), and Simon and Goldberg (1984). Coleman (1934) studied the phantom double and its psychological significance, and Wolstein (1974) differentiated between the 'I' and 'me' patterns of the self.

I believe that the characters in novels and plays, to say nothing of the denizens of our dreams by night and our active lives by day, constitute dilemmas of categories for us insofar as we are in a dialectical doubt as to whether they are concordant, complementary or preternaturally opposing, although disguised, portions of ourselves uniting at our existential doorway for us to be receptive to their return; or whether they are strangers, the anxiety about whom caused us to 'familiarize' them with cursorily improvised self-awareness ('He reminds me of . . .'). Thus all our relationships – whether in the internal world or in outer reality – are with persons who are either known aspects of ourselves, lost aspects, or relationships with strangers who remind us of aspects of ourselves, or of strangers proper. Alter objects (or images) are an extension of our need to cast the shadow of familiarity onto newly acquired experiences with people and to diffuse stranger anxiety by connections with familiarity.

Whereas poets, novelists, and dramatists depict the alter ego phenomenon in literary form, psychiatrists and neurologists have studied it from a medical perspective, especially in such phenomena as autoscopy (heautoscopy), the phenomenon of experiencing the image of oneself as a double (Wigan, 1844; Galton, 1883; Dewhurst, 1954; Dewhurst and Pearson, 1955). Janet and Charcot, Freud's mentors at the Salpêtrière in Paris, began the detailed investigation of hysteria. Janet observed that hysterics were characterized by a splitting of consciousness, a phenomenon he ascribed to decomposition or weakness of integration.[3] Breuer and Freud (1893–95), continuing the investigation of hysteria, also observed a 'double conscience' (double consciousness) and created the field of psychoanalysis from this observation. Thus, psychoanalysis owes its origin to the eighteenth- and nineteenth-century preoccupation with the alter ego. As Freud continued the development of psychoanalytic theory, however, these splits of consciousness rotated from the vertical to the horizontal so that splitting became transformed into topographical repression in which consciousness superordinated and repressed the unconscious, which became first more arcane and closed-off and was later organized into a concept of instinctual drives.

The introduction of this concept of instinctual drives was the second major step in depersonifying the alter ego and, once stripped of its personalness, the id became the seat of the impersonal but universal power attributed to a mystical nature by German Romanticism. It seems most likely, moreover, that Freud's notion of the instincts was his own way of 'objectifying' into scientific terms the concepts more attributable to Schopenhauer's 'Will' and Nietzsche's 'Dionysiac Power' (O'Shaughnessy, 1982). In other words, the idea that instinctual drives were the principal content of the unconscious may be due largely to Freud's biological background and his logical-positivistic attempt to link mental phenomena with neurobiology, which found its apogee in his 'Project for a scientific psychology' (Freud, 1895/1950). Psychoanalysis thus became a science dealing with this duality of human nature but at the expense of the dehumanization of the repressed internal self.

The intra-personal 'sociology' of alter egos was practically spelled out in Freud's (1915/1917) 'Mourning and melancholia' when he discussed the relationship of the ego ideal (a 'gradient in the ego') to the ego in terms of the respective identifications each has with the narcissistically lost object. Certainly it is apparent in 'The ego and the id' (1923), where he formalizes the components of the psychic apparatus and their interrelationships, and in 'On narcissism: an introduction' (1914) where he refers to the ego as the id's first object choice. He returned to the concept of the double in his paper 'The uncanny' (1919), in which he formally recognized the existence of the alter ego, but failed to recognize its more profound and universal significance.

As Freud further formulated his ideas about the split between consciousness and unconsciousness, he employed consciousness and unconsciousness as formal systems occupying a vertical topographical gradient which preempted the vitalism and humanness of the unconscious self. The latter thereafter became alienated as the Unconscious, while consciousness seemed to imply 'I'-ness in its subjectively felt sense. This alienation of the Unconscious, rather than its postulation as 'the other "I"', continued in Freud's move from the topographic to the structural hypothesis where 'I' (ego) was counterposed to 'it' (id) (see Freud, 1923). Both then are ruled over by a super-'I' which seems, like the id, not to have 'I' status as a subjectively felt entity. It is a force which is ambiguously within and yet comes from without – like the id.

The phenomenon of the double was revived somewhat in the work of Melanie Klein and by the British object relations school when they began to explore mental phenomena more primitive than repression, for example splitting and projective identification. Klein evolved a theory of the internal world comprising of internal objects which were formed, in the first instance, by splitting-off of aspects of the self and of the experience of the object, projectively identifying them within the object, and then introjecting them and identifying with this 'alchemic amalgam'. Because of the initial splitting which accompanies projective identification, internal objects are experienced as alien to the self but at the same time familiar since they contain transformed portions of the self. These split-off, projected, and then introjected objects are experienced as independent subjective selves ('I's), each speaking from within the domain of an object within the domain of the self. Implicit in her theory is the conception that all human beings consist of unresolved splits within the ego, and an analysis is required to shepherd the patient into the depressive position where these splits within the ego can be reconciled.

Fairbairn (1944) highlighted the possibility of other selves within the individual when he described the 'internal saboteur' (the rejecting object and the anti-libidinal ego), the libidinal ego, and the 'exciting object' as endopsychic structures. Winnicott's concept of the 'true' and 'false selves' (1952) was later reformulated as the pathological legacies of the 'being' self and the 'doing' self respectively (Winnicott, 1963). I would think of introjections generally, and of internal objects specifically, as strange/familiar 'I's within us seeking reunion and integration.

The alter ego phenomenon is explicit in the phenomenon of the imaginary companion of childhood and is implied in Bion's (1967) conception of the 'imaginary twin', a defensive construct in phantasy which seeks to arrogate selfness to everything that the infant's eyes can behold in order to deny separation. Bion's (1975, 1977, 1979) concept of fetal 'somite consciousness', whose fate is either to remain unborn or to become transformed into psychosomatic or group personality attributes is another alter ego. Katan (1954) and Bion (1957) distinguished the presence of non-psychotic and psychotic personalities in the same patient, and Rosenfield (1967) described a 'mad omnipotent self' alongside the normal personality. Kohut's (1971, 1977) and Kernberg's (1975) conception of the 'pathological grandiose self', which Kernberg further subdivides into aggressive and libidinal subpersonalities, can also be thought of as an alter ego.

The literature on multiple personality has alluded to the concept of the alter ego but not in detail. Salley (1988) describes a single patient with multiple personalities in which he found subpersonalities with separate dreaming functions. The psychoanalytic concepts of 'symbiosis' (Mahler et al., 1975) and 'at-one-ment' (Silverman et al., 1982) seem also to touch on the concept of the alter ego insofar as they both allude to the simultaneity of the experience of oneness and otherness. Emde (1987) addresses this issue from the standpoint of infant development in his formulation of the development of the 'ego' and the 'we-go' in the infant. These concepts, however, miss the dual subjective experience of 'I'-ness, which is essential to the alter ego phenomenon.

I contend that psychoanalysis may have suffered from Freud's failure to grasp the deeper significance of his discovery, that of dual consciousness or dual 'I'-ness, in which consciousness and unconsciousness, or ego and id (and superego), are each individual 'I's separately and compositely. In other contributions (Grotstein, 1997) I sought to reinterpret the analysand's inner experience of internal persecutors, what I have referred to as 'demons', 'monsters', 'phantoms', or 'chimerae' – often 'ghosts'. The deceptive characteristic of internal objects is that they do not represent the internalization of external objects (actually, individuals) *per se*. They represent chimerical third forms which have been altered in the process of splitting and projective identification. An internal object is an alienated aspect of the projecting subject cast into a projectively altered perception of the external object, both of which then are internalized and undergo transformative changes once more when introjective identification occurs (Grotstein, 1997). I have proposed (Grotstein, in press) that the term 'internal object' does not convey the vitality and separate sense of selfhood of these chimerical phantoms. Malignant or benign, they behave as if they have a separate sense of personality along with a sense of agency, intentionality (purpose or will), and especially *subjectivity*. They are 'alters' in the true sense of the term and behave as virtually separate entities. When the infant or analysand employs defensive projective identification, what is split off and projectively re-identified in the (image of the) object is part of the projecting subject's own subjectivity. Consequently, at the end of the cycle of transformations when the object is introjectively installed back within the projecting subject's ego, the infant or patient now contains an 'alien' or 'rogue', misrecognized subjectivity which persecutorily hounds the projecting subject and demands repatriation.

Ogden observed: 'Internal objects do not think. Only egos do' (1983: 229), and he leaves room open for the idea that the subjectivity of the object *can* be internalized and identified with. Ogden (1984, 1986) conceives of 'dyadic subjectivity' and the 'analytic third' as amalgams of the subjectivities of the analysand and the analyst. Bion (1959, 1962) conveyed the same idea in his concept of the container and the contained when he stated that the mother (and analyst) must 'dream her infant' (patient), implying a momentary merger. In light of Bion's and Ogden's conceptualizations of merged subjectivities, I now propose that *the rogue subject consists of the alienated subjectivity of the projecting subject and the projectively and then introjectively altered subjectivity of the external object.*

My hypothesis is that the human being, seemingly a single entity, comprises a series of dualities of selves – both normally and abnormally – and that these dualities of being are multifarious (for example, the duality of right and left brain consciousnesses, the duality of existential being, the bilateral representation of the sense organs of the body, etc.). Not only are we multiply dualistic in our *subjective* nature, but the very objects we perceive in the 'real' world are dualistic in at least two ways. First, we perceive them via two different data-processing systems: primary process (personal meaning) and secondary process (detached observation). Secondly, the very objects in the so-called world of reality may themselves be duplicates of each other, not only in the sense of being differing objects to each sense organ (for example, left and right eye, left and right ear) but also may be doubly existent in a variety of ways ranging from the emotional to the ultra-abstract. Thus, the self is not only an individual entity in its own right but is also, at the same time, a montage of sub-selves experiencing a world which itself is a montage of objects and alter objects. Further, I believe that Freud's (1915) concept of the primal unconscious, that portion of the personality which is subjected to repression prior to experience and therefore never undergoes 'after repression', represents the alter ego phenomenon insofar as the primal unconscious is that portion of ourselves which we always sense exists but can never experience directly. We can see it only in shadows and reflections; it knows us without our ever being able to know it.

The alter ego phenomenon actualizes the Hegelian notion of dialectical relationships as one ego is confronted by a quasi-alien counterpart, first presupposing a mysteriously common origin (déjà vu) and then enacting either a concordant, a complementary, or a conflictual (antithetical) relationship with the other, to be followed, hopefully, by a reconciling synthesis. The alter ego phenomenon, like all dialectical relationships, is not only based fundamentally on the premise of a common origin, but also results from negation, as one aspect confronts, contradicts, or opposes the other. It also depends upon displacement (splitting), projective identification, and decomposition.

We are less consciously aware of alter ego experiences, not only because of repression, but also because of the strictures imposed upon our perceptual apparatus by a universal tendency to concretize binocular schemata into monocular (cyclopeian) over-simplification. In our childhood we knew alter egos as imaginary playmates, as guardian angels, as fairy-godmothers, etc. Our siblings and friends seemed to take over those roles and the mysterious archetypes disappeared into the substance of real people. They may reappear in varying forms during lonely times, during bouts of self-criticism, through our secretive talking to ourselves (sometimes out loud when no one else is around), in our yearning for an archetypal 'couch' to stretch us to our more excellent selves, or even in the quiet talks we have with our pets, or those we have with ourselves when engaging in our hobbies. In short, the alter ego phenomenon is the personification of a transitional object and, therefore, mitigates the terror of the 'me/not me' interface.

The alter ego phenomenon represents, consequently, the confluence of dual subjectivity ('co-I-ness') and dual experience of the self (personal and objective). Through it we approach the data of our personal experiences, and apply the categories of our inherent and applied preconceptions in order to still the anxiety of newness and strangeness. Since psychoanalytic technique is constructed to emphasize transference, most analysts emphasize familiarity – that is, how the transference demonstrates repetition of familiar, although repressed, experiences from earlier times. The alter ego (and alter imago) phenomenon may be a transitional phenomenon whereby the infant, child, or patient can defend against neophobia by assigning categories of familiarity, consciously or unconsciously. A passage quoted from the transcript of an analytic hour illustrates this dilemma:

PT: It's funny, Dr Grotstein, but why don't I have transference images towards you as if you were my father or my mother or something? I used to have these frequently with my previous therapists. M. was certainly like my mother, and L., before her, was very much like my father. But you're like nobody I ever met.

JG: I may represent the 'transference' of the person or persons you have never met – a stranger you 'knew about' from an early age, even when you were adoring your father, that you knew you had to meet in your later life to link up with to form your own family or to have as an archetypal foster parent.

PT: That makes me scared! You seem to elude every category I try to place you in. I've always been afraid of strangers and yet always longed to leave where I live and go to see people on the other side of the mountain.

JG: I am the one who always has and still lives on the other side of the mountain who seems to elude your attempts to make me familiar. Yet, in so doing, allows you to re-explore your future.

PT: It is as if this analysis is a journey undertaken by two intimate strangers.

The alter ego experience can be seen when patients wonder: 'What might have been?' or 'What would have happened if I had only . . .?' It is also demonstrated in the awareness of some unwritten agenda which hovers over one as a parallel track of measurement. People in the twilight of their lives frequently attempt to 'put their affairs in order', which often means assessing or appraising the distance between their real accomplishments and their ambitions. It is as if an invisible runner races parallel with us and somewhat ahead, periodically looking back to say, 'What? Haven't you caught up yet?'

The alter ego phenomenon belongs to the realm of narcissistic object relations. Freud's conception of narcissistic object relations presupposed the ego's identification with a narcissistically cathected object (incompletely separated, or, as we might currently say, symbiotically – or in a state of projective identification with). Following this state of identification with the narcissistically cathected object, the ego might choose an object which would be similar to the self (narcissism in the *choice* of object) because of an identification with the mother who loved the self (narcissism as the *subject* of choice) because of an identification with an object who narcissistically cathected the self (subject as its narcissistic object). Narcissistic relations are based on the needs and choices of a subjective self ('I') which does not yet experience a sufficient separation from the object and sufficient individuation in its own development to make independent and autonomous choices. The phenomenon of homosexuality is a specific instance of the alter ego phenomenon on a narcissistic basis – when it is immature or pathological. Other homosexual relationships may be alter ego phenomena on a mature basis.

My concept of narcissistic object relations includes Freud's (1912–13/ 1914) ideas (in which the ego relates to an object with which it is identified) and those of Kohut. I see the subjective self ('I') as always experienced as separate and autonomously individuated as well as not; that is, it is also experienced as primally bonded with a background subject-object of primary identification (to constitute primary narcissism) to comprise a dual-track. As a nascent 'I' (subject) contemplates its self (as object), this self-as-object is, at first, indistinguishable from mother's self. All experiences with self and with other objects constitute object relations proper, whereas all relations with the self and with objects employed as self-objects, constitute variations in the experience of subjective 'I'-ness, which can only be contemplated in reflections from the self – since the subjective 'I' can be only the subject of contemplation, never the object. Practically speaking, all experiences with objects not only enhance our inventory of object representational knowledge but also enhance our knowledge of ourselves, particularly of the subjective alter egos which those object experiences reflect. Each experience illuminates a different aspect, facet, or alter ego within the subcontinent of always emerging yet always inscrutable and ineffable 'I'-ness.

The conception of identification has obtruded on our understanding of the alter ego ('other "I"s') because of the implication that the ego projectively identifies with an object, which is then internalized as an internal object, which is then identified with once more but now internally (Klein, 1963; Grotstein, 1981). Thus dissociations of self are assigned, consequently, to identification with internalized objects. My theory includes that process but adds another theory of identification: that of the investment of the cathexis of 'I'-ness (the combined subjectivities of the projecting subject *and* of the object) in one or more of the myriad possibilities of alter egos – of disparate 'I's (subjectively) and of disparate selves (objectively) which are in our inherent and/or acquired repertoire of experience or pre-experience. All experience – and pre-experience – affects, is affected by, and/or relates to alter egos.

Contributions from neurobiology

Wigan (1844), an English psychiatrist, attended the post-mortem examination of his best friend and was puzzled to find that his friend, who had lived a normal life, had only one cerebral hemisphere. Wigan posed the question, 'Why are there two cerebral hemispheres when one is enough?' He conjectured that the two hemispheres normally have a harmonious relationship with each other, the breakdown of which duality leads to insanity. Geschwind (1983) reports a case of Kurt Goldstein's: a middle-aged woman tried to strangle herself with her left hand, while her right hand attempted to relieve the strangling grasp of her left hand. On post-mortem examination she was found to have a tumor of the corpus callosum which had severed the connection between the two hemispheres so that she was operating as two separate, self-inimical personalities.

LeCours (1975) and LeMire et al. (1975) report that the corpus callosum and the deep cerebral commissures (the major tracts which unite the two hemispheres) do not begin to myelinate (and therefore to develop) until about three to four months of age, and this myelination is not complete until adolescence, if not later. This time of onset correlates with Klein's timing for the onset of the depressive position (1952), with Mahler's (1968) conception of the development of 'hatching', and approximates Parens's concept of the development of normal aggressive assertiveness (1979). This point of onset also approximates to Winnicott's conception of the development of transitional phenomena and the beginning of the playspace of illusion (Winnicott, 1951). This delay of myelination also compels us to contemplate the infant as having two separate minds which are only slowly coming together. This delayed union of the two minds may also serve to reduce the impact of the data of personal experience and mute the intensity of feelings that may have resulted had the two mind-brains been able to comprehend the full significance of their infantile helplessness. In other words, the delayed myelination of the corpus callosum and the deep cerebral commissures may facilitate infantile innocence and omnipotence. Gazzaniga and LeDoux (1978) selectively anesthetized one cerebral hemisphere at a time and conclusively demonstrated that the normal human functions with two separate consciousnesses – one for each hemisphere, so to speak – grasping the data of experience between them, like between a thumb and a

forefinger. Phenomenologically, however, we experience only one consciousness because of the limits of our inferred sensory capacity. Gazzaniga
and LeDoux state at the end of their book:

> The last implication of this model that we would like to consider surfaces right on
> the question of the nature of personal responsibility. Most of our social insti-
> tutions are built on the notion that man is personally responsible for his actions,
> and implicit in that statement is a notion that man has a unitary nature embodied
> in the self. What are we now to do with that view, given the possibility that
> multiple selves exist, each of which can control behavior at various moments in
> time? . . .
>
> We are faced, it seems, with a new problem in analyzing the person. The
> person is a conglomeration of selves – a sociological entity. Because of our
> cultural bias toward language and its use, as well as the richness and flexibility
> that it adds to our existence, the governor of these multiple selves comes to be the
> verbal system. *Indeed, a case can be made that the entire process of maturing in
> our culture is the process of the verbal system's trying to note and eventually
> control the behavioral impulses of the many selves that dwell inside of us.* (1978:
> 159–61, my italics)

Alter ego and déjà vu

Freud dealt with the déjà vu phenomenon in terms of wish-fulfillment. He
states:

> In some dreams of landscapes or other localities, emphasis is laid in the dream
> itself on the convinced feeling of having been there once before. (Occurrence of
> 'déjà vu' in dreams have a special meaning.) These places are invariably the
> genitals of the dreamer's mother; there is indeed no other place about which one
> can assert with such conviction that one has been there once before. (Freud, 1919:
> 244)

Bion (1962, 1963, 1965, 1970) introduced the term 'inherent preconception' into psychoanalytic thinking; borrowed from Plato's Theory of Forms,
it is the belief that ideal forms existed before there were human beings to
contemplate them. This concept found its way into Kant's theory of the
noumenon, the abstract but incomprehensible notion of the thing-in-itself
prior to its becoming a phenomenon of experience to the senses. Freud
(1912–13/1914) touched on the theme of inherent preconception in his
notion of the primal horde phenomenon, alluding to our capacity to inherit
the memory trace of an ancient catastrophe – the horde of the brothers
slaying the father. Freud's concept of primal repression may designate an
inherent aspect of the self that is fated never to achieve consciousness and is,
therefore, never knowable.

Klein (1959) postulated that the infant inherited preconceptions of sexual
intercourse and of the parental genitals. Bion added the preconception of the
breast. When he formulated the notion of inherent preconceptions as a gen-

eral theorem, however, he was amplifying for psychoanalysis the premise
that we never discover anything new, we only rediscover it. As Freud stated:
'The finding of an object is in fact a re-finding of it.' (1905: 222). For Bion
the inherent preconception is mobilized when a beta element (the initial
sensory element of emotion) encounters an alpha function (our capacity to
transform the registration of the stimulus into an alpha element suitable for
'mental digestion', as dreams, emotions, thoughts, etc.). In other words, if
we accept the emotional impact of our experience, the experience is
transformed into meaningful elements for our awareness; but, at the same
time, it mobilizes the data from previous experiences with events similar to
this phenomenon – going all the way back to pre-experience, that is, to
inherent preconceptions themselves. Thus, we never encounter anything
new; we are programmed, as it were, to re-encounter yet another version of
that which has already been encountered at least once before.[4]

I would add that every time an inherent or acquired preconception mates
with its counterpart in experience and becomes realized as a conception, the
déjà vu phenomenon is enacted, and a rendezvous occurs with the ego and
its alter ego. I suggest that this process may underlie a fundamental theory of
learning and that many learning difficulties may pertain to the dread of this
rendezvous. Further, we may presume that primary process thinking, which
dominates the mind of the infant virtually to the exclusion of secondary
process, creates a cosmic view for the infant in which it is everyone and
everything, as in the 'at-one-ment' tenets of Taoism. Later the infant
descends in the world of separateness, and a newer cosmic view ensues
which includes separated others. Déjà vu thereafter constitutes the senti-
mental but uncanny link with 'Once upon a time . . .'.

The déjà vu phenomenon represents that uncanny, numinous paradox of
strange familiarity, an indescribable trick of memory, in which one feels
mysteriously connected to a strange other being. The inchoate sense of this
strange familiarity must certainly belong to the phenomenon of primal
repression (Freud, 1915), that is, to that aspect of ourselves which was repressed prior to experience and therefore comprised another self. In addition,
we are also bound to the earliest split-off aspects of selves which have
undergone different algorithmic life scenarios, for example the id, the ego
ideal, and the superego. The mysterious connection between these entities or
selves can be likened to the Möbius strip in which there is a mysterious twist
so that one feels continuity and discontinuity simultaneously.

Clinical aspects

Alter egos, both subjective and objective, comprise a great portion of our
analytical work. Patients in analysis invariably experience hitherto split-off
aspects of the self which first come to light, often, as unpleasant experiences
of self: 'I don't like that envious me.' or 'I didn't know that I was so petty.'
Often our alter egos are recovered from the analysis of our projective

identifications with objects and have hitherto been experienced as the bearers of unwanted traits within the self. Similarly with alter objects – we seldom experience the object as it is but rather confuse it with a variety of images from our own alter ego, alter object, archetypal past. 'I', 'self', and 'objects', are montages of perceptions and conceptions – and our belief in the individuality of the self and of the objects we experience is a benevolent yet costly and ill-founded illusion which allows us to navigate in a world of randomness, pretending that we know our way.

The alter ego phenomenon is demonstrable in psychotherapy and psychoanalysis as the unconscious becomes engaged and the infantile neurosis becomes transformed into the transference neurosis, with its hitherto entrapped and entrapping arcane internal objects to which ancient selves have been attached. Contrastingly innocent and demonic, infantile and mature, moral and disingenuous, healthy and regressed counterparts of the personality – each struggling for its 'day in court' – spring forth.

Frequently, patients describe their analytic progress as a contest between a regressed self and a progressing self, and experience the struggle as an internal 'political power play' between two subpersonalities. One of the goals of analysis may be to help our patients re-own alienated impulses and feelings, and to return them to consciously ambivalent integration – a process that occurs best when the separate 'I'-ness and subjectivity of the other self is acknowledged.

Child molestation and abuse frequently seem to lead to the development of multiple personalities (Kluft, 1984; Putnam, 1984). In primitive mental disorders, particularly hysteric and borderline personalities, psychical dissociation is common. In the psychoanalytic treatment of primitive mental states it seems easy to offer these patients interventions such as the following: 'Your vulnerable, dependent self is frightened by the strides made in analysis by your progressing, developing self', or 'Your petulant, defensive self seems to be envious of the you who can have a good, cooperative relationship with me', or 'When you did not perform more successfully in your recital yesterday, I believe that you were undermined by an "internal saboteur".' Interventions with this sort of phrasing address second selves which seem to insinuate themselves into the clinical picture. More dramatically, we may see patients who are violently abusive to themselves in grotesque physical ways or who mutilate themselves. Frequently it seems as though one personality is abusing another.

There are innumerable examples of alter ego and alter object phenomena in our practices. It is common for patients who have regressed to the infantile neurosis to 'recover' images of themselves as helpless infants; as wounded, disfigured victims; and so on. A number of examples follow.

A 24-year-old borderline patient finally confided in me that he has had an 'advisor' as a mythical companion and has used this secret companion since earliest childhood. As a child, he and the companion would play many games. He would seek the companion's advice and finally related to this companion as an idealized older brother (ego ideal) who would provide advice in all matters of daily life. As the analysis progressed and the transference deepened, the advisor seemed to recede into the shadows.

A 57-year-old mathematician-entrepreneur, 'Type-A' in personality character, seems to have grown up by himself, according to his view of things, because he could not depend upon his mother or father. As the analysis progressed and his dependency feelings came into prominence, he began to have more feelings about his mother but would ward them off. He once told me about a trip he had recently taken to Israel. During this trip he encountered his mother's niece (who looked exactly the way he remembered his mother thirty to forty years earlier). He experienced a deep emotional reaction at seeing this 'alter object'. He then remembered that his own mathematical abilities were stimulated by his mother teaching him mathematical exercises when he was very young. The recovery of this lost memory seems to have been stimulated by his meeting with the 'alter object', his cousin, but then dovetailed with the other 'alter object', the other mother.

R.W. is a 38-year-old male screenwriter who has recently acquired wealth after a long period of failure. He reports a pathos for poor people and still considers himself one of them. His pathos represents both empathy for others and also for his former self which is still present. He believes that his poor self is his persistent alter ego which sometimes challenges and at other times jeopardizes his new-found self.

A diffident, self-effacing patient frequently finds himself taken over by dissociative autoscopic phenomena in which he vacillates between two personalities: a weak self which seems to be his more pervasive false self, and an inner stronger self (true self) which, paradoxically, is the weaker of the two. He is ambiguous, therefore, about the identity of his 'false self' and believes that one is a 'mamma's boy' who has always been close to mother and who has been ridiculed by father, whereas the other one is the one who can do things and accomplish things in the world but rarely exerts the effort. Sometimes he feels himself to be outside his body and can see himself as a double (heautoscopy).

A physician patient who is concerned about his problem with alcohol presented the following dream: 'My wife and I were vacationing in an elegant holiday resort in Europe where we encountered a group of other Americans who were also vacationing there. One of them was about my age, was elegantly dressed, appeared to be suave and poised, and was quite knowledgeable about the subject we were talking about, the nature of which I now forget. I recall one scene in which we are walking through the courtyard and encounter him at a window on the second floor. I am aware that I am carrying an alcoholic drink and hide it embarrassedly so that he cannot see me carrying it. In the next moment, he comes down to the first floor, walks up to me, and conspiratorially whispers in to my ear, "Sinuses".' The patient's associations to the dream dealt not only with the patient's difficulty with alcohol but also with a unique theory he had developed that afflictions of the prostate gland had some effect on the nasal mucosa and the sinuses because of the similarity in their tissue composition. He stated that this was an idiosyncratic theory held by no one but himself. Thus, the elegant, suave stranger in the dream was not only an image of the analyst but also an image of his alter ego acting as helpful ego ideal. Even though the patient tried to hide the drink from him, the polite alter ego informed him via a riddle that he really knew after all but was not being critical.

B.G. is a 65-year-old owner and chief operating officer of a large chain of retail stores. He is a devout believer in reincarnation and has many dreams, as well as phantasies, of having lived previous lives. Analysis revealed these to be alter ego experiences which could be linked up to traumatic dissociation of self secondary to a manic psychosis. Although the example in this case is specific to the patient, it is conceivable that the whole gamut of reincarnation beliefs may belong in the realm of the alter ego phenomenon.

Finally, I will describe the details of a dream reported by a 54-year-old married woman, but I shall not give the associations, in order to portray the doubling process which takes place in terms of the objects and of the self in the manifest content of the dream:

Through most of the dream, I am the woman, though she doesn't look like me at all. It was all like a foreign art film (*film noir*). It began with a man having accidentally killed someone. I think in a car; I think he ran over a child. The man is outside an open window or door. It is dark and raining outside. He is very upset. I feel very sorry for him. He is thin, has straight black hair (now disheveled), rain on his glasses, kind of aesthetic-looking, of indeterminate age (perhaps mid-thirties). Through about half of the dream, he has a young boy of about six (and I do also) [alter ego, alter object]. They are only intermittent figures. They are perfectly dressed in Curzean style. The children never say anything.

Initially, there is another woman. The man is full of rage if anyone goes near her. He stalks her constantly. Eventually, he shoots her with a rifle when she is talking to another man. I replace the woman as his possession. I must avoid talking to anyone else or he will murder the other person (man or woman). He murders several people I come into contact with. I live in perpetual fear. He stalks me constantly, appearing in train windows, once on a window ledge walking toward my apartment. I see him from a crowded street. I know my little boy is in there. He knows that I am watching him. He taunts me. He always taunts me in a parasitic and evil way. He plays at murdering me, but he doesn't. He plays at murdering my child but doesn't. At one point, I realize he will not murder my boy because he is a companion for his own boy.

The longest and most terrifying period, seemingly lasting forever, is where I am in a huge house, alone. I know he is there waiting to kill me. I am so terrified that after a while I wish he would kill me and get it over with. He appears several times, but doesn't kill me.

There is a later scene in which there is a huge kitchen of a restaurant. Suddenly I see that he and his companions are the bakers. He is covered with flour and is watching me from inside a dumbwaiter, upstairs on rafters with a rifle.

Throughout, with his taunting, he is very charming, in a black humorous but sardonic way. At the end, I find that he and she (she is no longer me because I am now a different she – we both look the same, but there are two of us) kill just for the love of killing. He throws a knife at me. I am out on a city street, pleading for help; no one will help me.

A particular psychopathological perspective on the alter ego phenomena occurs in the relationship between the normal and the abnormal personalities of dysthymic, cyclothymic, and unipolar and bipolar disorders, to say nothing of some borderline, schizophreniform, and schizotypal disorders. Frankly dissociated states may occur in hysteria and in temporal lobe epilepsy (what was once called the 'Jekyll/Hyde' phenomena). Katan (1954) and Bion (1957) have described borderline and psychotic patients in whom they could detect a difference between a normal or neurotic personality and a psychotic one as the former's twin. It is easy to discern this alternation in the affective disorders when the patient reports a psychotic self as a twin and in affective disorders when patients report that their 'gloomy', 'panicky', or 'manicky' self has left and now they feel 'normal'. The transformation of the normal or neurotic personality and that of the 'biochemical alter ego' may follow different psychoanalytic agendas.

Actual consciously available alter ego phenomena are seldom available to us, however, so we have only 'visitation rights' with them in the projective screen of everyday reality – when we experience them incognito in the form of our loved ones, our friends, our colleagues, our patients, and our enemies. Analysis, particularly when projective identification is emphasized, depends for its success on our being able to recognize our lost twin self, our alter ego, in the other.

Conclusion

The alter ego phenomenon is a testimony to the arcane and uncanny 'we-ness' of 'I' and suggests that 'I' is both a single and a plural noun. The alter ego is comprised of concordant, complementary, and opposing counterparts and constitutes a template of predictability for our future and a balance in our daily lives. We encounter alter ego, as well as alter object derivatives in our daily lives when we experience the whole cast of our daily dramas. Alter ego and alter object phenomena are extensions of the psychoanalytic concept of transference. The psychoanalyst is the medium, in the more ancient sense of that word, who reintroduces the patient to the lost second self, which has made itself known through the primitive argot of symptoms – symptoms that, from another perspective, can be seen as oracular, ambiguous charades in which the alter ego pantomimes from the far country into which it had been exiled. We are linked to our alter ego(s) via a Siamese twin connection, analogous to the Möbius strip, a phenomenon denoting strangeness and simultaneous familiarity, the two together comprising the phenomenon of the uncanny. The déjà vu phenomenon unites with the alter egos.

The alter ego (and alter object) phenomenon was more widely experienced in the Romantic period when imagination was still highly respected. In today's more materialistic and 'scientific' culture, imaginal life has been eclipsed by the more concrete demons of certainty and tangibility. Nevertheless, one need only consult one's dreams to realize that the alter ego (and alter object) phenomenon is eternally present and defies the culture-bound limitations of perception and imagination. Alter ego and alter object phenomena are, in sum, counterparts in or out of counterpoint with the self. It is a critical imbalance which brings them to our awareness.

Notes

1 Heautoscopy or autoscopy is the phenomenon of being able to visualize one's own double through imagination, illusion, or hallucination. It is reported less commonly today than formerly and does not necessarily convey grave diagnostic significance. For an in-depth study of the phenomenon, see N. Lukianowicz, 'Autoscopic phenomena', *Archives of Neurology and Psychiatry*, 80 (1958), pp. 199–220; J.S. Grotstein 'Autoscopic phenomena', in Claude Friedmann and Robert Faguet (eds), *Extraordinary Disorders of Human Behavior* (Plenum Press, New York, 1982), pp. 65–78; and G.O. Gabbard and S.W. Twemlow, *With the Eyes of the Mind. An Empirical Analysis of Out-of-Body States* (Praeger, New York, 1984).

2 See Richard Rosenthal's analysis of Dostoyevsky's *The Double* in terms of the use of splitting and projective identification: R. Rosenthal, 'Dostoyevsky's experiment with projective mechanisms and the theft of identity in *The Double*', in M. Lazer (ed.), *The Anxious Subject: Nightmares and Daymares in Literature, Art, and Film* (Undena Publishers, Los Angeles, 1983), pp. 13–40.

3 It is interesting to note that this view went into eclipse with the advent of psychoanalysis but has become revived, without allusion to its origins in Janet's work, by Kohut's views on self disorders.

4 An example of an inherent preconception can be seen in physical medicine in the form of inherited immune antibodies which seem to 'know' their inimical counterparts even before their first real experience with them, e.g., bacteria. The bacteria in this case would be an example of the mysterious stranger self-object which is anticipated by its inherent preconception on the inherited template of immunity.

References

Bion, W.R. (1957) 'Differentiation of the psychotic from the non-psychotic personalities', in W.R. Bion *Second Thoughts*. London: Heinemann, 1967. pp. 43–64.

Bion, W.R. (1959) 'Attacks on linking', in W.R. Bion, *Second Thoughts*. London: Heinemann, 1967. pp. 93–109.

Bion, W.R. (1962) *Learning from Experience*. London: Heinemann.

Bion, W.R. (1963) *Elements of Psycho-Analysis*. London: Heinemann.

Bion, W.R. (1965) *Transformations*. London: Heinemann.

Bion, W.R. (1967) 'On arrogance', in W.R. Bion, *Second Thoughts*. New York: Jason Aronson. pp. 86–92.

Bion, W.R. (1970) *Attention and Interpretation*. London: Tavistock.

Bion, W.R. (1975) *A Memoir of the Future. Book 1: The Dream*. Rio de Janeiro, Brazil: Imago Press.

Bion, W.R. (1977) *A Memoir of the Future. Book 2: The Past Presented*. Rio de Janeiro, Brazil: Imago Press.

Bion, W.R. (1979) *A Memoir of the Future. Book 3: The Dawn of Oblivion*. Perthshire: Clunie Press.

Breuer, J. and Freud, S. (1893–1895) 'Studies on hysteria', *Standard Edition*, vol. 2: 1–309. London: Hogarth Press (1955).

Coleman, S.M. (1934) 'The phantom double: its psychological significance', *British Journal of Medical Psychology*, 14: 254–73.

Cox, S.D. (1980) *'The Stranger Within Thee': Concepts of the Self In Late-Eighteenth-Century Literature*. Pittsburgh, PA: University of Pittsburgh Press.

Dewhurst, K. (1954) 'Autoscopic hallucinations', *Irish Journal of Medical Science*, 263–7.

Dewhurst, K. and Pearson, J. (1955) 'Visual hallucinations of the self in organic disease', *Journal of Neurology, Neurosurgery, and Psychiatry*, 18: 53–7.

Dodds, E.R. (1951) *The Greeks and the Irrational*. Berkeley and Los Angeles, CA: University of California Press.

Emde, R.N. (1987) 'Development: terminal and interminable. I. Innate and motivational factors from infancy; II. Recent psychoanalytic theory and therapeutic considerations'. Paper presented to the International Psychoanalytic Congress, Montreal, Canada, July 1987.

Fairbairn, W.R.D. (1944) 'Endopsychic structure considered in terms of object-relationships', in W.R.D. Fairbairn, *Psychoanalytic Studies of the Personality*. London; Henley; and Boston, MA: Routledge & Kegan Paul, 1952. pp. 82–136.

Fairbairn, W.R.D. (1952) *Psychoanalytic Studies of the Personality*. London; Henley; and Boston, MA: Routledge and Kegan Paul.

Frazer, J. (1922) *The Golden Bough: A Study in Magic and Religion*. New York: Macmillan.

Freud, S. (1905) 'Three essays on the theory of sexuality', *Standard Edition*, vol. 7: 125–245. London: Hogarth Press (1953).

Freud, S. (1912–13/1913) 'Totem and taboo', *Standard Edition*, vol. 13: 1–161. London: Hogarth Press (1957).

Freud, S. (1914) 'On narcissism: an introduction', *Standard Edition*, vol. 14: 67–104. London: Hogarth Press (1957).

Freud, S. (1915) 'Repression', *Standard Edition*, vol. 14: 141–58. London: Hogarth Press (1957).

Freud, S. (1915/1917) 'Mourning and melancholia', *Standard Edition*, vol. 14: 237–60. London: Hogarth Press (1957).

Freud, S. (1919) 'The "Uncanny"' *Standard Edition*, vol. 17: 217–52. London: Hogarth Press (1955).

Freud, S. (1923) 'The ego and the id', *Standard Edition*, vol. 19: 3–68. London: Hogarth Press (1961).

Freud, S. (1895/1950) 'Project for a scientific psychology', *Standard Edition*, vol. 1: 283–398. London: Hogarth Press (1966).

Gabbard, G.O. and Twemlow, S.W. (1984) *With the Eyes of the Mind. An Empirical Analysis of Out-of-Body States*. New York: Praeger.

Galton, F. (1883/1908) *Inquiries into Human Faculty and its Development*. New York: Dutton Press.

Gazzaniga, M.S. and LeDoux, J.E. (1978) *The Integrated Mind*. New York: Plenum Press.

Geschwind, N. (1983) 'The organization of the living brain', in Jonathan Miller (ed.), *States of Mind*. New York: Pantheon Books. pp. 116–35.

Grotstein, J.S. (1979a) 'Demoniacal possession, splitting, and the torment of joy', *Contemporary Psychoanalysis*, 15 (3): 407–53.

Grotstein, J.S. (1979b) 'The soul in torment: a newer and older view of psychopathology', *The Bulletin for Catholic Psychiatrists*, 25: 36–52.

Grotstein, J.S. (1981) *Splitting and Projective Identification*. New York: Jason Aronson.

Grotstein, J.S. (1982) 'Autoscopic phenomena', in Claude Friedmann and Robert Faguet (eds), *Extraordinary Disorders of Human Behavior*. New York: Plenum Press. pp. 65–78.

Grotstein, J.S. (1997) ' "Internal objects" or "chimerical monsters?": the demonic "third forms" of the internal world', *The Journal of Analytical Psychology*, 42: 47–80.

Grotstein, J.S. (in press) *Who is the Dreamer Who Dreams the Dream?*. New Jersey: Hillsdale.

Guerard, A.J. (ed.) (1967) *Stories of the Double*. Philadelphia and New York: J.B. Lippincott Co.

Jung, C.G. (1953) *Psychology and Alchemy*. (Trans. R.F.C. Hull.) Bollinger Series XX, vol. X. New York: Pantheon Books.

Katan, M. (1954) 'The importance of the non-psychotic part of the personality in schizophrenia', *International Journal of Psycho-Analysis*, 35: 119–28.

Kernberg, O. (1975) *Borderline Conditions and Pathological Narcissism*. New York: Jason Aronson.

Klein, M. (1952) 'Some theoretical conclusions regarding the emotional life of the infant', in M. Klein, P. Heinemann, S. Isaacs and J. Riviere (eds), *Developments in Psycho-Analysis*. London: Hogarth Press and the Institute of Psycho-Analysis. pp. 198–236.

Klein, M. (1959) *The Psycho-Analysis of Children*. London: Hogarth Press.

Klein, M. (1963) 'On identification', in M. Klein, P. Heinemann and R. Money-Kryle (eds), *New Directions in Psycho-Analysis*. New York: Basic Books. pp. 3099–345.

Kluft, R. (1984) 'Multiple personality in childhood', *Psychiatric Clinics of North America*, 7: 121–34.

Kohut, H. (1971) *The Analysis of the Self*. New York: International Universities Press.

Kohut, H. (1977) *The Restoration of the Self*. New York: International Universities Press.

LeCours, A.R. (1975) 'Myelogenetic correlates of the development of speech and language', in *Foundations of Language Development: A Multi-Disciplinary Approach*, vol. 1. New York: Academic Press. pp. 121–34.

LeMire, R.J., Loesser, J.D., Leech, R.W. and Alvord, E.C. (1975) *Normal and Abnormal Development of the Human Nervous System*. Hagerstown, MD: Harper & Row.

Lukianowicz, N. (1958) 'Autoscopic phenomena', *Archives of Neurology and Psychiatry*, 80: 199–220.

Mahler, M.S. (1968) *On Human Symbiosis and the Vicissitudes of Individuation*. New York: International Universities Press.

Mahler, M.S., Pine, F. and Bergman, A. (1975) *The Psychological Birth of the Human Infant: Symbiosis and Individuation*. New York: Basic Books.

Ogden, T. (1983) 'The concept of internal object relations', *International Journal of Psycho-Analysis*, 64: 227–41.

Ogden, T. (1984) 'Instinct, phantasy, and psychological deep structure', *Contemporary Psychoanalysis*, 20 (4): 500–25.

Ogden, T. (1986) *The Matrix of the Mind*. Northvale, NJ/London: Jason Aronson.

O'Shaughnessy, B. (1982) 'The id and the thinking process', in: Richard Wollheim and James Hopkins (eds), *Philosophical Essays on Freud*. London: Cambridge University Press. pp. 106–23.

Parens, H. (1979) *The Development of Aggression in Early Childhood*. New York: Jason Aronson.

Pirandello, Luigi (1995) *Six Characters in Search of an Author and Other Plays*. London/New York: Penguin Books.

Putnam, F. (1984) 'The psychophysiologic investigation of the multiple personality disorder', *Psychiatric Clinics of North America*, 7: 31–40.

Rogers, R. (1970) *A Psychoanalytic Study of the Double in Literature*. Detroit, MI: Wayne University Press.

Rosenfeld, R. (1987) *Impasse and Interpretation*. London: Tavistock.

Rosenfield, C. (1967) 'The shadow within: the conscious and unconscious use of the double', in A.J. Guerard (ed.), *Stories of the Double*. Philadelphia, PA and New York: J. B. Lippincott Co. pp. 311–31.

Rosenthal, R. (1983) 'Dostoyevsky's experiment with projective mechanisms and the theft of identity in *The Double*', in M. Lazar (ed.), *The Anxious Subject: Nightmares and Daymares in Literature, Art, and Film*, vol. II of *Interplay*. Los Angeles: Undena Publishers. pp. 13–40. Reprinted in D. Rancour-Laferriere (ed.) (1988) *Russian Literature and Psychoanalysis*, vol. I. Amsterdam: Benjmins.

Salley, R.D. (1988) 'Subpersonalities with dreaming functions in patients with multiple personalities', *The Journal of Nervous and Mental Disease*, 176 (2): 112–15.

Silverman, L.H., Lachmann, F.M. and Milich, R.H. (1982) *The Search for Oneness*. New York: International Universities Press.

Simon, J. and Goldberg, C. (1984) 'The role of the double in the creative process and psychoanalysis', *Journal of the American Academy of Psychoanalysis*, 12 (3): 341–62.

Steiner, J. (1993) *Psychic Retreats*. London: Routledge.

Stevenson, R.L. (1886/1992) *Dr. Jekyll and Mr. Hyde and Other Stories*. New York: Knopf.

Whitman, Walt (1921/1932) *The Uncollected Poetry and Prose of Walt Whitman, much of which has been but recently discovered, with various early manuscripts now first published, collected and edited by Emory Holloway*. New York: P. Smith.

Wigan, A. (1844) *The Duality of the Mind: A New View of Insanity*. London: Longman, Brown, Green & Longman.

Winnicott, D.W. (1951) 'Transitional objects and transitional phenomena', in D.W. Winnicott, *Collected Papers: Through Paediatrics to Psycho-Analysis*. New York: Basic Books, 1958. pp. 229–42.

Winnicott, D.W. (1952) 'Psychosis and child care', in D.W. Winnicott, *Collected Papers: Through Paediatrics to Psycho-Analysis*. New York: Basic Books, 1958. pp. 219–28.

Winnicott, D.W. (1963) 'Communicating and not communicating leading to a study of certain opposites', in D.W. Winnicott, *The Maturational Processes and the Facilitating Environment. Studies on the Theory of Emotional Development*. New York: Basic Books, 1965. pp. 179–92.

Winnicott, D.W. (1971) *Playing and Reality*. London: Tavistock.

Wolstein, B. (1974) ' "I" processes and "me" patterns: two aspects of the psychic self in transference and countertransference', *Contemporary Psychoanalysis*, 10 (3): 347–57.

3 IF YOU CAN'T BE JEKYLL BE HYDE: AN EXISTENTIAL-PHENOMENOLOGICAL EXPLORATION OF LIVED-PLURALITY

Mick Cooper

[L]ate one accursed night, I compounded the elements, watched them boil and smoke together in the glass, and when the ebullution had subsided, with a strong glow of courage, drank off the potion.

The most racking pains succeeded: a grinding in the bones, deadly nausea, and a horror of the spirit that cannot be exceeded at the hour of birth or death. Then these agonies began swiftly to subside, and I came to myself as if out of a great sickness. There was something strange in my sensations, something indescribably new, and, from its very novelty, incredibly sweet. I felt younger, lighter, happier in my body; within I was conscious of a heady recklessness, a current of disordered sensual images running like a mill race in my fancy, a solution of the bonds of obligation, an unknown but not an innocent freedom of the soul. I knew myself, at the first breath of this new life, to be more wicked, ten fold more wicked, sold a slave to my original evil; and the thought, in that moment, braced and delighted me like wine.

(Stevenson, 1886/1993: 50)

The image of Dr Jekyll, the prototypical Victorian gentleman, transforming into the grotesquely hunched Mr Hyde, is all but etched on our cultural imagination. And yet, viewed from this perspective – as an outside, 'objective' observer – an understanding of Dr Jekyll's metamorphosis is inevitably limited. From witnessing the writhing limbs and strangled shrieks we may grasp something of Dr Jekyll's agony, but it is only when we are presented with Dr Jekyll's own, subjective account of his experiences, as above, that we can begin to gain a deeper and more detailed insight into the nature of his transformation: the nausea-becoming-sweetness, the flood of sensual images, the experience of delight. Equally, while the question of self-plurality has been explored from a variety of external, 'objective' perspectives – for example, neuropsychology (e.g., Gazzaniga, 1985), cognitive psychology (e.g., Martindale, 1980), social psychology (e.g., James 1890/1981) – without an exploration of self-plurality from the perspective of the subjectively-experiencing individual, our understanding of this phenomenon may inevitably remain limited.

The importance of examining this phenomenon in terms of the subject's own experiencing, however, is more than, 'a mere matter for soaring speculation about the most general or generalities' (Heidegger, 1926/1962: 29). Rather, from an existential-phenomenological perspective, the question of how individuals experience their world is the primordial question, the question that must be asked and answered before any other question can be tackled, '*the most basic and the most concrete*' (Heidegger 1926/1962: 29) of all questions. As Merleau-Ponty argues, prior to any psychological theorizing, prior to any empirical experimentation, there is an existent, embodied human being – psychologist or otherwise – who is encountering his or her world in an immediate and unreflective way: existing at 'the layer of living experience through which other people and things are first given to us' (1962: 57). First there is human Being; then there are theories, research, concepts – the latter cannot exist other than as a project of the former. Rather than our experiences, then, being mere epiphenomena, from an existential-phenomenological perspective they are the very grounds from which all other knowledge emerges. What we know is what we experience, and to reflect on our lived-experiences is to return 'to the things themselves': 'the ultimate court of appeal in our knowledge of things' (Merleau-Ponty, 1962: 23).

In this respect, the question is not whether self-plurality is objectively measurable from the standpoint of an 'objective' measurer, but whether it is possible to experience self-plurality from the standpoint of a subjective-experiencer. Are you experiencing self-plurality, for instance, as you read this chapter? Do you feel like there are different parts of you feeling different things right at this moment: for example, an 'exploratory self' which is hoping to understand an existential-phenomenological perspective on self-plurality, a 'critical self' which is thinking, 'What the hell is he on about!', and a 'lazy self' which is more concerned with what is currently being broadcast on television? Or would it be more veridical to state that the 'self' which is currently experiencing this chapter (for example, an 'exploratory self') is qualitatively different from a 'self' that may emerge at a later date (for example, a 'lazy self')?

At the level of lived-experiences, the notion of a plurality of coexistent, independent selves – as proposed, for instance, by Freud's (1923) theory of id, ego and superego, or Beahrs's (1982) theory of 'co-consciousness' – is profoundly problematic. Existentially, 'Being-in-the-world is a structure which is primordially and constantly whole' (Heidegger, 1926/1962: 225), a unified living-through which cannot be fragmented, 'for the simple reason that human Being-in-the-world is by nature indivisible' (Boss, 1979: 147). Such indivisibility arises from the fact that the experience of Being-in-the-world is a 'field' (Rogers, 1959) – 'A totality of coexisting facts which are conceived of as mutually interdependent' (Lewin, 1951: 240) – in which it is the relationship between the parts, and not the parts themselves, which constitutes the lived-experience. Hence, a plurality of simultaneous-yet-independent 'part-experiences' is inconceivable, as it is the interrelationship between the 'different' experiences which constitutes the very essence of that experiencing. In other words, it would not be possible for you to experience the reading of this chapter simultaneously-yet-independently as an 'exploratory self' and as a 'lazy self', because, at the level of lived-experiences, some relationship must necessarily exist between these two different self-experiences, and it is the relationship which co-constitutes the actual experience. While feelings of laziness and feelings of interest may coexist therefore, they could only coexist as interdependent feelings: for example, as a subjectively-felt laziness against a background of interest, or as a subjectively-felt interest against a background of laziness, or as a subjectively-felt interest which was trying to block out feelings of laziness. To simultaneously-yet-independently experience both feelings of laziness and feelings of interest, on the other hand, would be like simultaneously-yet-independently perceiving both the young woman and the old woman in the classic gestalt illustration.

Yet remaining at the level of lived-experiences, one encounters an intriguing paradox. For while experiences would appear to be unpluralizable, it is by no means uncommon for individuals to describe their subjectively-felt lived-experiences in fundamentally self-pluralistic terms. Within the consulting room, clients (both from a clinical and subclinical population) regularly – and quite spontaneously – talk about experiencing different 'parts'/'sides'/'aspects' to themselves: for example, their 'vulnerable side', their 'critical part', their 'inner adult'; even Carl Rogers (1986), the quintessential phenomenological psychotherapist, has described a piece of person-centred therapy in which he helped a client to identify – and befriend – a 'naughty little girl' inside of her. Equally, clients may talk about how they switch from one personality to another, describing themselves as 'schizophrenic', 'Like the woman/man in the book/film *Sybil/The Three Faces of Eve/The Minds of Billy Milligan*' or, indeed, 'Like Jekyll and Hyde'. One such client was Joan,[1] a 35-year-old teacher, who came into psychotherapy saying that she had always experienced substantial difficulties in her relationships with men, and was currently on the verge of splitting up with a man who she really loved. Much of the time around her boyfriend, she explained, she felt like a 'good little girl' – desperately trying to win his approval and affection by being considerate, letting him watch his television programmes, and making numerous sacrifices for him. But there were also times when she said that she turned into what she described as 'the bitch from hell' – screaming at him that he was no good, that he didn't pull his weight around the house, and that he ought to 'get his shit together' or leave. After such 'outbursts' she said she would then feel incredibly guilty and go back to being a 'good little girl' in an attempt to win back his affections. Furthermore, when Joan was teaching, she experienced herself as neither a 'little girl' nor a 'bitch', but as a capable, rational and sophisticated woman, who had the capacity to deal effectively with those around her. If only, she said, she could be a bit more of a 'teacher' in the relationship, and a lot less of a 'good girl' and a 'bitch'.

The purpose of this chapter, then, is to find a way of resolving the paradox of a unity that appears to have the potential to be plural. The chapter begins by presenting a Rogerian, phenomenological theory of how an individual may come to be divided against him or herself, and then goes on to develop Rogers' work in a more pluralistic direction. The final part of this chapter looks at the subjectively-lived implications of this self-pluralism.

Self-experience and self-concept: the divided self

In exploring how unified experiences may become pluralized, Rogers' (1951, 1959) developmental theory provides a useful starting point. For Rogers, the unity of the organism is not just a unity of experiencing but a unity of motivation, in which the individual, as a whole, strives for just one goal – that of actualization: 'the inherent tendency of the organism to develop all its capacities in ways which serve to maintain or enhance the organism' (1959: 196). And yet, within this profoundly holistic framework, Rogers outlines a process whereby this wholeness may come to be fundamentally divided against itself.

Rogers' (1951, 1959) developmental narrative begins with a child who experiences its world through the totality of its phenomenal field. As the child develops, however, Rogers argues that their phenomenal field becomes increasingly differentiated. As part of this process, those experiences related to the child's own awareness of his or her Being become differentiated off from the rest of the phenomenological field as 'self-experiences'. Thus a young boy might begin to develop a primitive concept of him-self, as 'someone who likes playing the piano', or 'someone who gets scared of monsters'. For Rogers, however, this self-concept is not simply a collection of independent, distinctive characteristics – even in the form of a multi-faceted hierarchy (see Hattie, 1992). Rather, the self-concept, as a perceptual experience like any other experience, is a patterned, coherent, integrated, organized gestalt. From this perspective, then, the young boy does not experience him-self as a person who is 'creative', plus 'scared', plus 'x'; rather, he experiences him-self as a person who is 'creative-scared-x' – as an interdependent, uniquely-constellated configuration of characteristics which cannot be broken down to its constituent parts. Furthermore, for Rogers, this unity of the self-concept is not just a given but a goal towards which the individual constantly motivates him or herself. This hypothesis is based on the work of Lecky (1945/1961), who argued that the fundamental motive of the organism is to maintain its unity. Because, as Lecky proposed, the individual's 'valuation of himself' acts as the 'nucleus' of this system, a consistent sense of self becomes a central motive of the organism as a whole.

Ideally, according to Rogers (1951, 1959), the child's self-concept should correspond to their self-experiences. However, Rogers argues that a fundamental divide arises from the fact that the child, as part of his or her actualizing tendency, has a need for positive regard: being loved, liked, valued, respected, accepted – the experience of 'making a positive difference in the experiential field of an other' (1959: 208). Because of this need – both from others and from self – the child increasingly turns his or her attention to the positive regard evoked in others, and begins to associate his or her self-experiences with certain levels of acceptance, warmth, and so on. In some very rare cases, a child will experience positive regard in relation to all their self-experiences – what Rogers refers to as 'unconditional positive regard'. More likely, however, the child will begin to discover that certain of his or her self-experiences are associated with positive regard while others are not: for example, 'People seem to like me when I play the piano; but when I tell them that I'm terrified of monsters, they just tell me to grow up and stop being silly.' Hence, the child develops what Rogers refers to as a 'regard complex': 'all those self-experiences, together with their interrelationships, which the individual discriminates as being related to the positive regard of a particular social other' (1959: 209).

According to Rogers (1951, 1959), however, this experience of positive regard, the need for it, and the regard complex do not exist only at the interpersonal level. Rather, as the child develops, the associations between self-experiences and positive regard are internalized, such that the child comes to experience 'positive self-regard' independently of the positive regard transactions from external others. Hence, no longer does the child need others to 'reward' him for playing the piano to experience positive regard – he 'rewards' himself, through the medium of the total 'self-regard complex'. The child has come to selectively view his self-experiences as more or less worthy of self-regard – he has acquired what Rogers terms 'conditions of worth'. And because, as an internalization of the need for positive regard, the child has a need for positive self-regard, he comes selectively to seek those self-experiences which are associated with positive self-regard and avoid those self-experiences which are not. Thus the child is quite happy to practise on the piano because it gives him a good feeling about himself; but when he feels fear at night and a desire to run away he does not act on it, because to do so would fail to invoke positive self-regard: 'Why are you such a scaredy-cat!', he might say to himself.

Furthermore, Rogers (1951, 1959) argues that, because of the need for positive self-regard, the child begins to *perceive* his or her self-experiences selectively. Those self-experiences consistent with the child's conditions of worth will evoke feelings of positive self-regard. For this reason the child should feel quite comfortable with reflecting on these self-experiences, symbolizing them accurately at the level of conscious awareness, and integrating them into the overall self-concept. But those self-experiences contrary to the child's conditions of worth will fail to evoke feelings of positive self-regard. Hence, the child is less likely to feel comfortable with reflecting on these self-experiences. Rather, the child may leave the self-experiences at a pre-reflective level, refraining from symbolizing them accurately at the level of conscious awareness, and failing to integrate them into his or her overall self-concept. Rogers refers to this process of discrimination without reflective awareness as 'subception', achieved through such strategies as denial and distortion. At the same time, the child may introject experiences associated with positive self-regard which lie entirely outside the realms of their own self-experiencing. The consequence of this selective perception is that a discrepancy 'develops between the self as perceived, and the actual experience of the organism. Thus the individual may perceive himself as having characteristics a, b, c, and experiencing feelings x, y, z. An accurate symbolisation of his experience would, however, indicate characteristics c, d, e and feelings v, w, x' (Rogers, 1959: 203). The young boy begins to believe that he is someone who likes playing the piano, and someone who is not afraid of the monster under his bed.

Having developed a sense of self which is discrepant with the organism's actual experiencing, the desire for self-consistency (Lecky, 1945/1961; Rogers, 1951, 1959) then reinforces the individual's tendency to avoid both those behaviours and experiences which challenge this sense of self. The self-concept thus becomes a selective screen (Burns, 1979), filtering out self-experiences and possibilities that do not fit in with the individual's beliefs about who they are. Spinelli (1994) terms this 'disowning' of experiences that the self-construct cannot accommodate 'dissociation', and suggests that the re-attribution of the phenomenological experiences to someone or something else may be one particularly prevalent means by which the organism attempts to maintain the integrity of its self-construct. He gives the example of one of his clients, Clive, a fundamentalist lay preacher who 'experienced sexual arousal when in the presence of certain female members in his religious commune'. Believing, however, that he had, in his own words, ' "overcome the temptations of the flesh" ', Clive was required to 'explain his experience as that of "temporary possession by Satan" ' (1994: 345). Through this process of disowning, then, along with other strategies of denial and distortion, the believed-in self-concept becomes more and more reified: the individual dissociates themselves from particular self-experiences, these dissociated self-experiences are not integrated back into the self-concept, and so the sense of self moves further and further away from that which is not associated with positive self-regard. The result is a self-concept that becomes narrower and narrower, and less and less able to incorporate the totality of the individual's lived-experiences.

If an individual could align their lived-experiences with their believed-in self-construct – for example if the young boy could actually stop being scared at night – then the discrepancy between self-experiences and self-construct might be dissolved. But because, as Rogers (1951, 1959) argues, the organism tends towards actualizing the *totality* of its Being – not just those aspects consistent with the self-concept – then the organism-as-a-whole will continue to experience and act towards its world in ways that are incongruent with the believed-in self-concept. For this reason, though the young boy may attempt to deny or distort his fears, the needs and feelings of his organismic totality cannot be discarded. As he lies in his bed, he feels something hollow and gnawing in the pit of his stomach. He ignores it, tells him-self that he's a big boy now, that he shouldn't be afraid of monsters, but the gnawing eats away at him from the inside. He wants to move, wants to run for support and comfort, but he is pinned down by the need for positive self-regard and self-consistency. If the fear becomes so overwhelming that, at some point the organism-as-a-whole does decide to leap out of bed, on reflection – and in relation to his self-construct – the young boy may still attempt to disown these experiences: 'I can't believe I ran to my parents', 'I don't know what came over me'. In this sense, then, the individual becomes a 'divided personality' (Rogers, 1959): torn between the motive to actualize its self-as-perceived ('who I should be') and the motive to actualize the totality of its organismic Being ('who I fully am'). Only by de-constricting the self-concept, only by returning it to a 'fluid gestalt, changing flexibly in the process of assimilation of new *experience*' (1959: 234), can the individual overcome this 'basic estrangement', and once more return to being the fully functioning individual that he or she has the capacity to become.

Plural self-concepts

Rogers' (1951, 1959) theory of the 'divided personality' provides a means of understanding self-plurality while maintaining the integrity of the experiencing whole. For Rogers, experiencing at any one moment is always a totality – whether reflective or pre-reflective – but the totality of what is reflected upon need not be the totality of what is experienced at a pre-reflective level. Hence, the split that Rogers is proposing is not a synchronic one (that is, between two simultaneous-yet-independent parts) but a diachronic one (between what is reflectively experienced, and the totality of the reflective possibilities). In this respect, a Rogerian notion of self-plurality accords with the statement by the philosopher Galen Strawson (1997: 416) that: 'the experience of multiplicity can at most affect . . . the sense of the mental self as diachronically single. . . . It cannot affect . . . the sense of the mental self as synchronically single'.

Yet, in itself, what Rogers (1951, 1959) is describing is not a plurality of experiences but a duality – a one-way splitting between the believed-in self-construct and the phenomenologically-experiencing organismic totality. In the case of Dr Jekyll, such a theory of self-estrangement goes some way to making sense of his experiences, but it cannot explain the whole story. In the totality of his organismic Being, Dr Jekyll is Dr Jekyll-and-Mr Hyde. Indeed, as he notes: 'all human beings . . . are commingled out of good and evil' (Stevenson, 1886/1993: 51). But through a concern 'for the respect of the wise and good', Dr Jekyll develops a self that, 'wears a more than commonly grave countenance before the public', denying the 'impatient gaiety' and wildness that characterized his youthful self-experiencing. 'Hence it came about', writes Dr Jekyll, 'that I concealed my pleasures; and that when I reached years of reflection, and began to look round me, and take stock of my progress and position in the world, I stood already committed to a profound duplicity of life' (Stevenson, 1886/1993: 48). So far so good, but if this desire for positive self-regard, denial of self-experiences and realization of self-estrangement was the complete picture, then the tale of Dr Jekyll and Mr Hyde would end here: with a repressed and lifeless Victorian gentleman, struggling against the constant calling of his organismic needs. (Alternatively, had Dr Jekyll entered person-centred therapy, the tale might end with a Victorian gentleman increasingly able to actualize his wilder potentialities.) But instead, the story takes a twist that would seem entirely incompatible with Rogers' theory of human development. For instead of continuing to reify his self-concept against the onslaught of his organismic yearnings, Dr Jekyll does something entirely incompatible with Rogerian theory: he sacrifices his original self-concept, and instead develops an entirely new self-concept which is its complete antithesis – that of the 'malign', 'bestial', 'villainous' and 'depraved' Mr Hyde.

Such radical self-concept switching is not limited to fiction. Joan, for instance, also experienced profound shifts in her concept of self: from 'child' to 'bitch' to 'adult'. Other clients speak of other switches in self-concept: from a sense of self as fearsome to a sense of self as easy-going; from a sense of self as omnipotent to a sense of self as helpless; from a sense of self as open to a sense of self as defensive. Indeed Rogers, too, writes that:

> in the process of change which appeared to occur in therapy, it was not at all uncommon to find violent fluctuations in the concept of the self. A client, during a given interview, would come to experience himself quite positively. He felt that he was worthwhile, that he could meet life with the capacities he possessed, and that he was experiencing a quiet confidence. Three days later he might return with a completely reversed conception of himself. The same evidence now proved an opposite point. The positive new choice he had made now was an instance of silly immaturity; the valid feelings courageously expressed to his colleagues now were clearly inadequate. Often such a client could date, to the moment, the point at which, following some very minor incident, the balance was upset, and his picture of himself had undergone a complete flip-flop. During the interview, it might suddenly reverse itself again. (1959: 201)

Such 'violent fluctuations' in the concept of self suggest that the theory of a single self-concept which filters out aspects of the experiencing-organism's lived-world propounded by Rogers (1951, 1959) would appear to be somewhat unidimensional. Rather, what these experiences seem to suggest is that the individual may have the possibility of accessing – and switching between – a *plurality* of qualitatively distinctive self-concepts, each of which may filter out aspects of the individual's lived-world in qualitatively distinctive ways. This is acknowledged by David Brazier, editor of *Beyond Carl Rogers*, who writes: 'It is perfectly possible to have a multitude of different self-concepts' (1993: 85); and in recent years, a picture of the person 'as possessing a multiplicity of credible self conceptions' (Gergen, 1982: 138) has become increasingly supported by empirical research. Lester (1992), for instance, asked undergraduates to describe their 'different selves', and found that 84 per cent were able to describe more than one self, with a mean of 3.46 selves per student. In a more complex study, Rosenberg and Gara (1985) asked professional women to describe, in their own terms, from twenty to fifty of their personal identities: for example as 'psychologist', 'historian', 'overeater'. Responses were entered into a two-way matrix and then subjected to a constrained Boolean factor analysis, such that an identity structure could be determined for each woman. As hypothesized, the traits by which the women described themselves varied enormously from personal identity to personal identity, but in contrast to a haphazard spread of personal-definitions from identity to identity that might be predicted from a situationist perspective (Mischel, 1968), Rosenberg and Gara found that the personal identities tended to cluster around a small number of higher-order identities.

A plurality of self-concepts have also been identified in the self-narratives that people relate. McAdams (1985) asked subjects to think about their life as a book, and to divide it up into chapters, describing the content of each chapter. McAdams found that many of the subjects described two or more 'imagoes': 'idealized and personified image of self that functions as a main character in an adult's life story' (1985: 116). Similarly Gregg found that, 'Life-history interviews show narrators to shift among multiple, often contradictory self-representations' (1995: 617). Gregg gives the case-example of Skip, an American assembly-line worker, whose self-narrative twists and turns around three 'highly elaborated' images of self:

> At times he describes himself as an exploited, humiliated, and defeated 'factory rat', at times as the leader of a guerrilla war against his foreman by day and a rebellious folk singer by night; and at times as a tyrant – if only briefly in fantasy, in humour that often takes aim at ethnic minorities, and in the authoritarian fashion with which he equates full democracy with chaos and insists that people need strong leaders. (1995: 623)

If one accepts, then, the possibility that the individual may possess a plurality of possible self-constructs, one is left with the question of how such self-plurality may develop at the level of lived-experiences. That is, how is it possible that an existent human Being can come to form a plural understanding of themselves – particularly given Rogers' (1959) assertion that the self-concept is experienced as a consistent and unified whole?

A first possible explanation revolves around the distinction between synchronic and diachronic self-consistency. According to Rogers (1951, 1959), an individual with a relatively narrow and rigid sense of self will tend towards dealing with self-concept-inconsistent self-experiences by attempting to 'realign' the self-experiences with the self-concept. Yet, a closer reading of Lecky (1945/1961) suggests that this is not the only possibility for such an individual. Rather, Lecky writes that, 'Any value entering the system which is inconsistent with the individual's valuation of himself cannot be assimilated; it meets with resistance and is likely, *unless a general re-organization occurs*, to be rejected' (1945/1961: italics added). In other words, along with the possibility that an individual may attempt to realign self-experiences with self-concept, there is also the possibility that the individual will radically reorganize their self-concept to match the new self-experiences. Such a transformation might violate the diachronic consistency between the individual's present self-concept and their past self-concept, but it would at least serve to maintain the synchronic consistency between the individual's current self-experiences and their self-concept – a consistency which the process of denial or distortion of self-experiences fundamentally violates. Paradoxically, then, identifying with a new sense of self may be one means of maintaining self-consistency. As Joan's organismic feelings of anger and irritation towards her boyfriend start to find behavioural expression she has two avenues for maintaining a consistent sense of self. Either she can hold on to her 'good little girl' self-concept and experience the anger as something external and alien: 'He's making me act like this', 'I don't know what I'm doing', 'It's not like me at all'; or, she can detach herself from her initial self-concept and temporarily reorganize her sense of self into a new self-concept which is entirely compatible with the emergent self-experiences: 'I feel like I'm a screaming harpy', 'I just want to destroy', 'I don't care about anyone else'. In Joan's case, it is the latter alternative which she seems to turn towards. Equally, when Dr Jekyll starts to experience feelings of recklessness and freedom, he can experience him-self in two possible ways: either as Dr Jekyll who is having some very un-Jekyll-like experiences, or else as a new self which is consistent with the emergent self-experiences. Again, it is the latter option to which Dr Jekyll turns, defining him-self at the breath of these new experiences to be someone tenfold more wicked than the original Dr Jekyll.

But why is it that individuals may choose to maintain diachronic self-consistency in one instance, and synchronic self-consistency in another? Based on Lecky's thinking (1945/1961), what we can predict is that the individual will choose the way which least violates the principle of self-consistency as a whole. If subception of the self-experiences can occur without too much threat and anxiety to the individual, then this may be the preferred option. But if the inconsistent self-experiences and behaviours are continual and unremitting – if they are less one-off self-inconsistent bursts of anger or panic and more a persistent, inescapable gulf between self-concept and self-experience – then it may be that a temporary yet radical transformation into a new self-concept is the only way that the individual can actualize the totality of their Being, while protecting themselves from a total breakdown in the self-structure. Joan bursts out in anger at her boyfriend and initially she has a sense of disconnected-ness, as if it is not her at all who is being angry. She feels apart from her Being, as if her body has been taken over and she is somewhere separate from it. If the conflict ended here, perhaps Joan would never dis-identify with her 'good little girl' self-concept. But her boyfriend argues back: he says that he does do things, that she shouldn't always be having a go at him, that she should just get out of the way so he can watch television. And now, being outside of her self is not enough – it is too empty, too fragile, too decentred. She needs to be behind her-self: consistent, congruent, like an arrow that can shoot out the rage through her-self that she is feeling inside. She is coming back into her body, her-self, but it is a new self – a self which encompasses and legitimates her feelings of rage. She is right. He is a pig. She isn't going to take this any more. She's someone who can stand by her position and, by God, she's going to. She's committed, stern, fierce. She doesn't care what he thinks. She doesn't care if she screams at him and the neighbours hear it and she wakes up the baby next door.

What's more, when her boyfriend starts to apologize, when he says that perhaps he could do a bit more around the house and that he can be pretty lazy at times, Joan will have none if it. She's in 'bitch from hell' mode now, and the same rules of self-consistency and subception apply. He says that perhaps he could do more washing and she says, 'What about always picking your socks up from every goddamn corner of the house!' He says that maybe he could pick his socks up, and she says, 'And you never get up from that bloody television set!' Somewhere at the fringes of her phenomenal field she is aware that perhaps he is trying to sort things out, that perhaps she should let her anger drop, but she feels determined to stay consistent with who she now is. Only when her 'bitch from hell' self-concept becomes entirely incompatible with the love and affection she is experiencing towards him does she finally let it go, and switch back into 'good little girl' mode.

The 'switch' into a new self-concept that Joan experiences, however, would appear to be very different from the smooth and fluid assimilation of new self-experiences that Rogers' fully-functioning person is said to go through (Rogers, 1951, 1959, 1961). As with Rogers' interviewee, as with Dr Jekyll and Mr Hyde, the shift is a violent fluctuation – a sudden, staccato-like, 'flip-flopping' between qualitatively different selves. Such 'switching' only makes sense in the context of Rogers' assertion that the self-concept is not 'an entity of slow accretion, of step-by-step learning, of thousands of unidirectional conditionings' (1959: 201), but 'a gestalt, a configuration in which the alteration of one minor aspect could completely affect the whole pattern' (1959: 209). In the example of Rogers' interviewee, then, the initial self-concept might be something along the lines of a total immature-inadequate-negative-worthless gestalt. Having begun to experience a degree of positivity following his interview with Rogers, therefore, it is not possible for him simply to take out 'negative' from his self-concept configuration and insert 'positive' instead. Rather, he must invoke a whole new self-concept gestalt configuration which is complete within itself.

Such a configuration *already* exists, however, by virtue of the fact that a gestalt formation does not exist in isolation, but in terms of its relation to what it is not (Gregg, 1995; Spinelli, 1994). As Gregg writes: 'identity must not be viewed as a set of self-attributions. . . . Instead, identity consists of a system of self versus anti-self, or Me versus not-Me contrasts, so the meaning of a quality attributed to Me cannot be known without discovering the contrary not-Me representation(s) which define it' (1995: 637). In other words, Rogers' (1959) interviewee does not just start off as seeing himself as immature-inadequate-negative-worthless, but immature-inadequate-negative-worthless against the background of mature-adequate-positive-worthwhile. Hence, in experiencing himself as positive, the individual may tend towards invoking the entire gestalt configuration of which this positivity is a part; just as Dr Jekyll, in experiencing a certain recklessness and freedom, may invoke the whole gestalt to which Dr Jekyll – and Victorian middle class society as a whole – configurated these qualities: recklessness-freedom-evil-bestiality-villainy as opposed to gravity-repression-goodness-humanity-morality. (Indeed, it is interesting to note that there is no mention of feelings of villainy or malice in Dr Jekyll's youth – only a certain playfulness, gaiety and unruliness. Mr Hyde's 'evil', therefore, would seem to be less a consequence of Dr Jekyll's 'true nature', and more a consequence of a society which constellates order with goodness and disorder with badness.)

The implication, then, is that a 'not-me', an alter (Grotstein, Chapter 2, this volume), is already implicit in every 'me' – a shadow that every self-concept casts across its phenomenal field, a hidden (Hyde-n) Being which stalks each self's existence. As an entity which can only be defined in relation to what it is not, the self-concept is not a thing but an outline between figure and ground: a configuration which, as the gestalt psychologists recognized, is always open to reversal. As Rogers writes, in relation to his interviewee's self-concept switching: 'One was forcibly reminded of the favourite textbook illustration of a gestalt, the double picture of the old hag and the young woman. Looked at with one mind set, the picture is clearly that of an ugly old woman. The slightest change, and the whole becomes a portrait of an attractive girl' (1959: 201). Hence, while Lecky (1945/1961) writes that the introduction of self-inconsistent values may lead to a general reorganization of the self, in fact, in this figure–ground reversal, a remarkable degree of consistency is actually preserved. The boundary between self and not-self remains fixed, the only difference is that the individual is now viewing it 'from the other side of the fence'. As Gregg writes, the individual simply, 'changes identity by reversing the meaning of a single system of self-representational symbols' (1995: 631).

Furthermore, the more fixed and inflexible the self–not-self boundary, the more violent and startling any transformations are likely to be. If there is some fluidity, then the self-concept may be able to bend its outline to incorporate new self-experiences; but the more rigid it is, the more there is only self and alter self, with no transitional possibilities in between. Paradoxically, then, the greater the desire for an organismically-incongruent self-unity – or what Ross (Chapter 10, this volume) refers to as 'pathological pseudo-unity' – the greater and more dramatic a self-duality may emerge. As Dr Jekyll notes: 'it was thus rather the exacting nature of my aspirations, than any particular degradation in my faults, that made me what I was' (Stevenson, 1886/1993: 48).

Through the development of one overly-narrow self-concept, then, emerges the possible identification with its 'shadow' – as rigid and incongruent with the totality of the lived-experiences as the first, but with the inverse characteristics. Having identified with this second self-concept, the individual may then go on to fluctuate between these two selves, in a frantic attempt to maximize both synchronic and diachronic self-consistency. At one moment, for instance, 23-year-old Mark feels himself to be omnipotent; he feels proactive, engaged, as if he could conquer the world. But when he starts to experience things as 'going wrong', his omnipotent sense of self can no longer hold; and because it is so tightly constellated (defended?), the possibility of developing an integrated 'successful-with-the-possibility-of-failing' self-concept is experienced as deeply inconsistent and uncomfortable. Rather, by shifting into a sense of self as 'complete failure' – as a total lack of omnipotence and success – he can at least manage to salvage his self–not-self boundary and maintain a consistent sense of who he is. So he identifies with his shadow self-concept, and it is only when this self-as-failure becomes entirely incompatible with his self-experiences that he chooses to flip back into his 'omnipotent' self-concept. From omnipotence to impotence and back again – such a flip-flopping between figure and ground can last a lifetime.

Like the story of Dr Jekyll and Mr Hyde, however – along with Rogers' (1951, 1959) own narrative of human development – such an understanding of self-plurality is somewhat embedded in a structuralist, modernist worldview. Bipolar switching between self-concept and shadow-self-concept may be a recurrent phenomenon for some individuals but, as Rowan (1990), Gergen (1971, 1991), and many others have noted, self-plurality is not restricted to two selves, nor is it necessarily the case that these two selves are structural opposites. In the case of Joan, for instance, there does seem to be something of a polarity between her 'good little girl' self-concept and her 'bitch from hell' self-concept; but her 'teacher' self-concept seems to be something altogether different: borrowing elements from both her other self-concepts, as well as configuring into the overall gestalt characteristics that seem relatively independent.

How, then, can this more post-structuralist self-plurality be explained at the level of lived-experiences? One aspect of Rogers' thinking which seems to be frequently overlooked is his assertion that the regard-complex – and hence the internalized self-regard complex – is related to the positive regard 'of a *particular* social other' (1959: 209, italics added). In other words, while Rogers generally refers to the regard complex as a unified entity, the positive regard that the individual experiences from a particular social other may be very different to the positive regard that they experience from another social other. While Joan as a child, for instance, may have experienced positive regard from her parents in relation to such self-experiences as self-sacrifice, 'cuteness', and passivity; in relation to fellow teachers and pupils, such self-experiences may have had little association with positive regard – indeed, they may have been seen as quite inappropriate. Rather, within this context, Joan may have experienced positive regard in relation to such self-experiences as maturity, calmness and a certain authoritativeness. If one assumes, then, that in many cases these particular social others will constellate into a relatively limited number of groups, each of which positively regard in relatively similar ways – for example parents/family, friends, work colleagues, political affiliates, lover/partner – then it can be proposed that the positive regard complex is not a single gestalt, but a collection of gestalt formations, between which clearly defined structural relationships need not necessarily exist.

Following through with Rogers' theory of development (1951, 1959), this experience of plural, qualitatively distinct positive regard complexes may lead to the internalization of plural, qualitatively distinct positive *self*-regard complexes. As a result, the individual may then go on to develop a plurality of self-concepts: that is, a different self to maximize positive self-regard in relation to each social grouping – self-sacrificial in intimate relationships, self-assertive in the classroom, etc. This is a possibility that Rogers certainly considered, writing that others in his research circle had 'felt that a plural definition [of the self-concept], indicating many specific selves in each of various life contexts, would be more fruitful' (1959: 203). What is more, given the relational nature of the self-concept and the possibility of figure/ground reversal, one can predict that each of these social selves may well cast their own 'shadow'. Hence, while it seems that Joan's 'bitch from hell' self-concept is the shadow of her 'good little girl'; there is also the possibility that her 'teacher' self-concept will have a shadow too – an authority-less, incapable, immature sense of self – perhaps a feared self-concept that haunts Joan's teaching self, emerging only briefly in moments of panic in front of her students.

The development of multiple self-concepts through figure/ground reversal, through a plurality of self-regard complexes, and through a combination of these two processes, however, is probably only some of the way in which different self-concepts may emerge. The existential psychotherapist R.D. Laing (1960), for instance, talks about the development of a 'false self system': mask-like part-selves that the individual erects as a means of defending his or her inner self against the perceived threat of annihilation. Symbolic interactionists such as Mead (1934), on the other hand, argue that self-concepts develop through the subjective interpretation of the feedback one receives from social others – a process of internalization which need not necessarily be based on the desire for positive self-regard. Berne (1961) proposes two further means of acquiring self-concepts: an individual may retain selves from earlier periods in their life (that is, child selves), and they may also develop selves as a consequence of the introjection of significant others (that is, parental selves). Gergen (1991) extends this notion of internalization further, suggesting that in a postmodern world, characterized by the technologies of mass social communication – telephones, televisions, videos, electronic mail, etc. – we are increasingly bombarded with a multiplicity of possible self-concepts with which to identify and embody: film stars, friends, soap opera characters, electronic mail correspondents, video conferencing colleagues, and so on. The consequence of this, argues Gergen, is a state of 'multiphrenia', as, 'each of us comes to harbor a vast population of hidden potentials – to be a blues singer, a gypsy, an aristocrat, a criminal. All the selves lie latent, and under the right conditions may spring to life' (1991: 71).

Gergen's (1991) social constructionist perspective is, perhaps, in danger of losing the phenomenological livedness of human Being. Yet what it does emphasize, a point which can be easily lost in a more Rogerian perspective, is that the acquisition of self-identities is not something thrust on to the person, but something which the individual proactively chooses as a means of actualizing the totality of his or her Being – a totality which includes the motive for positive self-regard and self-consistency. '[T]here is no character,' writes Sartre, 'only a project of oneself' (1943/1958: 552). In encountering his or her world, the individual – reflectively or pre-reflectively – delves into their toolbox of self-concepts, and chooses the one which may most effectively help to maximize their potentiality. Joan comes home from work and, to maximize the positive regard she receives from her boyfriend, she turns to her 'good little girl' self-concept. It may not be a perfect fit but, within her phenomenological frame of reference, it seems to her the best tool that she has for the job. But as her organismic anger builds in relation to her boyfriend's perceived laziness, the 'good little girl' self-concept no longer maximizes her actualization – by virtue of the self-inconsistency it is generating. By switching into her 'bitch from hell' self-concept, she can express her organismic disgust while at the same time maintaining a consistency between self-concept and self-experience. The existence of plural self-concepts, then, is not an inevitability but an intentional construction. It is a strategy through which the individual attempts to maximize the fullness of his or her Being. Dr Jekyll does not just become Mr Hyde, he chooses it as a means of being who he most wants to be in the context of a particular sociocultural milieu. In a highly repressive society, his duplicity is a proactive strategy through which he hopes to resolve his conflict between gravity and gaiety. As he tells himself:

> If each could be housed in separate identities, life would be relieved of all that is unbearable; the unjust might go his way, delivered from the aspirations and remorse of his more upright twin; and the just could walk steadfastly and securely on his upward path, doing the things in which he found his pleasure, and no longer exposed to disgrace and penitence by the hands of this extraneous evil. (Stevenson, 1886/1993: 49)

'Modes' of Being

If an individual can encounter their world through a plurality of qualitatively distinct self-concepts, then what evolves is the picture of an organismic being who has the potential to encounter their world in a plurality of qualitatively distinctive ways. As one particular self-concept comes 'on-line' (Markus and Wurf, 1987) – that is, becomes figure – so the individual actualizes potentials and reflects on experiences that are consistent with this self-concept, while keeping pre-reflective those potentials and experiences which are inconsistent with this on-line sense of self. When she sees her-self as a teacher, for instance, Joan chooses to act towards her students in a respectful and authoritative manner and acknowledges her feelings of satisfaction with her work; at the same time, she chooses away from childish or flirtatious behaviours, and subceives those feelings of wanting to give up responsibility, of just wanting to sit with the students and stop being the teacher. With her 'good little girl' self-concept on-line, on the other hand, Joan chooses to act towards her boyfriend in a way that is deferential and 'cute' and can easily acknowledge her feelings of insecurity in front of her class; at the same time, more challenging and assertive behaviours are avoided, as is an acknowledgement of her teaching abilities: 'I can't believe I actually stand up there and do that!'. What is denied and disowned from the position of one self-concept, then, may seem entirely everyday from the position of another. Furthermore, recent research suggests that the self-concept not only influences an individual's choice of behaviours and perceptions, but acts as the 'central structure and first structure through which all information flows' (Markus and Sentis, 1982: 65). Hence, as the individual shifts from one self-concept to another, so the very way in which they interpret and make sense of their world may be fundamentally transformed. For Rogers' interviewee, for instance, what seemed like a positive choice from the position of one self-concept was, from the standpoint of another, just an example of 'silly immaturity' (1959).

What is being proposed, then, is that many – if not all – individuals, encounter their world through a variety of different 'modes' (Cooper, 1996). These modes of Being are not 'things' within a 'psyche', but stances: tendencies towards particular constellations of behavioural, affective, and cognitive acts-in-the-world. What is pivotal to each of these modes, however, is the existence of a specific, qualitatively discrete self-concept, and it is this that differentiates a 'mode' of Being from a mood or emotion. This self-concept, however, need not necessarily be the explicit object of attention – indeed, in most instances it will be at the fringes of phenomenological awareness. Rather, the experienced-self-concept can be considered more akin to a somewhat ephemeral – almost ghostly – sense of 'me-ness', an ineradicable presence through which the individual acts towards their world. If, then, existence can be likened to 'a light which luminates whatever particular being comes into the realm of its rays' (Boss, 1963: 37), the self-concept can be likened to a coloured filter – a structure which in itself is not the object of attention, yet which comes fundamentally to modify the individual's 'world-illuminating' Being. When, for instance, the on-line self-concept of Rogers' interviewee is 'immature-inadequate-negative-worthless' (1959), it is like he is experiencing his world through a grey filter, where the vibrantly coloured positive choices he makes are darkened out. But, viewed through the rosier filter of his mature-adequate-positive-worthwhile self-concept, the same experiences are seen in a very different light – in the fullness of their vibrancy and potentiality – while his feelings of negativity and hopelessness are reduced to indiscernible shadows. Developing the analogy, Rogers' fully-functioning individual (1961) is not filter-less, but has a filter which is fluid and flowing – somewhat like the coloured oil filters in the projectors of the 1960s and 1970s. This contrasts with the more 'flip-flopping' individual, who has a discrete number of fixed and possibly quite different filters, such that the world is pink, or blue, or grey – or, in the worst case scenario, just black and white.

Conclusion

From an existential-phenomenological perspective, the model of self-plurality presented above suggests a means of resolving the paradox of an experienced unity which can be experienced as a plurality. As 'modes' of Being, the principle of the unity of human experiencing that Rogers (1951, 1959), Heidegger (1926/1962), Merleau-Ponty (1962) and other phenomenologists insist on is not violated – Being is always a complete gestalt configuration – yet there exists the possibility that this wholeness can be experienced in a plurality of ways: a diachronic plurality of synchronic unities. In this sense, there is neither a one (for example John, 1990) nor a many (for example Gergen, 1991) nor a many-within-the-one (for example Janet, 1889), but a one-with-the-potential-to-be-many: a unified Being-towards-the-world which has the possibility of Being-towards-its-world from a variety of self-positions. Hence, the position developed here is somewhat akin to the 'polyphonic self' of Hermans et al., in which the experiencing human being is posited to shift around 'a dynamic landscape of relatively autonomous "I" positions' (1993: 215).

Contrary to Holdstock's (1993) critique of Rogerian 'individuocentrism', however, the phenomenologically-experiencing 'one' need not necessarily be equated with an autonomous, individual and pre-social Self. Rather, as the more intersubjectivist phenomenologists have argued (for example, Heidegger, 1926/1962; Merleau-Ponty, 1962), the unity of experiencing is the unity of Being-in-the-world-with-others – a total configuration from which an isolated 'Self' cannot be extracted. A theory of self-plurality based on Rogers' phenomenological approach, therefore, is not tied to a particular conception of the experiencing-'I'; what it is tied to is the proposition that this experiencing-'I', in whatever form it takes, tends towards limiting itself through the construction of one or more self-concepts. Individuocentrism, as a Western liberal 'condition of worth', may become an integral part of the constructed sense of self, but the nature of the organismic Being which underlies this self-construct may be of a very different order.

As well as suggesting a plural answer to the question of the unity/plurality of the self, the position outlined here suggests a plural answer to the question of whether self-plurality is psychologically 'healthy' or 'dysfunctional'. In essence, what seems to emerge is that it depends on how that self-plurality develops. Where the self-plurality emerges as a consequence of the individual's inability to squeeze their self-experiences into a rigidly defined self-concept – what one might call a 'repressive plurality' – then it would seem that something rather ineffectual is going on. As a means of actualizing the totality of its Being, the creation of a shadow self-concept may counterbalance the one-sidedness of the initial self-concept; but the existence of two self-concepts, each equally incongruent with the organismic Being (albeit in different directions), is still likely to be less actualizing than the existence of one, congruent self-concept. In terms of actualizing the totality of the organismic Being, another somewhat ineffective form of lived-plurality would seem to be a plurality which emerges from a plurality of self-regard complexes – what one might term an 'approval-based plurality' – in which the individual attempts to be everything for everyone, while sacrificing so many other aspects of their self-experiencing and potential. Yet, given the thinking of Gergen (1991) and also Rappoport, Baumgardner and Boone, there may also be a form of self-plurality which allows the individual to maximize their potentialities – what we might call a 'creative' or 'adaptive' (Rappoport et al., Chapter 5, this volume) plurality – in which the individual takes on different self-concepts primarily because a singular self – however fluid – simply cannot make the most of the multiple opportunities that a postmodern world presents. As Camus writes, today's absurdist hero 'multiplies . . . what he cannot unify', and thus, 'discovers a new way of being which liberates him' (1955: 70). Filters can darken important things out, but they can also darken what is unimportant so that what really matters can come to light; they can also make everything look much more exciting. By shifting from a 'real man' identity in his gym, to a 'new age man' identity in his men's group, to an 'intimate man' identity in his relationships, the postmodern man may be most fully able to engage with each of these diverse worlds, and most fully actualize the totality of his Being. Such a plurality, however, is characterized by playfulness and a mutual valuing from one mode of Being to another – in contrast to the deadly seriousness and mutual antagonisms of the more repressive form of lived-plurality.

Therefore, while plurality may be an existential choice, the sociocultural facticities within which this choice takes place may fundamentally affect its meaning and value. In a culture which enforces a rigid and repressive monopsychism, self-plurality is most likely to emerge as a 'failure' of the organismic Being to fit into a rigid sense of self. In a sociocultural milieu, on the other hand, which celebrates heterogeneity and diversity, self-plurality may emerge as a potential means of maximizing one's possibility for actualization. Dr Jekyll may have been right, therefore, to suggest 'that man will be ultimately known for a mere polity of multifarious, incongruent and independent denizens' (Stevenson, 1886/1993: 48–9); but whether or not we are all doomed to the same 'dreadful shipwreck' as Dr Jekyll may depend on how this plurality is lived-out: in a spirit of either/or-ness, repression and divisiveness, or in a spirit of both-ness, liberation, and dialogue.

Note

1 To ensure complete anonymity, a number of details in this case have been changed.

References

Beahrs, J.O. (1982) *Unity and Multiplicity*. New York: Brunner/Mazel.
Berne, E. (1961) *Transactional Analysis in Psychotherapy*. New York: Grove Press.
Boss, M. (1963) *Psychoanalysis and Daseinanalysis*. (Trans. L.B. Lefebre.) London: Basic Books.
Boss, M. (1979) *Existential Foundations of Medicine and Psychology*. (Trans. S. Conway and A. Cleaves.) London: Jason Aronson.
Brazier, D. (1993) 'The necessary condition is love: going beyond self in the person-centred approach', in D. Brazier (ed.), *Beyond Carl Rogers: Towards a Psychotherapy of the 21st Century*. London: Constable.
Burns, R.B. (1979) *The Self-Concept: in Theory, Measurement, Development and Behaviour*. London: Longman.
Camus, A. (1955) *The Myth of Sisyphus*. (Trans. J. O'Brien.) London: Penguin.
Cooper, M. (1996) 'Modes of existence: towards a phenomenological poly-psychism', *Journal for the Society of Existential Analysis*, 7 (2): 50–6.
Freud, S. (1923) 'The ego and the id', *Complete Psychological Works*, vol. 19. London: Hogarth Press.
Gazzaniga, M. (1985) *The Social Brain*. New York: Basic Books.
Gergen, K.J. (1971) *The Concept of Self*. London: Holt, Rinehart and Winston.
Gergen, K.J. (1982) 'From self to science: what is there to know?', in J. Suls (ed.), *Psychological Perspectives on the Self*, vol. 1. London: Lawrence Erlbaum Associates.
Gergen, K.J. (1991) *The Saturated Self: Dilemmas of Identity in Contemporary Life*. London: Basic Books.
Gregg, G.S. (1995) 'Multiple identities and the integration of personality', *Journal of Personality*, 63 (3): 617–41.
Hattie, J. (1992) *Self-Concept*. London: Lawrence Erlbuam Associates.
Heidegger, M. (1926/1962) *Being and Time*. (Trans. J. Macquarrie and E. Robinson.) Oxford: Basil Blackwell.
Hermans, J.M., Rijks, T.I. and Kempen, H.J.G. (1993) 'Imaginal dialogue in the self: theory and method', *Journal of Personality*, 61 (2): 207–36.
Holdstock, L. (1993) 'Can we afford not to revision the person-centred concept of self', in Brazier, D. (ed.), *Beyond Carl Rogers*. London: Constable.
James, W. (1890/1981) *The Principles of Psychology*, vol. 1. London: Harvard University Press.
Janet, P. (1889) *L'Automatisme Psychologique*. Paris: Alcan.

John, O.P. (1990) 'The "big five" taxonomy: dimensions of personality in the natural language and in questionnaires', in L. Pervin (ed.), *Handbook of Personality Theory and Research*. New York: Guildford Press.

Laing, R.D. (1960) *The Divided Self*. London: Tavistock.

Lecky, P. (1945/1961) *Self-consistency: a Theory of Personality*. London: Shoe String Press.

Lester, D. (1992) 'The disunity of self', *Personality and Individual Differences*, 13 (8): 947–8.

Lewin, K. (1951) *Field Theory in Social Sciences*. New York: Harper and Row.

McAdams, D.P. (1985) 'The "Imago": a key narrative component of identity', in P. Shaver (ed.), *Self, Situations, and Social Behaviour*. Beverly Hills, CA: Sage.

Markus, H. and Sentis, K. (1982) 'The self in social information processing', in J. Suls (ed.), *Psychological Perspectives on the Self*, vol. 1. Hillsdale, NJ: Lawrence Erlbaum.

Markus, H.A. and Wurf, E. (1987) 'The dynamic self-concept: a social psychological perspective', *Annual Review of Psychology*, 38: 299–337.

Martindale, C. (1980) 'Subselves: the internal representations of situational and personal dispositions', in L. Wheeler (ed.), *Review of Personality and Social Psychology*, vol. 1. Beverly Hills, CA: Sage.

Mead, G.H. (1934) *Mind, Self and Society*. (Ed. C.W. Morris.) London: University of Chicago Press.

Merleau-Ponty, M. (1962) *The Phenomenology of Perception*. (Trans. Colin Smith.) London: Routledge.

Mischel, W. (1968) *Personality and Assessment*. New York: Wiley.

Rogers, C.R. (1951) *Client-Centred Therapy*. London: Constable.

Rogers, C.R. (1959) 'A theory of therapy, personality and interpersonal relationships as developed in the client-centred framework', in S. Koch (ed.), *Psychology: A Study of Science*, vol. 3. New York: McGraw-Hill.

Rogers, C.R. (1961) *On Becoming a Person: A Therapist's View of Psychotherapy*. London: Constable.

Rogers, C.R. (1986) 'Client-centred therapy', in I.L. Kutash and A. Wolf (eds), *Psychotherapist's Casebook*. San Francisco: Jossey-Bass.

Rosenberg, S. and Gara, M.A. (1985) 'The multiplicity of personal identity', in P. Shaver (ed.), *Self, Situations, and Social Behaviour: Review of Personality and Social Psychology*, vol. 6. Beverly Hills, CA: Sage.

Rowan, J. (1990) *Subpersonalities: The People Inside Us*. London: Routledge.

Sartre, J.-P. (1943/1958) *Being and Nothingness: An Essay on Phenomenological Ontology*. (Trans. H. Barnes.) London: Routledge.

Spinelli, E. (1994) *Demystifying Therapy*. London: Constable.

Stevenson, R.L. (1886/1993) *The Strange Case of Dr Jekyll and Mr Hyde*. Hertfordshire: Wordsworth Editions Ltd.

Strawson, G. (1997) 'The self', *Journal of Consciousness Studies*, 4 (5–6): 405–28.

Vargiu, J.G. (1974) 'Psychosynthesis workbook: subpersonalities', *Synthesis*, 1.

Watkins, M. (1990) *Invisible Guests*. Boston, MA: Sigo Press.

4 LIFE INSIDE DIALOGICALLY STRUCTURED MENTALITIES: BAKHTIN'S AND VOLOSHINOV'S ACCOUNT OF OUR MENTAL ACTIVITIES AS OUT IN THE WORLD BETWEEN US

John Shotter

A plurality of independent and unmerged voices and consciousness, a genuine polyphony of fully valid voices is in fact the chief characteristic of Dostoevsky's novels. What unfolds in each of his works is not a multitude of characters and fates in a single objective world, illuminated by a single authorial consciousness; rather a *plurality of consciousnesses, with equal rights and each with its own world*, combine but are not merged in the unity of the event.

(Bakhtin, 1984: 6)

To be means *to communicate* . . . To be means to be for another, and through the other, for oneself. A person has no internal sovereign territory, he is wholly and always on the boundary; looking inside himself, he looks *into the eyes of another* or *with the eyes of another.*

(Bakhtin, 1984: 287)

Language lives only in the dialogic interaction of those who make use of it.

(Bakhtin, 1984: 183)

A whole *dialogical* view of language, mind, meaning, and selfhood, focusing on events occurring out in the world between people, is slowly growing to displace the *monological* Cartesian conceptions, centered in mental states and acts 'in the mind' hidden inside people's individual heads, that have dominated our thought for so long here in the West. The changes in our conceptions of ourselves and of our relations to our surroundings that it will bring, are, I think, very deep and quite astonishing – so much so, that we shall find many of the conclusions reached in this chapter quite hard to accept. Many workers are contributing to this movement. Here, I shall claim that some of its essential features are most clearly expressed in the works of Bakhtin and Voloshinov. Elsewhere, I have emphasized the centrality of Wittgenstein's work in this sphere (see Shotter, 1996, 1997); Spinosa, Flores, and Dreyfus (1997) emphasize the importance of Heidegger's work

(1967, 1977); while the work of Merleau-Ponty (1962) is also very important. But we cannot pursue the interconnections between all these works here.
Suffice it to say that central to them all are, I think, three major themes: first,
they all take it that there is something very special about us being alive;
second, they focus on what occurs in those living moments when we are in
contact with others or othernesses in our surroundings; third, among the
many consequences of us being in the world as living, embodied beings, is
the fact that we cannot not be spontaneously responsive to each other in a
bodily way, prior to anything we might do deliberately and intellectually.
However, Bakhtin and Voloshinov are, I think, distinctive in suggesting a
fourth theme: that the outcomes of such responsive activity, in emerging
from the creative bridging of the momentary 'gaps' occurring between us as
we turn from 'addressing' others to 'inviting' them to address us, have a
complex, open, mixed, *dialogical* structure to them which cannot be completely captured in any finalized descriptions. In other words, all the workers
above suggest that we are not 'self-contained' selves (to use Sampson's
[1993] phrase), but, that we owe our character as the individuals we are to
our living, embodied relations to the others and othernesses around us.

We shall find the whole new approach to the problem of what is involved
in us coming to the new, *relational* understanding of ourselves that I want to
introduce below, implicit in the themes I mentioned above. But before we
explore them any further, if we are to grasp why they constitute such a new
approach to 'mind' (more properly, our mentality), it is necessary for us to
remind ourselves of our current Cartesian conception of mind – for we shall
find what I am calling Bakhtin's and Voloshinov's dialogical approach
contrasts with this monological conception in almost every detail.

The Cartesian monological concept of mind

In the Cartesian view of mind, the mind is not simply contained inside the
head of the self-contained individual as itself the container of our mental
powers or faculties, but is *radically hidden* in there (thus we can only ever
know of its existence by inference). Inside each normal person there is only
a single mind (multiple or split minds are abnormal). In this view, a mind is
something we are born with and, as we develop, it supposedly becomes
stocked with knowledge. When working properly, it is a unified, rational
system working according to logical laws or principles. Meaning and
understanding are done inside people's heads by mental acts: by intending,
we put our meanings into words, and by interpreting, we come to understand
the content of other people's words. All proper meanings – that is, rational
meanings – are, in the end, linguistic meanings; meanings which cannot be
put clearly into words, cannot be claimed to be rational. Like the mind, in
the Cartesian scheme of things, language is also thought of as a container: as
an orderly, unified system of forms combined according to rules, words are
related to meaning as form is to content. Furthermore, as a shared system

of forms whose representational content constitutes a shared conceptual scheme, language mediates between person and world. Yet, like the mind, language as a system of linguistic representations is a hidden or underlying system, its existence thus has to be inferred also; it can only be known intellectually, through reason. However, the notion of underlying or hidden *representations* as providing the only link between mind (or person) and world is so central that for many, including many social constructionists, we only come properly to know anything at all in terms of linguistically formulated representations – whether, as realists, we think of our representations as picturing objects in the world, or whether, as social constructions, we think of them as constituting what there is for us in it.[1] It is a world in which our theories have priority over our practices.

To understand how Descartes (1986) came to this view, thus to contrast his concerns with those we now feel important to us, it is worth turning to his original writings to examine them in more detail. He begins his *Meditations* – first published in 1641 – by saying that he was 'struck by' the large number of falsehoods he had accepted as true in his childhood, and that he realized 'it was necessary, once in the course of my life, to demolish everything and start again right at the foundations if I wanted to establish anything at all in the sciences that was stable and likely to last' (1986: 12). So, how can he achieve his goal of building up a body of incontrovertible, rational truth? With doubt as his tool, he begins to search for something that he can claim to know beyond all doubt. First to be rejected are those of our beliefs that are derived from the senses: for the belief that he is now, for example, sitting by the fire, wearing a winter dressing gown and so on, is no different from exactly similar thoughts he has had about himself in dreams. We are forced to conclude that, when considered in themselves, there is no way that we can tell true perceptions from ones that are false. What, of course, he is challenging here is whether there is anything in our sense-images that testifies indubitably to the truth of what they represent; he is not doubting their existence as ideas, only whether one's ideas *represent* something beyond themselves.

After our perceptions, he turns to another class of ideas that seem not to originate in nature but from within ourselves in some way: ideas to do with physics, astronomy, medicine, as well as those in arithmetic and geometry. These too he doubts, for 'firmly rooted in my mind is the long-standing opinion that there is an omnipotent God who made me the kind of creature that I am' (1986: 14). Thus he gives up his trust in all the empirical sciences, and in subjects like arithmetic. What can he trust, what can he be certain of? If he has convinced himself 'that there is absolutely nothing in the world, no sky, no earth, no minds, no bodies' (1986: 16), does it not follow that he too does not exist?

No: if I convinced myself of something then I certainly existed . . . I must finally conclude that this proposition, *I am, I exist*, is necessarily true whenever it is put forward by me or conceived in my mind. (1986: 17)

Once convinced of his own existence, he can now ask himself: 'What kind of thing am I?' And, admitting only what is necessarily true, he answers: 'I am, then, in the strict sense only a thing that thinks' (1986: 18). Thus he comes to the conception of the self-contained individual, able to aspire to a self-given certainty about things – a self that needs neither a body nor other people to be able to arrive at certain fundamental truths. Indeed, regarding our bodies, Descartes remarks:

> I now know that even bodies are not strictly perceived by the senses or the faculty of imagination but by the intellect alone, and that this perception derives not from their being touched or seen but from their being understood. (1986: 22)

He thus ends with a picture of nature that is amenable to rational, scientific investigation. It is a picture of the world as a vast and complicated machine, and of us as rational intellects: disembodied, unified minds who, rather than being in the world, are set over against it, with the task of seeking a view of its plan (much like engineers facing the task of building it).

Bakhtin's and Voloshinov's dialogical conception of the multi-voiced mentality

Descartes's purpose was, let us remind ourselves, to establish results in the sciences that were stable and likely to last. He sought certainty, generalities, stable repetitions, knowledge amenable to proof; in short, he sought the Truth. He was not interested in knowledge of particularities, of unique and fleeting things. Bakhtin and Voloshinov begin with quite different purposes in mind. Although they each have their own distinct emphases, as we shall see, their central concerns are identical: it is to come to a grasp of people's unique and particular lives from within an involvement or an engagement of some kind with them in their living of them. For, as they see it, something very crucial is lost when we take the uninvolved, disengaged, mechanistic stance toward people's activities suggested to us in the Cartesian approach. In keeping ourselves separate, in remaining 'outside' of any living involvement with their lives, we 'establish a fundamental split between the content or sense of a given act/activity and the historical actuality of its being, the actual and once-occurrent experiencing of it', says Bakhtin (1993: 2). As Cartesians, we are dialogically unresponsive to the others around us; our relations to them are *monologic* in the sense that 'with a monologic approach . . . *another person* remains wholly and merely an *object* of consciousness, and not another consciousness . . . Monologue is finalized and deaf to the other's response, does not expect it and does not acknowledge in it any *decisive* force' (Bakhtin, 1984: 292–3). Monologically observing an act only in terms of its form or content, we see people's activities only as instances of a kind: we categorize them, we ignore their detailed particularity, their relations to their surroundings. We notice a couple in earnest conversation. One laughs out loud in response to an utterance of the other. We can easily fail to grasp, however, that in the meaning for the recipient of that overheard laugh, was not that they had just done something humorous, but that their relationship with the one laughing was clearly at an end: the serious proposal they had just put forward for a better future together had occasioned derision from them. Lacking any involvement with those we look upon, we have no 'entry', so to speak, into their 'inner lives'. Observing what is going on around us as if from afar, we introduce a radical, Cartesian split between two worlds:

> the world of culture and the world of life, the only world in which we create, cognize, contemplate, live our lives and die or [to put it another way] – the world in which the acts of our activity are objectified and the world in which these acts actually proceed and are actually accomplished once and only once. (Bakhtin, 1993: 2)

Like the unbridgeable split between body and mind, we introduce a split between the world of what is objectively given and the world in which we are actually living out our lives, between the world of the old and repeatable and the world of what is yet-to-be-achieved, the world of new and 'first-time' events. How can this radical split be overcome? Where can these two very different worlds meet each other, come into contact with each other?

Inside the 'once-occurrent event of Being': utterances

Crucial to Bakhtin's and Voloshinov's whole approach is the possibility of two quite distinct worlds coming into living, dialogical contact with each other. At that moment, when a speaker in one world turns from addressing those in another and invites their creative bridging of the gap thus created in their responsive rejoinders, a new world is created between them, with influences from the unique worlds of both participants and from their shared cultural worlds at work in it. And it is only in 'the once-occurrent act of Being in the process of actualization that can constitute this unique unity' (Bakhtin, 1993: 2) that two people with their own unique worlds can meet; where, the special unity or wholeness that emerges when two or more different worlds, or different 'freedoms' (Steiner, 1989)[2] meet, exists only in the fleeting moment of their meeting. It is in their sustained focus on, and the special way in which they 'poetically' articulate the details of what occurs in fleeting interactive or dialogical moments – without the need to step out of such moments as if to observe and to describe them from a distance – that is so special in their non-theoretical approach. It is non-theoretical because, says Bakhtin:

> All attempts to force one's way from inside the theoretical world and into actual Being-as-event are quite hopeless. The theoretically cognized world cannot be unclosed from within cognition itself to the point of becoming open to the actual once-occurrent world . . . It is only from within the actually performed act, which is once-occurrent, integral, and unitary in its answerability, that we can find an

approach to unitary and once-occurrent Being in its concrete actuality. (1993: 12, 28)

And, as we shall see below, to point toward the complex, mixed, polyvocal nature of such only once-occurrent events from within our ongoing participation in them, methods of quite a different kind to those currently prevalent (in a scientific psychology) are needed.

Turning our attention to the character of such only once-occurrent events, one of the first features that becomes apparent to us is, as already mentioned, that we cannot not be responsive to each other; that in the background to everything we do is a great deal of unreflective, unthinking, but nonetheless culturally structured activity. In contrast the Cartesian approach, let us remember, would have us focus only on what was reflectively and intellectually accessible to us. For Bakhtin:

> . . . when the listener perceives and understands the meaning (the language meaning) of speech, he simultaneously takes an active, responsive attitude toward it. He either agrees or disagrees with it (completely or partially), augments it, applies it, prepares for its execution, and so on. And the listener adopts this responsive attitude for the entire duration of the process of listening and understanding, from the very beginning – sometimes literally from the speaker's first word. (1986: 68)

And the speaker too is expecting such an active responsive understanding:

> [The speaker] does not expect passive understanding that, so to speak, only duplicates his or her own idea in someone else's mind (as in Saussure's model of linguistic communication . . .). Rather, the speaker talks with an expectation of a response, agreement, sympathy, objection, execution, and so forth . . . Therefore, each kind of utterance is filled with various kinds of responsive reactions to other utterances of the given sphere of speech communication. (Bakhtin, 1986: 69, 91)

In other words, unnoticed in the background and spontaneously at work in all our communicative relations with each other is what might be called a *relational-responsive* kind of understanding – a form of understanding much more basic than the *representational-referential* kind of understanding of which we are, as individuals, consciously aware. Indeed, as Goffman (1967) remarks, the spontaneous, taken-for-granted way in which we do in fact respond to and reply to each other in a conversation is required! If our involvement seems contrived rather than spontaneous, rationally planned rather than fully responsive to the conversation's current 'shape', then the others around us take offence. 'Here, in a component of non-rational impulsiveness – not only tolerated but actually demanded – we find important way in which the interactional order differs from other kinds of social order' (Goffman, 1967: 115).

Let us examine the features is this spontaneously responsive relational activity further, for it has a number of very special features to it that makes it very different from either naturally *caused* activity or from actions done by individuals for a *reason*. It is activity which is, so to speak, *distributed* between us; it is *joint action* in the sense that it is action we do as a group, as a collective, as a 'we' or an 'us' (Shotter, 1980, 1984, 1993a, 1993b, 1996). Indeed, to the extent that everything done by any of the individuals involved in it is done in spontaneous response to the others or othernesses around them, we cannot hold any of them individually responsible for its outcome. It lacks a reason. Yet it is not brought about by any causes external to them either. It is produced only by 'their' activity. It is in fact a complex mixture of many different kinds of influences. This makes it very difficult for us to characterize its nature: it has neither a fully orderly nor a fully disorderly structure; neither a completely stable nor an easily changed organization; a neither fully subjective nor fully objective character. Indeed, in being already partly specified but not yet fully specified, it is to an extent open to being further specified by those involved in it. Thus, from within our involvement in such activities, we can develop and refine them – but only in certain, limited ways. From an exclamation of joy, say, song emerges; from a gesture of delight, dance develops; from a smile, a friendship is cultivated; from a scowl, an antagonism grows; from a hesitation, a puzzlement as to how to 'go on' further with another which goes on and develops into an enquiry; and so on. But such developments depend on all those involved each responsively interweaving their activities in with those of the others around them; they determine its character. And it 'takes shape', so to speak, in an unfolding sequence of interactive events occurring between them. Where each event occurs in responsive relation both to previous events, along with contemporaneously occurring collateral events, as well as being influenced by participants' anticipations of the yet-to-be-achieved aim of the interaction in relation to its origin:

> The performed act concentrates, correlates, and resolves within a unitary and unique and, this time, *final context* both the sense and the fact, the universal and the individual, the real and the ideal, for everything enters into the composition of its answerable motivation. The performed act constitutes a going out *once and for all* from within the possibility as such into *what is once-occurrent*. (Bakhtin, 1993: 29)

So, although in theory we may see a particular person's action in an exchange as open to many interpretations, in practice it is responded to in just one particular way at a particular moment.

Voloshinov (1976: 99) describes an incident between two Russians in late May: It has been a long and tiring winter, the snow has lasted a long time, summer seems far off, and, as they look out of the window, they see it beginning to snow again. One turns to the other and simply says: 'Well!' And in the intonation of that single word is expressed (but not explicitly said) all the tiredness, resentment, and helpless indignation the speaker feels. But it is responsively addressed by the speaker, not to the friend, but to their condition. And in always being responsive in this way to our conditions, our circumstances, it is always the case that a whole complex of influences are at work in 'giving shape' to our responsive utterances in their voicing. The kind of complexity that emerges from the confluence of all these influences is, however, more than just a static kind of complexity: the activity involved has what we might call a dynamic, continually changing, oscillating, pulsating character, such that its structure at any one moment is very different from its structure at another. In this sense it has, we can say, a *dialogical structure* to it. For, although it links us into a unitary 'we' of a certain kind 'through' (dia) the reciprocal exchange of meaning it affords between us, in occurring 'across' (dia) the space between us as distinct individuals, it also constitutes us as a 'plurality of unmerged conscious-nesses' (Bakhtin, 1984: 9). In other words, while it is a unity at one moment, at another it is a plurality. It is only in each unique interactive moment, as one individual ceases to address him- or herself to the others and becomes him- or herself an addressee, that a unity is formed. In each uncertain once-occurrent event of Being, in which we encounter others radically different and distinct from ourselves, they call out from us responses which we are incapable of calling out from ourselves. But it is in these moments also, that we are joined with them and *present* to each other as the distinct individuals we are. Thus such moments as these are very special indeed. Bakhtin emphasizes their importance thus:

> Even if I know a given person thoroughly, and I also know myself, I still have to grasp the truth of our interrelationship, the truth of the unitary and unique event that links us and in which we are participants. That is, my place and function and his [sic], *and* our interrelationship in the ongoing event of being . . . It is only from within that act as *my* answerable deed that there can be a way out into the unity of Being, and *not* from its product, taken in abstraction. It is only from within my participation that the function of each participant can be understood. (1993: 17–18)

Outside of such moments, we remain distinct and separate from each other.

The kind of active responsive understanding we exhibit in practice, in dialogue with others, is quite different, then, to the passive kind of representational understanding we think of ourselves as possessing in our more contemplative moments, when alone with ourselves. But even here, we need not be wholly monological beings. As Bakhtin (1984) points out, very often in both our thought and talk, a second speaker (or many others) are 'present invisibly'. Thus, in such a circumstance

> we sense that this is a conversation, although only one person is speaking, and it is a conversation of the most intense kind, for each present, uttered word responds and reacts with its every fibre to the invisible speaker, points to something outside itself, beyond its own limits, to the unspoken words of another person. (1984: 197)

Often we must express ourselves with, as Bakhtin puts it, to voice our utterances 'with a sideward glance' (1984: 208) toward certain absent others; that is, we speak not just with an awareness of how our immediate listeners are responding to what we say, but with a sense of how these absent others who are in some way significant to us might respond too. As an example, Bakhtin discusses the speech of Makar Devushkin, a poor man, a copying clerk, depicted by Dostoevsky in one of his stories in *Poor Folk*:

> In most cases Makar Devushkin's speech about himself is determined by the reflected discourse of another, 'other person', a stranger . . . [Makar Devushkin] is a poor man, but a man 'with ambition' . . . [and] he constantly senses the 'ill look' of this other upon him, a glance which is either reproachful or – perhaps even worse – mocking . . . Under this other's glance even Devushkin's speech cringes. (1984: 206)

Both his anger and resentment at the responses of this stranger/other to Devushkin's words are present in his words even as he utters them. This 'hidden dialogicality', as Bakhtin (1984: 197) calls it – or anticipatory dialogicality – is, of course, quite common in all those situations in which we must choose our words carefully in anticipation of how others will react to what we say.

The 'speech genres' that speak us

Speakers, in taking into account in the voicing of their utterances, the 'various kinds of responsive reactions to other utterances of the given sphere of speech communication', clearly cannot just speak as they please. Indeed, speakers must *address* their utterances to others, and in so doing, they must take into account who these others are, both their objective place in the relevant social hierarchy and what is currently happening to them in their 'inner lives'. Thus:

> both the composition and, particularly, the style of the utterance depend on those to whom the utterance is addressed, how the speaker (or writer) senses or imagines his addressee, and the force of their effect on the utterance. Each speech genre in each area of speech communication has its own typical conception of the addressee, and this defines it as a genre. (Bakhtin, 1986: 95)

> Each person's inner world and thought has its stabilized *social audience* that comprises the environment in which reasons, motives, values, and so on are fashioned . . . Orientation of the word toward the addressee has an extremely high significance. In point of fact, *word is a two-sided act*. It is determined equally by *whose* word it is and *for whom* it is meant . . . Each and every word expresses the 'one' in relation to the 'other'. (Voloshinov, 1986: 86)

Thus whatever we say can never be wholly up to us – all our utterances are to an extent jointly produced outcomes between ourselves and others. Yet our utterances are not responsive to just anyone. In being directed toward a stabilized social audience, they have their being within a particular 'form of life' (Wittgenstein, 1953), and to that extent have a generic form. Where, what it is that makes a whole set of utterances all hang together in a unity as members of a genre, is their capacity spontaneously and impulsively each to 'call out' another, so that 'any concrete utterance is a link in the chain of speech communication in a given sphere' (Bakhtin, 1986: 91). Indeed, 'nowhere is there a break in the chain, nowhere does the chain plunge into inner being, nonmaterial in nature and unembodied in signs' (Voloshinov, 1986: 11).

In other words, it is our actual or imagined ways of us responsively relating ourselves to each other – in what, as already mentioned, Wittgenstein calls our 'forms of life' – that are the basis for our ways of talking, which ultimately provide us with our ways of thinking and feeling, valuing and judging. These are the constraints we must take into account and struggle with in attempting to answer to others for ourselves; we cannot respond just as we please. Even when talking to oneself, one cannot just talk as one pleases:

> As living, socio-ideological concrete thing, as heteroglot opinion, language, for the individual consciousness, lies on the borderline between oneself and the other. The word in language is half someone else's, it becomes 'one's own' only when the speaker populates it with his own intentions, his own accent, when he appropriates the word, adapting it to his own semantic and expressive intention. Prior to this moment of appropriation, the word does not exist in a neutral and impersonal language (it is not, after all, out of a dictionary that the speaker gets his words!), but rather it exists in other people's mouths, in other people's contexts, serving other people's intentions: it is from there that one must take the word, and make it one's own. (Bakhtin 1981: 293–4)

In other words, even in our own inner dialogues, the dialogical relations with others and othernesses are at work in us, in which new reasons, new motives, new values, and so on can be fashioned (Shotter and Billig, 1998).

Indeed, it is not going too far to suggest that in each speech genre, both different selves and different worlds are created:

> Thus an illiterate peasant, miles away from any urban center, naively immersed in an unmoving and for him unshakable everyday world, nevertheless lived in several language systems: he prayed to God in one language (Church Slavonic), sang songs in another, spoke to his family in a third and, when he began to dictate petitions to the local authorities through a scribe, he tried speaking yet a fourth language (the official-literate language, 'paper' language). All these are *different languages*, even from the point of view of abstract socio-dialectical markers. But these languages were not dialogically coordinated in the linguistic consciousness of the peasant; he passed from one to another without thinking, automatically: each was indisputably in its own place, and the place of each was indisputable. He was not yet able to regard one language (and the verbal world corresponding to it) through the eyes of another language (that is, the language of everyday life and the everyday world with the language of prayer or song, or vice versa). (Bakhtin, 1981: 295–6)

And many of us remain, like this peasant, unable to pass easily from one form of talk in one part of our lives, on to another in another sphere.

However, it is not difficult also to imagine us beginning to talk from within our different selves with ourselves. In his study of Dostoevsky's novels, Bakhtin, for instance, comments on the first interior monologue of Raskolnikov – the central character in Dostoevsky's *Crime and Punishment*:

> [I]t was not a psychological evolution of an idea within a single self-enclosed consciousness. On the contrary, the consciousness of Raskolnikov becomes a field of battle for other voices; the events of recent days (his mother's letter, the meeting with Marmeladov), reflected in his consciousness, take on the form of a most intense dialogue with absentee participants (his sister, his mother, Sonya, and others), and in his dialogue he tries to 'get his thoughts straight' . . . As a result, Raskolnikov's idea appears before us in an inter-individual zone of intense struggle among several individual consciousnesses, while the theoretical side of the idea is inseparably linked with the ultimate positions in life taken by the participants in the dialogue. (1984: 88–9)

In this sense, then, we can say that here an individual's consciousness works not so much in terms of thoughts as in voices, in terms of a multiplicity or polyphony of voices – each with their own unique position in existence, each separately able to see things invisible to the others, and thus each with something of concern to say to the others. Thus thinking is responding to questions, discovering meanings in hearing possible responses to them, and so on; and, in all of this, the focus is on the only once-occurrent event of being, in which all these voices can meet and make a living, dialogical contact with each other. Indeed, 'an act of our activity, of our actual experiencing, is', says Bakhtin, 'like a two-faced Janus. It looks in two opposite directions: it looks at the objective unity of a domain of culture and at the never-repeatable uniqueness of actually lived and experienced life . . .' (1993: 2).

In contrast, without a sensitivity to such unique but unifying moments, in which two consciousnesses, two distinct voices, occupying two distinct positions in existence can come into responsive contact with each other, we remain like the peasant above: unable to bring the different forms of talk in the different parts of our lives into dialogical contact with each other. Thinking (talking to ourselves) only monologically, we are, to repeat, 'deaf to the other's response' (Bakhtin, 1984: 293). Because of this, those of us with an interest in psychological theory find that there is no easy passage from talk within its theoretical frameworks to talk that is responsively involved in life; nor do we often meet those to whom it is applied within a dialogically structured context, either. Usually, we listen to what 'the subjects' of our research have to say, in order to hear it *as* 'data', as representing something already well known to us in our theories. In remaining unresponsive to them, we remain only in a monologic relation to them. In such circumstances, our listening is partial in the double sense of it being both selective and preferential. It is in preferentially selecting only some aspects of people's expressions at the expense of others, that power can exert its influence in human relations. This is the function of official, authoritative genres, or ways of talking, in allowing only certain limited forms of expression; whereas, suggests Bakhtin, 'the single adequate form for *verbally expressing* authentic human life is the *open-ended dialogue*' (1984: 293). And interestingly, the turn to fully dialogic forms of talk can allow, not only for the verbal expression of authentic human life, but also for the development of familiar and intimate styles of address, in which people:

> perceive their addressees [as] . . . more or less outside the framework of the social hierarchy and social conventions, 'without rank', as it were . . . In familiar speech, since speech constraints and conventions have fallen away, one can take a special, unofficial, volitional approach to reality. This is why during the Renaissance familiar genres and styles could play such a large and positive role in destroying the official medieval picture of the world. (Bakhtin, 1986: 97)

Inside the 'inner lives' of both others and ourselves

Taking these emphases together – the emphasis on the only once-occurrent event of Being, on its dialogical structuring, and on its embedding in a speech genre or form of life – we can perhaps begin to see why Bakhtin's and Voloshinov's emphasis on what occurs in our relational encounters, in the dialogical moments occurring both between us and within us, is so important. For it is in just these momentary relational encounters, that the influences from many quarters – those from within us, from the past, from our expectations, from the expressions of our listeners, from the rest of our surroundings – can all meet and, in the way in which we responsively interrelate them, we can form a unique responsive answer to them. So, although in these moments of indeterminacy, the influences of others and of the othernesses in our circumstances partially 'shape' what we do, we also express ourselves in relation to them. This is why, in this approach, we are far less interested in looking back on repeatable patterns of 'already spoken words', and are much more interested in the unique, once-occurrent, moment-by-moment emergence of 'words in their speaking': for it is in our responsive speaking and bodying forth of our expressions that we can *create* (with others) a sense of the unique nature of our own inner lives, we can be 'present' to them – to the extent, that is, that they too are prepared to play a proper responsive part in the process. For it is in our utterly unique and novel uses of language, our own special way of populating our words with our own accents, our own rhythms, our own ways of juxtaposing them, and so on, that we can offer or afford others the chance of a responsive understanding of our own unique inner lives.

To grasp how this can be so, let us remind ourselves of Bakhtin's and Voloshinov's emphasis on the primacy of responsive understandings. In other words, in practice, we do *not* primarily understand another person's speech by a non-material process of first grasping 'the inner ideas' they have supposedly put into their words by us interpreting their 'content'. This view of how we understand each other must be seen as a special case; most of time, I suggest, we do not fully understand each other in that way at all. Indeed, in practice, shared understandings occur only occasionally, and if they occur at all, it is by people testing and checking each other's talk, by them questioning and challenging it, reformulating and elaborating it, and so on – as Bakhtin and Voloshinov suggest. In practice, shared understandings are developed, negotiated or 'socially constructed' between participants over a period of time, in the course of an ongoing conversation, guided by a felt sense of understanding. Indeed, what our felt understanding 'is' for us, what something 'is' for us in our 'inner lives', is revealed, not in how we talk *about it* when reflecting upon it, but in how 'it' necessarily 'shapes' those of our everyday communicative practices in which it is in fact involved. Indeed, 'it' has its being in the 'movement' of our voices as we speak our words. A friend proposes a vacation. I reply, 'Well', in a special intonation, and he knows straightaway that there is 'a difficulty', and he asks, 'What's the difficulty?'. I say to another, 'I've a good new idea for the group: we should all do X', and my friend replies, 'I see your little game. You just want to be master, that's all'. One Russian seeing snow in May says an indignant, 'Well!' to another, and the other concurs. And so on. In short: the 'things' in our 'inner' lives are not to be found inside us as individuals, but out 'in' the moment-by-moment shaping of the relational spaces occurring between ourselves and an other or otherness in our surroundings. Where, out in such a space, 'they' are, or 'it' is, just as much an influence in shaping what occurs there as we ourselves. In other words, the contents of our 'inner' lives are not radically hidden 'inside' us as individuals; they are 'in' our living of our lives, 'in' the responsive ways in which we relate our momentary activities to all else occurring around us; they are 'shown' or 'exhibited' in the *internal relations* (philosophers would say) present in our activities. And this gives rise to the strange consequence that, as Voloshinov puts it, 'the processes that basically define the content of the psyche occur not inside but outside the individual organism, although they involve its participation' (1986: 25).

Thus, adopting this dialogical or relational view of people's psychic life suggests that people's 'inner lives' are neither so private, nor so inner, nor so orderly, logical, or systematic as has been assumed. Instead, our 'thinking' not only reflects essentially the same ethical, rhetorical, political, and poetic features as those exhibited in the dialogical transactions between people, out in the world (Billig, 1996), but it does not go on wholly 'inside' us as individuals either. This is because, as Voloshinov claims, what we call our thoughts are not first organized at the inner center of our being (in a non-material 'psyche' or 'mind'), later to be given adequate outer expression, or not, in words; they only become ordered and organized in a moment-by moment, back and forth, formative or developmental process at the boundaries of our being, involving similar linguistically mediated negotiations as those we conduct in our everyday dialogues with others. Indeed, if they did go on wholly within us, then it would be difficult to see how they could still, nonetheless, be related to our surrounding circumstances. However, in being 'in' the living of our lives, in being internally related to what goes on around us, their relation to our surroundings is somewhat less mysterious.

> 'What sort of reality pertains to the subjective psyche? *The reality of the inner psyche is the same reality as that of the sign.* Outside the material of signs there is no psyche . . . By its very existential nature, the subjective psyche is to be localized somewhere between the organism and the outside world, on the *borderline* separating these two spheres of reality . . . Psychic experience is the semiotic expression of the contact between the organism and the outside environment. (Voloshinov, 1986: 26)

Thus, even our own psychic experience must be dialogically structured, consisting mainly in only once-occurrent events of Being. Traditionally, we have thought of thinking as the inner, rational manipulation of logical symbols – hence the adherence to the computational model of thought in cognitive psychology, and the idea of a separate and special 'language of the mind'. But if thought is dialogically structured, then, as Billig shows so well, 'humans do not converse because they have inner thoughts to express, but they have inner thoughts to express because they are able to converse' (1996: 141). The idea of an orderly language of the mind is a theoretical invention; our orderly thought emerges from inner dialogues as disorderly as our outer ones.

Why poetic methods are needed and theories are of no help in 'entering into' each other's lives

This, I think, is the startling conclusion. Traditionally, we have always been concerned with patterns and order, with what is stable and repeatable, with what can be calculated and measured, with understanding things by finding the hidden laws or principles determining their nature. We are quite unused to the idea that the events of importance to us in our investigations are unique, novel, unmeasurable events, not repetitions. Yet, isn't this what is involved in making history, in doing something that has never been done before? And further, isn't it terribly difficult for us to maintain any stable orders in the world; don't we have to make continual efforts – not only to establish courts of law and to institute continual review procedures, but, in fact, continually to monitor our every action for its legitimacy – if we want our social orders to endure? Isn't stability maintained only through the continual introduction of novelty? But if this is so, how in the world are we to understand such novelties? Well, we cannot by acting theoretically, as isolated, scientific thinkers; but we can practically, as dialogically involved, ordinary, everyday, embodied persons – if we are prepared to *enter into* dialogical relations with them.

I have already mentioned Steiner's (1989) remark that the experiencing of the special unity that emerges in dialogical relations, is a meeting between freedoms. In other words, there is no compulsion, no requirement, no necessity that we understand what another merely *offers* us. Only if we, so to speak, go out to meet them and responsively (and responsibly) enter into relation with them, is meaning between us possible. Cartesian meaning, as Bakhtin (1986) points out, gives rise to only a passive, abstract under-standing – an understanding that does not call out for a response from us; while all active responsive understanding does, and does so spontaneously. A statement like: 'The cat sat on the mat. The mat was red, the cat was black', sits dead on the page, so to speak. We can only say in response to it: 'So what, I get the picture, but what's the point, what follows from it?' But if I say (slowly and with pauses): 'The night was dark . . . the man was dressed in black . . . he walked along the road alone', we want to know what happens next, why he was there, what was special about the road, and so on. The pauses (and the intonational style) 'invite' us, spontaneously, into a relation to the scene, without us having to 'work out', intellectually, what that relation *is*. Articulating its details can come later. But unless we take up the initial offer of relation, responsive understandings cannot occur.

Like Bakhtin and Voloshinov, Steiner wants, he says, 'to delineate, as directly as I can, the characteristic immediacies of the "happening to us" of created forms in poetics and the arts' (1989: 179). And he tells us of their spontaneous nature, himself in a poetic idiom:

> That which comes *to call on us* – that idiom, we saw, connotes visitation and summons – will very often do so unbidden. Even when there is a readiness, as in the concert hall, in the museum, in the moment of chosen reading, the true entrance into us will not occur by an act of will . . . But each and everyone of us, however bounded our sensibility, will have known such unbidden, unexpected entrances by irrevocable guests . . . I picked up and leafed through, scarcely attentive, a very thin book of poems [while waiting for a train] . . . I do not now recall whether I caught the intended train, but Paul Celan has never left me. (1989: 179–80)

Steiner's use of poetic language here is crucial. For, if we are to learn to grasp more of people's 'inner lives' in the momentary and fleeting but responsive ways in which they relate themselves to their surroundings, then we must learn to 'look over' and be responsive to their activities, on the surface, so to speak. We must search for the internal relations and connec-tions these unique events might actually have both within themselves and with the rest of their surroundings. To do this, we not only need to have our attention 'called' to the actual events themselves, but also at the same time, to talk of them in such a way that at least some of the further possible relations and connections they might have to the circumstances of their occurrence are also drawn to our attention. And to stabilize our ability to notice such things, we need to use the words again and again to 're-call' our attention to them again and again.

This is the function of poetic forms of talk. For these forms of talk at first 'strike' us or 'arrest' us; they put reality, so to speak, on 'freeze-frame', and then 'move' us to search that freeze-frame for ways in which to relate ourselves responsively to aspects of it that might not otherwise have occurred to us. Steiner, in saying that our dialogical relations with others are like 'a meeting between freedoms' (1989: 152); or like 'the stranger's entrance' into our home (1989: 176); or, that 'it does seem to be words that rap most surely on the door [that is, that "strike" us]' (1989: 191), uses poetic forms of talk. In saying such things he brings two bits of knowledge familiar to us all – to do with offered understandings, meetings, callings, and entrances – together into new juxtapositions: and in reading them, we imagine an other visiting us, and all the things that might and might not happen as a result. We begin to grasp the non-required, non-guaranteed nature of our dialogical relations, but also the 'gifts' they can make available to us if we have the trust to 'enter into' them.

Bakhtin puts it thus:

> When I experience an object actually, I thereby carry out something in relation to it; the object enters into relation with that which is to-be-achieved, grows in it – within my relationship to that object. Pure givenness cannot be experienced actually. Insofar as I am actually experiencing an object, even if I do so by thinking of it, it becomes a changing moment in the ongoing event of my experiencing (thinking) it, i.e., it assumes the character of something-yet-to-be-achieved. Or, to be exact, it is given to me within a certain event-unity, in which the moments of what-is-given and what-is-to-be-achieved, of what-is and what-ought-to-be, of being and value, are inseparable. All these abstract categories are here constituent moments of a certain, living, concrete, and palpable (intuitable) once-occurrent whole – an event. (1993: 32)

And as we stare at a painting – at, perhaps, Van Gogh's *Sunflowers* – we begin to look it over, first this way and then that way, up close, from afar, responsively relating ourselves to it first this way and then that, thinking of the other paintings like it, of sunflowers we have actually seen, of the rest of our lives, and so on. We don't have to spend the time on it, but if we do, 'the "otherness" that enters into us makes us other' (Steiner, 1989: 188). But as soon as we fall out of our two-way, living, dialogically structured relationship to such an otherness, and begin just to view the other as a thing to be externally observed, then we can no longer 'enter into' its 'inner life'. 'From inside this [objective or external kind of] seeing,' says Bakhtin simply, 'there is no way out into life' (1993: 14). With only a passive understanding that, so to speak, creates a theoretical picture inside someone's head, we have no access to that active kind of meaning which moves us, which calls us this way and that, so that we come to traverse over the 'inner structure' of a whole new meaningful world.

Conclusion: putting a new practice into our practices

Inside the multi-voiced, dialogical world, then – if we open ourselves up to 'entering into' it, accept the 'invitations' to participate in it – the 'inner lives' of other living beings can become apparent to us. Inside such a world, instead of dead pictures that can only be passively understood, that we need to make efforts of inference and interpretation to grasp, there are living movements – activities which 'call out' responses from us, activities that, so to speak, 'look to' us for a response. In such a world as this, all our truly mental activity is primarily 'out there' in the world between us: that is where it originates, and that is where it has its most meaningful expression. Even within ourselves, if we can actually hide our responsive reactions to a sufficient extent to achieve an inner privacy, we can find the results of such spontaneously conducted inner dialogues at work on the boundaries between the others and othernesses within us. To repeat Steiner's remark: 'the "otherness" that enters into us makes us other' (1989: 188).

As I mentioned at the beginning of this chapter, the Cartesian mind is a single, unified rational mind which, when working properly, is a rational system with all its parts interrelated in an orderly way according to logical laws or principles. With such a mind, if we are to be instructed into a new practice, it is thought best to instruct us by first teaching us its rational principles; it is a matter, as we say, of 'putting theory into practice'. The Bakhtinian/Voloshinovian mentality is, however, structured in a quite different way: it is dialogically structured, and when working properly, all its parts are interrelated as people are interrelated, in myriad ways in countless meetings – all of which require the taking up of offerings, the issuing of invitations, tact, trust, helpfulness, disquiet, joy, and so on. With such a mentality as this, to be instructed into a new practice, we require things to be pointed out to us from within our attempts to begin executing the practice, we require living examples to which we can relate. Our teachers must 'call' fleeting features of our ongoing circumstances to our notice that would otherwise pass us by unremarked – features we can ourselves 're-call' by using their words to 're-mind' us of them. Rather than putting a theory into practice, we can call this 'the putting of a special practice into our practices'. Where the special practice in question is to do with us using crucial words at crucial moments, to distinguish and relate, to place and position, to separate and to connect, certain crucial features in our current ways of doing things, so as to come to a grasp of their 'inner structure'. For, if we can *articulate* our activities in this way, so as to develop an 'inner landscape' of possible next 'places to go' in our performing them, then we can develop them into more refined and skillful forms. Paradoxical though it may seem, we learn a practice from within our doing of it.

Indeed this, I think, is precisely the function of Bakhtin's and Voloshinov's writings: they work in certain ways to make us more aware, to articulate our language-entwined activities more clearly to ourselves, so that we can come, not to a theoretical, but to a more elaborate and refined practical grasp of how to make sense of them than we have at present: where our greater practical grasp is exhibited in us being able, for instance, to attend to and to talk of their dialogical nature – an aspect of their nature that had until now been ignored. So, to conclude, I will list some of the methods Bakhtin and Voloshinov use in achieving this:

1   They use 'striking' or 'unusual' images or phrases that *arrest* or *interrupt* (or destabilize or deconstruct) the spontaneous, unself-conscious flow of our ongoing activity, to make us notice something fleeting that would otherwise have passed us by unnoticed.

2   By the careful use of selected poetic images, similes, analogies, metaphors, or 'pictures', they suggest *new ways of talking* that not only orient us toward sensing otherwise unnoticed distinctions and relations for the first time but which also suggest new connections and relations with the rest of our proceedings – as well as enabling us to 're-call' such relations, and to 'think over' them in such a way as to begin to construct from them a stable, living, 'inner relational landscape'.

3   If we are to get a grasp of the *order* of things in such a living, 'inner landscape', to grasp what 'goes with' what, so to speak, then we need a third method. By the use of *comparisons*, 'our' ways of doing things becomes visible by comparison with 'others':

> *Creative understanding* does not renounce itself, its own place in time, its own culture; and it forgets nothing . . . In the realm of culture, outsideness is a most powerful factor in understanding. It is only in the eyes of *another* culture that foreign culture reveals itself fully and profoundly . . . A meaning only reveals its depths once it has encountered and come into contact with another, foreign meaning: they engage in a kind of dialogue, which surmounts the closeness and one-sidedness of these particular meanings, these cultures. We raise new questions for a foreign culture, ones that it did not raise itself; we seek answers to our questions to it; and the foreign culture responds to us by revealing to us its new aspects and new semantic depths. (Bakhtin, 1986: 7)

Both Bakhtin and Voloshinov follow this maxim in their own writings, by introducing their view always in contrast with those of others. And I have followed it here in by introducing their views in contrast with those of Descartes.

4   As a result of dialogically bringing two (or more) views together in novel or strange combinations, a number of special events seem to occur. We are 'struck by' the combination of words we hear; the ordinary routine flow of our thought and understanding is 'arrested'; our everyday, taken-for-granted practices are suspended; for a moment, the flow of activity in which we are involved seems to come to a halt, and we begin to look over the extent of the momentary 'freeze-frame' thus created, to see present circumstances in the light of the shifting and oscillating relations between the juxtaposed utterances of the 'voices' that 'struck' us. The combinations suggest connections and relations between features of the circumstances to which they are applied not previously apparent. And in the 'interactive' or 'moving moments'

created, we begin to survey whatever circumstances happen currently to be before us, with a new 'movement of thought', a new way of looking, so to speak. And as we look over and dwell on our surroundings in this way, we see, not beyond them into a radically hidden reality (a supposedly 'more real' reality only knowable through inference in terms of a theory), but extensively over the actual reality around us. We begin to look over its everyday complexity, its tangled richness, its particular details, with a greater sensitivity, and to notice in them the not-previously-apparent hints of unique but possible new ways of 'going on' available to us. We see these new features *through* our words, so to speak. Here, instead of an *image of* something already well known to us, they provide an *image for* seeing something for the very first time.

5   Finally, we can note the fact that none of these methods ever leads to a final, fixed account of what something 'really' means. One's investigations are never over. There is always 'more' to come. By continually shifting one's stance and position in relation to one's surroundings, yet further unnoticed aspects become visible.

> At any moment in the development of the dialogue there are immense, boundless masses of forgotten contextual meanings, but at certain moments . . . they are recalled and invigorated in renewed form (in a new context). Nothing is absolutely dead: every meaning will have its homecoming festival. (Bakhtin, 1986: 170)

All these methods taken together, can be called a 'social poetics' (Katz and Shotter, 1996a, 1996b; Shotter, 1996, in press; Shotter and Katz, 1996).[3]

Behavior informed by this kind of dialogically structured, polyvocal understanding is to be contrasted with people acting monologically, as Cartesians in accord with a theory – in which we take it for granted that we first have thoughts which we then put into words. In Bakhtin's (1986) and Voloshinov's (1986) view, our inner psychic lives are only fully manifested in our practical activities as we body them forth, dialogically, out into the world. Indeed, 'consciousness [only] takes its shape and being in the material of signs created by an organized group in the process of its social intercourse' (Voloshinov, 1986: 13); or, to put it another way, 'people do not "accept" their native language – it is in their native language that they first reach awareness' (ibid.: 81). Even what we call *introspection* is for Bakhtin and Voloshinov a dialogical process, in which we 'dialogically develop' the initial, vague 'sense' that we have of a circumstance into something determinate, in a back-and-forth process between our sense of it and the specific formulations we offer ourselves and our responsive attempts to give voice to it in a socially intelligible and legitimate manner. Thus a person's psyche (if such an entity can be said to exist at all) is, according to surrounding social conditions, an entity with constantly contested and shifting boundaries; something we can re-collect in one way one day, and in another the next. And even when 'thinking' all alone, these considerations of our relations to others are still the ones to which we must address ourselves –

that is, if we want what we do or say to be acceptable to, and to have point for, others.

In the Cartesian mind, however, instead of being able to work toward a sense of the fittingness of one's actions to one's circumstances in an embodied, responsive, back-and-forth, dialogical fashion, at least partially out in the world, over time, one is supposed to work things out, 'in one's mind', cognitively, as if by calculation. Instead of one's understanding being of an active, *relational-responsive* kind, to do with understanding the detailed connections and relations between things, it is of a passive under-standing of a *representational-referential* kind, to do with accurately pictur-ing an outer state of affairs internally. And whereas relational kinds of understanding are lived out in one's life, representational forms of under-standing must be argued for and justified. By contrast, in their more poetic, dialogical forms of talk, Bakhtin and Voloshinov have tried to help us to come to a very different kind of understanding. They have sought the kind of immediate, practical grasp of our own talk-entwined activities as the kind of knowledge that we have, say, of our own dwelling places, our own homes, when we know where everything is placed and where to look for something we have not used for a while. It is this same kind of 'at-homeness' in our own dialogically-structured practices that they seek. This is what a social poetics can do for us when put to work within our practices: it can give us a better knowledge of our 'way about' inside them, and to enable us to see in their details and subtleties, possibly new ways forward – ways that are easily obscured by an insistence on external rules and principles that are already in place for their 'supposed' good ordering. Instead of living our lives from within theories, systems, narratives, or dreams, they bring us back to living our lives within life itself.

Notes

1   Among social constructionists, the quintessential version of this thesis is given by S. Woolgar, *Science: the Very Idea* (Tavistock Publications, London and New York, 1987), p. 65: 'The argument is not just that social networks mediate between the object and observational work done by participants. Rather, the social network constitutes the object (or lack of it). The implication for our main argument is the inversion of the presumed relationship between representation and object; the representation gives rise to the object'. But many other con-structionists also simply invert Cartesianism: thus, while Cartesianism radically splits mind from body, they radically separate language from world. It is our total enclosure in our own linguistic forms, in this still representationalist view of language, that is both the main (argumentative) strength of this form of social constructionism and its main weakness: it makes it impossible for us to connect our language with our lives – a concern, as we shall see, that is central for both Bakhtin and Voloshinov.
2   'The experience of created form is a meeting of freedoms' (G. Steiner, *Real Presences* (University of Chicago Press, Chicago, IL, 1989), p. 152.

3   In these papers, we show how these methods can be used to illuminate events occurring both in medical diagnostic interviews and in the conduct of mentoring programs in medical education.

References

Bakhtin, M.M. (1981) *The Dialogical Imagination*. (Ed. M. Holquist; trans. C. Emerson and M. Holquist.) Austin, TX: University of Texas Press.

Bakhtin, M.M. (1984) *Problems of Dostoevsky's Poetics*. (Ed. and trans. Caryl Emerson.) Minneapolis, MN: University of Minnesota Press.

Bakhtin, M.M. (1986) *Speech Genres and Other Late Essays*. (Trans. Vern W. McGee.) Austin, TX: University of Texas Press.

Bakhtin, M.M. (1993) *Toward a Philosophy of the Act*. (Trans. and notes by Vadim Lianpov; ed. M. Holquist.) Austin, TX: University of Texas Press.

Billig, M. (1996) *Arguing and Thinking: a Rhetorical Approach to Social Psychology*. (2nd edn) Cambridge: Cambridge University Press.

Descartes, R. (1986) *Meditations on First Philosophy: with Selections from Objections and Replies*. (Trans. J. Cottingham, with intro. by B. Williams.) Cambridge: Cambridge University Press.

Goffman, E. (1967) *Interaction Ritual*. Harmondsworth: Penguin.

Heidegger, M. (1967) *Being and Time*. Oxford: Blackwell.

Heidegger, M. (1977) *Basic Writings*. (Ed. D.F. Krell.) San Francisco: Harper.

Katz, A.M. and Shotter, J. (1996a) 'Hearing the patient's voice: toward a "social poetics" in diagnostic interviews', *Social Science and Medicine*, 43: 919–31.

Katz, A.M. and Shotter, J. (1996b) 'Resonances from within the practice: social poetics in a mentorship program', *Concepts and Transformation*, 2: 97–105.

Merleau-Ponty, M. (1962) *Phenomenology of Perception*. (Trans. C. Smith.) London: Routledge and Kegan Paul.

Sampson, E.E. (1993) *Celebrating the Other; a Dialogic Account of Human Nature*. Boulder, CO: Westview Press.

Shotter, J. (1980) 'Action, joint action, and intentionality', in M. Brenner (ed.), *The Structure of Action*. Oxford: Blackwell. pp. 28–65.

Shotter, J. (1984) *Social Accountability and Selfhood*. Oxford: Blackwell.

Shotter, J. (1993a) *Cultural Politics of Everyday Life: Social Constructionism, Rhetoric, and Knowing of the Third Kind*. Milton Keynes: Open University Press.

Shotter, J. (1993b) *Conversational Realities: Constructing Life through Language*. London: Sage.

Shotter, J. (1995) 'In conversation: joint action, shared intentionality, and the ethics of conversation', *Theory and Psychology*, 5: 49–73.

Shotter, J. (1996) 'Living in a Wittgensteinian world: beyond theory to a poetics of practices', *Journal for the Theory of Social Behavior*, 26: 293–311.

Shotter, J. (1997) 'Dialogical realities: the ordinary, the everyday, and other strange new worlds', *Journal for the Theory of Social Behaviour*, 27: 345–57.

Shotter, J. (1998) 'Social construction as social poetics: Oliver Sacks and the case of Dr. P.', in B. Bayer and J. Shotter (eds), *Reconstructing the Psychological Subject: Bodies, Practices and Technologies*. London: Sage.

Shotter, J. and Billig (1998) 'A Bakhtinian psychology: from out of the heads of individuals and into the dialogues between them', in M.M. Bell and M. Gardiner (eds), *Bakhtin and the Human Sciences: No Final Words*. London: Sage.

Shotter, J. and Katz, A.M. (1996) 'Articulating a practice from within the practice itself: establishing formative dialogues by the use of a "social poetics" ', *Concepts and Transformation*, 2: 71–95.

Spinosa, C., Flores, F. and Dreyfus, H.L. (1997) *Disclosing New Worlds: Entreprenueurship, Democratic Action, and the Cultivation of Solidarity*. Cambridge, MA: MIT Press.

Steiner, G. (1989) *Real Presences*. Chicago, IL: University of Chicago Press.

Voloshinov, V.N. (1976) *Freudianism: a Critical Sketch*. Bloomington and Indianapolis: Indiana University Press.

Voloshinov, V.N. (1986) *Marxism and the Philosophy of Language*. (Trans. L. Matejka and I.R. Titunik.) Cambridge, MA: Harvard University Press.

Wittgenstein, L. (1953) *Philosophical Investigations*. Oxford: Blackwell.

Woolgar, S. (1987) *Science: the Very Idea*. London and New York: Tavistock Publications.

5 POSTMODERN CULTURE AND THE PLURAL SELF

Leon Rappoport, Steve Baumgardner and George Boone

One of the many ironies of postmodern life, at least in psychology and the other social sciences, is that ever since the term 'postmodern' first came into general usage, its meaning has become increasingly problematic. And yet its use has also become increasingly unavoidable as a way of indicating certain sociocultural and philosophical trends occurring in the First World or 'high tech' societies of North America, Western Europe and Japan. Despite the ambiguity of the term (which will be addressed in some detail below), we consider it essential to our thesis that social-emotional adjustment to life in postmodern societies encourages, and all but requires, development of a pluralistic sense of self. While acknowledging that plural self-concepts or subpersonalties may not yet be normative, we will argue that such pluralism is becoming more and more prevalent, particularly among young adults.

The general basis for this argument resides in well-established understandings of the relationship between culture and personality which generally emphasize that the very ground of personhood is defined by culture. The technologies, language forms, values, and other representational systems delimiting the range of meanings through which persons come to understand themselves and others are all rooted in their culture (Geertz, 1973; Bruner, 1990). Accordingly, insofar as significant changes in culture take place, it appears axiomatic that significant changes in self understanding will occur. An outstanding example can be seen in the effect of feminism on the self-concepts of women. As the norms and values that previously discouraged women from entering and competing in the socio-economic domains traditionally dominated by men have been eroded, young women have become more assertive, independent, and self-confident.

In the following pages, we first discuss the mixture of popular, intellectual and economic culture changes generally lumped together under the heading 'postmodern' so as to clarify some of the ambiguity associated with this term. At the same time, those changes with manifest implications for personality development are noted. Relevant theoretical and empirical work in psychology is then reviewed, with particular attention to material concerning formulations of the self. Finally, we conclude with discussion of specific criticisms that have been levelled against the concept of a pluralistic sense of self, and suggest the need for a revised epistemological approach to personality theory.

Postmodern culture

The 'short course' on postmodernity is simple: metaphorically, it is bracketed at the popular or 'low' end by hypermodern music television videos (MTV), Madonna, McDonalds and films like *Pulp Fiction* and at the 'high' or intellectual end by Baudrillard, biotechnology, and chaos theory. (For a more detailed discussion of postmodern culture, see Boyne and Rattansi, 1990; for its relevance to psychology, see Kvale, 1992). Once this polarity is understood, much of the confusion that many critics associate with the concept of postmodernity evaporates. At the popular level, the key factor is electronic media saturation and the so-called technoporn world-view this fosters. Briefly, at this level it can be said that if modernity penetrated much of the world via the introduction of Coca-Cola, Hollywood films and transistor radios, postmodernity is now penetrating much of the world via the introduction of satellite TV, the world wide web, and McDonalds.

The primary, overarching effect of such penetration follows from its emphasis on diversity, constant change, and 'linkage'. Thus, McDonalds constantly reinvents the hamburger while linking promotion of its products to the latest Disney film creations. Madonna and MTV stars like Michael Jackson constantly appear in new incarnations linked to changing styles in music, clothing, and language forms. And in the world of the Internet or cyberspace, it seems that every product – from the computer hardware and software that becomes obsolete within a year or two, to the home pages, databases, and consumer services that are changed or upgraded on a near daily basis – is characterized by diversity, change and linkage.

In other words, at the level of popular culture, postmodernity equates to a condition of flux, multiplicity, and transformation: whatever 'is' today, is not likely to be the same tomorrow. Important contributing factors intrinsic to this condition are the increasing priority accorded to imagery over material substance (sometimes called 'hyperrealism'), and of non-linear over linear narratives. These qualities are particularly apparent in films, TV productions and media-driven politics such as the 1996 presidential contest between Bill Clinton and Bob Dole. Can there be any doubt that Clinton is the archetype of the postmodern politician, just as *Pulp Fiction* is the archetype of postmodern films?

Moreover, given this general condition of popular culture, which shows itself in various forms on television situation comedies and talk shows as well as MTV, films and magazines, can there be any doubt that the personality development of youth immersed in it will be profoundly influenced? Insofar as flux, multiplicity, and transformation have emerged as dominant values in postmodern society, and are celebrated as admirable qualities in the personalities of public figures all across the spectrum of society, from Beavis and Butthead, to Madonna, to Bill Clinton, these qualities inevitably take on the status of important developmental values – criteria of self-evaluation – for young people. In short, our point is that at the level of popular culture, the models and styles defining successful person-ality development emphasize the qualities associated with postmodernism. But this emphasis is not limited to, and does not stop at, the level of popular culture alone. It is directly supported and encouraged by the theoretical and philosophical perspectives emerging from high culture.

Kvale (1992) epitomizes the general intellectual world-view of post-modernism by suggesting that it is basically defined by abandonment of the Enlightenment faith that progress can best be achieved through the accumula-tion of objective, scientific knowledge. In a more specific historical dis-cussion, Rappoport and Kren (1996) suggest that the modern ideal of progress through rationality, efficiency and social control died at Auschwitz, and that certain foundation principles of postmodern thought such as the critique of positivist science and the deconstruction of language can find their justification in the failure of modern institutions to prevent or compre-hend the Holocaust. Apart from such problematic generalizations, however, there is substantial agreement about epistemological issues central to the understanding of culture processes and science. Indeed, it is no longer unusual to find philosophers and historians describing science itself as a culture process.

Thus, Baudrillard (1995) has pushed the idea of the social construction of reality to its limit by arguing persuasively that material reality is increas-ingly and primarily apprehended through 'simulacra': simulations, repre-sentations, or images. In this view, moreover, it is no accident that scientific research of all kinds is now presented in the form of 'models' open to whatever modifications may be suggested by the most recent results. For Baudrillard and many students of semiotics, however, the more radical general rule is that the intrinsic properties of objects and events have become less significant than their sign qualities (the designer label on clothing can be more important than its fit or comfort). Meanwhile, the postmodern move-ment in science takes its inspiration from findings in quantum theory (Wolfe, 1984; DeBerry, 1993), where pluralism is a well accepted basis for explana-tion, and from biology (Prigogine and Stengers, 1984), where dissipative structures, randomness and uncertainty are accepted properties of non-equilibrium systems. Chaos theory, with its emphasis on systemic rather than pointed predictability, also stands as an important feature of post-modernity in science (Barton, 1994).

In sum, there are both implicit and explicit ways in which the high culture forms of postmodern thought lend credibility to the postmodern qualities of popular culture. The apparent randomness of music video productions and the uncertainty imposed on film audiences have their counterparts and justification in chaos theory; the multiform presentations of self enacted by Madonna or Bill Clinton reflect principles of both chaos theory and quantum theory; and the relative priority of imagery over substance emphasized by Baudrillard is readily observable. Consequently, beneath their surface differences, the intellectual and popular strains of postmodernism appear mutually supportive and interpenetrating insofar as both reflect the values of diversity (multiplicity), change (flux) and linkage (transformation). These are the values that can be understood as cultural forces or vectors towards development of the plural self.

Psychosocial precursors

It should be noted at the outset that the idea of pluralism as a fundamental characteristic of personality or the self is not new. The Freudian tripartite formulation of id, ego and superego is nothing if not pluralistic, and the same may be said of George Herbert Mead's (1934) description of the social self and the active self, Erikson's (1950) developmental theory with its specification of conflicting ego qualities at every stage of the lifespan, and Berne's (1964) view of the self as consisting of parent, child, and adult selves. What *is* new, and essentially postmodern, is the idea that pluralism is not necessarily bad, or something to be reduced or eliminated in favor of hierarchical integration.

Freud's famous aphorism emphasizing hierarchical organization of the psyche, 'where id was, there shall ego be', has in one form or another been at the center of modern personality theories, all of which consider healthy social adaptation to require an integrated sense of self, with the ego or normatively rational self fully in command. It is no mere coincidence, moreover, that virtually all modern systems, whether social, economic or psychological, have been characterized by the value placed upon vertical, hierarchical integration. This is one of the features of modernity that distinguishes it from the postmodern emphasis on diversity.

Furthermore, in addition to its prominence in popular culture, diversity – in the form of diversification – has also become a major trend in business, education, and economic systems, and is closely associated with the postmodern critique of hierarchical integration in such systems. The practical reason or justification for this general trend of organizational change is, in a word: 'adaptation'. Whether in industry, education or government, it is widely accepted that flexible adaptation to rapidly changing environments is at a premium, and this means that the responding systems must themselves be capable of rapid change – a capability that can best be realized by diversified, relatively horizontally integrated systems.

The psychosocial implications of this general condition for individuals are quite clear: if they are to function effectively, they too must be diversified and operate in a horizontally integrated fashion. In the economic sphere, for example, the downsizing, outsourcing, and global realignments of industry facilitated by postmodern technologies have made it all too plain that persons maintaining a hierarchically integrated, unitary sense of self may often lack the flexibility required for successful psychosocial (emotional, social and cognitive) adaptation to their changing circumstances. The essential logic of our thesis concerning the conditions of postmodernity conducive towards the development of a plural self can now be briefly summarized as follows.

Adaptation to rapidly changing socio-economic environments increasingly *requires* a pluralistic sense of self; the popular culture increasingly encourages *development* of a plural self and provides attractive, instructive models towards this end; and the discourses of leading-edge theories in philosophy, social science, physics and biology increasingly *support* pluralism as a foundation principle of contemporary epistemology. As will be noted below, psychology has not been untouched by this state of affairs.

Psycholosocial theory and research

Theory and research supporting recognition of a pluralistic self-concept has been spread across three different areas or domains: clinical, theoretical-philosophical, and personality-social psychology. The clinical area deserves precedence, for it was Prince (1905) who first described treating a patient showing the pathological form of pluralism that would become known as multiple personality disorder. Apart from the literature on pathology, however, it was only in the early 1980s that clinical practitioners such as Beahrs (1982) began suggesting that a pluralistic sense of self or multiple identities could be part of a normal individual's adjustment to society. Subsequently, Rowan (1990) organized a substantial body of clinical observations and theoretical material in support of his thesis that the individual self could be understood as consisting of a collection of distinctive 'subpersonalities'. Since much of the relevant clinical work is reviewed elsewhere in this volume, it will not be elaborated upon here.

In the same time frame, however – early 1980s through the 1990s – discussions of personality pluralism and multiplicity appeared in a number of speculative theoretical and philosophical discourses. Thus Wolfe (1984), Zohar (1990), and DeBerry (1993) have all appealed to quantum theory as the basis for assertions that individuals may have more than one persona. Other noteworthy theoretical-philosophical discussions relevant to pluralism include Sampson's (1989) critique of the ideal of 'self contained individualism' prevalent in modern American psychology; Lather's (1990) suggestion that in postmodern society, the self should be understood as an 'empirical contingency', and Hermans et al. (1992) formulation of a 'dialogical self'.

The foregoing citations are by no means exhaustive; a valuable, detailed review of relevant literature is available in Hill (1996). Within academic psychology, however, no theorist has advanced the pluralistic perspective more forcefully or consistently than Kenneth Gergen. In an article aptly entitled 'Multiple identity: The healthy, happy human being wears many masks', Gergen (1972) was apparently the first mainstream theorist to assert that a pluralistic conception of self need not be seen as symptomatic of pathology, but could be a perfectly appropriate form of social adjustment. He subsequently articulated this view in greater depth (Gergen, 1988), by discussing it in the context of narrative theory and suggesting that personal identity could be construed in terms of a 'relational self': that is, a multi-faced self or set of selves based on the many different ways individuals stand in relation to their social and material environments. A few years later, in a detailed review and elaboration of his seminal analyses of how sociocultural forces impact upon the individual (the social construction of the self), Gergen (1991) epitomized his conclusions under the heading of 'the saturated self'. This is a self that owes its pluralism or multiplicity to exposure to the constant barrage of imagery and information produced by postmodern communication technologies. An individual saturated in this fashion with diverse, often contradictory sociocultural material can hardly be expected to develop a sense of self or identity that is not diversified, and in many respects, variable or inconsistent.

Finally, in what seems to be a further elaboration of his formulation of the relational self, as well as the saturation dynamic (1992, 1996), Gergen suggests that the whole modern conception of an individual personality grounded on a 'singular, coherent and stable self' may be disappearing under the impact of 'socializing technologies' which are eroding beliefs in individual uniqueness. If this actually happens, Gergen concludes that it might have the effect of reducing various group conflicts by facilitating mutual understanding across the barriers of race, ethnicity, and social class that have traditionally helped maintain the idea of uniqueness.

The pluralistic perspective in psychology has also been supported by the empirical findings of social-personality investigators. Some of the earliest and most provocative work was accomplished by Linville (1985) who reported that self-complexity was a measurable form of self representation based on the range of self-concepts maintained by individuals. Subsequently, Linville (1987) found that persons with more complex (or in the present context, pluralistic) self-concepts were better able to cope with stress. This was attributed to the fact that such persons were able to compensate for stress in any particular self domain by finding 'relief' in other domains.

Additional supportive evidence can be found in Markus and Nurius (1986), Fiske and Taylor (1991), Gottschalk (1993), and Boone (1995). Boone administered a 23-item scale designed to measure self multiplicity or pluralism to a large sample of college students who also completed a measure of childhood stress. In keeping with clinical reports that multiplicity could be understood as a defense against severe childhood experience, Boone found a highly significant correlation (.53) between these measures. He also found that a small sub-sample of black students showed significantly higher multiplicity scores than others. The latter result is directly in line with a discussion by Gaines and Reed (1995) of the 'two souls of black folk'. These authors note that Afro-Americans typically manifest distinctively different identities or self-concepts in predominantly white or black social environments. In this instance, pluralism can be seen as an adaptive mechanism for coping with racism.

The emergent pluralistic individual

Much of the foregoing theoretical material can be recast as follows: insofar as personality development is concerned, the difference between the modern and postmodern eras may be epitomized as the distinction between serial and simultaneous pluralism. Serial pluralism, in which individuals may transition through clearly different self-concepts as they move through different stages of the life span, has become a widely acknowledged phenomenon of modernity. Profound alterations of the self occurring as people experience major changes in their careers, marriages, metaphysical values, and cultural or geographic environments are commonplace. It is our contention that in the postmodern era, simultaneous pluralism will also become widely acknowledged: that is, it will be generally understood that people can benefit by maintaining a dynamic portfolio of alternative self-concepts as they move through the life span.

The already observable conditions of life in postmodern societies appear to be such that ready access to alternative views of the self is necessary for effective adaptation. In the face of rapid change, reinvention of the self cannot wait upon gradual development 'starting from scratch'. Instead, individuals require the capacity to draw upon prepared alternatives or, in military jargon, 'prepositioned resources'. This does not necessarily mean fully formed alternative personas, but armatures: skeletal structures that can be quickly fleshed out to meet the demands of new situations. Given this general theoretical context, the question then arises: 'What kind of portrait can be drawn of the pluralistic postmodern individual?'

Broadly viewed, the underlying values of postmodern culture and the body of contemporary theory and research relevant to pluralism suggest a portrait with the multiple, flowing qualities of early Picasso cubism rather than the sharp-edged randomness of abstract expressionism. More specifically, when construed as an 'ideal type', the characteristics of the pluralist postmodern individual are anticipated to include: (a) a globally-oriented world-view emphasizing complexity and uncertainty; (b) a high degree of cognitive and behavioral flexibility, as indicated, for example, by the term androgyny; (c) a preference for friendships and peer relations characterized by diversity; (d) a high level of moral relativism or situation ethics, including tolerance of mood-altering drugs; and (e) an absurdist sense of humor geared to irony, satire, and parody (the Monty Python style).

In addition to these attributes, we would also suggest that certain psychodynamic adjustment mechanisms are likely to be prominent. The most obvious would be defensive reactions to internal conflicts or threats to self-esteem based on compartmentalization. DeBerry (1993) refers to this more broadly as a 'schizoid' or divided consciousness, whereas Lifton

(1986) has described the near-pathological compartmentalization reported in his study of Nazi physicians as a form of dissociation he calls 'doubling'. This is clearly an extreme, 'worst case' formulation. However, what is generally implied is a dynamic in which anxieties may be distributed across the individual's alternative selves, and either worked out via internal dialogues among them, or compressed and walled up within one particularly relevant alternative.

Another likely psychodynamic quality of the postmodern pluralist would be some variety of escapism via paranoid or wish-fulfilling fantasies. The former tendency may be apparent today in the growing popularity of complex conspiracy theories whereby threatening events are attributed to the malevolent schemes of government officials, global corporations, or more remote entities. In the latter case of wish-fulfilling fantasies, a familiar example involves outer space visitor theories, whereby either threatening or redemptive scenarios are based on the idea of advanced life forms arriving from other planets. The pattern suggested here is probably too simplistic and extreme, but may be justified by an already observable general trend towards distrust of government, large corporations, and experts in the fields of science and medicine. Noteworthy, in this connection, is the TV series *The X-Files* involving themes that blend together *both* paranoid and wish-fulfilling fantasies. The fact that this series is reported to be especially popular among relatively well-off, well-educated young adult professionals is directly in line with our forecast.

Although the foregoing outline of the postmodern pluralist individual is incomplete and clearly speculative, some degree of anecdotal verification can be found by considering public figures who embody many of the qualities suggested above as prototypical. The obvious candidates here would be entertainers, such as Elton John and Madonna, who have virtually made pluralism their careers. But at least two world-class public figures with no direct financial incentive towards pluralism bear a close fit to our outline: Bill Clinton and the late Princess Diana. Since most readers will be familiar with the range of diverse if not contradictory qualities attributed to the President and the Princess, no detailed discussion appears necessary. It deserves emphasis, however, that both of them have suffered substantial criticism for their apparent multiplicity: Clinton for his shifting political positions and variable personal morality; Diana for her diverse manifestations as concerned mother, abused wife, glamour queen, and exponent of charitable causes. Not the least aspect of these criticisms is the implicit accusation that anyone showing such diversity cannot be sincere; that they must be either fooling themselves or deliberately trying to fool others. Yet viewed from the perspective of our pluralist thesis, such an accusation may be dismissed as reactionary. In principle, there is no reason why individuals cannot display sincere, empathic behaviors and emotions while functioning in one or another of their self incarnations.

A final caveat concerning our sketch of the hypothetical 'ideal type' postmodern individual relates to social class and socio-economic status. The foregoing sketch is admittedly oriented towards a reasonably well-educated, middle class 'everyman'. But we do not anticipate that class distinctions will disappear. Postmodernity, like modernity, will have its plutocrats, proletarians and lumpen, and although pluralism will likely be manifest to varying degrees in each of these categories, it will probably assume different forms. Further speculation about how pluralism may be mediated by social class differences, however, is beyond the scope of the present discussion.

Theoretical implications and controversies

The material presented to this point adds up to an emphatic argument for the thesis that the conditions of life in postmodern societies encourage and virtually require the development of a pluralistic sense of self. We consider this movement towards pluralism to be an evolving adaptation to the cultural and technological changes occurring in these societies, as suggested by Gergen. Our view is also in accord with Sedikides and Skowronski's (1997) application of evolutionary theory to the development of the modern self. Their conclusion is that the modern, polymorphous, symbolic self has evolved based on adaptation to proliferating linguistic and other abstract representations of human qualities. Insofar as evolution of the self continues, however, we see a transition from the polymorphous but unitary symbolic self, to a plurality of distinctive alternative symbolic selves. Moreover, we have argued that such self-pluralism is celebrated in popular culture, implicitly supported by contemporary scientific, theoretical and philosophical discourses recognizing the central importance of pluralism as a principle in nature and human societies, and that it has gained at least preliminary empirical credibility from psychosocial research studies. Nevertheless, strong arguments can and have been made against our thesis and deserve consideration.

The broadest of these arguments is based on rejection of the pluralistic epistemology associated with postmodernism, and, therefore, rejection of the idea that pluralism should be recognized as a legitimately adaptive process in personality development. Indeed, Smith (1994) has attacked Gergen's views, arguing that they represent an unjustified radical relativism undermining fundamental beliefs in human progress. The evidence we have cited in support of a plural self may appear radical and subversive of human values to some, but we understand it to be more of an affirmation than a denial of beliefs in human progress.

The most substantial theoretical arguments against the view that postmodern conditions foster the development of a pluralistic self are based on two prominent themes in modern psychosocial theory: social role playing and the development of identity. As promulgated in sociology and social psychology, the role theory theme maintains that in every society, individuals are required to play out a variety of more or less prescribed social roles, and that persons learn to vary their behavior according to the expectations or scripts associated with these roles. The criticism made against the concept of a pluralistic self is that such pluralism is simply a matter of role playing. Like a professional actor, one may play various roles while still maintaining a unitary, integrated sense of self. According to this view, for example, persons who can see different 'possible selves' in the future, or acknowledge different 'subpersonalities' in the present, are only envisioning – perhaps in a reified way – different social roles for themselves.

Ideally, this criticism might be addressed by designing a study to determine if role playing can be distinguished from self-pluralism. But until such a study may be accomplished, the answer to this criticism must rest partly on suggestive empirical findings and partly on observations of common experience. Thus, Linville's (1987) finding that persons with more complex, that is pluralistic, self-concepts are better able to cope with stress implies that something more than role playing is at work. Multiple roles do not equate to multiple, pluralistic, or more complex self-concepts. Furthermore, Biddle (1986) reported that multiple roles, or multiple demands relevant to a single role, can produce a condition of 'role strain' which increases rather than reduces stress. Also noteworthy is Boone's (1995) finding that persons with high personality multiplicity scores typically agreed with an item specifying that, on different occasions, they often felt like a different person.

Common experience suggests that a pluralistic sense of self goes beyond role playing. That is, role playing is often a relatively superficial behavior, as when a person may be required by circumstances to act in an unaccustomed or novel capacity. In academia, for example, it is not unusual to hear a new instructor say that their role as teacher feels artificial and they feel uncomfortable in class, like an imposter. It is only after some years of experience that the role is internalized to the point of seeming very natural. Our view is that at this point the role becomes a relatively independent dimension or alternative form of self. Thus, it is fairly common to observe a significant degree of disorientation or mourning when circumstances (illness, retirement, reduction in force, etc.) require an individual to relinquish a role that has become an alternative self. In general, perhaps the most conservative way to summarize the role-playing vs plural self issue is by suggesting that they are probably coterminous rather than dichotomous. A role may initially be just that, but if it is internalized and becomes a reflexive, authentic pattern of thought and behavior definitive of the individual, it can become a separate self, or a semi-autonomous subpersonality. Nor is there any apparent reason why such a transformation cannot involve more than one role. When the first author served in the army, for example, his off-duty self-concept was that of alienated intellectual, whereas on duty in field maneuvers it became (rather surprisingly and quite totally) that of combat ready infantryman. On rare occasions, the latter self still pops up.

The second theoretical criticism against self-pluralism derives from Erikson's extensive work (1950, 1968, 1974) on the development of a sense of identity among older adolescents and young adults. The developmental crisis of this age period is said to be based on the polarity between a sense of individual identity and identity confusion. Without going into the details of this formulation, it should be clear enough why it can be cited against self-pluralism: young people in a state of identity confusion would presumably show a pattern of inconsistent, variable behaviors and values, and a high level of uncertainty or multiplicity concerning their sense of self. This state would also appear conducive to preoccupation with a range of 'possible selves'. Consequently, the notion of a pluralistic self has been seen by some critics as equivalent to identity confusion.

Here again, as with the role-playing critique, one might try to design an empirical study that could settle the issue by pitting measures of identity confusion and multiplicity or pluralism, against each other. In the absence of such a study, however, certain empirical and theoretical considerations are still available, indicating substantial non-equivalence. Foremost among these are studies showing that young people in the confused state tend to be withdrawn, self-conscious and depressed (Clancy and Dollinger, 1993), and likely to be involved in drug abuse (Jones, 1992). In short, identity confusion is associated with serious adjustment problems, whereas research findings cited earlier in connection with pluralism indicate that it can serve as an adaptive form of stress coping.

Another theoretical consideration relevant to identity formation is Erikson's view that the conflict between identity achievement and confusion can be resolved through a central process of role experimentation. Accordingly, young people are encouraged to try out different social and occupational roles in order to discover what works for them as a route towards achievement of a satisfying unitary sense of identity. This is considered to be a healthy, normal process. It requires no great leap of imagination, however, to conclude that if role experimentation becomes a permanent feature of everyday life promulgated, as has been suggested, in popular culture and fostered by economic policies, then it may be better understood as a route towards the achievement of a plural self or identity.

Not to be neglected in this discussion of identity and the self-pluralism we see as emerging in postmodern societies is the pathbreaking Berger et al. (1974, first published 1973) psychosocial analysis of modernity and consciousness. Here they speak of the 'pluralization of social life worlds' and its effects on the 'subjective consciousness' (for our purposes, self-concepts) of individuals: 'modern man' – would they today say postmodern men and women? – 'is afflicted with a *permanent identity crisis*' (1974: 77–9, italics original). In 1973, this was perhaps as close as one could come to the idea of a pluralistic self. At present, however, it seems to us that an effective adjustment to permanent identity crisis lies in the development of a relatively stable set of alternative self-concepts. And once a certain range of these alternatives is delimited and becomes familiar, the person becomes free to shift from one to another, and/or consciously to negotiate priorities across the range of alternatives as circumstances may warrant.

Conclusions: understanding the plural self

There is more than one way to understand the meaning and implications of a pluralistic sense of self. Depending on one's perspective, its meaning can vary from a liberatory, normative adjustment view, in which subpersonalities or alternative selves are seen as an adaptation to the diversity of postmodern societies, to a quasi-pathological view, in which such pluralism is seen as symptomatic of a tendency towards schizoid fragmentation of the psyche. Although both views are defensible, our perspective emphasizes the former. This is not to deny that schizoid fragmentation with moderate or serious pathological consequences can be seen as the 'shadow' or dark side of adaptive pluralism. One study (Ross, 1991) already points to an increase in the frequency of multiple personality or dissociative disorders. But the existence of such pathology does not necessarily undermine the idea of adaptive pluralism. As Gergen suggested more than twenty years ago, the healthy, happy human being can wear many masks; in the present context, it is not surprising to see evidence that unhealthy, unhappy human beings can get their masks confused.

Although the larger theoretical implications of psychosocial pluralism concerning the self are at this point quite problematic, the pluralism we have described clearly poses a challenge to established representations of personality as a hierarchically integrated system dominated by a unitary self or ego. As argued in more detail elsewhere (Baumgardner and Rappoport, 1996), it now seems plausible to consider replacing the hierarchically integrated system formulated by Freud and other pioneers of modern psychology, with a more decentralized, horizontally integrated system.

In closing, it seems useful to reiterate and extend the evolutionary perspective on the self presented by Sedikides and Skowronski. They describe the self as having evolved through stages of subjective, objective, and finally symbolic self-awareness. The latter, symbolic self, 'refers to both the language-based and abstract representation of one's own attributes and the use of this representation for effective functioning' (1997: 83). Our contention is that the multifaceted information and communication technologies characterizing postmodern culture allow new information and communication-based representations that are already beginning to shape the self of the future. Our conclusion is that this future self has arrived, and it is pluralistic.

References

Barton, S. (1994) 'Chaos, self-organization, and psychology', *American Psychologist*, 49: 5–14.
Baudrillard, J. (1995) 'The virtual illusion: Or the automatic writing of the world', *Theory, Culture and Society*, 12: 97–107.
Baumgardner, S.R. and Rappoport, L. (1996) 'Culture and self in postmodern perspective', *The Humanistic Psychologist*, 24: 116–40.

Beahrs, J. (1982) *Unity and Multiplicity*. New York: Bruner/Mazel.
Berger, P.L., Berger, B. and Kellner, H. (1974/1973) *The Homeless Mind*. New York: Vintage Books.
Berne, E. (1964) *Games People Play*. New York: Grove Press.
Biddle, B.J. (1986) 'Recent developments in role theory', in R.H. Turner and S.F. Short (eds), *Annual Review of Sociology*, vol. 12, pp. 67–92.
Boone, G.D. (1995) 'Personality multiplicity: Developmental antecedents and behavioral implications'. PhD dissertation, Kansas State University.
Boyne, R. and Rattansi, A. (1990) 'The theory and politics of postmodernism: By way of an introduction', in R. Boyne and A. Rattansi (eds), *Postmodernism and Society*. New York: St Martin's Press. pp. 1–45.
Bruner, J.S. (1990) 'Culture and human development: A new look', *Human Development*, 33: 344–55.
Clancy, S.M. and Dollinger, S.J. (1993) 'Identity, self, and personality: 1. identity status and the five-factor model of personality', *Journal of Research on Adolescence*, 3: 227–46.
DeBerry, S.T. (1993) *Quantum Psychology: Steps to a Postmodern Ecology of Being*. Westport, CT: Praeger.
Erikson, E.H. (1950) *Childhood and Society*. New York: Norton.
Erikson, E.H. (1968) *Identity, Youth and Crisis*. New York: Norton.
Erikson, E.H. (1974) *Dimensions of a New Identity*. New York: Norton.
Fiske, S.T. and Taylor, S.E. (1991) *Social Cognition*. New York: McGraw Hill.
Gaines, S.O. and Reed, E.S. (1995) 'Prejudice: from Allport to Dubois', *American Psychologist*, 50: 96–103.
Geertz, C. (1973) *The Interpretation of Cultures*. New York: Basic Books.
Gergen, K.J. (1972) 'Multiple identity: The healthy, happy human being wears many masks', *Psychology Today*, 5: 31–5, 64–6.
Gergen, K.J. (1988) 'Narrative and self as relationship', in L. Berkowitz (ed.), *Advances in Experimental Social Psychology*, vol. 21. New York: Academic Press. pp. 17–56.
Gergen, K.J. (1991) *The Saturated Self*. New York: Basic Books.
Gergen, K.J. (1992) 'The decline and fall of personality', *Psychology Today*, Nov.–Dec.: 59–63.
Gergen, K.J. (1996) 'Theory under threat: Social construction and identity politics', in C.W. Tolman, F. Cherry, R. van Hezewijk and I. Lubek (eds), *Problems of Theoretical Psychology*. North York, Ontario: Captus Press. pp. 13–23.
Gottschalk, S. (1993) 'Uncomfortably numb: counterculture impulses in the postmodern era', *Symbolic Interaction*, 16: 351–78.
Hermans, J.M., Kempen, J.G. and Van Loon, R.J.P. (1992) 'The dialogical self: Beyond individualism and rationalism', *American Psychologist*, 47: 23–45.
Hill, D.B. (1996) 'The postmodern reconstruction of self', in C.W. Tolman, F. Cherry, R. van Hezewijk and I. Lubek (eds), *Problems of Theoretical Psychology*. North York, Ontario: Captus Press. pp. 265–73.
Jones, R.M. (1992) 'Ego identity and adolescent problem behavior', in G.R. Adams, T.P. Gullota and R. Montemayor (eds), *Adolescent Identity Formation*. Newbury Park, CA: Sage. pp. 216–33.
Kvale, S. (1992) 'Postmodern psychology: A contradiction in terms?', in S. Kvale (ed.), *Psychology and Postmodernism*. Newbury Park, CA: Sage. pp. 31–57.
Lather, P. (1990) 'Postmodernism and the human sciences', *Humanistic Psychologist*, 18: 64–84.
Lifton, R.J. (1986) *The Nazi Doctors: Medical Killing and the Psychology of Genocide*. New York: Basic Books.
Linville, P.W. (1985) 'Self-complexity and affect extremity: Don't put all your eggs in one cognitive basket', *Social Cognition*, 3: 94–120.

Linville, P.W. (1987) 'Self-complexity as a cognitive buffer against stress-related illnesses and depression', *Journal of Personality and Social Psychology*, 52: 663–76.

Markus. H. and Nurius, P. (1986) 'Possible selves', *American Psychologist*, 41: 954–69.

Mead, G.H. (1934) *Mind, Self and Society from the Standpoint of a Social Behaviorist*. Chicago, IL: University of Chicago Press.

Prigogine, I. and Stengers, I. (1984) *Order Out of Chaos*. New York: Bantam.

Prince, M. (1905) *The Dissociation of a Personality*. New York: Longmans Green & Co.

Rappoport, L. and Kren, G. (1996) 'The Holocaust and the postmodern trend in human science', in C.W. Tolman, F. Cherry, R. van Hezewijk and I. Lubek (eds), *Problems of Theoretical Psychology*. North York, Ontario: Captus Press. pp. 274–9.

Ross, C.A. (1991) 'Epidemiology of multiple personality disorder and dissociation', *Psychiatric Clinics of North America*, 14: 503–17.

Rowan, J. (1990) *Subpersonalities: The People Inside Us*. New York: Routledge.

Sampson, E. (1989) 'The challenge of social change for psychology: Globalization and psychology's theory of the person', *American Psychologist*, 44: 914–21.

Schwartz, R. (1987) 'Our multiple selves', *Networker*, March–April: 25–31; 80–3.

Sedikides, C. and Skowronski, J.J. (1997) 'The symbolic self in evolutionary context', *Personality and Social Psychology Review*, 1: 80–102.

Smith, M.B. (1994) 'Selfhood at risk: Postmodern perils and the perils of postmodernism', *American Psychologist*, 49: 405–11.

Wolfe, F. (1984) *Star Wave: Mind, Consciousness and Quantum Physics*. New York: Macmillan.

Zohar, D. (1990) *The Quantum Self*. New York: Quill/William Morrow.

PART II

RESEARCH

---

6   THE POLYPHONY OF THE MIND: A MULTI-VOICED AND DIALOGICAL SELF

Hubert J.M. Hermans

Anyone who has ever attended a concert is familiar with the musicians tuning their instruments before they start to play. Each of them makes their own specific sound, yet not tuning in to the sounds of the other musicians, and together producing that stimulating cacophony that evokes the expectation of pleasures to come. However, as soon as they start to play, the cacophony is transformed into a well-organized composition of consonants and dissonants, that can only be produced by musicians who respond to each other in precise and structured ways.

The instruments in an orchestra, like the voices in a choir, are organized in two dimensions: one temporal, the other spatial. From the temporal perspective, any instrument or voice produces a particular sequence of sounds, typically taking the form of a melody. From the spatial perspective, different instruments or voices accompany and oppose one another in such a way that they are able to produce chords in which harmonies and tensions between the voices come to expression. In a musical composition, the combination of temporal and spatial forms organize the sounds on higher levels of complexity. A symphony, oratorio, canon or fugue are all musical forms in which melodies develop on a temporally-structured, horizontal dimension, whereas chords are organized along a spatially-structured, vertical dimension (Gregg, 1991).

In this chapter I will elaborate on the multi-voiced, dialogical nature of the self in which both temporal and spatial dimensions are included. The main inspirational source is Bakhtin's (1929/1973) metaphor of the polyphonic novel, providing a fertile starting point for the exploration of the multi-voicedness and dialogicality of the human mind.

Bakhtin's polyphonic novel

In his book *Problems of Dostoevsky's Poetics*, originally published in Russian, Bakhtin (1929/1973) developed the thesis that Dostoevsky – one of the most brilliant innovators in the history of literature – created a new form of artistic thought: the polyphonic novel. Its principal feature is that it is composed of a number of independent and mutually-opposing viewpoints embodied by characters involved in dialogical relationships. In playing their part in the novel, each character is 'ideologically authoritative and independent', that is, each character is perceived as the author of his or her own view of the world, not as an object of Dostoevsky's all-encompassing, artistic vision. Instead of being 'obedient slaves' in the service of Dostoevsky's intentions, the characters are capable of standing beside their creator, disagreeing with the author, even rebelling against him. It is as if Dostoevsky enters his novels wearing different masks, enabling him to present different and even opposing views of self and world, representing a multiplicity of voices of the 'same' Dostoevsky.

Bakhtin's metaphor of the polyphonic novel symbolizes, as Spencer (1971) calls it, the retreat of the omniscient author in the literary tradition. Becoming part of the text and giving up his or her privileged and centralized position, the author may take the role of one or more characters, often with contrasting world-views. These characters may, at times, enter into dialogical relations of question and answer, agreement and disagreement, so that new constructions may emerge. As in a polyphonic composition, the several voices or instruments have different spatial positions, and accompany and oppose each other in a dialogical relationship.

Logical versus dialogical relationships

For a proper understanding of Bakhtin's conception of dialogue it is necessary to establish the difference between logical and dialogical relationships. Bakhtin gives the following examples (see also Vasil'eva, 1988). Consider two phrases that are completely identical, 'life is good' and, again, 'life is good'. From the perspective of Aristotelian logic, these two phrases are related in terms of *identity*; they are one and the same statement. From a dialogical perspective, however, they may be seen as two remarks expressed by the voices of two spatially-separated people in communication, who in this case entertain a relationship of *agreement*. Here we have two phrases that are identical from a logical point of view, but different as utterances: the first is a statement, the second a confirmation. Similarly, the phrases 'life is good' and 'life is not good' can be compared. In terms of logic, one is a *negation* of the other. However, as utterances from two different speakers, a dialogical relation of *disagreement* exists. For Bakhtin, the relationship of agreement and disagreement are, like question and answer, basically dialogical. Bakhtin does not go so far that he rejects the rules of logic: 'Dialogical relationships are totally impossible without logical and concrete semantic relationships, but they are not reducible to them; they have their own specificity' (Bakhtin, 1929/1973: 152).

Logical relationships are 'closed', in that they do not permit any conclusion beyond the limits of the rules that govern the relationship. For example, once the identity or negation thesis has been applied to a set of statements, there is nothing left to be said, nor is an opening created to the domain of the unexpected. In Bakhtin's view, however, dialogue is conceived as an extremely *open* process: 'Consciousness is never self-sufficient; it always finds itself in an intense relationship with another consciousness. The hero's every experience and his every thought is internally dialogical, polemically colored and filled with opposing forces . . . open to inspiration from outside itself' (1929/1973: 26).

Dialogical relationships are not only open and 'unfinalized', but also highly *personal*. Dostoevsky's world is 'profoundly personalized' (Bakhtin, 1929/1973: 7) in that an utterance is never isolated from the consciousness of a particular character. Moreover, in Dostoevsky's novels, characters are always involved in communication with other characters. Because one particular character is always implicitly or explicitly responding to another character, the context of a particular utterance is always highly personalized.

Spatialization of characters in The Double

The notion of dialogue makes it possible to differentiate the inner world of one and the same individual in the form of an interpersonal relationship. When an 'inner' thought of a particular character is transformed into an utterance, dialogical relations spontaneously occur between this utterance and the utterance of imaginal others. In Dostoevsky's novel *The Double*, for example, the second hero (the double) was introduced as a personification of the interior thought of the first hero (Golyadkin). By the externalization of the interior voice of the first hero in a spatially-separated opponent, a fully-fledged dialogue between two independent parties develops. In Bakhtin's terms: 'This persistent urge to see all things as being coexistent and to perceive and depict all things side by side and simultaneously, as if in space rather than time, leads him [Dostoevsky] to dramatize in space even the inner contradictions and stages of development of a single person' (1929/1973: 23). Along this narrative spatialization, Dostoevsky constructs a plurality of voices representing a plurality of worlds that are neither identical nor unified, but rather heterogeneous and opposed. As part of this narrative construction, Dostoevsky creates ever-changing perspectives, portraying characters conversing with the Devil (Ivan and the Devil), with their alter egos (Ivan and Smerdyakov), and even with caricatures of themselves (Raskolnikov and Svidrigailov).

The multi-voiced, dialogical self

Drawing on Bakhtin's polyphonic metaphor and its implication of spatialized dialogue, Hermans et al. (1992) and Hermans (1996) proposed defining the self in terms of a dynamic multiplicity of relatively autonomous *I* positions. In this conception, the *I* has the ability to move, as in a space, from one position to the other in accordance with changes in situation and time. For example, in actual or imaginal conversations I can move back and forth between my own position and the position of my actual or imaginal interlocutor. In the case of imaginal conversations, the *I* has, moreover, the capacity imaginatively to endow each position with a voice so that dialogical relations between positions can be established (for example, I converse with my image in the mirror, with the photograph of somebody I miss, with my conscience, with a character from a book, or with myself who is writing this chapter at this moment). The voices function like interacting characters in a story, involved in a process of question and answer, agreement and disagreement. Each of them has a story to tell about their own experiences from their own standpoint. As different voices, these characters are able to exchange information about their respective *Mes*, resulting in a complex, narratively-structured self. (For a more detailed discussion of the relationships between *I* positions see Hermans, 1996 and Hermans and Kempen, 1993; for another view on the spatial characteristics of the self, see Jaynes, 1976.)

In line with Bakhtin's polyphonic novel, the dialogical self combines temporal *and* spatial characteristics. This combination marks a difference with Labov and Waletzky (1967), Sarbin (1986), Bruner (1986), Gergen and Gergen (1988), and McAdams (1993) – advocates of a narrative approach – who have focused on the temporal dimension of narratives (for example, as a sequence of episodes, periods or stages). The dialogical self certainly acknowledges the temporal dimension as a constituent feature of narratives or stories. However, for the dialogical self, time and space are equally important as basic constituents. The spatial nature of the self is expressed in the terms 'position' and 'positioning', terms that are, moreover, more dynamic, flexible, and personalized than the traditional term 'role' (see Harré and Van Langenhove, 1991).

In the preceding sections I have described how a novelistic metaphor (the polyphonic novel) has led to the formulation of a psychological concept (the dialogical self). Now I will further develop this concept by presenting a more specific theory (valuation theory) and a method (the self-confrontation method) which allow a research strategy to be devised that can be used for the empirical study of the multi-voicedness and dialogicality of the self.

Valuation theory: multi-voiced meaning structures

Valuation theory (Hermans, 1987a, 1987b, 1988, 1989; Hermans and Hermans-Jansen, 1995) is inspired by such philosophical thinkers as James (1890), Merleau-Ponty (1945), and Bakhtin (1929/1973) and conceives of the self as an *organized process of valuation*. The 'process' aspect refers to the historical nature of human experience and implies a spatio-temporal orientation. The individual lives in a present situation and is, from a specific position in space and time, oriented to past and future and to the surrounding world. This position is voiced; that is, from this particular perspective (for example, a significant other, myself as an intellectual, or myself as a dreamer) I can tell a particular story about myself and the world. More specifically, from different positions I can remember different aspects from the past and see different possibilities in the future. The 'organizational' aspect points to the fact that the individual not only orients to the world from different positions, but also brings the meanings emerging from these positions together in a multi-voiced self-narrative. In this narrative the several voices and experiences are placed as parts in a composite whole, in which one voice or experience is accorded a more influential place than another.

The concept of 'valuation' refers to any unit of meaning that is seen as relevant from a particular position. It has a positive (pleasant), negative (unpleasant) or ambivalent connotation for the individual from the perspective of a particular position. Personal valuations, as subjective constructions of personal experiences, refer to a broad range of phenomena such as: a dear memory, a disappointment in the contact with somebody, a good talk with a friend, an exciting project, a physical handicap, an unreachable ideal, etc. From different positions different valuations may emerge and the same experiences may receive different weight or relevance because the individual's reference point may alternate or change from one position to another. Through the acts of dialogue and self-reflection, the valuations emerging from different positions are organized in a complex, composite self-narrative that develops through time with some parts more changeable and other parts more stable.

A central assumption in valuation theory is that voices do not exchange information in neutral ways but, rather, that they express and exchange affect-laden concerns. That is, people, as passionate storytellers, express particular concerns which they feel as personally relevant and may deeply involve them. The implication is that each valuation carries an affective connotation; that is, each valuation reflects a particular set of feelings (a particular profile of affect). When we know which types of affect are characteristic of a particular valuation, we know something about the valuation itself. This also implies that the affective meaning of a valuation cannot be separated from it.

Manifest versus latent level of organization

The variety of voices and their personal valuations, which may vary not only between individuals but also within a single individual across time and situations, are on the manifest level of the self. At the latent level, however, a limited number of basic motives exist that are reflected in the affective component of the valuations. Study of the affective component can, therefore, reveal which particular motive is active in a particular valuation.

Two basic motives, in particular, have been taken into consideration to characterize the affective component of the valuations: the striving for self-enhancement or S motive (self-maintenance and self-expansion), and the longing for contact and union with the other or O motive (participation with other people and the surrounding world). This distinction has been present in various forms in the writings of authors who have discussed the duality of human experience: Bakan (1966) viewed agency and communion as fundamental dynamic principles; Angyal (1965) proposed the concepts of autonomy (or self-determination) and homonomy (or self-surrender); Klages (1948) relied on *Bindung* (solidification) and *Lösung* (dissolution) as the two basic human motives; McAdams (1985) has distinguished power and intimacy as fundamental motives in a narrative context. Recently, the dimensions of individualism-collectivism and idiocentricism-allocentrism, again suggesting the basic character of the S and O motives, have been extensively discussed and investigated (Triandis et al., 1988; Schwartz, 1990; Lau, 1992).

In valuation theory, it is assumed that the basic motives are reflected in the affective component of a valuation. This can be explained using two different valuations:

> 'At home I often get my way by pushing just a little bit'
> 'I feel marvellous when I paint a good picture'

On the assumption that feelings of 'strength' and 'pride' are general indicators of the self-enhancement motive (S motive), the presence of these feelings in both of the valuations is evidence that they are expressions of the same, underlying motive. Put differently, the valuations pertain to quite different aspects of the self (they differ on the *manifest* level), although they are rooted in the same basic motive (they are similar on the *latent* level). In this theoretical construction, the affective component provides the bridge between motivation and valuation. The affect associated with a valuation can be considered as an expression of the basic motives from the *latent* level.

Let us look now to some valuations representing the longing for contact and union with the other (O motive):

> 'During stormy weather on the North Sea, I felt a real bond with
>   my brother: I felt lost in the elements, and yet was able to stand
>   upright without having to struggle to be strong'
> 'Singing in a group: the way that I express most of my feelings'

Both of the valuations from the same client – although clearly different manifestations of her self-narrative – imply strong feelings of intimacy and love. If we assume feelings of intimacy and love to be indicators of the O motive, then the two valuations can, again, be seen to differ on the manifest level but not on the latent level.

As will be seen later in my research examples, the distinction between the manifest and latent levels has an important advantage. It enables not only a study of the ways in which valuations change, depending on the changing of positions, but even an exploration of the extent to which a change of position implies a change on the deeper, latent level.

Closely related to S and O feelings, *well-being*, in the form of the difference between positive and negative feelings, plays a central role in valuation theory. The rationale is that, on their path towards fulfilment of basic motives, people meet obstacles. When it is difficult or impossible to overcome obstacles, *negative* feelings are aroused. On the other hand, overcoming obstacles and hindrances results in *positive* feelings. Each valuation is associated with a pattern of positive and negative feelings, so that the emphasis of one of the two types of affect gives information about the extent to which basic motives are fulfilled.

Generalization and idealization

Two concepts in particular, generalization and idealization, represent the dynamic nature of valuations as an organized process and play a central role in the methodology presented in the next section of this chapter. The more a particular valuation *generalizes* as part of the valuation system that belongs to a particular position, the more it determines the 'general feeling' that the person experiences from the perspective of a particular position as a whole (for example, 'How do I generally feel, as a student?'). When one asks a person how he or she feels in general, it is highly probable that particular experiences color this general feeling more than others. If the person has, for example, failed an important examination, there is a good chance that the feelings associated with this failure are more likely to determine the student's general feelings in this period than, for example, the good memories of his or her last vacation. In other words, not all valuations are equally influential: the more generalizing power a valuation has, the more influential the affective component of this valuation is in coloring the way the person generally feels from the perspective of a particular position.

Valuations may also differ in the extent of *idealization*. That is, certain valuations fit more with the way an individual would ideally like to feel from the perspective of a particular position. Valuations that color the ideal feeling are often different from those that influence the general feeling. Typically, this is found when people are actually going through a period in which they are faced with personal problems. Under such circumstances, the ideal feeling shows an affective modality that is in contrast to the affective modality of the general feeling.

In summary, in the presented theoretical framework the multi-voicedness of the self is expressed in the supposition that there is a multiplicity of positions or voices, each associated with their particular system of valuations. Each valuation, in turn, is associated with a particular set of feelings, in which basic motives are expressed. It is assumed that a repositioning of the self implies a shift from one voice to another with a concomitant change in the content and organization of valuation and affect.

The self-confrontation method: exploring a multiplicity of meanings

The self-confrontation method is an idiographic assessment procedure based on valuation theory. The method is designed to study the relation between valuations and types of affect and the way in which these variables become organized within and between positions (Hermans and Hermans-Jansen, 1995). The procedure involves elicitation of a set of valuations for each position and then association of these valuations with a standardized set of affect terms. The result is an individualized matrix in which each cell represents the extent to which a specific affect is characteristic of a specific valuation (for an example of a matrix of a subject see Table 6.1; note that one subject may fill in more matrices for more positions).

The valuations (that is, rows in the matrix) are elicited through a series of open-ended questions. The main questions, outlined in Table 6.2, are intended to bring out the important units of meaning for the past, the present, and the future. The questions invite individuals to reflect on their life situations in such a way that they feel free to mention those concerns that are most relevant from the perspective of a particular position. The subjects are free to interpret the questions in any way they want; they are also encouraged to phrase the valuations in their own terms, in order that the formulations are as much as possible in agreement with the intended meaning. The typical form of expression is the sentence (that is, the basic unit of text). In a sentence the subject brings together those events that the person feels belong together as elements of a personal unit of meaning. A quick response is not required, and there is no one-to-one relation between

TABLE 6.1   *Matrix of valuation × affect; raw ratings of a subject*

Valuation number	Affect terms															
	1	2	3	4	5	6	7	8	9	10	11	12	13	14	15	16
1	4	3	1	2	1	0	4	5	0	0	1	3	0	1	1	0
2	0	3	0	0	0	0	0	0	3	0	0	0	2	0	2	1
3	3	4	2	0	4	0	3	0	0	0	3	1	0	3	0	3
4	0	0	0	2	0	0	0	0	3	0	0	0	2	0	0	0
5	4	4	4	0	2	0	3	4	1	3	3	2	0	0	1	5
6	0	0	0	0	0	0	0	1	3	0	1	1	1	2	3	0
7	5	3	4	0	2	5	0	0	0	2	4	1	0	0	0	5
8	4	4	4	1	4	4	3	2	0	2	4	0	1	3	1	5
General feeling	2	1	3	4	0	2	3	1	3	0	1	0	2	3	4	0
Ideal feeling	5	4	5	0	4	5	4	5	0	4	3	3	0	5	0	5

Note: Rows represent valuations and columns represent affect terms used for the indices S, O, P, and N, where S = affect referring to self-enhancement, O = affect referring to contact with the other, P = positive affect, and N = negative affect.

Affect terms: 1 = joy (P); 2 = self-esteem (S); 3 = happiness (P); 4 = worry (N); 5 = strength (S); 6 = enjoyment (P); 7 = caring (O); 8 = love (O); 9 = unhappiness (N); 10 = tenderness (O); 11 = self-confidence (S); 12 = intimacy (O); 13 = despondency (N); 14 = pride (S); 15 = disappointment (N); 16 = inner calm (P).

TABLE 6.2 *Questions used to elicit valuations in the self-confrontation method*

Set 1: The past

These questions are intended to guide you to some aspect of your past that is of great importance to you:

- Was there something in your past that has been of major importance or significance for your life and which still plays an important part today?
- Was there, in the past, a person, an experience or circumstances that greatly influenced your life and still appreciably affect your present existence?

You are free to go back into the past as far as you like.

Set 2: The present

This set is also composed of two questions that will lead you, after a certain amount of contemplation, to formulate a response:

- Is there in your present life something that is of major importance for, or exerts a great influence on, your existence?
- Is there in your present life a person or circumstances which exert a significant influence on you?

Set 3: The future

The following questions will again be found to guide you to a response:

- Do you foresee something that will be of great importance for, or of major influence on your future life?
- Do you feel that a certain person or circumstances will exert a great influence on your future life?
- Is there a goal or object that you expect to play an important role in your future life?

You are free to look as far ahead as you wish.

---

question and answer. The individual is encouraged to mention all valuations that come to mind and, typically, each question leads to more than one valuation.

In the second part of the investigation, a standard list of affect terms (columns in the matrix) is presented to the subject. Concentrating on the first valuation, the subject indicates on a 0–5 scale the extent to which he or she experiences each affect in relation to the valuation (0 = *not at all*, 1 = *a little bit*, 2 = *to some extent*, 3 = *rather much*, 4 = *much*, and 5 = *very much*). The subject, working alone now, rates each valuation with the same list of affect terms, and the different valuations can then be compared according to their affective profiles. The list of affect terms found at the bottom of Table 6.1 has proved to provide the maximum amount of affective information with the minimum number of terms (Hermans and Hermans-Jansen, 1995). Once the affective ratings for the different valuations have been obtained, a number of indices that represent the motivational structure of the valuation system are calculated.

1 Index S is the sum of the scores for four affect terms specifically expressing self-enhancement: numbers 2, 5, 11 and 14 of Table 6.1.

2   Index O is the sum of the scores for four affect terms specifically expressing contact and union with the other: numbers 7, 8, 10 and 12 of Table 6.1. For each valuation, moreover, the S–O difference can be determined. When the experience of self-enhancement is stronger than the experience of contact with the other, S > O. When the feeling of contact with the other prevails, O > S. When both kinds of experiences coexist, S = O.

3   Index P is the sum of the scores for four general–positive (pleasant) affect terms: numbers 1, 3, 6 and 16.

4   Index N is the sum of the scores for four general–negative (unpleasant) affect terms: numbers 4, 9, 13 and 15. For each valuation, the P–N difference can be studied. This indicates the degree of well-being the person experiences in relation to the specific valuation. Well-being is positive when P > N, negative when N > P, and ambivalent when P = N. (Note that the scores for each of the four indices S, O, P and N range from 0 to 20 for each valuation.)

5   The extent of *generalization* (G) of a valuation within a particular position is assessed by asking the following question at the end of the valuation construction phase: 'How do I generally feel these days?'. This question does not ask for a specific valuation but is devised to assess the 'general feeling'. The person answers directly with the list of affect terms that was used for the characterization of the valuations. The product–moment correlation between the pattern of affect that belongs to a specific valuation and the pattern of affect that belongs to the general feeling is a measure of the extent of the generalization of this valuation. The more positive the correlation, the more this valuation is supposed to generalize within a particular position. For example, when a person is, from his or her position as a student, worrying all the time about his or her studies, it is expected that a valuation referring to this problem (for example, 'Wherever I am, I am always worrying about failing in my studies') has a high degree of generalization within this position. That is, the correlation between the affective profile belonging to this valuation and the affective profile belonging to the general feeling is expected to be high.

6   The *idealization* (I) of a valuation is assessed by asking this question: 'How would I like to feel?'. The correlation between the affective profile belonging to a specific valuation and the affective profile belonging to the ideal feeling indicates the ideal quality of this valuation. The height of the correlation indicates the extent of the idealization of the valuation. The more positive the correlation, the higher the idealization. When a valuation has an affective profile that contrasts with the ideal feeling, this is expressed in a negative (minus) correlation. (General feeling and ideal feeling represent the last rows in the matrix, see Table 6.1; for reliability and validity data of S, O, P, and N indices see Hermans, 1987b: 166, 169–71).

A second self-investigation is often performed, usually after some months, in order to document any changes in the valuation system. In this case, however, the subjects do not start 'from scratch'. Instead, they are confronted with the statements they had constructed in the first session. The interviewer reads the original question and then presents the statements provided in the first session. The subjects are instructed to consider, for each statement separately, whether they would still come up with the same response to the question. When this is not the case, the interviewer explains that there are various options available: an old valuation may be reformulated (modification); replaced (substitution); discarded altogether (elimination); or a completely new statement added (supplementation). This procedure allows the subjects considerable freedom to point to both the constant and the changing constituents in their valuations. For a third investigation the same procedure as in the second investigation is followed.

Note that the multi-voiced nature of the self-narrative implies that for each position (voice) a specific valuation system may be constructed and a specific matrix filled in. In this way the differences between the positions can be assessed concerning the formulation of the valuations, their affective organization, and their changes and constancy over time. This allows us to study the multi-voiced self as an organized process.

Research examples

Two idiographic studies are presented: one that shows how a well-functioning person entertains a long-lasting relationship with an imaginal other; and a second one which discusses a client with a dysfunctional split between herself and another figure in herself which she calls 'a witch'. The purpose behind these examples is not only to illustrate the proposed methodology as a research tool for the multi-voiced, dialogical self, but also to demonstrate the difference between a functional and dysfunctional organization of a multi-voiced self.

Consulting an internal guide

In her book *Invisible Guests*, Watkins (1986) argues that a great deal of our experience is based on 'imaginal dialogue'. She refers, for example, to Petrarch who wrote letters to the eminencies of classical antiquity, to Machiavelli who had imaginal dinner conversations with historical personages, to Landor who wrote volumes of imaginal dialogues between sages of different countries, and to Pablo Casals who said to his listeners, 'Bach is my best friend'. Watkins vividly portrays how art, drama, poetry, music, as well as the spontaneous appearance of personifications, keep us in conversation with imaginal others. Indeed, imaginal others affect our interactions with 'actual' others just as surely as the other way around.

TABLE 6.3 Kathy's own valuations and the valuations of her imaginal figure and their scores on the affective indices at investigations 1 and 2

	Kathy's own valuations at investigation 1	S	O	P	N	G	Kathy's own valuations at investigation 2	S	O	P	N	G
1.	I always had to conform to the image my parents and the nuns had of me.	0	0	0	18	.06	[Same formulation as at Investigation 1]	0	0	0	18	-.83
2.	When I was alone, I constructed a fantasy world where I made myself a very strong person.	16	12	16	2	.11	[Same formulation as at Investigation 1]	16	13	16	2	.80
3.	I've always searched for my own opinion, my own values.	16	0	2	7	.60	[Same formulation as at Investigation 1]	16	0	4	7	.11
4.	When I was 17, I ran away from home; I left a poem of which the last two lines were 'I have to leave, I love you too much.'	7	5	0	18	.30	[Same formulation as at Investigation 1]	7	5	0	19	-.71
5.	I have a strong will to survive; they can't easily break me.	13	0	4	3	.41	[Same formulation as at Investigation 1]	13	0	10	1	.55
6.	I really want to finish my studies.	7	0	4	2	.66	I really want to finish my studies; I want to be good in the field I've chosen.	10	0	8	4	.41
7.	I have a guide who helps me to find my way.	12	10	14	10	.04	I have a guide who helps me to find my way; I've recognized and become more accepting of him; we have become better friends.	12	13	16	6	.77
	General feeling	11	6	9	10	–	General feeling	11	10	14	2	–
	Ideal feeling	17	15	20	0	-.08	Ideal feeling	20	18	20	0	.84

	Valuations from Kathy's imaginal figure at investigation 1	S	O	P	N	G	Valuations from Kathy's imaginal figure at investigation 2	S	O	P	N	G
8.	I am the other one in Kathy. Sometimes she needs a good kick.	3	8	2	0	.06	I am the other one in Kathy. Sometimes she needs a good kick, or she needs a hand to hold and take her along.	8	11	9	6	.56
9.	As a child Kathy was quiet and reserved; I played with her in her own world.	3	8	16	0	.04	[Same formulation as at Investigation 1]	7	8	15	0	.45
10.	Sometimes I had to protect Kathy from her fantasies.	6	12	0	5	.37	[Same formulation as at Investigation 1]	8	4	0	4	.00
11.	I stimulated Kathy to opposition during her adolescence: 'Let's *not* do that for a change; you don't have to do everything they say.'	15	1	7	5	.36	[Same formulation as at Investigation 1]	16	1	7	3	.26
12.	Between her 18th and 22nd year Kathy pushed me away; she didn't want to be bothered by me.	4	6	0	14	-.08	[Same formulation as at Investigation 1]	0	2	0	14	-.25
13.	Kathy looks to her work through my eyes.	7	5	7	1	.42	[Same formulation as at Investigation 1]	11	8	10	2	.24
14.	I must be careful not to dominate Kathy; I must also listen to her.	9	6	0	11	.42	We are together; we have both accepted that.	13	15	14	4	.41
	General feeling	15	11	10	9	–	General feeling	9	11	12	9	–
	Ideal feeling	18	14	19	0	.32	Ideal feeling	20	19	20	0	.22

Note: S, affect referring to self-enhancement; O, affect referring to contact with the other; P, positive affect; N, negative affect; G, generalization index. From Hermans, Rijks and Kempen (1993). Copyright 1993 by Duke University Press. Reprinted with permission.

An imaginal figure can be seen as 'another persona' with a specific valuation system that is different from, and at the same time meaningfully related to, the 'usual' valuation system of the person him- or herself. Such a construction is certainly possible because it depicts the person as being involved with the imaginal figure in a process of question and answer, and agreement or disagreement. In other words, the imaginal figure behaves like an antagonist belonging to a highly dynamic, multi-voiced self (Hermans, 1996). Guided by this idea, two valuation systems were collected from the life of one and the same person, whom we shall call Kathy: one from her usual position, and one from the position of an imaginal figure with whom she had contact from an early age.

Kathy, a divorced woman of thirty-one years of age and brought up in a lower-class family, worked as a graphic designer. She had no psychiatric history. She participated in a self-investigation project on the multivoicedness of the self because she was interested in exploring the role of an imaginal figure that played an important role in her life. She described this figure as 'a guide who helps me to find my way in life', and explained that she has been in touch with this figure since her early nursery school years.

According to the described procedure, Kathy performed two self-investigations: one from the perspective of her familiar position (as Kathy), and one from the perspective of her imaginal position (her guide). In the latter case, she performed the self-investigation as if she were the imaginal figure, using the same questions and affect terms which she had earlier used from her familiar position as Kathy. The two valuation systems, as they have developed over six months after the initial investigation, will also be presented in order to assess the extent to which they have changed. Kathy formulated 27 valuations from the usual *I* position and 27 valuations from the imaginal position. In Table 6.3 a representative sample of the two groups of valuations at investigation 1 and their development at investigation 2 is presented.

The main characteristics of Kathy's valuation systems can be summarized as follows.

- When focusing on investigation 1, it can be seen that both the content and the affective organization of the valuations are markedly different between the two positions. Whereas the valuations from Kathy's own position refer mainly to her relation with the world (for example, parents, studies), all the valuations from her imaginal other are focused on the relation with Kathy. This suggests that the imaginal figure has a clear function for Kathy, as her protector (no. 10) and as a figure who compensates for her lack of contact (no. 9). Moreover, we can see that not only Kathy's own valuations, but also those from her imaginal other, show a clear temporal organization. The content of the valuations suggests that the imaginal figure had quite different meanings for Kathy in different time periods (compare, for example, nos. 11 and 12). In a nutshell, we see in this example the two basic ingredients of both the polyphonic novel and the dialogical self: the temporal dimension (a developing melody) and the spatial multiplicity of positions (the simultaneous sounding of a chord), where valuation no. 9 sounds as a consonant, valuation no. 8 as a dissonant, both having their function in the composition of a multifaceted self-narrative.

- The two positions tend to differ not only from the perspective of the manifest level, but also from the latent level. Kathy's own valuations tend to be associated with more self-enhancement affect than affect referring to contact and union and, moreover, these valuations have a strong generalizing potential in the system (for example, valuations nos. 3 and 6). The valuations from her imaginal figure, in contrast, include several valuations with more affect referring to contact and union than self-enhancement affect (for example, valuations nos. 8–10). This suggests that the guide has a helping attitude towards Kathy, whereas Kathy is more involved in her struggle with the world.

- There is a considerable constancy in the valuations: 5 of the 7 valuations from Kathy receive the same formulation at investigation 2 as at investigation 1, and also the scores on the affective indices S, O, P, and N are remarkably stable. Furthermore, for Kathy's imaginal figure, 5 of the 7 valuations receive the same formulation in both investigations.

- Nevertheless, there are some significant changes from investigation 1 to investigation 2. Of particular interest is the improved cooperation that is experienced, both from the side of Kathy (no. 7) and from the side of her imaginal figure (no. 14). This improved cooperation is also expressed in the increase of positive affect and the decrease of negative affect (nos. 7 and 14) from investigation 1 to investigation 2. These findings suggest that the imaginal figure plays a constructive and stimulating role in Kathy's life. (The changes are spontaneous, that is, there were no psychotherapeutic interventions of any kind.)

Fragmentation of the self: the case of the witch

When the question is raised about the difference between functional multi-voicedness and dysfunctional fragmentation of the self, the notion of 'multiple personality' becomes particularly relevant. As Watkins (1986) has argued, in (abnormal) multiple personality there is sequential monologue, whereas in the case of functional multi-voicedness there is rather simultaneous dialogue. Paradoxically, in the case of *multiple personality disorder* (MPD), there is only one and not several personalities active at a particular moment. The personality that is dominant at a specific point is found to take full control of the individual's behavior (cf. American Psychiatric Association, 1987, *Diagnostic and Statistical Manual of Mental Disorders-III-R*: 272). More recently, the concept of *Dissociative Identity Disorder* (DID) is proposed which is also characterized by a serious impediment in dialogical relationships between the 'host personality' and the diversity of 'alters'. In the clinical literature, it is concluded that the alters typically represent 'rejected parts of the original self' (Carson et al., 1996: 267). In MPD and DID a sequential, monolithic succession of personalities is found rather than a cooperative and productive relationship between different subpersonalities.

Dysfunctions such as MPD and DID delineate an inability to establish dialogical relationships between the subparts of the self. In healthy functioning there is a simultaneity of positions among which the *I* is moving back and forth, so that question and answer, agreement and disagreement between the several positions becomes possible. In the dysfunctional case, there are also several positions (for example, 'Eve White' and 'Eve Black' in the famous case of Thigpen and Cleckly, 1954). However, the dialogical relationship between these positions is seriously impoverished. The client with a multiple personality is often able to tell something about the person in the other position, but does so in a rather objectifying way. The frivolous Eve Black, for example, said about the decent Eve White: 'When *I* go out and get drunk, *she* wakes up with the hangover' (Thigpen and Cleckly, 1954: 141). In the clinical dysfunction the person is doing in the one position things that are entirely beyond control of the person in the other position.

In the light of the preceding considerations, I present the case of a client who was, during the period of investigation, very close to suffering from a multiple personality dysfunction. I discuss this case in some detail because I want to demonstrate that the notion of the dialogical self provides not only a conceptual framework for the assessment of a dysfunction, but also a strategy for moving the self into the direction of more integration.

Mary is a 33-year-old woman, who has bad memories about her father who was an alcoholic. When she smelled alcohol, she was overwhelmed by disgust and panic. She remembered her adolescent years with the same panic and disgust because she joined a drug scene, in which she was sexually abused. It was still difficult for her to tell how she was forced to have sex, sometimes even under armed threat. As a reaction, she 'protected' herself by always wearing a tampon and by bathing overfrequently in order 'to clean herself'. Her problems became acute when she married a man whom she loved very much. In strong contrast to her intimate feelings for him, there were moments that she was troubled by strong feelings of disgust for him. Quite suddenly, she could feel a fierce aggression toward him that was entirely beyond her control. When she saw her husband sleeping, she felt an almost uncontrollable urge to murder him. When he was sick, she felt hate and a complete lack of any compassion (as when she saw her father sleeping off his debauch, as she later realized). At some moments she felt like a witch – an alien experience that frightened her, particularly because the witch took almost total possession of her. It was this frightening experience that was the reason for her contacting a psychotherapist.

After intensive discussion of her case, we (Els Hermans-Jansen as her therapist and me as a personality psychologist) decided to propose that Mary perform a self-investigation from the perspective of two positions: one from her usual position as 'Mary', and the other from the position of 'the witch'. We expected that, given the split between the two positions, her fragmented self would improve if: (a) the two positions were to be clearly distinguished with regard to their specific wishes, aims, and feelings; and (b) a process of dialogical interchange could be established between the two positions, so that the witch could have the opportunity to tell what she wanted and Mary could take account of her wishes.

The therapist and I decided to first distinguish the two valuation systems (from Mary and the witch) as sharply as possible, and then to relate them in dialogical ways. Therefore, we selected from each valuation system a number of valuations: 4 from Mary and 4 from the witch (these valuations are presented on the left side of Table 6.4). Next, Mary was invited to rate the affective meaning of her own valuations (nos. 1–4, Table 6.4), followed by the witch who was also invited to give her affective experience of Mary's valuations (compare the affective indices on the left side of Table 6.4). For example, Mary liked valuation no. 1 (P = 17, N = 2), whereas the witch disliked the same valuation (P = 0, N = 8). Apparently, Mary and the witch strongly disagreed about the affective meaning of this valuation. Mary's and the witch's contrasting feelings are further expressed by the correlation (r) between the two affective ratings. The more positive the correlation between the ratings from Mary and the witch, the stronger their agreement. The more negative the correlation, the stronger their disagreement (see the correlation of $-.45$ for valuation no. 1 indicating a rather strong disagreement between Mary and the witch). As the correlations for the other valuations show, there are more cases of disagreement between the two positions. These contrasting affective responses are not only found with Mary's valuations (upper-left part of Table 6.4) but also with the valuations from the witch (lower-left part of Table 6.4). A notable exception is found with valuation no. 4, which calls forth a clear agreement between the two positions ($r = .74$). Apparently, in the work situation in which a certain hardness is welcome Mary could cooperate quite well with the witch. The same hardness, however, was extremely dangerous in the intimate relationship with her husband. This is well illustrated by valuation no. 6, which indicates that the witch enjoyed 'breaking' Mary's husband, whereas for Mary this was a very negative experience.

Note that also from the perspective of the latent, motivational level there are strong differences between Mary's and the witch's valuations. Mary shows a great deal of variation in her valuations: for some of them S affect is higher than O affect (for example, valuation no. 4), in other valuations S and O affect coexist (for example, valuations nos. 1 and 3). The valuations from the witch, on the contrary, show consistently higher patterns for S than O. This suggests that the witch was largely focused on self-enhancement and did not bother very much about Mary's well-being (compare this with Kathy's imaginal other who was strongly devoted to Kathy's well-being).

The psychotherapist discussed two ideas with Mary that were based on an analysis of her twofold self-investigation. First, the psychotherapist advised her to become more active (for example, to take up sport, cycling or walking), in order to expand her imaginal space and to give expression to the

TABLE 6.4 Valuations from Mary and Mary's witch and their mutual affective responses at investigations 1 and 2

Valuations from Mary at investigation 1

Valuation		S	O	P	N	r
1. More and more I am permitting myself to receive.	Mary	12	12	17	2	−.45
	witch	4	0	0	8	
2. I want to try to see what my mother gives me: there's only one of me.	Mary	12	9	12	6	−.14
	witch	10	2	3	12	
3. For the first time in my life I am engaged in making a home ('home' is also coming home, entering into myself).	Mary	16	13	17	4	.41
	witch	12	2	11	8	
4. In my work I can be myself. I am planning from which angles I can enter. The trust that I receive gives me a foothold, more self-confidence.	Mary	14	7	18	2	.74
	witch	16	0	13	0	
General feeling	Mary	15	13	14	6	−.33
	witch	8	0	0	15	
Ideal feeling	Mary	20	17	19	2	.94
	witch	19	18	20	5	

Valuations from Mary at investigation 2

Valuation		S	O	P	N	r
1. I dare to take care of myself more and more: receiving and asking.	Mary	15	10	16	1	.96
	witch	13	9	14	0	
2. I have something solid under my feet and I take more responsibility for my feelings and attitudes. When my mother doesn't see me, that is an injury, but she is not the only determining factor.	Mary	12	10	14	2	.83
	witch	13	6	13	2	
3. It more often feels safe inside myself.	Mary	17	14	19	0	.95
	witch	14	11	15	2	
4. As soon as I can be loyal to myself in my work, I will start again.	Mary	14	4	12	2	.69
	witch	14	4	10	5	
General feeling	Mary	14	11	13	3	.87
	witch	12	7	10	3	
Ideal feeling	Mary	17	16	16	1	.95
	witch	16	13	16	2	

Valuations from Mary's witch at investigation 1		S	O	P	N	r
5. With my bland, pussycat qualities I have vulnerable things in hand, from which I derive power at a later moment (somebody tells me things that I can use so that I get what I want).	witch	14	0	13	0	-.09
	Mary	6	1	3	10	
6. I enjoy when I have broken him [husband]: from a power position entering the battlefield.	witch	18	0	19	0	-.55
	Mary	0	0	0	16	
7. When Fred becomes vulnerable, it makes me even more hard.	witch	16	0	8	4	-.08
	Mary	5	1	0	20	
8. I am there, and I am gone again.	witch	10	2	6	9	.43
	Mary	5	2	7	13	
General feeling	witch	8	0	0	15	-.33
	Mary	15	13	14	6	
Ideal feeling	witch	19	18	20	5	.94
	Mary	20	17	19	2	

Valuations from Mary's witch at investigation 2		S	O	P	N	r
5. I [M+w] want to be clear, don't want to manage along the game of the sweet pussycat; sometimes, however, my [w] reactions are too fierce.	witch	12	9	12	3	.97
	Mary	12	8	12	3	
6. When I [M] feel that I [M] get in touch with my [w] power, I [M] use all my [M] energy to fight against this. I [M] don't want that power; it is too painful.	witch	13	8	12	6	.64
	Mary	10	6	9	7	
7. When Fred becomes vulnerable, and I [M] feel this harshness, then I [M] enter into a fight with myself [w] and I [M] want to be there for him.	witch	16	14	16	4	.81
	Mary	14	12	13	5	
8. When this hard side comes and I [M] recognize it, I [M] get in touch. I [M] can look at it and examine from which it is a signal. I [M] then make a good use of it.	witch	13	11	13	4	.93
	Mary	15	10	13	1	
General feeling	witch	12	7	10	3	.87
	Mary	14	11	13	3	
Ideal feeling	witch	16	13	16	2	.95
	Mary	17	16	16	1	

Note: S, affect referring to self-enhancement; O, affect referring to contact with the other; P, positive affect; N, negative affect; r, product moment correlations between the affective profile from Mary and the affective profile from the witch; M, Mary; w, witch. From Hermans and Hermans-Jansen (1995). Copyright 1995 by Guilford Press. Reprinted with permission.

witch's dammed-up energy. Second, the psychotherapist proposed she keep a written diary of her daily experiences, in order to sharpen her perception. In particular, Mary trained herself to make fine discriminations between the impulses, reactions and emotions of the witch and those of herself. The psychotherapist considered it important for her to see, at an early stage, during which situations the witch entered the scene and took control of the situation. Mary found out, to her surprise, that the witch appeared in situations that looked at first sight quite innocent but that she soon tended to take control over the situation.

In a later stage, she started trying out new actions. Here, in her own words, is an example of the type of strategy she developed to cope with the witch:

> A few days ago Fred was sick, with 104 degrees temperature in bed; he even had blisters on his lips. I made breakfast for him and brought it upstairs. When I entered the room and saw him lying in bed, I loathed him, and I thought, 'Don't think that I'm staying at home for you!' (I was planning to leave for an overnight visit with friends in Amsterdam). Standing in front of the bed, I was thinking about this (with increasing venom) and became aware that the witch was coming up again. I left the tray with Fred and left the house for a walk. During this walk I felt that I could discharge a great deal of the energy of the witch. At the same time, I had the time to quietly reflect on the situation as it was: 'He is sick, he needs me, and I want to care for him.' I decided to buy a newspaper for him. When I came home, I explained to him that I would stay the night at home and would go to Amsterdam the next morning. (So, I did not leave the decision up to him but proposed it myself). Fred accepted this, and the next morning I went out to visit my friends. (Hermans and Hermans-Jansen, 1995: 191)

In this way, Mary not only made a clear perceptual distinction between her position and that of the witch but also developed a concrete strategy to deal with her opponent. This strategy implied that Mary did not split away from or suppress the witch, but rather tried to be as alert as possible to her appearance. When she came, Mary decided to take a break, walked first (moving was important for the witch), and then made a more balanced decision.

One year after the first investigation, Mary performed a second one in order to evaluate the changes. Between the two investigations there were a limited amount of sessions with the psychotherapist, in which Mary discussed her daily experiences. The modified valuations are presented on the right-hand side of Table 6.4. The main change is that there is more agreement among the affective responses from Mary and the witch (see the high to very high correlations among the affective profiles). This suggests that Mary has developed a more integrative valuation system with less tension between the two positions.

It is notable to see how Mary proceeded in the second investigation. According to the procedure she was instructed to first take the 'usual' position of Mary, and then the position of the witch. Indeed, she very seriously attempted to do this, but discovered that it was almost impossible for her to let the witch speak in the same way as one year before. When she was confronted with the valuations from the witch from investigation 1 (left side of Table 6.4), she was able to modify these valuations in accordance with present experiences (right side of Table 6.4). However, the person who was speaking was not simply the witch, but some combination ('Mary-witch') or even primarily Mary. The psychotherapist checked this change more systematically by inviting Mary to indicate for each of the valuations on the lower-right part of Table 6.4, if the words 'I' or 'my' were indications of Mary or the witch (see the indications between brackets). It was found that, in most cases, the words 'I' and 'my' were indications of Mary and not of the witch. One of the exceptions was valuation no. 5, in which the word 'I' was seen as a combination of Mary and the witch, and the word 'my' as a reference to the witch. This is an intriguing result from a psychotherapeutic point of view: the valuations that were originally formulated by the witch (with strong disagreement from the side of Mary), were developed in such a way that one can recognize at the time of investigation 2 the original (time 1) formulations from the witch, whereas the (modified) valuations at the time of investigation 2 are primarily from Mary! This suggests that Mary has taken the lead, even in situations that were originally under the control of the witch.

It would be a misunderstanding to think that, at the time of the second investigation, a perfect dialogical interchange exists between Mary and the witch. Apart from the fact that Mary's reactions were sometimes 'too fierce' (valuation no. 5), there were, at the time of investigation 2, signs of the continuing struggle between the two positions. This is most clearly expressed in valuation no. 7: 'then I [M] enter into a fight with myself [w]'. Although there are still signs of a struggle, there is at the same time a cooperative relationship. This can be observed in valuation no. 8, in which Mary does not simply suppress her hard side, but proceeds to get in touch with it and examines the nature of 'the signal'. See also her next remark: 'I then make good use of it.' In other words, she uses the witch's energy for her own purposes.

It is useful to consider Mary's case from a theoretical perspective. The dialogical self has two main defining features: intersubjective exchange and dominance (Hermans and Kempen, 1993). In Mary's case, both forces are at work. First, dialogical exchange is stimulated by inviting not only Mary, but also the witch to tell their story – each from their own position. In this way the *I* has the opportunity to move back and forth between positions, and to consider the differences, contrasts, contradictions, agreements and disagreements. Second, the two positions were involved in a struggle for dominance during the total period that this case was followed. Whereas the witch was, certainly at times, more dominant than Mary during the period of the first self-investigation, Mary took control over the witch during the period of the second investigation. It is in this field of tension, between exchange and dominance, that dialogical relationships between positions develop.

It follows from the notion of dialogue that an incompatible position is not simply 'cured' or treated as an undesirable symptom, but taken seriously as a partner with whom it is possible to meet 'on speaking terms'. The dialogical process, in its combination of interchange and dominance, is then a road to the integration of incompatible positions as part of a multi-voiced self. (For a more complete discussion of Mary's case, see Hermans and Hermans-Jansen, 1995: 187–95.)

The constructive meaning of contradiction

In this chapter I started with a discussion of Bakhtin's metaphor of the polyphonic novel and described how this metaphor led to the formulation of the dialogical self as a dynamic multiplicity of voices. Next, I elaborated on the dialogical self by presenting a more specific theory – valuation theory – which assumes that people are passionate storytellers who select and organize events in their lives in such a way that a multiplicity of personal meanings (valuations) emerge. The meanings expressed by the different voices show a great variation on the manifest level of self-organization, but they are, at the same time, organized under the influence of basic motives at the deeper latent level. The distinction between the two levels allows a distinction to be made between more superficial differences and changes, and more fundamental differences and changes in one's self-narratives.

Using a self-confrontation method, based on valuation theory, two idiographic studies were presented: one of an imaginal figure which played, as an imaginal guide, a constructive role in a person's life; and another in which a 'witch' manifested herself in more destructive ways. Both cases were followed over time, so that constancy and changes could be observed. Self-oppositions, self-negotiations, and self-contradictions functioned as central processes in the dynamic multiplicity of voices.

A specific feature of the notion of the dialogical self is that contradictions and discrepancies between voices are seen as having constructive and even innovative potential. This is in contrast to Higgins' (1987) theory, which is based on the assumption that discrepancies between several domains of the self (for example, the actual, ideal, and ought selves) are associated with emotional vulnerabilities (for example, dejection or agitation). This theory is implicitly based on the mechanistic supposition that discrepancies are (automatically) associated with negative feelings and that, in order to achieve well-being, it is necessary to reduce these discrepancies. In the dialogical self, on the other hand, self-discrepancies and self-contradictions between voices are seen as intrinsic to a healthy functioning of the self and as contributing to its innovation. Although multi-voicedness may be associated with anxiety or depression (see the example of the witch), the tension, contradiction, and opposition between voices express the self's inherent capacity to create new and integrative constructions (Hermans, 1996).

An example of a new, integrative construction is valuation no. 14 at the right side in Table 6.3: 'We are together, we have both accepted that.' This statement, that starts with the word 'we', can only be made when there has been a preceding process of negotiation between Kathy and her guide. Apparently there have been some tensions between the two positions (see valuation no. 14 at the left side in Table 6.3), but these tensions have resulted in a modified valuation with a novel element (mutual acceptation) in the second self-investigation.

For me, as a psychologist, one of the most fascinating observations I have made in everyday life is that people can express a firm opinion on some matter in one situation, and at some later moment they can express, in an equally firm way, the opposite opinion. Somebody may, for example in a conversation with a family member, come to the conclusion that she is quite satisfied with her career as it has developed up to the present, being entirely sure that she has reached some valuable goals in her life. However, the same person may be, at a moment of critical self-interrogation, for example, strongly dissatisfied with her career. The reason for this contradiction is that different voices, using different criteria, arrive at opposite opinions and associated affective connotations. The person may be not aware of this contradiction because she may have forgotten what she has said or thought at an earlier moment in time. My point, however, is that it is useful and enriching when the person has the opportunity to compare the divergent positions and reflect on their implications. In doing so, the person is involved in a process of self-extension which may lead to integrative and innovative constructions. In our career example, this may mean that the person does not only reflect on 'my career was successful' *or* 'my career was unsuccessful', but on the contradictory nature of the two statements itself. This juxtaposition of two contradictory statements creates an opening for a new construction which may bring novelty in the self (for example, 'I will give special attention to certain goals in my career, which I've neglected up to now'). This constructive and reconstructive process of self-negotiation is typical of the open-ended character of the polyphonic novel as proposed by Bakhtin.

Finally, in the presented idiographic studies I have focused on the relationship between *two* voices, whereas in my theoretical introduction I have taken the notion of *multi*-voicedness as a starting point. Would not this notion imply the necessity of more than two voices? Indeed, as Rowan (1990) has argued in his review of the psychological literature, the self can be portrayed in terms of a larger number of subpersonalities or subselves. The point I want to make is that dialogical relationships may exist between *any* of a multiplicity of voices that are available and open for dialogue at a certain moment in time and in a particular situation. However, this availability may be seriously constrained by social, personal or biological factors. One person's repertoire of voices may be limited by the existence of particular cultural norms, circumstances in personal history or biological factors that prevent particular voices from birth or, once born, do not keep them alive, so that they eventually expire. Moreover, certain voices may actively avoid contact with other voices because, like real persons, they do not feel at ease in each other's company. For example, two people involved in an intimate sexual contact may not feel very motivated to start an intellectual discussion. The intellectual voice may easily disturb the sexual voice and bring it 'out of the mood', so that sexual feelings simply disappear. In other words, there may be a variety of reasons why dialogical relationships do not emerge, but under certain circumstances they do. On the basis of these considerations one may reach the preliminary conclusion that, given a certain repertoire of voices, some of them are, under specific circumstances, available for dialogical contact.

In this contribution I have focused on the multi-voiced and dialogical nature of the self, and presented a theory and method for its assessment and research. There are, however, some challenging questions that have to be answered in future thinking and research: which voices enter in a dialogical relationship with which other voices, why do they do so and under what circumstances? These questions can be labeled as a 'neglected area' in the study of the dialogical self. In musical terms, we may hear which instruments are playing together but do not know much about the question: why did these particular instruments come together, and not others?

Note

I thank Sue Houston for her detailed editorial comments. Correspondence concerning this chapter should be addressed to Hubert J.M. Hermans, University of Nijmegen, Department of Clinical Psychology and Personality, P.O. Box 9104, 6500 HE Nijmegen, The Netherlands. E-mail: HHermans@psych.kun.nl
Homepage: http://www.socsci.kun.nl/~hermans/index.html

References

American Psychiatric Association (1987) *Diagnostic and Statistical Manual of Mental Disorders-III-R*. Washington, DC: American Psychiatric Association.
Angyal, A. (1965) *Neurosis and Treatment: A Holistic Theory*. New York: Wiley.
Bakan, D. (1966) *The Duality of Human Existence*. Chicago, IL: Rand-McNally.
Bakhtin, M. (1929/1973) *Problems of Dostoevsky's Poetics* (2nd edn). (Trans. R.W. Rotsel.) Ann Arbor, MI: Ardis. First edn 1929: *Problemy tvorchestva Dostoevskogo* [Problems of Dostoevsky's Art].
Bruner, J.S. (1986). *Actual Minds, Possible Worlds*. Cambridge, MA: Harvard University Press.
Carson, R.C., Butcher, J.N. and Mineka, S. (1996) *Abnormal Psychology and Modern Life*. (10th edn) New York: HarperCollins.
Gergen, K.J. and Gergen, M.M. (1988) 'Narrative and the self as relationship', *Advances in Experimental Social Psychology*, 21: 17–56.
Gregg, G.S. (1991) *Self-Representation: Life Narrative Studies in Identity and Ideology*. New York: Greenwood Press.
Harré, R. and Van Langenhove, L. (1991) 'Varieties of positioning', *Journal for the Theory of Social Behaviour*, 21: 393–407.

Hermans, H.J.M. (1987a) 'Self as organized system of valuations: Toward a dialogue with the person', *Journal of Counseling Psychology*, 34: 10–19.

Hermans, H.J.M. (1987b) 'The dream in the process of valuation: A method of interpretation', *Journal of Personality and Social Psychology*, 53: 163–75.

Hermans, H.J.M. (1988) 'On the integration of idiographic and nomothetic research methods in the study of personal meaning', *Journal of Personality*, 56, 785–812.

Hermans, H.J.M. (1989) 'The meaning of life as an organized process', *Psychotherapy*, 26: 11–22.

Hermans, H.J.M. (1996) 'Voicing the self: From information processing to dialogical interchange', *Psychological Bulletin*, 119: 31–50.

Hermans, H.J.M. and Hermans-Jansen, E. (1995) *Self-Narratives: The Construction of Meaning in Psychotherapy*. New York: Guilford Press.

Hermans, H.J.M. and Kempen, H.J.G. (1993) *The Dialogical Self: Meaning as Movement*. San Diego, CA: Academic Press.

Hermans, H.J.M., Kempen, H.J.G. and Van Loon, R.J.P. (1992) 'The dialogical self: Beyond individualism and rationalism', *American Psychologist*, 47: 23–33.

Higgins, E.T. (1987) 'Self-discrepancy: A theory relating self and affect', *Psychological Review*, 94: 319–40.

James, W. (1890) *The Principles of Psychology*, vol. 1. London: Macmillan.

Jaynes, J. (1976) *The Origin of Consciousness in the Breakdown of the Bicameral Mind*. Boston, MA: Houghton Mifflin.

Klages, L. (1948) *Charakterkunde* (Characterology). Zürich, Switzerland: Hirzel.

Labov, W. and Waletzky, J. (1967) 'Narrative analysis', in J. Helm (ed.), *Essays on the Verbal and Visual Arts*. Seattle, WA: University of Washington. pp. 12–44.

Lau, S. (1992) 'Collectivism's individualism: Value preference, personal control, and the desire for freedom among Chinese in Mainland China, Hong Kong, and Singapore', *Personality and Individual Differences*, 13: 361–6.

McAdams, D.P. (1985) *Power, Intimacy, and the Life Story: Personological Inquiries into Identity*. Chicago, IL: Dorsey Press (reprinted by Guilford Press).

McAdams, D.P. (1993) *The Stories We Live by: Personal Myths and the Making of the Self*. New York: William Morrow.

Merleau-Ponty, M. (1945) *Phénoménologie de la Perception* [Phenomenology of Perception]. Paris: Gallimard; (1962) *Phenomenology of Perception*. (English trans. Colin Smith.) London: Routledge & Kegan Paul.

Rowan, J. (1990) *Subpersonalities: The People Inside Us*. London: Routledge.

Sarbin, Th.R. (1986) 'The narrative as a root metaphor for psychology', in Th.R. Sarbin (ed.), *Narrative Psychology: The Storied Nature of Human Conduct*. New York: Praeger. pp. 3–21.

Schwartz, S.H. (1990) 'Individualism-collectivism: Critique and proposed refinements', *Journal of Cross-Cultural Psychology*, 21: 139–57.

Spencer, S. (1971) *Space, Time, and Structure in the Modern Novel*. New York: New York University Press.

Thigpen, C.H. and Cleckley, H. (1954) 'A case of multiple personality', *Journal of Abnormal and Social Psychology*, 49: 135–51.

Triandis, H.C., Bontempo, R., Villareal, M.J., Asai, M. and Lucca, N. (1988) 'Individualism and collectivism: Cross-cultural perspectives on self-ingroup relationships', *Journal of Personality and Social Psychology*, 54: 323–38.

Vasil'eva, I.I. (1988) 'The importance of M.M. Bakhtin's idea of dialogue and dialogic relations for the psychology of communication', *Soviet Psychology*, 26: 17–31.

Watkins, M. (1986) *Invisible Guests: The Development of Imaginal Dialogues*. Hillsdale, NJ: Erlbaum.

7 THE MULTIPLE BRAIN AND THE UNITY OF EXPERIENCE

Brian Lancaster

Any analysis of the relationship between the brain and psychological processes must confront what might be construed as the central paradox of psychophysics. While the brain is characterized by multiplicity at all levels from the intracellular to that of its processing systems, our immediate experience bears the hallmark of unity, as exemplified in William James's famous construct of the 'stream of consciousness'. Recognizing this paradox, a solution would seem to require one or more of the following logical possibilities: (a) the multiplicity in the brain is subject to some form of super-ordinate integrative brain system; (b) our experience of unity is illusory; (c) our experience of unity, if not illusory, derives from a level of organization which in some sense is not reducible to the physical brain.

As a generalization, these positions can be viewed as drawing respectively on three different levels of explanation, namely the neurophysiological, the psychological, and the transcendental. Although, as Wilber (1979) argues, applying the approach of one level to the experience of another can be misleading, this chapter will draw on each of these levels where appropriate. Neither the levels of analysis nor the three possibilities noted above are mutually exclusive. Indeed, there is an important distinction between, on the one hand, *reducing* the experience of one level to the categories employed in a lower level, and, on the other hand, drawing on the categories of the lower level in order to clarify the nature of the experience at the higher level. It is in this latter sense that explorations of psychological or psychoanalytic concepts frequently draw on relevant research in neuroscience (for example, Reiser, 1984; Stevens, 1982). Even theological or spiritual concepts have been examined from the vantage point of neuroscientific observations (Ashbrook, 1996; D'Aquili and Newberg, 1993), and it may be claimed that both sides of the divide can potentially gain from such dialogue. A more complete understanding of brain states can clarify the distinctions between conscious and unconscious states, and potentially further illumine our appreciation of those states traditionally described as spiritual. Furthermore, if – as Neoplatonic traditions suggest – there is a relationship of correspondence between the different levels of being from the divine to the physical, then analyses of brain function should be valued for the insight they can give into 'higher' manifestations of mind. Jung (1954), for example, thought of the archetypes as paralleling the structure and operation of the physical brain.

In this chapter I shall review contemporary understanding of the brain as a multiple system, and suggest a possible integration of the three positions specified above. In essence, I shall argue that an integrative brain system underlies the generation of our sense of self, or 'I'; that this 'I' is, however, not as unified as it seems; and, finally, that a greater degree of personal integration may be achieved through contact with the transcendental dimension.

Multiplicity in perceptual and memory systems

The brain system which has been most fully researched is the visual system, and it can be assumed that the principles of organization and operation evident here generalize across the brain as a whole. The system is characterized by functional specialization, with anatomically distinct areas processing the visual signals in parallel. Different regions are specialized in the sense that they respond selectively to specific aspects of the visual signals, including colour, movement, and orientation of visual elements. In fact, the retinal image is mapped onto a number of distinct regions in the visual area of the cortex at the rear of the brain. Recent research suggests that there may be as many as thirty-two separate visual maps in the brain (Fellerman and Van Essen, 1991). Moreover, the entire visual system seems to be divided into two major pathways: one focusing on form and colour, the other on spatial vision (Ungerleider and Mishkin, 1982). A picture emerges of a highly ordered system, where division of labour is the *modus operandi*. What is missing from the picture is some kind of end structure, sitting – as we might simplistically envisage it – at the top of a hierarchy of analysing systems, where the whole set of processed information comes together into a unified visual image. Zeki makes this point in relation to our knowledge of the anatomy of the brain. We find no cortical area which receives only inputs, as might be expected of a terminus of some kind. All areas are characterized by both inputs and outputs, implying that the principle of dynamic interaction is operative at all levels of the brain. 'There is no single cortical area to which all other cortical areas report exclusively, either in the visual or in any other system' (Zeki, 1993: 296).

The conception we have today of the cerebral basis of integration is much more dynamic than is implied in the notion of a single terminus-like brain centre, or homunculus. It has often been remarked that our concepts of the brain and its functions have always owed a great deal to the cultural and technological images available at the time. The medieval cell doctrine, for example, which located functions in the cavities – or ventricles – of the brain, reflected the Church's vision of the non-physical realm, and especially its trinitarian focus (the doctrine being that of *three* cells in the brain). As Finger remarks, 'it probably made more sense to an early Christian theologian to place the ethereal spirits responsible for the highest functions in hollow cavities of the brain than in the flesh itself' (Finger, 1994: 18). Moving forward a few centuries, the emphasis in phrenology on the localization of function clearly reflected the thrust towards division of labour and regional specialization which the Industrial Revolution had ushered in. More recently, the computer has been the pre-eminent image employed in modelling brain function. This relativity in concepts of brain function is particularly poignant when it comes to the nature of integration in the brain. The history of civilization until the Second World War testifies to the quest for centralized power structures. Integration meant a single locus of authority. A nation or empire could be judged in terms of the strength of its centralized rule and the effectiveness of its channels of communication in enabling the centre to be in touch with all parts of the nation or empire. Today these values have changed and moves towards more devolved systems are evident. Indeed, as the power of communication systems has grown, so the need for centralization has decreased.

Our understanding of integration within the brain mirrors this devolved view. The functional areas should not be thought of in hierarchical terms; rather, each contributes in its own way towards our experience. Current research suggests that integration is signalled in terms of *temporal* aspects of neuronal firing patterns. The spatial dimension of neuronal organization may be of somewhat lesser significance. To put it in more philosophical terms, we are no longer looking for a 'Cartesian theatre' (Daniel Dennett's term for a site where the brain plays out its cohesive patterns for the mind to observe; see Dennett, 1991), but seek rather to comprehend the logic of oscillatory patterns in neuronal activity, which seem to signal the relationship of parts to the whole. '[B]rain function is conceived as anatomically dispersed over specific sensory and motor maps, but bound together by time, in the sense of being capable of temporal resonance' (Llinás, 1993: 49).

Interestingly, our understanding of this temporal dimension in brain dynamics is dependent on something of a shift in the scientific approach required. Traditionally, as von der Malsburg (1997) notes, science advanced through penetrating into ever smaller aspects of the subject under study. Studies of temporal resonance in the brain, by contrast, require scientific analysis on a larger scale, ideally correlating patterns in neuronal responses across the whole brain. Delving into the workings of the individual neurone cannot yield helpful information in this context. As with other advances in our understanding of the brain, developments in technology have made these ideas feasible, for it is only with complex imaging systems and computers capable of intercorrelating dynamic patterns from diverse sites that relationships in neuronal oscillations have been detected. A parallel with developments in our understanding of the physics of *chaotic* systems is appropriate here. A similarly large-scale view of system dynamics has given rise to greater understanding of the ways in which perturbations are magnified and coherent patterns established. Indeed, it may well be that the functioning of brain systems can best be understood from the vantage point of chaos theory, and progress in our understanding of the integrative nature of brain function may be expected to follow from advances in the relevant areas of mathematics and physics (see, for example, Freeman and Barrie, 1994; Hardcastle, 1996; McKenna et al., 1994).

There has been considerable interest in the *binding problem*, as it has been called (see Singer, 1994, for a recent review). At its simplest level, the problem concerns any sensory event, for how does the brain 'know' that the responses of its neurones to the different parts of what is a singular entity in the physical world belong together? This question, with which philosophy has grappled since the eighteenth century (see Hardcastle, 1994), is now receiving answers on the basis of electrophysiological studies. Gray et al. (1989) demonstrated that responses from spatially distinct neurones display phase synchrony in their oscillations when, and only when, they are triggered by features of a single stimulus. The research paradigm here involved monitoring electrical responses of neurones in the visual cortex while the neurones' receptive fields were stimulated with light of the appropriate orientation and direction of movement. When separate light bars were used to stimulate the receptive fields of two neurones 7 mm apart, little phase-locking was evident in the oscillatory patterns of the neurones' activity. However, under the condition in which the light stimulating the two neurones derived from a single elongated light bar, responses were strongly phase-locked. In other words, it seems that *resonance* in the oscillation patterns of neuronal responses constitutes the binding code used by the brain.

A further argument in this area holds that the oscillatory binding system serves as the cerebral basis of consciousness (Crick and Koch, 1990; von der Malsburg, 1997). The logic of this argument follows from the experiential unity of consciousness. Just as the object I perceive as a singular entity is so perceived on the basis of temporal binding mechanisms, so the stream of thought within which the perceived object takes its place may be unified through a more all-embracing level of synchronization. Von der Malsburg suggests further that the state of *highest* consciousness would be one characterized by maximal coherence across the brain's diverse systems, a state of 'global order'. Using magnetoencephalography on human subjects, Llinás and Paré (1991) have observed global waves of 40 Hz oscillations sweeping across the entire brain cortex from rostral to frontal regions. They postulate that these global waves – a neuronal 'humming' as they term it – serve to highlight the occurrence of unpredicted events which disturb the system. Global levels of analysis have similarly been attempted by John and his colleagues (John et al., 1997). They studied voltage 'landscapes' over the entire cortex derived from event-related potentials recorded from multiple sites on the skull. They claim that these landscapes show evidence for the temporal integration of widespread neuronal assemblies, and that the time-course of changes in the landscapes suggests that the assemblies signalling current sensory input are continually and dynamically being compared with memory systems.

While these sorties towards concepts of global integration are interesting, the fact remains that the available data lag behind the more ambitious claims which have been made for the role of oscillatory binding in the brain. Evidence for small-scale binding – in terms of parts of visual stimuli, for example – cannot necessarily be extrapolated to include more global integration. And the claim that consciousness might be attributable to such oscillatory binding systems merely represents the latest in a historical series in which the most fashionable feature of brain function is seized upon as *the* key to consciousness. What *is* clear, however, is that widespread brain regions are engaged in even relatively trivial cognitive operations. Such a claim is supported by several complementary lines of evidence including positron emission tomography (PET) and other techniques for imaging functional brain systems, neuropsychological studies of the consequences of brain damage, and electrophysiological studies of neuronal activity. The brain operates as a 'parallel distributed system', and the argument that 'association areas' (beloved of brain cartographers from earlier this century) might integrate spatially segregated neuronal data, has largely been laid bare by recent research. As more is discovered about the functional architecture of the brain, it is apparent that very little of the cortex is sufficiently non-specialized to take on such 'associative' roles. Moreover, it is doubtful whether sufficient spatial integrative power could be housed within the confines of the human skull.

These challenges to any simple unitary quality in the brain may be reinforced when we consider its larger subdivisions in functional terms. Considerable interest was generated in the differences in function of the two hemispheres following the early split-brain operations. Studies of these patients, as well as a wealth of information from patients with unilateral brain damage and from studies on normal subjects, suggested that considerable functional specialization was evident between the hemispheres. Such specialization was not only apparent at the level of specific cognitive abilities, but seemed to reflect a difference in overall processing styles employed by each hemisphere. The left hemisphere was described as being analytic and rational in its style; the right, more holistic (Levy-Agresti and Sperry, 1968). Again, some degree of historical relativity may have been at work here, for these observations were being reported at a time – in the 1960s – when many were exploring non-rational and more intuitive dimensions of the mind. Indeed, the primary observations were seized upon within the popular imagination and seen to reflect a plethora of dichotomies, ranging from the conscious-unconscious mental split to Western-Eastern divisions in thought patterns.

The studies on split-brain patients were seminal in the reintroduction into mainstream psychology of concepts of mental multiplicity and dissociation (Hilgard, 1977). Patients acted as if two independent spheres of consciousness were operating within their heads concurrently. While Sperry argued that normal individuals are characterized by one unified sense of self and a single stream of consciousness, others considered his split-brain studies to imply that the normal human condition was one of divided consciousness (Natsoulas, 1995; Puccetti, 1981). For Sperry, the inter-hemispheric pathways are critical in bringing about an integration between the diverse activities of the two hemispheres, consciousness itself being an emergent property of the *whole brain* (for example, Sperry, 1984; see also Dimond, 1980). While the notion of emergent properties is strongly defensible, relating as it does to my earlier comments about levels of explanation, the jury must remain out on the question of whether the normal brain is as totally integrated as Sperry suggests. Consciousness may well represent an integrative phenomenon, but there can be little doubt that such integration can be relative at best, and the split-brain condition probably constitutes an extreme case of the everyday lack of integration witnessed in the average human condition.

In terms of arguments for multiplicity of brain function based on large-scale divisions of the brain, a series of divisions in the brain's vertical axis should be considered in addition to this horizontal split between the cerebral hemispheres. MacLean's model of the *triune brain* emphasizes the divisions in evolutionary terms between successive layers of the human brain (see MacLean, 1990, for recent discussion). The primitive *reptilian brain* includes primarily brain stem regions and controls instinctual functions; the *paleo-mammalian brain* includes the limbic system and deals with internal stimuli, especially feelings; and the *neomammalian brain*, the neocortex, is directed to analysis of the external world. According to MacLean, the threefold nature of our brain can result in behaviour being controlled from inappropriate regions, as for example when people commit atrocities that normally seem unimaginable. Historically, such instances have occurred when individuals slavishly follow a charismatic leader, such as Hitler (MacLean, 1969; Koestler, 1976). In its threefold conceptualization of human nature, the model bears comparison with the psychoanalytic approach of Freud and the metaphysical analyses of Plato. A further comparable analysis of human nature is that provided by the Russian mystical philosopher, Gurdjieff, who argues strongly that the human mind is multiple, and that three separate brains are responsible for intellect, emotion, and movement (Ouspensky, 1950). For our purposes, the importance of both models – the triune and the hemispheric – lies in their emphasis on systems of neural organization which are sufficiently independent to count effectively as sub-brains.

As suggested already, the contemporary emphasis on dynamic binding in temporal terms adds an additional dimension of multiplicity to the spatial one inherent in these models. Systems integrated within an oscillatory coherent pattern in one moment may be divergent in the next, and such systems may include neurones both within and across the hemispheric and triune boundaries. Moreover, distinctions between 'input' and 'output' systems are becoming blurred. As far as vision is concerned, for example, the input line goes from the retina to the thalamus and into the visual areas of the cortex. However, the number of fibres proceeding from the thalamus to the cortex is actually exceeded by those going in the reverse direction.

These backwards, or *efferent* fibres, are presumed to underlie interactions between previously recognized patterns of information and the current stimulus array (Damasio, 1989; Harth, 1995; Zeki and Shipp, 1988). Such memory read-out is central not only to imagery processes but also to perception of objects or events in the outside world.

The involvement of memory in relation to proposed neuronal binding mechanisms is a corollary of the requirement to generate meaning, the task to which brain perceptual systems are directed (Lancaster, 1991). When I experience a visual image, say that of a car moving down the road, its unitary nature is not simply a consequence of diverse systems of visual processing being integrated, but, equally fundamentally, it arises from memory read-out interacting with the sensory processes. As I perceive the car approaching while I stand ready to cross the road, my prior experience of cars – including the knowledge I have built up of the consequences of their motion, for example – becomes incorporated in the percept. This is where the self-relatedness of the percept comes in, for memory is essentially egocentric. Items in memory are stored not as islands of information but according to their meaning, which is determined in large measure by the information's relation to the self – a point to be discussed further in the next section. 'To count as a memory a cognitive experience, or thought, must contain the conviction that I myself was the person involved in the remembered scene' (Warnock, 1987: 59). To pursue the car example, if the percept encourages me to begin running to the other side of the road, it is because the memory read-out includes a sense of *my* body and of the far pavement in relation to *my* movement, etc. Sensory data become meaningful only when they have been embedded into an egocentric framework provided by memory. Since similar arguments may be advanced in relation to emotion and thought, it follows that memory is the touchstone of mental life, and of our sense of the unified nature of experience.

But is memory itself unitary? While specific structures, especially the hippocampus and other components of the brain's limbic system, are known to be critically involved in aspects of memory, no single unified brain structure suggests itself as *the* memory centre of the brain. The brain *as a whole* must be conceived of as the organ of memory. Studies of brain-damaged patients, as well as experimental research with intact humans and animals, have led some to propose that distinct systems of memory exist. Tulving (1995), for example, posits five separate systems, which are distinguished according to the type of performance the memory underlies and the time course of its effective function. Looking to memory as the basis for unification in the brain-mind system would, therefore, seem to be unfounded.

A critical distinction may be drawn between memory operating with, and without *consciousness*. Early this century, Claparède (1911/1995) noted this distinction in his patients suffering from Korsokoff's syndrome, which is characterized by dense amnesia. His patients' behaviour suggested that it was not the memories *per se* that had been lost, but the patient's ability to consciously connect to those memories. He describes, for example, a patient whom he greeted by shaking her hand while holding a pin so that she received a prick. When he returned to her some time later, the amnesia was evident in her total failure to recognize him. Nevertheless, she noticeably withdrew her hand as he approached to shake it. When questioned, she even suggested that, 'Sometimes pins are hidden in people's hands.' She could not, however, relate to such a possibility as a memory. Clearly, the earlier event had been stored and continued to affect the patient's behaviour and thinking, but in a fashion which was effectively unconscious.

The nature of this distinction between conscious and unconscious memory performance has been extensively researched over recent years (for recent reviews, see Graf, 1994; Schacter, 1995). Disagreements over the precise meaning of the terms 'conscious' and 'unconscious' in such contexts have led to the use of alternate terminology. Thus the conscious-unconscious dichotomy in cerebral processing is generally replaced by *explicit-implicit* (Graf and Schacter, 1985) or *intentional-incidental* (Richardson-Klavehn and Bjork, 1988). In particular, use of a term like 'implicit' avoids any implication that a dynamic unconscious of the kind envisaged by Freud and others is engaged in the relatively simple tasks which have been researched. As Greenwald (1992) has emphasized, if one regards these studies as yielding evidence of an unconscious then it is a decidedly 'simple and dumb' unconscious by comparison with that described by Freud or Jung, for example. Moreover, Kihlstrom suggests that, by comparison with the psychoanalytic unconscious, the unconscious of contemporary psychology is 'kinder and gentler . . . and more reality bound and rational, even if it is not entirely cold and dry' (Kihlstrom, 1992: 789; see also Stein, 1997). Bearing in mind this caveat, I will use the terms implicit and unconscious as applied to brain processing interchangeably.

Returning to the discussion of temporal binding within neural systems, we may postulate that implicit processes are ones which have not been integrated into the binding system to the same degree as have explicit ones. There must be a degree of relativity here. Clearly, a stimulus to which an individual responds unconsciously (as, for example, in the case of subliminal perception) is itself a unified entity; the neuronal responses to which its parts give rise must have been bound together in order for appropriate actions to be elicited. However, as Kinsbourne (1997) argues, the implicit status of such events suggests that the neuronal activity concerned has not become integrated within the dominant focus of neural activity. By the phrase, 'the dominant focus of neural activity', Kinsbourne is referring to those widespread but integrated neuronal systems which are responsible for the contents of consciousness at any given time. In this sense, then, neuronal systems engaged in processing of unconscious material are *dissociated* from the dominant (*conscious*) system by virtue of their different oscillatory rhythm. It is worth noting that Freud presciently arrived at a similar formulation in his *Project for a Scientific Psychology* of 1895 (see Pribram and Gill, 1976), before abandoning the neurological approach to explaining the nature of unconscious and conscious processes. In this work, he regarded *periodicity* of neural discharge as the critical feature distinguishing the conscious from the unconscious system.

The brain is increasingly seen as being a *modular* system, to which the concept of dissociation is appropriately applied (Hilgard, 1977; Schacter, 1989; Gazzaniga, 1985, 1988). The modularity of the brain is seen in the way in which brain damage can interfere with specific, encapsulated functions. For example, the ability to recognize faces may be lost, without any decrement in other aspects of visual recognition; or memory for living things is compromised while memory for artificial objects remains. The model of brain function advanced to explain these kinds of dissociation is one in which a specific domain of information processing is limited to a fixed brain locus – a module of the brain, with each module characterized by a high degree of autonomy (Fodor, 1983; Shallice, 1988). The question remains of how to reconcile the seeming unity in our experience of the world with the evident multiplicity of the modular brain. Periodicity, or temporal binding may represent an adequate *mechanism* at the neuronal systems level. But it is only when we consider the level of *psychological meaning* that we can relate brain systems to experience. And, strangely enough, this move from the physiological to the psychological level of analysis is precisely the one made by Freud when he rejected his *Project* over a hundred years ago. *Plus ça change, plus c'est la même chose.*

An integrative self system?

The advantage we have over Freud is that a considerable knowledge base has accumulated in which changes in psychological experience relating to the conscious-unconscious dichotomy are understood in relation to brain structures. A syndrome such as blindsight (Weiskrantz, 1986) is illustrative of this knowledge base. A blindsight patient is phenomenally blind over one half of visual space on account of damage to the contralateral area of V1 (primary visual receiving area of the cortex). Despite such 'blindness', patients report that visual stimuli in the blind field may give rise to non-visual sensations such as 'sharpness' or 'smoothness', and they are often able to guess accurately about basic properties of the visual stimulus. Such residual abilities must be attributable to the activity of remaining visual areas of the brain. The critical issue concerns the reason why such activity generally remains unconscious.

Following earlier ideas of William James and Ernst Claparède, it has been suggested that the unconscious status of material in cases such as this is a consequence of a dissociation between the neuronal systems processing the material and those systems responsible for the representation of self (Claparède, 1911/1995; Kihlstrom, 1993, 1997; Lancaster 1991, 1997a). On this view, the neural representation of self becomes the touchstone of consciousness. As Kihlstrom suggests, 'When a link is made between the mental representation of self and the mental representation of some object or event, then the percept, memory or thought enters into consciousness; when this link fails to be made, it does not' (Kihlstrom, 1993: 152).

There seem to me to be good reasons for accepting this view of the critical role played by the self system in relation to mundane consciousness. The self system underpins the meaningfulness of perceived objects, memories and thoughts, which is the hallmark of consciousness. An entity is rarely perceived as an abstraction; its status as an object with a meaningful function, or place in the world of experience, derives in the first place from my connection to it. The rich network of interconnections between the self and objects, people, and events is built up from early infancy, and even though a particular conscious thought may not overtly include any reference to 'I', the very framework in which it arises is invariably egocentric. 'Every psychic manifestation, whether perception, bodily sensation, memory, idea, thought or feeling carries *this particular aspect of "being mine"* of having an "I" – quality, of "personally belonging", of it being one's own doing' (Jaspers 1923/1963: 121, italics in original).

I have proposed the term *'I'-tag* to convey this special relation between neuronal representations of events in the outer or inner worlds and the representation of self (Lancaster, 1991, 1993, 1997a). In the 'I'-tag model there is no assumption of unity in the nature of self. On the contrary, the model addresses specifically the superficiality in our mundane sense of 'possessing', or 'being', a unitary self. My emphasis on the multiplicity of 'I'-related processing derives from two sources. In the first place, as dis-cussed above, objective neuropsychological data supporting the modularity of brain systems and the dynamically changing binding of neural systems mitigates against a unitary self. Secondly, spiritual traditions with a highly developed emphasis on disciplined introspective analysis invariably criticize the concept of a coherent personal self. Given that neuroscientific data are effectively filtered through researchers' intuitive understanding of the nature of mind, the suggestion from these spiritual traditions that such under-standing may be flawed should be given due consideration. I have argued that an integrative approach is required, in which the data employed to generate models of the processes and states of the mind are expected to have been subject to the appropriate validation. In the case of neuroscientific data, the validation criteria of science must be met; in the case of introspective data, the approaches to validation of a long-standing tradition such as Buddhism should also be met.

The 'I'-tag is a feature of memory. It is clear that neuronal representations of perceived events or thoughts become stored as memories which have a network of appropriate interconnections to the representations of associated events and thoughts. In the case of my perception of a pen, for example, associated memories might include those of other writing implements, or of the occasion on which the pen was given to me, etc. In addition, we may assume that the sense of self, or 'I', active at the particular time of per-ceiving the pen will also be stored in association with the memory of the pen. It is the associative bond between the memory of the event and that of 'I' which the term *'I'-tag* is meant to convey.

In neurological terms a broad distinction may be drawn between brain modules concerned with processing of specific categories of information and those systems necessary for consciousness of the information. The former would seem to require the cerebral cortex, whereas the latter are undoubtedly extra-cortical since even large-scale lesions of the cortex do not compromise consciousness. A site which has been strongly implicated in the cerebral basis of consciousness is the higher brainstem including the thalamus (Bogen, 1995; Newman, 1995; Penfield, 1975). However, such a view can be sustained only when taken together with data suggesting the involvement of more disparate sites in the complex of operations involved in conscious processing. Indeed, the evidence of blindsight indicates that visual consciousness cannot be dependent on solely extra-cortical systems. This syndrome suggests that multiple interactions between diverse sites, including brainstem areas and cortical area V1, are necessary for visual consciousness.

Furthermore, studies of amnesia suggest that the hippocampus and related structures in the temporal lobe are essential for conscious (explicit) memory function (Markowitsch, 1995; Squire, 1987). There is good evidence to suggest that these temporal lobe structures are critical also to the sense of self (Mandell, 1980). Coons (1996) notes that, while a wide variety of biological and psychological factors may trigger symptoms of depersonalization, the temporal lobe and its various cerebral connections represent the final common pathway. Cases of temporal lobe epilepsy, for example, can cause states of depersonalization as well as other disturbances of consciousness. It seems likely that this hippocampal system is responsible for contextual information essential for the access of memories, at least until memories are firmly established. In non-human animals such contextual information may include spatial coordinates (O'Keefe and Nadel, 1978) or the orderly relationships between stimulus elements (Dusek and Eichenbaum, 1997), for example. In humans, however, it is the self system which becomes the overarching contextual system for memory. As Rosenfield argues: 'injury to the hippocampus, in destroying the relation between external and internal stimuli, destroys the ability to create a "memory" that will have a meaningful relation to self' (Rosenfield, 1995/1992: 72). On the basis of neuropsychological evidence, then, we may suggest that the hippocampal system is necessary for the incorporation of 'I'-tags as a kind of index of memory traces.

It would be a mistake to think of these tags as passive, as the image of something like a card index might suggest. They do not become inert elements once 'filed', or 'stored' as engrams. Rather, ongoing cognitive processing would be continually reactivating and reorganizing the 'I'-tag system. When a memory becomes activated due to a related current situation – to return to the earlier example, perhaps I have to hunt for the pen because I've mislaid it – associated memories will become activated. The 'I'-tag will be one such reactivated memory feature. It is proposed that 'I'-tags active at any given time provide the elements from which the experience of self at that time is synthesized. This synthesized self, or *unified 'I'*,[1] which gives the unitary quality of experience, emerges as a consequence of the brain's attempt to generate a coherent level of interpretation to all the diverse modular outputs at the given time. The self system is, then, paradoxically both *integrative* and *divisive*, for its function is to integrate diverse 'I'-tags but, in doing so, it will ignore or reinterpret data that do not fit, leaving them dissociated from the current unified 'I'.[2]

I consider the left hemisphere system that Gazzaniga (1985, 1988) has termed 'the Interpreter' to be responsible for the synthesis of the unified 'I'. His experiments on split-brain patients led him to the view that this brain system is continually monitoring the outputs of other modules and synthesizing interpretations to account for behaviour. A stimulus presented to the right hemisphere only will be unavailable to the interpreter on account of the surgically divided inter-hemispheric pathways. However, should the patient react to the stimulus, either behaviourally or emotionally, the reaction will be picked up by the interpreter, which will accordingly invent an explanation for its occurrence. When, for example, an emotionally disturbing film was projected to a patient's right hemisphere only, she later stated, 'I feel jumpy. I think maybe I don't like this room, or maybe it's you, you're getting me nervous.' As Gazzaniga comments, such a phenomenon 'represents an extreme case of an event that commonly occurs to all of us. A mental system sets up a mood that alters the general physiology of the brain. The verbal system notes the mood and immediately attributes cause to the feeling' (Gazzaniga, 1997: 75). I have argued that 'I-ness' is effectively the putative cause of causes in this context. As Minsky notes: 'If you're compelled to find some cause that causes everything you do – why, then, that something needs a name. You call it "me." I call it "you." ' (Minsky, 1985: 232). The unified 'I' is generated as the central focus of all interpretations. It is the hypothesis of a unified receiver of impressions and instigator of actions. In reality there is no such core inner 'I' in control. The unified 'I' is a *post hoc* interpretation; it is merely a story we tell ourselves (for a more detailed discussion of this view of 'I', see Lancaster, 1991; see also Dennett, 1991; and Bruner, 1997, illustrates the important role cultural factors play in the narrative construction of self).

All this raises questions about the *function* of 'I'. Why does the brain generate such an ubiquitous illusion? The question is particularly acute since, as Buddhism stresses, much suffering is associated with this illusion of 'I'. Angst of one form or another is handmaiden to the human cult of personality. I believe the answer is bound up with the workings of memory, as will be evident from the role that 'I'-tags are thought to play. Memories which affect current processing without introducing 'I'-tags are, by definition, operating implicitly. It follows that the question of the function of 'I' can be rephrased in terms of the function of explicit memory. Moscovitch has proposed that, 'Consciousness may be necessary to allow us to have memories without acting on them and to retrieve them without the need of an external stimulus cue. In this way, we can think about and manipulate memories until we are ready to act' (Moscovitch, 1994: 1353). Adapting Moscovitch's view, we may suggest that 'I' enables a distinctive form of access to memory. Implicit memory operates by direct association and can operate only in connection with stimuli which are currently present in some form. According to the 'I'-tag model, the unified 'I' would be capable of activating memories unconnected with the present stimulus array via those memories' 'I'-tags. Much as Jaynes (1976) proposed, 'I' brings into being a metaphorical mind-space in which hypothetical connections may be explored.

As has been observed by poets and mystics alike, however, the price we pay for this advantage in the ability to reflect upon and conceptualize our experience is an inevitable distancing from the present. 'I' necessarily lives in the past and/or the future. In those rare moments when we truly make contact with the present moment, the metaphorical mind-space collapses and 'I' is transcended.

Transcending 'I'

While the sphere to which spiritual traditions point is primarily non-physical, their insights also bear relevance to the mundane level of the mind-brain. For Buddhism, insight into the non-unified nature of 'I' is a necessary step towards spiritual growth. There are significant parallels between the understanding of the mind in Buddhist philosophy and that drawn from contemporary cognitive neuropsychology (Lancaster, 1997a, 1997b; Varela et al., 1991). Most notably, the Buddhist view that the mind comprises elementary units bound together through association equates strongly with cognitive neuropsychology's emphasis on modularity and dynamic binding. Furthermore, the doctrine of no-self[3] is consistent with the many dissociation syndromes which have been described in neuropsychology.

The 'I'-tags, which play a critical role in limiting the sphere of memory to which the individual has conscious access, may be presumed to be grouped into broad constellations. These constellations would determine our personality structure, divided as it is into subpersonalities (Rowan, 1990). When we are operating from a subpersonality which is discontinuous from the one which had become bound into a given set of memory traces as their 'I'-tag, our ability to recall the memories will be compromised. The extreme of this phenomenon is found in multiple personality states, and such deficits in explicit memory performance across alter personalities have indeed been demonstrated by Nissen et al. (1994). One approach to transcending the limits on consciousness and memory function imposed by this fragmentation of 'I' would be fostered by detachment from the unified 'I', a state of affairs to which Buddhist practice is clearly directed. Over a prolonged period of such detachment, the circularity in the 'I'-tagging system would be broken, leading to a progressive liberation from egocentricity in memory and resolution of conflicts attributable to subpersonalities.[4]

The other approach to overcoming our limitations caused by fragmentation of the 'I' system is to subject 'I'-tags to a more all-embracing concept of oneness, an aspiration promoted in monotheistic religions by introjection of the vision of God. By emphasizing the notion that humans are 'in the image of the divine', Judaism, for example, holds that the human mind reflects God's mind. The divine name 'I will be that which I will be' (Exodus 3: 14) asserts that the 'I-ness' of God is in an endless process of becoming.[5] In mystical thought, the human 'I' becomes integrated through participation in this divine process of becoming. It is notable in this context that a major class of Jewish meditative practices are known as *unifications*. While the focus of these practices is on promoting the reunification of the divine, at a psychological level the practices may be conceived of as unifying diverse strands within the personality. Wholeness at the cosmic level is, in this reciprocal statement of the human–divine relation, dependent on wholeness within the individual.

A favoured symbol in Jewish mystical texts for these processes of unification is provided by the knot of the head *tefillin*.[6] The author of the Zohar, the most authoritative text of Jewish mysticism, writes:

> This is the mystery of unification. One . . . must unify the Name of the Holy One, blessed be He, unifying the upper and lower levels, integrating all parts and binding them at the place where the knot is found. (Zohar 2: 216a)

The role of knots as symbolic of binding and integration is self-evident. What is less obvious is the relation to the brain implicit in the Zohar's formulation. The Zohar emphasizes a threefold division of the divine 'brain',[7] a pattern which the human brain is said to follow. The 'place where the knot is found' is the lower of these three divisions, corresponding to the brainstem region. Accordingly, in the Zohar's scheme of things a critical role is being assigned to the brainstem in the process of unification. Whether or not this assignation possesses any validity in neuroscientific terms (Lancaster, 1988) is, of course, not the point. What is of interest is the implication that by the thirteenth century or earlier a 'cerebral binding problem' was, at least symbolically, being addressed.

It seems appropriate to close this chapter by reference to such imagery of unification. The emphasis on unification in these spiritual terms provides evidence of a different kind for the chapter's major argument, namely that the human brain – and, by implication, our mental life – is characterized by a *lack* of unification. In the Jewish mystical narrative of transcendence, it is this lack which the individual aspires to heal.

More generally, both the Buddhist and Jewish mystical traditions assert that our knowledge, especially that of our own minds, is limited by the delusions inherent in our view of ourselves as being naturally endowed with a unified 'I'. The path to deeper knowledge requires untying the strings of attachment to that illusory 'I', and establishing a clearer connection to the real world (which, in the case of monotheistic religion, includes the world of the divine). As Idel remarks in his study of the thirteenth-century Jewish mystic, Abulafia, 'The process of loosening and tying is identified with the process of enlightenment' (Idel, 1988: 136).

Notes

1 The term *unified 'I'* is used in distinction to *unified self*. The experienced sense of 'I' is viewed as the output of the interpreter system. It is a fact of experience that it is unified. Indeed that is the essential job which the interpreter performs. However, this experience of a unified 'I' does not mean that any kind of an inner unified self, continuous and unchanging, exists.

2 A degree of circularity will be evident in these proposals. The *unified 'I'* becomes an *'I'-tag* which becomes a determining element in subsequent constructions of the unified 'I'. To some degree this circularity is a realistic analysis of the automaticity in cognitive systems, and reflects the notion of 'I' as a kind of self-fulfilling prophecy. However, it will be obvious that there must be more to the system than this, otherwise how could 'I' arise in the first place? Certainly, non-'I'-tag-related operations are involved in the generation of the sense of 'I' in infancy and continue to influence this sense in later years (discussed in B.L. Lancaster, *Mind, Brain and Human Potential: The Quest for an Understanding of Self* [Element Books; Shaftesbury, Dorset and Rockport, MA, 1991]).

3 Rahula succinctly captures this teaching as follows: 'What we call "I", or "being", is only a combination of physical and mental aggregates, which are working together interdependently in a flux of momentary change within the law of cause and effect, and . . . there is nothing permanent, everlasting, unchanging and eternal in the whole of existence' (W. Rahula, *What the Buddha Taught* (Gordon Fraser, London and Bedford, 1967), p. 66).

4 This prediction based on the 'I'-tag model would also suggest that detachment from 'I' could lead to impaired memory performance in the mundane spheres of personal memory. Anecdotal reports support this suggestion. Kempf (personal communication) notes that 'absentmindedness' seems to be a characteristic of some individuals who have been deeply immersed in meditative traditions. He cites, for example, Suzuki Roshi, one of the major figures in bringing Soto Zen to the USA, as being 'endearingly' absentminded.

5 The mistranslation of this name in the King James version of the Bible as 'I am that I am' misses this key emphasis. Of course the spectre of historical relativity raises its head here also, for the seeming certainty of self implied by the mistranslation accorded with the predominant scheme of things in this early seventeenth-century period.

6 Ritual boxes containing scriptural texts worn on the head and arm during weekday morning prayers.

7 Such anthropomorphic concepts of the divine are common in Jewish mysticism. It should be understood that the intention is not to impose any image on divine features. Rather, references to divine attributes are couched in these terms since they are intended to indicate realities which can be understood only through correspondences with human features.

References

Ashbrook, J.B. (1996) 'Interfacing religion and the neurosciences: A review of twenty-five years of exploration and reflection', *Zygon: Journal of Religion and Science*, 31: 545–82.

Bogen, J.E. (1995) 'On the neurophysiology of consciousness: I. An overview', *Consciousness and Cognition*, 4: 52–62.

Bruner, J. (1997) 'A narrative model of self-construction', *Annals of the New York Academy of Sciences*, 818: 145–61.

Claparède, E. (1911/1995) 'Recognition and selfhood', *Consciousness and Cognition*, 4: 371–8.

Coons, P.M. (1996) 'Depersonalization and derealization', in L.K. Michelson and W.J. Ray (eds), *Handbook of Dissociation: Theoretical, Empirical and Clinical Perspectives*. New York: Plenum Press.

Crick, F.H.C. and Koch, C. (1990) 'Towards a neurobiological theory of consciousness', *Seminars in the Neurosciences* 2: 263–75.

Damasio, A.R. (1989) 'Time-locked multiregional retroactivation: a systems-level proposal for the neural substrates of recall and recognition', *Cognition*, 33: 25–62.

D'Aquili, E.G. and Newberg, A.A. (1993) 'Religious and mystical states: A neuro-psychological model', *Zygon: Journal of Religion and Science*, 28: 177–200.

Dennett, D.C. (1991) *Consciousness Explained*. London: Penguin Books.

Dimond, S.J. (1980) *Neuropsychology: A Textbook of Systems and Psychological Functions of the Human Brain*. London: Butterworths.

Dusek, J.A. and Eichenbaum, H. (1997) 'The hippocampus and memory for orderly stimulus relations', *Proceedings of the National Academy of Sciences USA*, 94: 7109–14.

Fellerman, D.J. and Van Essen, D.C. (1991), 'Disinhibited hierarchical processing in the primate cerebral cortex', *Cerebral Cortex*, 1: 1–47.

Finger, S. (1994) *Origins of Neuroscience: A History of Explorations into Brain Function*. Oxford: Oxford University Press.

Fodor, J.A. (1983) *The Modularity of Mind*. Cambridge, MA: MIT Press.

Freeman, W.J. and Barrie, J.M. (1994) 'Chaotic oscillations and the genesis of meaning in cerebral cortex', in G. Buzsaki, R. Llinás and W. Singer (eds), *Temporal Coding in the Brain*. Berlin: Springer-Verlag.

Gazzaniga, M.S. (1985) *The Social Brain*. New York: Basic Books.

Gazzaniga, M.S. (1988) 'The dynamics of cerebral specialization and modular interactions', in L. Weiskrantz (ed.), *Thought Without Language*. Oxford: Oxford University Press.

Gazzaniga, M.S. (1997) 'Why can't I control my brain? Aspects of conscious experience', in M. Ito, Y. Miyashita and E.T. Rolls (eds), *Cognition, Computation and Consciousness*. Oxford: Oxford University Press.

Graf, P. (1994) 'Explicit and implicit memory: a decade of research', in C. Umilta and M. Moscovitch (eds), *Attention and Performance XV: Conscious and Non-conscious Information Processing*. Cambridge, MA: MIT Press.

Graf, P. and Schacter, D.L. (1985) 'Implicit and explicit memory for new associations in normal and amnesic subjects', *Journal of Experimental Psychology: Learning, Memory, and Cognition*, 11: 501–18.

Gray, C.M., König, P., Engel, A.K. and Singer, W. (1989) 'Oscillatory responses in cat visual cortex exhibit inter-columnar synchronization which reflects global stimulus properties', *Nature*, 338 (6213): 334–7.

Greenwald, A.G. (1992) 'New look 3: Unconscious cognition reclaimed', *American Psychologist*, 47: 766–79.

Hardcastle, V.G. (1994) 'Psychology's binding problem and possible neuro-biological solutions', *Journal of Consciousness Studies*, 1: 66–90.

Hardcastle, V.G. (1996) 'How we get there from here: Dissolution of the binding problem', *Journal of Mind and Behaviour*, 17: 251–66.

Harth, E. (1995) 'The sketchpad model: A theory of consciousness, perception, and imagery', *Consciousness and Cognition*, 4: 346–68.

Hilgard, E.R. (1977) *Divided Consciousness: Multiple Controls in Human Thought and Action* (expanded edn 1986). New York: Wiley.

Idel, M. (1988) *The Mystical Experience in Abraham Abulafia*. Albany, NY: State University of New York Press.

Jaspers, K. (1923/1963) *General Psychopathology*. (Trans. J. Hoenig and M.W. Hamilton.) Manchester: Manchester University Press.

Jaynes, J. (1976) *The Origins of Consciousness in the Breakdown of the Bicameral Mind*. Boston, MA: Houghton Mifflin.

John, E.R., Easton, P. and Isenhart, R. (1997) 'Consciousness and cognition may be mediated by multiple coherent ensembles', *Consciousness and Cognition*, 6: 3–39.

Jung, C.G. (1954) *The Development of Personality*. (Trans. R.F.C. Hull.) *Collected Works*, vol. 17. London: Routledge & Kegan Paul.

Kihlstrom, J.F. (1992) 'The psychological unconscious: found, lost, and regained', *American Psychologist*, 47: 788–91.

Kihlstrom, J.F. (1993) 'The psychological unconscious and the self', in *Experimental and Theoretical Studies of Consciousness*, Ciba Foundation Symposium no. 174. Chichester: Wiley.

Kihlstrom, J.F. (1997) 'Consciousness and me-ness', in J.D. Cohen and J.W. Schooler (eds), *Scientific Approaches to Consciousness*. Mahwah, NJ: Lawrence Erlbaum.

Kinsbourne, M. (1997) 'What qualifies a representation for a role in consciousness?', in J.D. Cohen and J.W. Schooler (eds), *Scientific Approaches to Consciousness*. Mahwah, NJ: Lawrence Erlbaum.

Koestler, A. (1976) *The Ghost in the Machine*. London: Hutchinson.

Lancaster, B.L. (1988) 'Tefillin, mind and brain: Illustrating the principle of resemblance in Jewish symbolism', *Journal of Psychology and Judaism*, 12: 21–43.

Lancaster, B.L. (1991) *Mind, Brain and Human Potential: The Quest for an Understanding of Self*. Shaftesbury, Dorset and Rockport, MA: Element Books.

Lancaster, B.L. (1993) 'Self or no-self? Converging perspectives from neuropsychology and mysticism', *Zygon: Journal of Religion and Science*, 28: 509–28.

Lancaster, B.L. (1997a) 'On the stages of perception: Towards a synthesis of cognitive neuroscience and the Buddhist Abhidhamma tradition', *Journal of Consciousness Studies*, 4: 122–42.

Lancaster, B.L. (1997b) 'The mythology of anatta: Bridging the East–West divide', in J. Pickering (ed.), *The Authority of Experience: Essays on Buddhism and Psychology*. Richmond, Surrey: Curzon Press.

Levy-Agresti, J. and Sperry, R.W. (1968) 'Differential perceptual capacities in major and minor hemispheres', *Proceedings of the National Academy of Sciences USA*, 61: 1151.

Llinás, R.R. (1993) 'Is dyslexia a dyschronia?', *Annals of the New York Academy of Sciences*, 682: 48–56.

Llinás, R.R. and Paré, D. (1991) 'Of dreaming and wakefulness', *Neuroscience*, 44: 521–35.

MacLean, P.D. (1969) 'The paranoid streak in man', in A. Koestler and J.R. Smythies (eds), *Beyond Reductionism*. London: Hutchinson.

MacLean, P.D. (1990) *The Triune Brain in Evolution: Role in Paleocerebral Functions*. New York: Plenum Press.

von der Malsburg, C. (1997) 'The coherence definition of consciousness', in M. Ito, Y. Miyashita and E.T. Rolls (eds), *Cognition, Computation and Consciousness*. Oxford: Oxford University Press.

Mandell, A.J. (1980) 'Toward a psychobiology of transcendence: God in the Brain', in J.M. Davidson and R.J. Davidson (eds), *The Psychobiology of Consciousness*. London: Plenum Press.

Markowitsch, H.J. (1995) 'Anatomical basis of memory disorders', in M.A. Gazzaniga (ed.), *The Cognitive Neurosciences*. Cambridge, MA: MIT Press.

McKenna, T.M., McMullen, T.A. and Schlessinger, M.F. (1994) 'The brain as a dynamic physical system', *Neuroscience*, 60: 587–605.

Minsky, M. (1985) *The Society of Mind*. New York: Simon and Schuster.

Moscovitch, M. (1994) 'Recovered consciousness: A hypothesis concerning modularity and episodic memory', *Journal of Clinical and Experimental Neuropsychology*, 17: 276–90.

Natsoulas, T. (1995) 'Consciousness and commissurotomy VI. Evidence for normal dual consciousness?', *Journal of Mind and Behavior*, 16: 181–206.

Newman, J. (1995) 'Thalamic contributions to attention and consciousness', *Consciousness and Cognition*, 4: 172–93.

Nissen, M.J., Ross, J.L., Willingham, D.B., Mackenzie, T.B. and Schacter, D.L. (1994) 'Evaluating amnesia in Multiple Personality Disorder', in R.M. Klein and B.K. Doane (eds), *Psychological Concepts and Dissociative Disorders*. Hillsdale, NJ: Lawrence Erlbaum.

O'Keefe, J. and Nadel, L. (1978) *The Hippocampus as a Cognitive Map*. Oxford: Oxford University Press.

Ouspensky, P.D. (1950) *In Search of the Miraculous*. London: Routledge & Kegan Paul.

Penfield, W. (1975) *The Mystery of the Mind: A Critical Study of Consciousness and the Human Brain*. Princeton, NJ: Princeton University Press.

Pribram, K.H. and Gill, M.M. (1976) *Freud's 'Project' Re-Assessed: Preface to Contemporary Cognitive Theory and Neuropsychology*. New York: Basic Books.

Puccetti, R. (1981) 'The case for mental duality: Evidence from split-brain data and other considerations', *Behavioral and Brain Sciences*, 4: 83–123.

Rahula, W. (1967) *What the Buddha Taught*. London and Bedford: Gordon Fraser.

Reiser, M.F. (1984) *Mind, Brain, Body: Toward a Convergence of Psychoanalysis and Neurobiology*. New York: Basic Books.

Richardson-Klavehn, A. and Bjork, R.A. (1988) 'Measures of memory', *Annual Review of Psychology*, 39: 475–543.

Rosenfield, I. (1995/1992) *The Strange, Familiar and Forgotten: An Anatomy of Consciousness*. London: Picador.

Rowan, J. (1990) *Subpersonalities: The People Inside Us*. London: Routledge.

Schacter, D.L. (1989) 'On the relation between memory and consciousness: Dissociable interactions and conscious experience', in H.L. Roediger and F.I.M. Craik (eds), *Varieties of Memory and Consciousness: Essays in Honor of Endel Tulving*. Hillsdale, NJ: Lawrence Erlbaum.

Schacter, D.L. (1995) 'Implicit memory: A new frontier for cognitive science', in M.A. Gazzaniga (ed.), *The Cognitive Neurosciences*. Cambridge, MA: MIT Press.

Shallice, T. (1988) *From Neuropsychology to Mental Structure*. Cambridge: Cambridge University Press.

Singer, W. (1994) 'The organisation of sensory motor representations in the neocortex: A hypothesis based on temporal coding', in C. Umilta and M. Moscovitch (eds), *Attention and Performance XV: Conscious and Nonconscious Information Processing*. Cambridge, MA: MIT Press.

Sperry, R.W. (1984) 'Consciousness, personal identity, and the divided brain', *Neuropsychologia*, 22: 661–73.

Squire, L.R. (1987) *Memory and Brain*. New York: Oxford University Press.

Stein, D.J. (ed.) (1997) *Cognitive Science and the Unconscious*. Washington, DC: American Psychiatric Press.

Stevens, A. (1982) *Archetype: a Natural History of the Self*. London: Routledge & Kegan Paul.

Tulving, E. (1995) 'Organization of memory: Quo vadis?', in M.S. Gazzaniga (ed.), *The Cognitive Neurosciences*. Cambridge, MA: MIT Press.

Ungerleider, L.G. and Mishkin, M. (1982) 'Two cortical visual systems' in D.J. Ingle, M.A. Goodale and R.J.W. Mansfield (eds), *Analysis of Visual Behavior*. Cambridge, MA: MIT Press.

Varela, F.J., Tompson, E. and Rosch, E. (1991) *The Embodied Mind: Cognitive Science and Human Experience*. Cambridge, MA: MIT Press.

Warnock, M. (1987) *Memory*. London: Faber and Faber.

Weiskrantz, L. (1986) *Blindsight: A Case Study and Implications*. Oxford: Clarendon Press.

Wilber, K. (1979) 'Eye to eye: Transpersonal psychology and science', *Revision*, 2: 3–25.

Zeki, S. (1993) *A Vision of the Brain*. Oxford: Blackwell Scientific.

Zeki, S.M. and Shipp, S. (1988) 'The functional logic of cortical connections', *Nature*, 335: 311–17.

8 MULTIPLICITY IN CROSS-CULTURAL PERSPECTIVE

Ruth-Inge Heinze

> [M]odern psychology has projected an image of man which is as demean-
> ing as it is simplistic . . . the mass dehumanization process which character-
> izes our time – the simplification of sensibility, the homogenization of
> taste, attenuation of our capacity for experience – continues . . . it should
> be psychology which combats this trend. Instead, we have played no
> small role in augmenting and supporting it.
>
> (Sigmund Koch, quoted by Brendan O'Regan, 1982: 1)

We all harbor multiple personalities in the recesses of our mind and do not
always know when one of them wants to come forth. Even when we aware
of some of the *potentials* inside of us, not all of us manage the switch from
one personality to another well. Sometimes, we surprise ourselves when an
emotionally charged situation brings out a personality we are not so familiar
with. We may also experience the same phenomenon in others when an
apparently dull-witted person surprises us with an inspiring insight we had
no indication he or she would be capable of. Are we deceived by wrong
notions and do we use defective terminology?

This chapter aims to provide cross-cultural evidence for multiplicity.
I intend to support my statements with data I collected during thirty-nine
years of fieldwork, mainly in South-east Asia. Because I have to use insights
and techniques from psychological anthropology, comparative religion, philosophy, and linguistics, my approach will necessarily be multi-disciplinary.

Fieldwork

During the last thirty-nine years in the field, for example in South-east Asia,
I observed that people still want to come into the presence of the Divine.
They want to establish contact with *other realities* and use trances to access
supernatural sources. These expectations are met by the belief that super-
natural entities decide to use human 'channels' to do 'salvation work'.
I witnessed, among others, that:

> clients . . . recognize the presence of divine powers, for example, in the
> 'possession trances' of shamans. In other cases, shamans become the actors and

retrieve otherwise inaccessible information during their 'magical flights' . . . World religions require . . . individuals who are trained and ordained to dispense the 'holy communion,' to confer blessings, and to perform religious rituals according to elaborate manuals. Shamans who, at times, assume priestly functions too, remain open to change . . . [and] continue to create new rituals. Shamans are less predictable because they adapt to the specific conditions at the time of consultation . . .

It is important to mention that, especially in Asia, shamans also act as spirit mediums. Among the folk religions I studied, the tradition of spirit mediums remained unbroken. It is believed that mediums can call spiritual entities into their body. The spirit of the individual is then considered to be displaced and may visit the spirit world while the individual's body is used by a spirit . . . [the rationale behind is that] a spirit may have difficulties to be reborn in this world and has to use the body of a living being to improve his/her own karma. (Heinze, 1991: 9–10; 1988: 50, 284–5; Zuehlsdorf, 1972: 85)

In other words, the different personalities speaking through a shaman are considered to be 'outside forces' which temporarily have taken over a human body (see also Salter, 1950 on trance mediumship).

In the West, glossolalia in Christian churches has been studied, among others, by Felicitas Goodman (1972). Furthermore, Christian priests continue to transform wine and bread into the blood and body of Christ during the Holy Communion. (Survivals of early animist and shamanic ritual can, indeed, be found in most world religion.)

According to my field notes, shamans, mediums, and channels keep emerging in modern cities like Bangkok and Singapore as well as in American and European cities. They fulfill age-old needs. When different personalities manifest in an individual for the first time, an expert will determine which spirit has descended or whether a spirit from a lower realm maliciously draws attention to him- or herself and requires exorcism.

During 1978–9 in Singapore I met, for example, a deified general from the Three Kingdoms (AD 220–80) who was using the body of a forty-year-old woman. In daily life, she was an outgoing and cheerful housewife and mother. She had been a model and a salesperson whose faculty to channel Taoist deities manifested one night while the family was sitting around the dinner table. The spirit was first evasive about his identity, but finally disclosed his name as *Kam T'ien Siong Teh*, one of the three brothers who swore the oath in the Peach Garden during the Third Kingdoms.

How unexpected was this possession? The family of seven, parents and five children, were living in close quarters with their in-laws. There had been health problems in that family and difficulties with the husband's and the wife's job. The uncertain future of the children gave reason for additional concern. The wife had consulted mediums and had also gone to various Chinese and Indian temples as well as Christian churches. She converted to Catholicism and, after more disappointments, became a 'free thinker,' resigned to the fact that she would have to cope with the family's uncertain socio-economic situation as best as she could.

While living with relatives, she took care of a house altar that her father-in-law had brought from China . . . [He] had been a devout worshiper of the deity but, after his death, the altar was left unattended. Because the altar stood in her room, the wife took it on herself to clean it and to occasionally put flowers in front of the deity's picture.

Why had a deified general, in the services of *Guanyin* [Goddess of Mercy in Taoism and Bodhisattva of *Avalokiteshvara* in Buddhism], chosen a modern-educated, non-believing housewife and mother to help others, also promising protection and assistance for her family. Since the medium could not recall what transpired during the trance, her husband related to me that his wife had been chosen because she was the purest in the family. (Heinze, 1993: 189)

At the time I met Mrs Y., she had been a full-fledged medium for six years. She practiced every night from 7–12 pm and twice on weekends. The spirit general instructed her how to serve and how to call him. Sometimes other entities appeared too, for example *Ong Teh Kong*, but *Kam T'ieng Siong Teh* never failed to make an appearance and continued to advise the medium even at times when she was not in trance.

She described the process of personality change as follows:

I light the joss [incense] sticks and just relax. I close my eyes and say, 'Kam T'ieng Siong Teh, you are summoned to do salvation work!' Then, gradually, it takes a few seconds to recognize it, he comes down. My body expands. It is like as if I were inside an iron armor. My body seems to be heavy and . . . becomes very big and very heavy . . . When he arrives, I feel a click, at the back of my neck. From then on, I know nothing, because he takes over. And when he is about to leave my body, I can feel my blood streaming back. I can feel how my blood enters all my organs again. Whether my astral body is back, I know by the feeling in the tips of my fingers. And I feel very fresh, as if I have awakened from a long sleep. (Heinze, 1993: 11)

The medium, indeed, appeared refreshed, even after long sessions or when she had been tired at the beginning. (Drawing from my two decades of experience as a professional actress, I can attest that I also felt refreshed and fully energized when a performance had been satisfactory. The energies spent during a performance apparently are returned in manifold ways when the audience resonates well. In other words, when the energy exchange takes a circular path, no loss of energy occurs and an increase of energy becomes possible.)

Though Mrs Y. did not remember what transpired during a trance when a spirit allegedly was using her body, she recalled clearly what her soul was experiencing at the same time. During the twelve months I was working with her, she gave me vivid descriptions of the different spiritual realms she visited in trance. To repeat, Mrs Y. experienced complete amnesia to what her body was experiencing during trance but in daily life, Mrs Y. had full recall of what her soul was experiencing during trance. (Multiple personalities in the West frequently do not know of each other [Allison, 1980; Keyes, 1981].)

In Singapore in 1979, I decided to tape record some of the sessions when the spirit general was using Mrs Y.'s body. The recordings were made with the permission of the spirit who told me that if his voice appeared on my tapes, it would be proof that he is blessing my research. (He was obviously interested in accurate reporting.) The stern and commanding spirit voice could, indeed, be heard on the tapes as clearly as it had come out of the mouth of Mrs Y. (I was told that other researchers had come home with empty tapes and unexposed films.) I took both voice tracks – the male spirit voice and Mrs Y.'s female voice outside of possession trance – to the Language Laboratory of the Department of Linguistics at the University of California in Berkeley and had them both analyzed. It could not be determined whether two different individuals were talking because the spirit was using the vocal cords of the medium. However, the two voices differed considerably in speech pattern and each pattern was maintained with great consistency. Such consistency cannot be found in the speech patterns of professional impersonators (personal communication, Language Laboratory, University of California, Berkeley, 1979).

Furthermore, while studying multiplicity, spirit mediumship, and glosso-lalia in Singapore, I was struck by the similarities between spirit language and glossolalia. There were often assistants who 'translated' for the clients what the spirits had said. After one such translation, I approached the translator and challenged him on the unintelligibility of the spirit's voice. His answer was that spirits speak a language which can be understood only by initiates (personal communication, Singapore, 1979). For me, the speech pattern of spirit voices showed striking similarities to glossolalia and appeared to be automatic and autonomic expressions of ecstatic states. A classical example of this phenomenon is the Pythia in Delphi whose utterances had to be interpreted by Greek priests.

I would like to add another observation. 'Automatic writing' has been practiced, in China, for example, for over two thousand years. In Singapore, there were two places where automatic writing was still practiced. The World Red Swastika Society was training several candidates when I visited them and in the Temple of the Keng Yeon Taoist Association in Jurong (based on a group from Medan, Indonesia), automatic writing took place every first and fifteenth day of the lunar month and also every Friday. Clients would:

> approach a small wooden table to ask their questions. The red stick, topped by a dragon head is . . . held by two school teachers. One of them is English educated. The temple committee has two substitutes in reserve in case one or both teachers are prevented from coming. It is said that nobody else but these four individuals can hold the writing stick with impunity.
>
> When I visited the temple . . . in 1979, both pen holders appeared to be very relaxed, The stick kept circling for a while over the table and then, although both holders were clasping the stick firmly, the stick seemed to have a life of its own and knocked the answer on the table. Sometimes the stick drew Chinese characters on the table. They had to be read following the movement of the stick. Or a brush was attached to the stick to automatically paint characters on joss [charm] paper, using red ink. (see Heinze, 1988: 217–18)

For cross-cultural information about 'automatic writing' (for example, Swendenborg, Sir Arthur Conan Doyle, the Fox-Taylor records and Patience Worth), I refer to my book on *Trance and Healing in Southeast Asia Today* (1988: 206–24); for automatism see also Janet, 1913/1889).

Over the last thirty-nine years, I have worked with 122 shamans (86 male and 36 female): 31 were ethnic Thai (14 male and 17 female), 7 Thai-Malay (6 male and I female), 1 female hilltribe (Meo), 4 ethnic Malay (3 male, 1 female), 10 Malay-Chinese (9 male and 1 female), 67 ethnic Chinese (52 male and 15 female), and 2 male ethnic Indians.

Paraphernalia and style varied considerably, according to the respective cultural tradition. The God Rama, for example, spoke through a simple Indian dock worker who would put burning camphor in his mouth when the deity departed. Most of the 67 Chinese mediums were 'vehicles' of Taoist deities. Departed Thai kings and nobility would speak through ethnic Thai who, in trance, dressed in royal brocade and silk.

One Thai-Malay (Muslim) fisherman whom I had asked whether the legend was true that tigers in the jungle teach future shamans, asked whether I wanted to see it. When I quickly said, 'yes', he transformed, after a lengthy evocation, into a tiger right in front of my eyes. He did, of course, not change his physical appearance but he assumed a tiger's nature, walking on all fours and jumping in giant leaps from one end of the room to the other. Another animal transformation occurred when Malay boys and girls performed the *kuda kepang* in Singapore. The *kuda kepang* comes from and is widespread in Indonesia. It is said that once a beautiful princess:

> lived in the State of Kediri in South Java. Having heard about her beauty, the Raja of Gerensong sent a delegation to ask for her hand. The father rejected the proposal because he found the Raja too ugly for his daughter. Infuriated, the Raja of Gerensong vowed revenge . . . When the warriors of Kediri saw themselves outnumbered by the Raja of Gerensong's army . . . they made horses out of bamboo and, after having charged the bamboo horse with spirit power, the soldiers behaved like horses themselves. (Heinze, 1988: 229–37)

The fifty-five Muslim boys and girls in Singapore rode on flat-bamboo horses which had been charged by burying them for forty-four days near a cemetery. To the trance-inducing sound of a gamelan orchestra, the group, indeed, behaved like horses. They asked to be whipped by their trainer. They jumped over rows of chairs, ate glass or danced on broken bottles with their bare feet, and broke coconuts with their head. They performed these feats to prove that spiritual powers were manifesting in their body. I asked the Mufti (Muslim leader) of Singapore about these folk practices and his answer was that as long they prayed five times a day and went to mosque on Friday, Allah (who is the one God for Muslims) would not be offended. So the old custom is tolerated. The *kuda kepang* group now performs at Muslim weddings and circumcisions to protect the community from evil forces; sometimes they dance even for tourists (Heinze, 1988: 230).

Trances in South-east Asia differed in depth and length, but all 'possession trances' brought about a visible, dramatic change in personality, facial expression, and speech pattern. The rationale behind this change in personality, however, was strikingly similar. All but one claimed to be 'called' by their spirit, only one male Thai shaman (a high government official in Bangkok) made the decision to train with a recognized group of mediums. All fulfilled the expectations of their clients who, as I had mentioned before, look for mediators between the Sacred and the Secular.

To add two cases from the West, I will now report on my work with the Spiritual Emergence Network (SEN) in California which has been founded by Stanislav Grof to assist individuals in spiritual crisis. The first case illustrates the kind of casualties neo-shamanic and soul-retrieval workshops may produce. After having taken a soul-retrieval workshop, a young woman performed a ritual to guide the soul of her brother into the other world (he had unexpectedly committed suicide). Having been told to tape record her work, she listened to the tape recording afterwards and found that she had taken the soul of her brother into her own body. Shortly after, she also incorporated the soul of a neighbor who had died suddenly of a heart attack. She was very confused and asked me to exorcise these two souls from her body (Anderson, 1981). I told her that it is not so easy to incorporate somebody else's soul, but we had to look at what her agitated mind and her fears had manifested in her body. She was greatly relieved and responded well to balancing exercises which included certain ways of breathing and movements.

The other case was a middle-aged woman with migraine headaches. She had consulted physicians and psychotherapists for years to no avail. The migraine worsened to the point where she could no longer work professionally. I suspected psychological causes but did not encourage her to talk further about her ailment so as not to reinforce the 'dis-ease' pattern. I showed her some breathing exercises to release physical and emotional tension and gave her a full-body Reiki (Japanese/Tibetan technique to move hands over a client's body which takes approximately one hour). She experienced some release during the breathing exercises and was surprised to feel her own energy rising during the Reiki treatment.

After a week, she returned. Being a desperate but intelligent woman, she had done the breathing exercises well and felt something had started to move. We did not talk much and again I gave her a full-body Reiki. The next morning she called to tell me that she was 'purging', literally – she was vomiting, had diarrhea, and a childhood trauma had come up. Now she could openly deal with her problem; I had 'shifted her attention' from the disease pattern to a point where change appeared to be possible. I had proven change to her when she felt her energy level rising, and I had shown her how to purge herself so that she could take over and interconnect on her own. She was now settling into a supportive pattern. The physical work on a traumatized patient removed the barriers to well-being and assisted in integrating different personality experiences.

The last point I want to present is that suggestions how everyone can cultivate personality changes are, for example, found in the manuals of

Hinduism (for example, *How to Know God*, 1969, Prabhavananda and Isherwood's translation of the Yoga Sutras collected by Patanjali) or Buddhism (for example, the *Abhidhamma*, 1968, Narada's translation, and numerous meditation manuals which clearly spell out the state-specific qualities of the different stages). A Western equivalent is Mottola's (1964) translation of *The Spiritual Exercises of St Ignatius* and the *Rites of the Catholic Church* (1614/1976).

Western psychologists and psychiatrists diagnose changes in personality to be 'dissociations' (West, 1967). The question then arises how consistency in speech pattern is produced and maintained within each fragment of a personality *after* dissociation.

Our autonomic nervous system already performs tasks we would need a great amount of information and skill to execute consciously. The main point in answering the above question is that we did not begin this life with a blank slate. Hindus and Buddhists believe that the quality of our present life is determined by our *karma* (the quality of past thoughts, words, and actions). In the West, scientists – for example geneticists – tell us that we are born with physical, emotional, mental, spiritual, and even social features imprinted on our DNA (Allport, 1986). That means, we are born with qualities developed in the past by our ancestors and our culture. We are born with an infinitely large amount of knowledge which if not triggered, for example by environmental stimuli, may remain unconscious. Our psyche seems to be ruled by already established, self-organizing principles which are capable of building a consistent personality from fragments dissociated from a whole which in many philosophical and religious systems is called the *Self*. In other words, the *Self* is not a solid whole but is composed of numerous sub-selves, each of them having the *potential* to become autonomous (see, for example, Bowers and Meichenbaum 1984; Dessoir, 1896; James, 1971; Pfeiffer, 1971). Dissociative tendencies can be found in everyone (Binet, 1986), but our autonomic nervous system protects our mind from overload. If we were to conduct a survey, I predict we would find a large number of physically quite healthy individuals who either have difficulties in differentiating their *selves* or who do not feel the need to prefer *one* identity over another.

I had to deal with this problem when I participated in an *American Identity Study*, conducted by the University of California, San Francisco, in 1975. To protect the informants I interviewed, I will use myself as an example. Born in Germany after World War I (1919), I came to the United States when I was 35 years of age. I 'think' and 'act' in situations as I am expected to do. At my seventieth birthday, I invited a large group of people, the majority of whom were surprised about my different activities which, they assumed, required different personalities. I must have convincingly fulfilled their expectations in assuming different personality roles as situations required. I did not consciously cultivate this ability during the forty-two years I had lived in America; I must, however, have resonated with whatever environment I had to work in. In other words, personality switches were triggered by different environments. Different character traits which we do not have the opportunity to display in one environment can be brought to the surface and sublimated in another.

I am adding here my experiences during two decades as a professional actress. Actors are trained to cue themselves, kinesthetically and psychologically, to produce different character traits – on demand – in a believable and consistent manner. The natural disposition to become an actress may explain why this step had been easy for me. Becoming an actress and 'acting on stage' offered, indeed, great emotional relief and encouraged me to test and use 'potentials' of which I had no overt knowledge.

I still remember my first public appearance in a large theater in Berlin which seated over three thousand. After the dress rehearsal, my stomach turned inside out. Do we have to get rid of impurities before we are able to transcend?

> Why had I ever become an actress? I would die, drowned by the laughter of three thousand people who would discover my incompetence on first glance. I did not even remember my first line. Somehow I managed the fifty steps to the center of the stage. Fainting seemed to be the only escape. But, then, the spotlights hit me . . . and . . . 'somebody' started to talk. *It was not me.* 'It' talked . . . using my vocal cords. ['It' (my body?) remembered what it had gone through during rehearsals.] There was no other sound. Was the audience still there? Time seemed to have stopped. And then, the wave of attention reached me, the audience had joined in the 'dance' and 'we' were carried to unknown heights. It was a perfect 'wedding night.' We interconnected! (Heinze, 1994: 27)

This was the first time I consciously experienced a personality change. But not all actors react the same way: some switch personalities with ease and gusto; others seem to be stuck in what I call *a single mold*. For some actors also the return to so-called *daily life* constitutes a problem. Most actors, however, thrive on this socially permissible opportunity to display multiple personalities. Incidentally, they share this gusto with shamans and mediums who are expected to produce transformations and who have learned to monitor personality changes professionally.

Different states of consciousness

Tart, who also compiled one of the first books on altered states of consciousness (1969), speaks of the state-specific qualities of each state, which is:

> a unique *configuration* or *system* of psychological structures or subsystems. The parts or aspects of the mind that we can distinguish for analytical purposes (such as memory, evaluation processes, and the sense of identity function) are arranged in a certain kind of pattern or system. . . . The nature of the pattern and the elements that make up the pattern determine what you can and cannot do in that state. (1986b)

Ludwig had mentioned already over twentier years earlier 'alterations in thinking, change in sense of time and body image, loss of control, change in

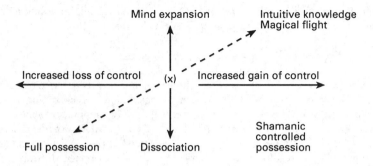

FIGURE 8.1 *Altered states of consciousness*

emotional expression, perceptual distortion, change in meaning and significance, a sense of ineffability, feelings of rejuvenation and hyper suggestibility' (1960: 225–34).

The range of possible altered states appears to be infinite and I offer Figure 8.1 as a working model. The (x) indicates the state of 'consensus reality'. On the horizontal line, I distinguish between increased gain of control versus increased lack of control. On the vertical line, an individual either moves toward increased awareness and mind expansion while gaining control or toward increased dissociation while losing control. Schizophrenics or fully possessed individuals have to be placed in the lower left quadrant, while shamans who retain some control of their dissociation, have to be placed in the lower right quadrant. The 'magical flight' of shamans, on the other hand, would be an excursion into mind expansion with increasing mastery and control and has to be placed in the upper right quadrant.

So far I have used mainly Western terms to describe the processes which may lead to multiplicity. Western scholars speak of *dissociation* or *fragmentation*. In Asia and other non-Western countries, only a few cases of multiple personality have so far been reported. When different personalities use a human body to express themselves, the event is called either *voluntary* or *involuntary possession*. In other words, it is inferred that an intrusion occurred – from the outside in; while Western terms like *dissociation* infer a *fragmentation* from the inside out. In the East, it is believed that entities, foreign to these individuals, have entered their body. In cases of *voluntary possession*, selected individuals become *vehicles* and can, afterwards, call the spirits to possess their body. These 'possessions' serve various needs of the community, for example healing, advising in inter- and intrapersonal affairs, job or business problems, divining, fertility, or longevity, etc. In cases of *involuntary possession*, the Eastern explanation is quite useful, because it shifts the responsibility away from the clients and:

> mobilizes the support of the extended family . . . by involving it in the ritual. The exorcist appeals for help to the positive 'good' beings of the respective society's

alternate reality. The evil possessing entity . . . is pushed into revealing its name and the reasons why it is plaguing the patient. (Goodman, 1988: 6)

Stanley Krippner, referring to Lewis (1971), speaks of:

> '*central possession*' [as] the way that the Brazilian spiritists describe 'incorporation.' Lewis sees the function of 'central possession' as upholding a social group's established power and morality. It is generally temporary, voluntary, and reversible . . . *Peripheral possession* . . . is taken to denote experiences which provide no direct support of the society's moral code, is typically long-lasting and involuntary, and results in dysfunctional behavior. (Krippner, 1987/1985: 16, italics added)

Referring to Ward (1980), Krippner also finds that 'spirit incorporation may be therapeutic in some cases as it can release inhibition and provide a source of esteem for the medium as well as emotional catharsis for the group' (1987/1985: 17).

In my book, *Trance and Healing in Southeast Asia Today* (1988: 9), I use Lewis's (1971) and Jones's (in Hitchcock and Jones, 1976: 1–5) definitions. *Peripheral possessions* are not necessarily seen in terms of a particular time or space, but, as has been said before, are mostly uncontrolled and unpredictable. *Reincarnate possessions* are for life and are experienced by practitioners who are connected with religious institutions or designated sacred spaces, being instrumental in rituals, curing, healing, divining, predicting and allaying misfortune. *Oracular possessions* by a spirit or god occur at a designated time and space. *Tutelary possessions* are called for when time is designated but space is not. An individual may, for example, call a tutelary spirit to possess him for the duration of a ritual (Jones in Hitchcock and Jones, 1976: 4). While *reincarnate possessions* rarely occur outside of the Tibetan and Hindu world, we find *tutelary* and *oracular*, but mainly *peripheral* possessions in other areas.

Bourguignon distinguishes between *possession* and *possession trance* (1973), because she maintains that *possession* does not necessarily involve alteration of consciousness. In 1976, she found also more differences than similarities between multiple personality cases and mediums in Latin America (quoted by Krippner, 1987/1985: 17). Mediums invite *intrusion of outside spirits*, voluntarily, on demand. They have learned to ritually control the entry into and the exit out of possession states. Multiple personalities, however, seem to split *from the inside out*. I agree with Bourguignon and Herskovits who, already in 1949, stated that 'the phenomenon of ritual spirit incorporation could not be equated with specific neurotic or psychotic conditions' (quoted by Krippner, 1987/1985: 17).

It may be worthwhile to note that Christian authorities themselves perpetuate the belief in spirits. In the framework of the Catholic Church (*Rituale Romanum* 1614/1976), it is permissible to confess 'spirit possession' which can then be exorcised. Thus, the anxieties of Christians who project their fears on to spirits are given a focus so the condition can be purged by an exorcism. Such a catharsis allows the release of repressed emotions.

A case of exorcism was performed as recently as in 1976 on a university student, Anneliese Michel, in Germany. It ended tragically with Anneliese's death. The church authorities went on trial but not the psychiatrists who had administered anticonvulsive drugs (Dilantin and Tegretal). Felicitas Goodman who studied this case, mentions the 'tremendous irritation' the drugs caused in the disturbed brain. In her opinion, the drugs interfered with the healing process when the brain was 'straining toward normalization' (1988: 9; 1981). In cases of spirit possession, the rationale of the Christian Church, therefore, does not differ much from the rationale behind cases of spirit possession in South America and Asia (Heinze 1985: 15).

We have to revise our opinions about multiple personalities (see Baldwin, 1984; McKellar, 1979; Prince, 1975) and study the 'divided self' of Hilgard (1979). We may gain some insights from Jung (1963, 1970/1957) and we can learn from studies on trance-inducing techniques (see for example, Kampman, 1976; Orzeck et al., 1948; Sutcliffe and Jones, 1962; and Thompson et al., 1937).

In sum, opinions about the different states of consciousness are culture-specific. People in non-Western countries distinguish between wanted or unwanted, that is controlled or uncontrolled, possession. Shamans and mediums have learned to control and use spirit possession professionally. They also know of a well-defined spiritual hierarchy on which they rely and from which they are able to call specific spirits for specific needs arising in their community. Spirits from the lower regions are considered to be more playful while more advanced spirits show greater moral fortitude. All spirits can punish or assist human beings. On account of their proximity to the earth and being elemental powers, spirits of the lower regions are more difficult to control, but, on the other hand, they are believed to be more effective in earthly affairs (Heinze, 1988: 98–116).

Undesirable spirit possession can be diagnosed in the East as the result of transgressing a cultural taboo or offending a spirit. In some cultures, it may also be considered to be the work of a sorcerer. Again, the guilt is removed from the client, because another human being has caused the distress. A *spirit master* will then be sought to drive out the *evil spirit* and return the *curse* to the sender. Each exorcism offers the client and the assisting group a cathartic release of emotions. The wrath of a spirit – high or low – or of another human being has to be appeased and the transgression amended, or demands of the spirit, especially unfulfilled wishes of a deceased relative, have to be carried out. The faith in the work of the *spirit master*, whether it is a placebo effect or not, guarantees the effectiveness of the treatment.

Recently the phenomenon of 'channeling' has become the object of serious scientific investigation. Channeling, obviously, shares features with a wide range of possession cases. Jon Klimo is presently revising his seminal book on *Channeling* (1987). He excludes, however, those who simply 'talk to themselves' or use telepathy. His definition is shared by Arthur Hastings, president of the California Institute of Transpersonal Psychology in Menlo Park, who says that channeling is 'the process in which a person transmits messages from a presumed discarnate source external to his or her consciousness' (1987: 4). For the discussion of 'channeling' as a historical phenomenon, I refer to Jon Klimo's book (1987). I already have mentioned the early *wu* in China who called Taoist deities into their bodies over two thousand years ago and the Pythia in Delphi who channeled early earth spirits, but was supervised and interpreted by the priests of the Greek invaders.

While mediumship has been used to solve many inter- and intrapersonal problems, foremost has been the use of mediumship in healing. Stanley Krippner (1987/1985: 6) discussed various therapies in Brazil, for example Mendes' *psicosintese*, where Mendes attempts to synthesize various aspects of his clients' psyche so that emotional 'linkages are formed between personalities'. He uses, for example, mediums who call the afflictions of his patients into their body and then ask the respective patients to heal the mediums. Mendes developed his method independently from Roberto Assagioli's *psychosynthesis* in Italy and Salvador Roquet's *psicosintesis* in Mexico.

'Intuitive diagnosis' is also practiced in the San Francisco Bay area, where training MDs put their interns at the foot of a patient's bed, hide all medical records, and invite them to 'tune into the patient'. The interns are then asked how they 'feel'. They are expected to absorb the patient's condition. This *additional* tool of Western diagnosis has proven to be quite successful because imbalances were discovered which had not yet been tested by Western procedures.

Conclusions

We have now reached the point where a bridge between Eastern and Western psychotherapeutic approaches seems to emerge. Has the West to revise its opinions on multiplicity? Shall we view the appearance of multiple personalities not only as the result of childhood trauma but as a lack of opportunity to realize different aspects of our *Self*? Do we have to look at cultural taboos? Have we closed doors to untapped *potentials* and, in closing off relief valves, created situations of increasing tension where 'demonic possessions' may erupt?

Personality appears to be a social convention. It is society's image of an individual's characteristics. Personality is also the concept we have of ourselves, of the way we want or should react to certain situations, of the way we think and of the way we handle our emotions, intuitions, dreams, of the way we fulfill needs and of the way we either ignore or sublimate certain trends. But personality can be much more. Tart says:

Essence is what is uniquely you. You were born as a unique combination of physical, biological, mental, emotional, and spiritual traits and potentials. Most of this is only potential at birth, and may never manifest unless the right circumstances are created by your world, or by you yourself later in life. (1986a: 5)

The Institute of Noetic Sciences is attempting to solve the 'puzzle of untapped potentials' (O'Regan, 1982: 1) in sponsoring research on multiple personalities. O'Regan speaks of the search for quantifiable explanations and the difficulty in dealing with the 'whole person'. Ornstein, in his work on the *Multimind* (1986), cities Hurley who confirms that:

> our minds are actually many 'small minds' that operate semi-independently of one another. Only one of these 'small minds' occupies the stage of conscious awareness at a time. Others wheel in and out as circumstances, habit, and conscious intention dictate, loosely controlled by a 'mental operating system' whose workings reflect the influence of evolution, culture, genes, and environment. The mind is a kind of bastard hybrid system; a collage comprising many fixed and innate routines, all of which serve the mental operating policies that stretch over millions of years, millions of organisms, and millions of situations. . . . The policies of mind can influence our thought and judgment over an extraordinary range. (Hurley, 1986: 24)

The *multimind* concept seems to gain popularity among brain/mind researchers. What is important to note is that it:

> does not assume that there is a single mind served by general processes like perception, learning and memory. It assumes that the mind is naturally split and that different parts of the mind communicate imperfectly with another. What one 'small mind' perceives or learns to do may not be perceived or learned by another part. (Hurley, 1986: 25)

The mind has to be seen as a multi-level system with consciousness being on the top of the hierarchy. However, major portions of the mind work unconsciously.

> Unconscious processes include not only the work of the sensory nerves and the modules of perception, but also the very selection processes involved in wheeling different talents and small minds in and out of operation. The father of psychoanalysis [Freud] was partially correct but he did not go far enough: 'We are not only the prisoners of our sexual and aggressive drives but of our particular assortment of small minds and more: of the chemicals in the food we have eaten, the position of the moon, the electrical charges in the air, the alcohol or drugs in our system, and even sunlight itself . . . The mind is systematically biased to attend to certain kinds of information. Strong emotions and events that are novel, unpredictable or striking make pre-emptory demands on our attention, for example. These are also cognitive strategies called 'heuristics' that bias the way we make judgments and solve problems. These mental 'rules of thumb' speed up decision making, although sometimes they sacrifice accuracy. The 'representativeness heuristic', for example, is involved when we make judgments about people based on the extent to which they match some preconceived idea we have about them. While this sometimes provides a helpful guide to behavior, it's misleading when we wrongly stereotype someone. (Hurley, 1986: 25)

Beahrs already argued in 1982 'that under some circumstances it is useful to look upon an individual as constituted of several parts, each with its own identity' (quoted in Krippner, 1987/1985: 18; see also Putnam and Pitblasdo, 1982).

That we should be careful in our diagnosis is obvious. Crabtree, for example, in his psychotherapeutic practice, has already distinguished correctly between *possession* which 'is the creation of a personality within an individual by a self other than that of the individual' (1985: 258) and *multiple personality* which 'involves the emergence of a personality manufactured within the psyche' (1985: 261). Are these two different states interconnected and how?

When repression becomes so strong that an eruption occurs, the door is opened toward the formless. Man has a deep-seated fear of chaos and the unknown. We dread to open ourselves to flooding of consciousness. We think that it takes a strong ego-axis and self-cultivation to recognize the Void of the Hindu and Buddhist, the unmanifest Divine Energy, or whatever name we may be using, as the unlimited *potential* all of us could access if we could lose the fear of losing our *Self*. Only artists, intuitives, and shamans seem to know how to approach the formless. Facing uncontrollable flooding and lacking familiar forms in our memory bank, belief in spiritual entities who can enter and 'possess' us appears to be a useful makeshift solution because the experience is objectified.

What forces us to undersell our *potentials*? Obviously, certain constellations ask for different social behavior. During socialization, as a child at home and at school and later in our professional career, we learn behavior appropriate to specific situations. Such rules vary with the country, the culture, and the religion we grow up with. Those who were born in one country and then moved to another country can attest to the veracity of this statement.

The society in which we live expects a certain *persona*. Even beyond these constraints, there seem to be quite a few character traits and emotions which are not encouraged by certain social environments, so they remain unused and, most of all, uncultivated. For one reason or another, we certainly are not taught how to access all of our *potentials*. How can we sublimate what unconsciously has been repressed? Sometimes, we do not even know what we have consciously suppressed. How can we come to know the multiple facets of our psyche?

The situation is compounded by the fact that we do not only have to take into account what we have repressed and suppressed in earlier years, but have to deal also with genetically transmitted imprints which may underlie character formation. I agree with Ornstein's statement that:

> Our mental apparatus is an amalgam of different circuits, of different priorities, and even of the evolutionary developments of different eras. The human brain, whose structures underlie the functioning of the mind, was not constructed of new elements. It is a compendium of circuits piled atop one another, each developed to serve a short-term purpose in millennia past. Evolution does not, unfortunately,

work for the long term, but rather for the immediate exigencies of survival for individual animals. . . .

The brain developed over a period of more than 500 million years. It is composed of quite separate structures that seem to be laid on top of each other, like a house being remodeled. So we do not have one single brain but a multilevel brain, built in different eras for different priorities. Many of these separate brains have, loosely speaking, 'minds of their own'. (1986: 33–4)

Each individual collection of talents, abilities, and capacities depends, therefore, not only on experiences in this life but also on what has been transmitted at the moment of conception. Each egg and each semen carries, with the physiological, also emotional/psychological, mental and spiritual memories of past generations. Predisposition to certain physical features or diseases as well as creative skills or destructive tendencies merge at conception and then 'materialize' at birth (Allport, 1986). We do not know the full extent of our inheritance.

I would like to refer briefly also to the research on '*cognitive dissonance*', for example, conducted by Leon Festinger (1957) who discussed people's reactions when they are holding inconsistent beliefs and strive to repair the interrupted connections.

I hope I have sufficiently challenged your belief that you are just *one* personality and would like to close with Ornstein's suggestion that 'many people may well be more able to respond to life as it really is, not as we would reduce it to fit one small-minded view' (in Hurley, 1986: 25). We are making many unconscious choices. Many psychodynamic defense mechanisms work unconsciously, so do intuition and aesthetics. Values arise from cultural patterns and may also subconsciously determine what we decide to do or how we act without any conscious decision. Decisions can be the result of authoritarian repression or the cultivation of genuine intuition. That this cultivation is possible gives us some hope.

The most important point I wanted to make in this chapter is that we have to be more accepting of our own multiplicity and that of others. We should encourage ourselves and others to escape expected 'molds' and follow the age-old knowledge which *materializes* again at the time of our birth and awaits further cultivation (see also Maslow, 1971; Ouspensky, 1949; Sargent, 1974; and Taylor, 1983). We should not neglect our natural multiplicity. In other words, a consciously lived multiplicity is not pathological at all but enriches our understanding of life and its purpose.

References

Allison, Ralph (1980) *Mind in Many Pieces*. New York: Rawson, Wade.

Allport, Susan (1986) *Explorers of the Black Box: The Search for the Cellular Basis of Memory*. New York: W.W. Norton.

American Psychiatric Association (1995) *Diagnostic and Statistical Manual of Mental Disorders* (4th rev. edn). Washington, DC: American Psychiatric Association.

Anderson, R. (1981) 'The therapist as exorcist', *Journal of the Academy of Religion and Psychical Research*, 4: 96–112.

Baldwin, L. (1984) *Oneselves: Multiple Personalities, 1811–1981*. Jefferson, NC: McFarland.

Beahrs, John O. (1982) *Unity and Multiplicity: Multilevel Consciousness of Self in Hypnosis, Psychiatric Disorder, and Mental Health*. New York: Brunner/Mazel.

Binet, Alfred (1986) *Alterations of Personality*. New York: D. Appleton & Co.

Bourguignon, E. (1973) 'Introduction: A framework for the comparative study of altered states of consciousness', in E. Bourguignon (ed.), *Religion, Altered States of Consciousness, and Social Change*. Columbus, OH: State University Press.

Bourguignon, E. (1976) *Possession*. San Francisco: Chandler & Sharp.

Bowers, Kenneth and Meichenbaum, Donald (eds) (1984) *The Unconscious Reconsidered*. New York: Wiley.

Crabtree, Adam (1985) *Multiple Man: Explorations in Possession and Multiple Personality*. New York: Praeger.

Dessoir, Max (1896) *Das Doppel-Ich*. Leipzig: Ernst Gunthers Verlag.

Festinger, Leon (1957) *A Theory of Cognitive Dissonance*. Evanston, IL: Row, Peterson.

Goodman, Felicitas (1972) *Speaking in Tongues: A Cross-Cultural Study of Glossolalia*. Chicago, IL: The University of Chicago Press.

Goodman, Felicitas (1981) *The Exorcism of Anneliese Michel*. Garden City, NY: Doubleday & Co.

Goodman, Felicitas (1988) *How About Demons? Possession and Exorcism in the Modern World*. Bloomington, IN: Indiana University Press.

Heinze, Ruth-Inge (1985) 'Consciousness and self-deception: the art of undeceiving', *Saybrook Review*, 5 (2): 11–27.

Heinze, Ruth-Inge (1988) *Trance and Healing in Southeast Asia Today*. Bangkok/Berkeley: White Lotus and Independent Scholars of Asia.

Heinze, Ruth-Inge (1991) *Shamans of the 20th Century*. New York: Irvington Publishers.

Heinze, Ruth-Inge (1993) 'The dynamics of Chinese religion', in Cheu Hock Tong (ed.) *Chinese Beliefs and Practices in Southeast Asia*. Selangor, Malaysia: Pelanduk Publications.

Heinze, Ruth-Inge (1994) *The Light in the Dark: the Search for Visions*. Berkeley, CA: Independent Scholars of Asia.

Hilgard, Ernest R. (1979) *Divided Consciousness: Multiple Controls in Human Thought and Action*. New York: John Wiley and Sons.

Hitchcock, John T. and Jones, Rex L. (eds) (1976) *Spirit Possession in the Nepal Himalayas*. New Delhi: Vikas Publishing House.

Hurley, Thomas J. III (1986) 'Review of Robert Ornstein's multimind: a new way of looking at human behavior', *Institute of Noetic Sciences Newsletter*, 14 (2): 24–6.

James, Williams (1971) *A Pluristic Universe*. New York: Dutton.

Janet, Pierre (1913/1889) *L'Automatisme Psychologique* (7th edn). Paris.

Jung, Carl Gustav (1963) *Memories, Dreams, Reflections* (ed. Aniela Jaffee). New York: Vintage Books.

Jung, Carl Gustav (1970/1957) *Psychiatric Studies*. (Trans. R.F.C. Hull.) Bollingen Series XX. Princeton, NJ: Princeton University Press.

Kampman, Reima (1976) 'Hypnotically induced multiple personality: an experimental study', *International Journal of Clinical and Experimental Hypnosis*, 24: 215–27.

Keyes, Daniel (1981) *The Minds of Billy Milligan*. New York: Random House.

Klimo, Jon (1987) *Channeling, Investigations on Receiving Information from Paranormal Sources*. Los Angeles, CA: Jeremy P. Tarcher.

Krippner, Stanley. (1987/1985) 'Cross-cultural approaches to multiple personality disorder: therapeutic practices in Brazilian spiritism', paper presented at the Second International Conference on Multiple Personality/Dissociative States.

Chicago, 25–27 October, 1985, and at the annual meeting of the Saybrook Institute, Belmont, California, 6 January, 1987.

Lewis, I.M. (1971) *Ecstatic Religion, An Anthropological Study of Possession and Shamanism.* Harmondworth, Middlesex: Penguin Books.

Ludwig, Arnold (1960) 'Altered States of Consciousness', *Arch. Gen. Psychiatrics,* 16: 225–34.

Maslow, A.H. (1971) *The Farther Reaches of Human Nature* (2nd edn). New York: Viking Press.

McKellar, Peter (1979) *Mindsplit. The Psychology of Multiple Personality and the Dissociated Self.* New York: J.M. Dent.

Mottola, Anthony (trans.) (1964) *The Spiritual Exercises of St. Ignatius.* New York: Doubleday & Company.

Narada, Maha Thera (1968) *A Manual of Abhidhamma.* Kandy, Ceylon: Buddhist Publication Society.

O'Regan, Brendan (1982) 'The puzzle of untapped potentials', *Institute of Noetic Sciences Newsletter,* 10: 1.

Ornstein, Robert (1986) *Multimind.* New York: Houghton Mifflin.

Orzeck, A.Z., McGuire, C. and Longenecker, E.D. (1948) 'Multiple self-concepts as effected by mood states', *American Journal of Psychiatry,* 115: 349–53.

Ouspensky, P.D. (1949) *In Search of the Miraculous.* New York: Harcourt Brace & World.

Pfeiffer, Wolfgang M. (1971) *Transkulturelle Psychiatrie.* Stuttgart, Germany: Thieme.

Prabhavananda, S. and Isherwood, C. (trans.) (1969) *How to Know God: The Yoga Aphorisms of Patanjali.* New York: Signet Books, New American Library.

Prince, Morton (1975) *Psychotherapy and Multiple Personality.* Boston, MA: Harvard University Press.

Putnam, Frank W. and Pitblasdo, Colin (1982) 'The three brains of Eve: EEG data', (Reviewer, W. Herbert), *Science News,* 121: 356.

Rites of the Catholic Church as Revised by the Second Vatican Ecumenical Council (1614/1976) (Orig. *Rituale Romanum,* 1614.) New York: Pueblo.

Salter, W.H. (1950) *Trance Mediumship.* London: Society for Psychical Research.

Sargent, W. (1974) *Battle for the Mind.* Garden City, NY: Doubleday.

Sutcliffe, J.P. and Jones, J. (1962) 'Personal identity, multiple personality, and hypnosis', *International Journal of Clinical and Experimental Hypnosis,* 10 (4): 231–69.

Tart, Charles (ed.) (1969) *Altered States of Consciousness. A Book of Readings.* New York: John Wiley & Sons.

Tart, Charles (1986a) 'Waking Up', *Institute of Noetic Sciences Newsletter,* 14 (2): 3, 5–8.

Tart, Charles (1986b) *Waking Up. Overcoming the Obstacles of Human Potential.* Boston, MA: Shambala, New Science Library.

Taylor, Eugene (1983) *William James on Exceptional Mental States.* New York: Charles Scribner's Sons.

Thompson, M., Forbes, T. and Bolles M. (1937) 'Brain potential rhythms in a case showing self-induced apparent trance states', *American Journal of Psychiatry,* 93: 1313–14.

Ward, C. (1980) 'Spirit possession and mental health: A psycho-anthropological perspective', *Human Relations,* 33: 149–63.

West, Louis Jolyon (1967) 'Dissociative reaction', in A.M. Freedman and H.I. Kaplan (eds), *Comprehensive Textbook of Psychiatry.* Baltimore, MD: Wilkins & Wilkins.

Zuehlsdorf, V. (1972) 'The witchdoctors of Chiangmai', Zeitschrift für Kultur und Geschichte Ost- und Suedasiens, 112: 79–87.

9 INDIVIDUAL DIFFERENCES IN PLURALISM IN SELF-STRUCTURE

John Altrocchi

> Do I contradict myself?
> Very well then, I contradict myself,
> (I am large, I contain multitudes).
>
> Walt Whitman (1992)

The study of the concept of the self started with William James (1890/1950), and has been a prominent subject of empirical research in psychology since Carl Rogers' trailblazing efforts more than forty years ago (Rogers and Dymond, 1954). In the late 1980s and 1990s there has been increasing attention paid to differentiating from each other, for research purposes, the *content* of the self-concept (for example, degree of self-esteem, specifics of self-identity) and the *structure* of the self-concept. This chapter focuses on investigations of the structure of the self-concept and how they contribute to conceptions of polypsychism, largely ignoring the content of what people say about themselves.

In narrowly focusing on the *self*-concept, this chapter is, by definition, focusing on people's *subjective view of themselves*, their conscious self-representations, as shared with investigators; it does not pay central attention to people's overt behavior – which may or may not be strongly related to their self-concepts – and will ignore whatever private or even unconscious ideas they may have about themselves. Furthermore, this chapter focuses on *individual differences* in how people view the structure of their selves – in pluralism in self-structure. To the extent that major individual differences in pluralism of self-structure can be demonstrated, the usefulness of nomothetic or universalist views of polypsychism (or monopsychism) need to be modified or elaborated.

History of ideas about self-structure pluralism

Pluralism in the structure of the self was proposed long ago by William James in a famous passage:

> A man has as many social selves as there are individuals who recognize him . . . [and] generally shows a different side of himself to each of these. (1890/1950: 294)

Other early psychologists accepted the existence of various or alternating selves, most particularly Edgar Swift in 1923, who examined the variety of selves that may be included in a personality. In contrast to such early kinds of acceptance of self-structure diversity, however, the dominant view from the 1930s into the 1970s was the posited tendency of individuals to seek unity and consistency in self and personality (Lecky, 1945; Murphy, 1947; Rogers, 1959; Erikson, 1968).

More recently, however, there has been a resurgence of interest in diversity in self-structure, notably by social psychologist Kenneth Gergen (1971; 1991), who spoke of 'multiple conceptions' of self and the 'populating of the self'; by Mair (1977), who suggested that a person can be thought of as a 'community of selves'; by Martindale (1980), who proposed a conceptualization of sub-selves; by Redfearn (1985), who spoke of sub-personalities and the many selves in all of us; by Markus and Wurf (1987) who summarized current views on the 'multifaceted self-concept'; most powerfully, by both Beahrs (1982) and Crabtree (1985) who wrote entire books with a major theme that we all have 'multiple personalities'; and finally, by one of the editors of this book, John Rowan, who wrote *Sub-personalities* (1990), which is a direct progenitor of the concept of poly-psychism. Clearly the psychological world is becoming more ready to consider and to integrate concepts of pluralism, including pluralism of the self-concept.

It can be postulated that both those who proposed diversity in self-structure and those who proposed that individuals seek unity and consistency in self-structure were correct. In the first place, what individuals seek is guided in major ways by the views of the culture of which they are a part: Western culture has been very integration-oriented; other cultures are not. In the second place, there may be major individual differences in integration versus diversity of self-structures.

Stability of self

> I enjoyed thinking of him as a sultan in the middle of his harem, where I was by turns each of his different favorites. (Choderlos de Laclos, 1782; quoted in Rowan, 1993: 4)

Empirical research in individual differences in pluralism in self-structure was begun by Morris Rosenberg (1965, 1979, 1989), a sociologist interested in studying the effects of social structure on personality. Rosenberg wrote extensively on the self-concept, and studied self-esteem and then self-consistency, guided by views like those of Lecky (1945) which proposed that people have a general motive to view themselves as, and to become, consistent. Rosenberg developed a five-item 'stability of self' scale with items such as: 'Does your opinion of yourself tend to change a good deal or does it continue to remain the same?'; 'Do you ever find that on one day you have one opinion of yourself and on another day you have a different opinion?'; 'I have noticed that my ideas about myself seem to change very quickly'. Rosenberg found *instability* of self to be related to young age, especially in females; to be modestly related to low self-esteem; and to be more highly, but still modestly related (for example a correlation of .37) to psychological disturbance and to psychological indices of anxiety. The four other sets of research, outlined more extensively below, all seem to have grown, in part, from Rosenberg's seminal ideas and efforts.

Self-pluralism

> It was during a time of painful conflict that I first began to experience myself as more than one. It was as though I sat in the midst of many selves. (O'Connor, 1971: 3)

In the mid-1980s, Paul McReynolds and I decided to put into investigative action our shared ideas, gained from research experience, clinical practice and university teaching, about normal variations in the structure of the self-concept. We perceived a discrepancy between the theories of the self that were current then, which usually portrayed the self as rather unchanging and monolithic, and observations of the changes in the self-concepts of patients in psychotherapy, as well as the variety of self-conceptions in patients with multiple personality disorder. Multiple personality disorder, now more appropriately called *dissociative identity disorder* (DID), always begins in childhood with multiple, horrendous traumas – almost always abuse – which are so unbearable that the child spontaneously dissociates or 'escapes' by creating one, and then additional parts or alters or subpersonalities to handle the traumas (Ross, 1989). The key original abnormality, of course, is the early abuse; the original dissociation was presumably protective and some-times may even have been life-saving (Ross, 1989), although recent data suggest that dissociation at the time of trauma tends to predict development of chronic post-traumatic stress disorders (van der Kolk et al., 1996). The dissociation process sometimes eventually produces multiple and separate identities, even to the extent that each subpersonality ultimately thinks of herself or himself as a totally separate person with a totally separate body. This can produce horrendous clinical problems in which a patient believes, for example, that killing an offensive alter will not harm himself at all. Thus the disorder that develops centrally entails amnesic barriers among the subpersonalities with very limited co-consciousness, and usually leads to a chaotic life with many interpersonal problems, multiple diagnoses and, often, frequent 'injuries', suicide attempts and hospitalizations (Ross, 1989).

We postulated that it was likely that the multiple, dissociative identity phenomenon, like most psychopathology, is an extreme of a dimension along which individuals differ. Therefore, we developed the concept of self-pluralism to provide a focused framework for research. We conceive of self-pluralism as a dimension of individual differences in the structure of the self-concept that includes: (a) relative variability versus relative consistency in how one describes one's behavior over time and across different situations; (b) diversity and heterogeneity versus unity and homogeneity in self-perceived personality structure; and (c) a relatively unstable versus a relatively stable concept of personal identity. *Self-pluralism is thus defined as the degree to which a person sees her- or himself as diverse and responding in different ways in different circumstances and at different times, or as unified and responding similarly in different circumstances and occasions.*

On rational considerations we (Altrocchi et al., 1990) developed a 30-item True–False measure called the 'self-pluralism scale' (SPS), with satisfactory reliability and a range of scores from 0–28, a mean of 10.28, Standard Deviation (SD) 7.07, and a moderate positive skew (N = 340). Later we reduced the scale to ten items (brief self-pluralism scale, BSPS), with satisfactory reliability and a range of scores of 0 to 10 (see Appendix A), a mean of 3.78, SD 2.89, alpha .83, correlation with SPS .92.

In a series of studies using 340 subjects – the majority, though not all, college students – the noteworthy (and highly significant) correlations with the 30-item self-pluralism scale (SPS) were:

College maladjustment scale	.51
Dissociative experiences scale	.51
NEO personality inventory, neuroticism	.45
Ego strength scale	−.40
Rosenberg's 'stability of self' (N = 56)	.53
(keyed so that high scores represent instability)	

It is clear from these results that self-pluralism is moderately correlated with measures of self-concept (in)stability, with maladjustment, and with the tendency to report that one comparatively frequently has (relatively normal) dissociative experiences.

Scores for 25 DID subjects (who were currently in psychotherapy) ranged from 16 to 29, with a mean of 25.3 on the 30-item scale; on the 10-item scale, they ranged from 1 to 10, with a mean of 8.2 (some of these data were reported in Altrocchi et al., 1990). Clearly we had succeeded in one of our goals: there are very large individual differences in self-pluralism, in a way that makes sense (see the results on DID subjects). People who share a kind of psychopathology that is defined by multiplicity of self-concept are far more polypsychic in structure of self-concept than most normal subjects.

In an attempt to extend the applicability of the concept of self-pluralism, we participated for a year in a long-term research project in our university which studied the relationship among diet, obesity, weight, weight variability, and cardiovascular functioning (Altrocchi and McReynolds, 1997). We conjectured that there may be a relationship between our measure of psychological variability (SPS) and their measures of one kind of biological variability – weight variability. We administered the SPS to 345 subjects, equally divided by gender and age (20s to 60s, mean age 54.7 in March 1997, SD 13.8), in the eighth year of the Reno Diet–Heart Study (eighth-year data were collected in 1993–4, so the mean age then was in the low 50s). The SPS mean was notably lower (3.6) than in any of our previous studies, perhaps because these subjects tended to be older and also, as people who had already stayed with the study for eight years, probably tended to be unusually dedicated, responsible, and organized (high ego strength).

SPS did not differ by gender but did relate to age: older subjects have slightly lower SPS scores, a result congruent with some of our earlier findings. SPS also related to measures of maladjustment, to number of 'life-change' experiences, and slightly but still *significantly to measures of weight variability*, although not to weight *per se*. Clearly, the relationships between psychological and biological variability warrant further research.

We also briefly studied the relationship between pluralism of self-concept and pluralism of behavior. We obtained the cooperation of 27 married couples and had them rate self and other on the same five-item pluralism of behavior description (with no communication until they were finished). One couple had known for years that they were opposite on self-pluralism (they did not learn this from us, and did not use our terminology). Even with their data included, the self-observer correlation was non-significant; and with this 'outlier' couple appropriately removed, the correlation was +.03. These modest data suggest that there is (usually) little relationship between one's rating of one's self-pluralism and an intimate other's rating of the pluralism of one's behavior.

Self-complexity

Linville's (1985, 1987) theoretical model suggested that 'representations of self are best conceived in terms of multiple self-aspects, or multiple cognitive structures, each with its own set of associations among features, propositions, affects, and evaluations' (Linville, 1987: 674). Self-complexity is defined (Linville, 1985) as a function of *the number* of aspects that one uses to cognitively organize knowledge about the self (polypsychism), and *the degree of relatedness* of these aspects; and she used the H statistic, representing the number of independent binary attributes needed to produce the self-description. Greater self-complexity entails more aspects that are independent of one another. Then, assuming that fewer and less independent aspects of self-representation (low self-complexity) would allow the effects of negative experiences relevant to one aspect to 'spill over' into other aspects, she hypothesized, and found, that high self-complexity moderated the affective effects of negative events, such as depression and physical symptoms.

These results can seem puzzling, given the relationship between high self-pluralism, low self-stability (and high self-concept differentiation and low self-concept clarity, see below) and measures of maladjustment. Pelham and Swann (1989), Showers (1992), Morgan and Janoff-Bulman (1994), and

Jordan and Cole (1996) helped to clarify Linville's results by using measurements that included features of both structure and content of the self-concept: (a) how important the subject thinks a particular aspect is; and (b) measuring positive and negative self-aspects separately. Self-complexity that was predominantly composed of positive and important aspects was associated with measures of adjustment (Showers, 1992); and positive self-complexity was not related to general adjustment but was associated with better adjustment to traumatic experiences (Morgan and Janoff-Bulman, 1994). The latter investigators suggest that Linville's otherwise puzzling finding of high self-complexity providing a buffer, may have occurred because her subjects were predominantly characterized by high complexity of positive features.

Range of number of sub-selves in Morgan and Janoff-Bulman's study ranged from 1 to 20 with a mean of 7 – again, suggesting a high degree of individual differences in monopsychism versus polypsychism in this area.

Self-concept differentiation

Donahue and her colleagues (Donahue et al., 1993; Roberts and Donahue, 1994) conceived of self-concept differentiation (SCD) as *the degree to which one sees oneself as having different personality characteristics in different social roles* – a modified kind of polypsychic outlook. Their measurement of SCD is much more complex than the simple questionnaire measures of stability of self, self-pluralism, and self-concept clarity (see below). They asked subjects to describe themselves, on eight-point Likert scales covering 60 personality attributes, in each of five social roles – student, friend, romantic partner, son or daughter, and worker. The descriptive ratings of themselves in different role identities were factor-analyzed for each subject separately. The percentage of variance accounted for by the first factor was then subtracted from 100 to produce SCD scores. Thus SCD represents the amount of variance in the ratings across roles that is *not* accounted for by co-variances across all five roles; with higher scores representing higher self-concept differentiation.

As was also true for self-pluralism, the distribution of SCD scores was skewed, with more subjects showing lower differentiation (monopsychism) and only 10 percent scoring over 40 percent. The mean was 24.6 percent, SD 12.4. Scores of men and women were not significantly different. Although range of scores was not given, the mean and SD imply that the range was from close to zero to more than 50 percent. As was true for self-pluralism and self-complexity (Morgan and Janoff-Bulman, 1994), this is a degree of variability that would be hard to reconcile with a narrow, universalist (generalized across all people) concept of other polypsychism or monosychism.

A major thrust of Donahue et al.'s (1993) first article was to test two differing views of the role of self-concept differentiation in adjustment. SCD was negatively correlated with self-esteem ($p<.01$) and positively correlated with two measures of maladjustment – MMPI Depression ($p<.01$) and NEO

Neuroticism ($p<.05$). Again, these results are closely parallel to those for self-pluralism and clearly contradict the frequently expressed view that SCD represents the possession of specialized identities that enable individuals to respond flexibly and adaptively to different role requirements. (That social-psychological view assumes a high correlation between one's view of structure of one's self and a complex feature of one's behavior. Such postulated correlations have received little support – see above on SPS and below.) In contrast, their results clearly support a more clinically oriented view in personality psychology that high differentiation indicates less-than-optimal integration, and sometimes fragmentation, of the self-concept.

These investigators also made another major contribution by studying longitudinal precursors of SCD. Subjects in this study were, instead of the college students used in the first study, women in their 50s who (naturally) had experienced various role-related conflicts, achievements, and changes – such as marriage, child rearing, divorce, career advancement, chronic illness, and deaths of parents, friends, and spouses – and who had first been assessed in a long-term research program when they were seniors in college, and then at later ages as well. California Psychological Inventory (CPI) scores from assessments at ages 21, 27, 43, and 52 and observer ratings at age 43, all assessing emotional adjustment and 'norm acceptance' (conventionality, conscientiousness), were correlated with SCD at age 52. The range of correlations can be summarized as follows:[1]

> age 21 – +.08 (NS) to +.25 ($p<.05$) (5 of 11 correlations $p<.05$)
> age 27 – +.20 (NS) to +.40 ($p<.01$) (6 of 11 correlations $p<.01$)
> age 43 – +.23 ($p<.05$) to +.49 ($p<.01$) (9 of 11 correlations $p<.01$)
> age 43 – (observer ratings) +.02 to +.35 (3 of 7 correlations $p<.01$)
> age 52 (concurrent with SCD measures) – +.26 to +.50, (all correlations $p<.01$)

Thus differences in SCD in middle adulthood can be modestly predicted from individual differences in personality dating back at least to the college years; and high levels of distress that characterize high SCD women in their 50s had characterized many of them for most of their adult lives.

Self-concept clarity

Campbell (1990) conceived of self-concept clarity (SCC) from pursuing research in self-esteem. Self-concept clarity is *the extent to which the contents of the self-concept, or self-beliefs, are clearly and confidently defined, internally consistent, and temporally stable* (Campbell et al., 1996). Of the measurers reviewed here, therefore, SCC is least directly related to self-multiplicity and most directly related to self-fluidity. Therefore, its relationship to the other measures reviewed here is of particular interest. SCC is measured by means of a simple 12-item, 5-point scale and the scale has been shown to have adequate reliability, so that, like SPS and SCD, SCC can be considered to be a stable trait (Campbell et al., 1996). SCC scores in several studies ranged from 12 to 60 (the maximum possible; see Campbell, 1996) and females tended to have slightly higher scores (clearer self-concepts) than males. SCC correlates with self-esteem because, according to Campbell and Lavalee (1993), there is a combination of, and reciprocal interaction among, low self-esteem; a cautious orientation to the environment (less likely to take risks or call attention to themselves); and a less certain, noncommittal, middle-of-the-road and more changeable view of the self. SCC is strongly (negatively) correlated with (Big-Five) Neuroticism (average correlations = −.64; see Campbell et al., 1996); and Campbell (1990) suggests that high SCC may, like high self-esteem, relate to controlled (conscious) flexibility of behavior (a clear adaptive advantage) and low SCC may relate to situational changeableness of behavior (possibly maladaptive in Western society).

Finally, Campbell et al. (1996) provided a first cross-cultural finding in this area. As predicted from the difference between the Western 'independent' construal of self and the Eastern 'inter dependent' construal of self (Markus and Kitayama, 1991), Canadians' SCC scores were higher than Japanese' SCC scores and were more closely related to their self-esteem scores. The assumption is that the Japanese' lower consistency and stability of self-concepts relates to their interdependent and contextual view of themselves.

Congruence of results

It is clear that most of the above results, from five different backgrounds and from several different groups of investigators, are quite congruent. Ignoring self-complexity because we were puzzled by Linville's initial results, we correlated self-pluralism and (in)stability of self (56 subjects, $r = .53, p<.001$); self-pluralism and self-differentiation (106 subjects, $r = .41, p<.001$); self-pluralism and self-concept clarity (56 subjects, $r = −.62, p<.01$); and self-concept clarity and stability of self (56 subjects, $r = −.70, p<.001$). Instability of self, self-pluralism, self-concept differentiation, and (lack of) self-concept clarity intercorrelate significantly, but not highly enough to be considered different measures of the same variable. As will be discussed more extensively below, they all correlate significantly with measures of maladjustment. All four measures – and Linville's – vary considerably and strikingly among individuals. There evidently are many individuals whose self-concepts are unstable, pluralistic, differentiated, and inconsistent; and others whose self-concepts are stable, integrated, undifferentiated, and clear – and there are others who span the dimensions in between. Thus, in this narrow area of the structure of the self-concept, *degree of polypsychism or monopsychism clearly varies among individuals.* Polypsychism and mono-psychism are evidently not concepts that apply approximately evenly to all people.

Furthermore, a dissertation by House (1991) makes matters even more complicated. She studied self-pluralism every day for 30 days in 30 subjects. Individuals not only varied in SPS and in variability of SPS but also in patterns of variation across time. Thus, in this area at least, we need to go beyond individual differences among people at static time periods and include *change across time,* and *varying patterns of the change.*

There are some other general features of the above results that deserve comment or raise questions. First, females sometimes (self-pluralism) have significantly higher scores in the instability-pluralism-differentiation-lack of clarity dimension, and sometimes have lower scores (higher self-concept clarity). At the present time we have no idea why.

Second, age is sometimes (for example, stability of self and self-pluralism) found to be related to lower pluralism. This needs to be investigated further. Many theorists (for example, Erikson, 1968) suggest that we tend to 'get it all together' better with maturity. Linville (1985), however, suggests that self-complexity is likely to increase with increasing life experiences; and Donahue et al. (1993), integrating some features of content and behavior, note that role satisfaction and role changes play a part in self-concept differentiation. Clearly age, like gender, needs to be investigated in a complex context of other variables, not by itself.

Third, there are intriguing suggestions that these measures relate to life history (we need to know more) and to other, seemingly distant realms such as weight variability. Perhaps (House, 1991), we need to start treating degree and kind of variability across psycho-social-biological realms as a basic variable for study.

Implications and questions for polypsychism and psychology

1 Do the findings of pluralism in self-structure suggest dimensions or polypsychic structuring? The concept of polypsychism was developed from a long background of considering multiple selves, or subpersonalities, in all of us. To what degree do conceptualizations and measurements reviewed in this chapter fit conceptions of subpersonalities, which are at least somewhat discontinuous and separate from each other; and to what extent, in contrast, do they emphasize dimensions and fluidity of self-concept (Cooper, personal communication, 1996)? Clearly the conception of self-pluralism arose from consideration of multiple subpersonalities by means of clinical work with and teaching about, an extreme, multiple, dissociative identity disorder. But, over a decade, the 'self-pluralism scale' evolved more and more toward measuring fluidity (see Appendix A). Similarly, Linville's (1987) early thinking focused on different 'aspects' of a self-concept; and Donahue's (Donahue et al., 1993) thinking concerned different self-concepts in different roles – so that both of these investigators seemed to be implying subpersonality thinking. Rosenberg's (1965, 1979, 1989) and Campbell's (Campbell et al., 1996) thinking seem based on a fluidity model; yet their measures seem similar to, and correlate with, SPS and stability. Morgan and Janoff-Bulman (1994), who derived their views from Linville, are even more clearly talking about dimensionality, and thus a 'fluidity' model. Thus this question has not been fully answered in this chapter and remains a question to be answered by future research. As an investigator who has been working in this area since the 1980s, however, I will hazard the prediction that *both the discontinuous and fluidity models apply – differently to different people.*

There is one sterling study that bears on this issue by suggesting that separateness of subpersonalities may be particularly related to dissociation. Waller et al. (1996) used taxometric statistical analysis of the 'dissociative experiences scale' (DES), the most frequently used measure of dissociation (that significantly correlates with self-pluralism), which is based on an assumption – going back at least as far as Janet – that there is a continuum between 'normal' dissociation and 'pathological' dissociation. Waller et al.'s findings justify a distinction: nonpathological dissociative experiences, represented by most of the DES items, can be validly arrayed along a continuum; but truly pathological dissociative experiences (such as feeling like two different people, hearing voices inside the head, or having no idea how you got somewhere) represent a non-continuous phenomenon, a 'taxon'. With those extreme dissociative experiences one probably has a true dissociative disorder. This is a possible climax to a considerable amount of research (cf. Ross, 1989) that suggests that trauma often leads to pathological use of dissociation which often leads to disordered separateness – that is extreme self-pluralism or polypsychism where the parts do not know (much) about each other; and the extreme of this dissociation is dissociative identity disorder (DID).

2 How, and under what conditions, does pluralism in self-structure change? Roberts and Donahue (1994) pointed out that William James, in addition to introducing pluralism, also said: 'For most of us, by the age of 30, the character has set like plaster and will never soften again (1890/1950: 124)'. But in order to explain how people may develop and maintain multiple, role-specific self-conceptions as well as some degree of self-consistency, Roberts and Donahue have conceptualized that there are different *facets* of personalities. Combining their terminology, which is congruent with the many views of multiplicity of selves that were reviewed earlier in this chapter, with the implications of the previous section of this chapter, I propose that we need to make our conceptualizations notably more complicated: we need to consider *variations (among people and) across time in polyfaceted polypsychism*; or we need to take a multidimensional, multi-faceted view (Showers, 1992) – including changes over time. This would mean vigorously *accepting both polypsychism and monopsychism.* We know very little about how such variations develop and change throughout the life cycle, although we know that behavior and experience can influence self-concept (Donahue et al., 1993; Morgan and Janoff-Bulman, 1994) – and even the structure of the self-concept – for example fragmentation as a result of trauma (Ross, 1989; van der Kolk et al., 1996).

3 What are the relationships between self-concept structure and overt behavior? Such possible relationships have rarely been studied and cannot blithely be assumed. Campbell's (1990) theory (see 'Self-concept clarity' section, above) about why self-concept clarity correlates with self-esteem (because of a cautious behavioral orientation to the environment) is one foray into this area; but so is our failure to find a relationship between self-pluralism and pluralism in behavior in married couples. The best kind of idea may be Markus and Kitayama's (1991) conception that how self-concept structure is related to behavior depends in part on a self-concept *content* variable – independence versus *inter*dependence of construal of self: self-concept and behavior are more likely to be related when the construal of self is (relatively) independent of others than when the construal of self is closely intertwined with construal of others.

4 Can we now afford to investigate the structure of self by itself? It is ironic that, if we take the findings of this chapter seriously, we may need to conclude that structure of the self-concept needs to be studied in conjunction with at least some features of content – for example, the importance or positivity of the content; and/or with some features of behavior (see point number 3 above) and culture (see point number 5 below).

5 How may culture relate to pluralism of self-structure? In my research, I (Altrocchi, 1993) was unable to find reliable differences in self-pluralism between idiocentric and allocentric or rural and urban Nevada high school students; or among Polynesians (for whom self-construal is not considered a key variable and, if considered, would be seen as interdependent) who differed in degree of acculturation to Western ways; nor between these groups and US medical students. However, the term *polyfaceted* fits very well with a study of acculturation among those groups (Altrocchi and Altrocchi, 1995). It is clear that we need more complex conceptualizations, as noted above in reference to Markus and Kitayama (1991).

It is also clear, however, that members of highly individualized Western cultures (Triandis, 1995), devoted to monotheism but also to a God in which several subpersonalities coexist (Miles, 1995), do not want to be called 'multiple' (Beahrs, 1982; Crabtree, 1985); and even that they tend to translate the experience of inconsistency into an illusion of wholeness (Ewing, 1991). This is a major sociocultural 'resistance' to polypsychism that this book will encounter.

6 Relationships between pluralism of self-structure and maladjustment. While we need to consider variations among people and across time in polyfaceted polypsychism, we also need to distinguish clearly between adaptive, usually conscious, flexibility in *behavior* across different situations with different people (a core of many cultural ideals, as in Polynesia) and variability in *self-concept*. Self-concept instability, high self-pluralism, high self-concept differentiation, and low self-concept clarity relate to maladjustment. Such findings may provide an interesting challenge to people who firmly believe that they, and all of us, are predominantly polypsychic, because many polypsychic people – unstable, unclear, pluralistic, differentiated – are evidently thrashing around and not doing very well in the world. Yet some – *à la* Linville – do very well. Therefore, evidently Rogers and Erikson and others were on *a* right track in proposing that the development of identity and integration of *self* (from the presumed multiplicity that we all start with) is *usually* useful adaptively. On the other hand, *to varying degrees* we may all be polyfaceted, polypsychic beings and we are presumably better off knowing about our many varying sides, because knowing means that we have better conscious control (Rowan, 1993).

Conclusion

This chapter covers a very narrow area of the psychology of personality – the structure of the self-concept. All the data presented here are based totally on persons' conscious, shared self-disclosure. This self-disclosure may be very influenced by culture; and our Western culture clearly still idealizes integration and *an* identity. Given these provisos, the data clearly suggest that individuals differ greatly in integration versus diversity of self-perceived self-structure; in pluralism of self-structure; in monopsychism *and* polypsychism.

Finally, let us see how monopsychism and polypsychism might coexist in the kind of person whom we would see as ideally well-adjusted *and* creative in our Western society – the ideal *result* of a full and a meaningful life in our culture, or of successful, growth-oriented psychotherapy. There would indeed be a solidity, a degree of consistency, continuity, and clarity of self and of identity. But there would presumably be considerable complexity too – as well as flexibility of behavior across social roles, and a self-aware knowledge of that flexibility so that one could be adaptive and creative. And that person would presumably have some self-differentiation and self-pluralism – and an openness to a wide variety of (and variability in) self-concepts and behavior in others.

> It is good to have many personae, to make collections, sew up several, collect them as we go along in life. As we become older and older, with such a collection at our behest, we find we can be anything, any day that we wish. (Estes, 1992: 477)

Notes

I am deeply indebted to my research colleague for the last decade, and friend for more than forty years, Professor Emeritus Paul McReynolds; and to former doctoral student Carolanne House, for their many and huge contributions to this research project; and to the research offices of the University of Nevada and the School of Medicine for their timely support for data analyses.

1   For simplicity of presentation here, the correlations using various CPI scores and observer ratings, such as depression, neuroticism, self-control, and ego resiliency are all presented so that positive correlations represent relationships between SCD and *mal*adjustment. None of the correlations were in the opposite direction.

References

Altrocchi, J. (1993) 'Self-pluralism and culture'. Unpublished paper.
Altrocchi, J. and Altrocchi, L. (1995) 'Polyfaceted psychological acculturation in Cook Islanders', *Journal of Cross-Cultural Psychology*, 26: 426–40.
Altrocchi, J. and McReynolds, P. (1997) 'The self-pluralism scale: A measure of psychologic variability', in S.T. St Jeor (ed.), *Obesity Assessment: Tools, Methods, Interpretations. A Reference Case: The Reno Diet–Heart Study*. New York: Chapman and Hall. Chapter 34, pp. 420–4.
Altrocchi, J., McReynolds, P. and House, C. (1990) 'Self-pluralism as a proposed contributing cause of multiple personality disorder'. Poster session at Seventh International Conference on Multiple Personality Disorder and Dissociation. Chicago, November.
Beahrs, J.O. (1982) *Unity and Multiplicity: Multilevel Consciousness of Self in Hypnosis. Psychiatric Disorder and Mental Health*. New York: Bruner/Mazel.
Campbell, J.D. (1990) 'Self-esteem and clarity of the self-concept', *Journal of Personality and Social Psychology*, 59: 538–49.
Campbell, J. (1996) Personal communication.
Campbell, J.D. and Lavelee, L.F. (1993) 'Who am I? The role of self-concept confusion in understanding the behavior of people with low self-esteem', in R.F. Baumeister (ed.), *Self-Esteem: The Puzzle of Low Self-Regard*. New York: Plenum Press. pp. 3–20.
Campbell, J.D., Trapnell, P.D., Keive, S.J., Katz, I.M., Lavelee, L.F. and Lehman, D.R. (1996) 'Self-concept clarity: Measurement, personality correlates, and cultural boundaries', *Journal of Personality and Social Psychology*, 70: 141–56.
Crabtree, A. (1985) *Multiple Man: Explorations in Possession and Multiple Personality*. Toronto: Praeger.
Donahue, E.M., Robins, R.W., Roberts, B.W. and John, O.P. (1993) 'The divided self: Concurrent and longitudinal effects of psychological adjustment and social roles on self-concept differentiation', *Journal of Personality and Social Psychology*, 64: 834–46.
Erikson, E.H. (1968) *Identity: Youth and Crisis*. New York: W.W. Norton.
Estes, C.P. (1992) *Women Who Run with the Wolves: Myths and Stories of the Wild Woman Archetype*. New York: Ballantyne Books.
Ewing, K.P. (1991) 'The illusion of wholeness; Culture, self, and the experience of inconsistency', *Ethos*, 19: 251–78.
Gergen, K.J. (1971) *The Concept of Self*. New York: Holt.
Gergen, K.J. (1991) *The Saturated Self*. New York: Basic Books.
House, C.K. (1991) 'Vicissitude in self-pluralism: A time series study of variation in variation'. PhD dissertation, University of Nevada.
James, W. (1890/1950) *Principles of Psychology*, 2 vols. New York: Henry Holt.
Jordan, A. and Cole, D.A. (1996) 'Relation of depressive symptoms to the structure of self-knowledge in childhood', *Journal of Abnormal Psychology*, 105: 530–40.

Lecky, P. (1945) *Self-consistency: A Theory of Personality.* New York: Island Press.

Linville, P.W. (1985) 'Self-complexity and affective extremity: Don't put all of your eggs in one cognitive basket', *Social Cognition,* 3: 94–120.

Linville, P.W. (1987) 'Self-complexity as a cognitive buffer against stress-related illness and depression', *Journal of Personality and Social Psychology,* 52: 603–76.

Mair, J.M.M. (1977) 'The community of self', in D. Bannister (ed.), *New Perspectives in Personal Construct Theory.* New York: Academic Press. pp. 125–49.

Markus, H. and Wurf, E. (1987) 'The dynamic self-concept: A social psychological perspective', *Annual Review of Psychology,* 38: 299–337.

Markus, H.R. and Kitayama, S. (1991) 'Culture and the self: Implications for cognition, emotion, and motivation', *Psychological Review,* 98: 224–53.

Martindale, C. (1980) 'Subselves: The internal representation of situational and personal dispositions', in L. Wheeler (ed.), *Review of Personality and Social Psychology,* vol. 1. Beverly Hills, CA: Sage. pp. 193–218.

Miles, J. (1995) *God: A Biography.* New York: Knopf.

Morgan, A.J. and Janoff-Bulman, R. (1994) 'Positive and negative self-complexity: Patterns of adjustment following traumatic versus non-traumatic life experiences', *Journal of Social and Clinical Psychology,* 13: 63–85.

Murphy, G. (1947) *Personality: A Biosocial Approach to Origins and Structure.* New York: Harper.

O'Connor, E. (1971) *Our Many Selves: A Handbook for Self-Discovery.* Princeton, NJ: Princeton University Press.

Pelham, B.W. and Swann, W., Jr. (1989) 'From self-conceptions to self-worth: On the sources and structure of global self-esteem', *Journal of Personality and Social Psychology,* 57: 672–80.

Redfearn, J.W.T. (1985) *Myself, My Many Selves.* New York: Academic Press.

Roberts, B.W. and Donahue, E.W. (1994) 'One personality, multiple selves: Integrating personality and social roles', *Journal of Personality,* 62: 199–218.

Rogers, C.R. (1959) 'A theory of therapy, personality, and interpersonal relationships as developed in the client-centered framework', in S. Koch (ed.), *Psychology: A Study of a Science,* vol. 3. New York: McGraw Hill. pp. 184–256.

Rogers, C.R. and Dymond, R.F. (eds) (1954) *Psychotherapy and Personality Change: Coordinated Research Studies in the Client-Centered Approach.* Chicago, IL: University of Chicago Press.

Rosenberg, M. (1965) *Society and the Adolescent Self-Image.* Princeton, NJ: Princeton University Press.

Rosenberg, M. (1979) *Conceiving the Self.* New York: Basic Books. (Reprinted by Robert E. Krieger Publishing, Malabar, Florida, 1986.)

Rosenberg, M. (1989) *Society and the Adolescent Self-Image,* rev. edn. Middletown, CT: Weslyan University Press.

Ross, C.A. (1989) *Multiple Personality Disorder: Diagnosis, Clinical Features, and Treatment.* New York: Wiley.

Rowan, J. (1990) *Subpersonalities: The People Inside Us.* London: Routledge.

Rowan, J. (1993) *Discover Your Subpersonalities: Our Inner World and the People In It.* London: Routledge.

Showers, C. (1992) 'Compartmentalization of positive and negative self-knowledge: Keeping bad apples out of the bunch', *Journal of Personality and Social Psychology,* 62: 1036–49.

Swift, E. (1923) *Psychology and the Day's Work.* New York: Charles Scribner's Sons.

Triandis, H.C. (1995) *Individualism and Collectivism.* Boulder, CO: Westview Press.

van der Kolk, B.A., Weisieth, L. and van der Hart, O. (1996) 'History of trauma in psychiatry', in B.A. van der Kolk, A.C. McFarlane and L. Weisieth (eds), *Traumatic Stress: The Effects of Overwhelming Experience on Mind, Body, and Society*. New York: Guilford.

Waller, N.G., Putnam, F.W. and Carlson, E.B. (1996) 'Types of dissociation and dissociative types: A taxometric analysis of dissociative experiences', *Psychological Methods*, 1: 300–21.

Whitman, W. (1992) *Song of Myself*, Stanza 51. Petrarch Press Edition.

Appendix A   Brief self-pluralism scale

Listed below are a number of statements concerning how you may *see yourself*. Please read each item and decide whether the statement is *True* or *False* for you personally. Circle T for true or F for False.

T   F   1. People who know me well would say I'm pretty predictable.

T   F   2. I act and feel essentially the same way whether at home, at work or with friends.

T   F   3. I'm the same sort of person regardless of whom I'm with.

T   F   4. I get along best when I act and feel like a totally different person at different times.

T   F   5. I am the same kind of person in every way, day in and day out.

T   F   6. People who know me say that my behavior changes from situation to situation.

T   F   7. People who know me well would say I act quite differently at different times.

T   F   8. Though I vary somewhat from time to time, in general I always feel much the same.

T   F   9. There have been times when I felt like a completely different person from what I was the day before.

T   F   10. I sometimes have conflicts over whether to be one kind of person or a different kind.

(High) self-pluralism scores are derived from T answers to 1, 2, 3, 5, 8 and F answers to 4, 6, 7, 9, 10.

10 SUBPERSONALITIES AND MULTIPLE PERSONALITIES: A DISSOCIATIVE CONTINUUM?

Colin A. Ross

Dissociative identity disorder (DID), formerly called multiple personality disorder, is described by the American Psychiatric Association (1994) in its official diagnostic manual, the *Diagnostic and Statistical Manual of Mental Disorders* (4th edn: DSM-IV). Multiple personality disorder first received official status in the third edition of the manual (DSM-III) in 1980, where it was for the first time grouped with other conditions in a separate section called 'Dissociative Disorders'.

DID is defined by the DSM-IV as a condition in which separate identity states take turns being in control of the body. There must also be some form of amnesia. DID can be diagnosed with a high degree of reliability (Ross, 1997; Steinberg, 1995), and has the same clinical symptom profile in Turkey, Norway, the Netherlands, Japan, Puerto Rico, Australia, Canada and the United States (Ross, 1997).

Despite its official recognition as a legitimate psychiatric disorder by the American Psychiatric Association, DID is not universally accepted as a valid diagnosis (Spanos, 1997). The two basic models of the disorder are: a trauma model, according to which the condition arises as a psychological strategy for coping with severe, chronic childhood trauma; and a socio-cognitive model, according to which the condition is an artifact of therapy, and caused by suggestive questioning, subtle cueing, demand characteristics and cultural influences.

The conflict between these two models centers on disagreement as to whether there are actual distinct psychological states in DID or only a variety of elaborated social roles. The onset of the condition is in childhood according to the trauma model, and in adulthood according to the socio-cognitive model.

The purpose of this chapter is to consider the implications of DID for polypsychism. What does it mean to have DID? If DID is a real and legitimate psychiatric disorder, how different are people with the condition from the rest of us? Is there a continuum of dissociation with normal dissociation at one end and DID at the extreme end, or is DID a discrete psychiatric disorder unrelated to normal psychology? Alternatively, is DID really nothing at all, from a psychiatric point of view – nothing more than a piece of misguided, transitory theatre played out by a suggestible patient and an incompetent therapist?

The basic conclusion of this chapter is that DID has little to teach us about polypsychism.

Theoretical foundations

Implications of the trauma and socio-cognitive models for polypsychism

If the trauma model of DID is incorrect, and if the socio-cognitive model provides a complete explanation of the disorder, then there are no discrete psychophysiological states in DID. If this is true, then DID is a form of social role-playing, and is not a legitimate psychiatric disorder. It would then follow that DID has nothing to teach us about polypsychism. DID is not an example of polypsychism, and its rules and social-psychological mechanisms have nothing to teach us about polypsychism. On the other hand, if the trauma model is accurate then DID does involve discrete psychophysiological states, and real dissociation between those states. In this scenario, DID is a pathological form of polypsychism, and potentially has a great deal to teach us about the phenomenology and mechanisms of normal polypsychism.

Because the conflict between the trauma and socio-cognitive models of DID is unresolved, any discussion of DID and polypsychism must be preceded by a review of the relevant conceptual and scientific disagreements between the two models.

Points of agreement between the trauma and socio-cognitive models

The trauma and socio-cognitive models are in agreement on a number of points. DID is the most complex and disabling of the dissociative disorders. Individuals who receive this diagnosis also meet criteria for many different disorders including depression, panic disorder, eating disorders and personality disorders. They often have extensive mental health treatment histories before the diagnosis of DID is made. Over ninety percent of DID patients describe serious childhood trauma in the form of sexual, physical and emotional abuse, and neglect. They often describe childhoods full of family chaos, loss, death, and violence.

No one disputes that individuals in treatment for DID have serious, chronic mental health problems. In large clinical series, seventy-five percent of people with the diagnosis have attempted suicide, and twenty-five to fifty percent have prior diagnoses of schizophrenia. Everyone is agreed that the goal of treatment is for the person not to have DID anymore. Once DID is defined as a psychiatric disorder, that must be the case, because it is never desirable to have a psychiatric disorder.

The clinical controversy centers on disagreement about the best diagnosis and treatment plan for people who meet DSM-IV criteria for DID. The only systematic, prospective treatment outcome data come from the trauma model (Ellason and Ross, 1997), while advocates of the socio-cognitive model have provided no data of any kind to support the efficacy of their vaguely defined treatment model.

Non-exclusivity of the two models

The basic problem in the dispute between the trauma and socio-cognitive models is threefold: (a) the dispute tends to be anecdotal and ideological in nature, rather than scientific; (b) advocates of each model tend to view the two models as mutually exclusive; and (c) no one has proposed a crucial experiment or piece of research that would definitively differentiate the two models, proving one and disproving the other.

In the absence of definitive scientific evidence, the two models are both supported by a variety of types of evidence, but most of the empirical data can be used to support either school of thought. No one from either of the two warring schools of thought has provided a compelling argument as to why the two schools of thought must be mutually exclusive. An alternative viewpoint is that the etiology of DID is a mix of different influences that varies from case to case (Ross, 1997). According to this approach, some cases are predominantly artifacts of therapy, others have arisen in childhood, and others represent a mixture of both forms of causality.

Empirical findings that must be accounted for by both models

One key empirical finding must be taken into account in any explanatory model of DID. Both trauma model proponents (Bliss, 1986) and socio-cognitive theorists (Merskey, 1995) have assumed that DID is a manifestation of high hypnotizability; and it is true that people with DID score high on standard measures of hypnotizability. From the trauma perspective, this has been interpreted to mean that DID is a naturally-arising auto-hypnotic strategy to cope with childhood abuse. From the socio-cognitive perspective, high hypnotizability means high suggestibility, therefore the same data are seen as supporting the artifactual nature of the disorder.

In fact there is no significant correlation between scores on the Dissociative Experiences Scale (DES) (Bernstein and Putnam, 1986) and standardized measures of hypnotizability. The DES is the most widely used and validated measure of dissociation. Whelan and Nash (1996) recently reviewed 11 studies in which correlations between DES scores and hypnotizability scores were in the range of 0.10. Any model which sees DID as a complex form of dissociation must take into account the fact that there is no intrinsic relationship between dissociation and hypnosis in nature. The two are separate constructs. Therefore DID cannot be explained, or explained away, by properties of hypnosis. Spanos (1997) is the only socio-cognitive theorist of DID to understand that hypnosis adds nothing to the socio-cognitive model of DID.

Another fact about DID must be taken into account by both schools of thought. DID is not a symptom of 'hysteria'. Hostile skeptics claim that people with DID have hysterical or histrionic personality structures, and as a result are theatrical, attention-seeking and impressionable. This, according to the skeptics, makes them susceptible to iatrogenic DID. Two studies, one using a structured diagnostic interview and the other a computer-scored interview, have demonstrated that histrionic personality disorder is an un-common comorbid diagnosis in DID, occurring in about 8 percent of cases (Ross, 1997). This is lower than the base rate of 10–15 percent for general adult psychiatric in-patients and outpatients cited in the histrionic person-ality disorder section of DSM-IV.

The only existing systematic data on the issue clearly demonstrate that DID patients are not characteristically histrionic in personality structure.

Empirical findings that do not differentiate the two models

Many pieces of evidence cited by both schools of thought do not in fact weigh in favor of either. For instance, it is an established fact that DID is diagnosed much more frequently inside North America than elsewhere. Socio-cognitive theorists cite this as evidence that DID is a culture-bound artifact, while trauma model advocates hold that clinicians outside North America are ideologically disinclined to make the diagnosis, and do not enquire systematically about it. The simple fact that DID is diagnosed clinically more often in North America does not weigh in favor of either model, however.

The question is, what would be a methodologically sound epidemiological test of the two competing hypotheses about the differential rates of DID diagnosis inside and outside North America? Citing the epidemiological facts as evidence for one model or the other is a conceptual and scientific error.

Essential requirements of the trauma model

What is it that is being alleged to be the case by trauma model advocates? Several stereotypes of the trauma model of DID can be dismissed. The trauma model does not require that the 'personalities' in DID be literally real. There is no need to assume that there is more than one person present. Likewise, the trauma model does not require that all or even the majority of trauma memories must be accurate; nor is it necessary that there be a history of sexual abuse. The trauma model also does not require a simple linear uni-causal relationship between specific traumatic events and the creation of alter personalities.

What are the essential requirements of the trauma model? They are that: (a) dissociation must be a real phenomenon in cognitive psychology. It must be true that mental contents can be actively compartmentalized from each other for strategic-defensive reasons that are not fully conscious. The dissociation must result in one set of mental contents being relatively inaccessible from the perspective of another set. The inaccessibility must be outside the range of normal; and (b) dissociation must occur between memory subsystems, resulting in amnesia.

Within a traumatized individual, all possible permutations and combinations of brain function could be dissociated from each other, including memory, sensation, perception, motor function and identity.

What are the key clinical observations that support the trauma model? The core clinical fact in DID is the amnesia that accompanies switching of alter personalities during face-to-face interviews by the clinician. Alleged amnesia for events in the remote past is also universal in DID, but difficult to test experimentally. The amnesia that occurs intra-session in DID therapy should be the primary target of systematic research. If this kind of dissociation in memory can be demonstrated in rigorous experiments, amnesia for the remote past becomes a plausible claim based on the proven amnesia for more recently acquired information.

The debate about the accuracy of traumatic amnesia for memories of childhood sexual abuse is scientifically barren and premature. The major research energy at this stage of scientific progress should be focused on intra-experimental dissociation in the present, including dissociations between procedural and declarative memory. If this phenomenon cannot be demonstrated, the trauma model of DID is bankrupt.

When a DID patient switches mid-session, the alter personality who has assumed executive control often claims complete amnesia for the preceding conversation. If this amnesia is genuine, it should not be very difficult to demonstrate in the laboratory. There are myriad experimental paradigms in cognitive psychology which could be brought to bear on the memory processes of people with DID (Cohen and Eichenbaum, 1993). It is necessary to demonstrate that information is compartmentalized in a way which cannot be explained by normal forgetting or role-playing.

Crucial tests of the trauma model of dissociative identity disorder

The methodological problem in this kind of research is that subjects can always guess the desired deficit in memory and enact it in response to socio-cognitive pressures exerted by the experimenter. The experiments must, therefore, be designed such that a superior performance can be obtained only with active dissociation. An experiment involving task interference in one form or another would be suitable. Task interference occurs when performance on one task interferes with performance on another task in normal subjects. Interference can occur in learning, recognition, cognitive, motor, perceptual and memorization tasks, or tasks of any kind.

Asked to enhance their performance by using any cognitive strategy they wish, normal subjects should be unable to reduce the task interference to the degree demonstrated by DID subjects. DID subjects could be tested without specific instructions, and also with the two tasks deliberately assigned to separate alter personalities. In one experiment, the alter personalities would be co-conscious, while in other experiments they would be separated by one-way and two-way amnesia barriers. In these experiments an even greater reduction in interference would be expected.

The prediction of the trauma model is that DID subjects can eliminate or markedly reduce task interference far more efficiently than normal subjects. The performance of DID subjects can be further enhanced by specific instructions that assign the tasks to alter personalities.

The second major core phenomenon in DID, after the cognitive dissociation, is the auditory hallucinations. DID patients hear the voices of alter personalities talking out loud to them inside their heads. These voices are experienced as fully ego-alien, as not-self. What would have to be true for these voices to be 'real'? They are obviously not real in the sense of being the voices of separate people.

Here, brain scanning technology should provide a definitive experimental test. The results hinge on the sensitivity of the available technology: if DID is real, then the voices must show up on a functional brain scan of sufficient sensitivity. There must be hyper-function of certain areas of the brain that cannot be duplicated by role-playing controls. The hyper-function must make anatomical sense. It must be turned on and off when cooperative alter personalities agree to talk out loud or be quiet inside the head during the scanning.

Integrated DID subjects should be unable to produce the phenomenon on brain scan and should be indistinguishable from role-playing controls.

If these two lines of experimental evidence were obtained, the core assumptions of the trauma model would have been proven. However, it is possible that purely iatrogenic cases of DID could exhibit the same experimental performances as childhood-onset cases. If this were so, we would have profound evidence for the functional plasticity of the brain, and its ability to create its own internal reality in response to environmental cueing. It would then be clear that DID is 'real' in a real sense, though it is not literally real. Demonstrating the voices of alter personalities on brain scan would not prove that they are separate people. It would, however, disprove the socio-cognitive theory that there is no discrete psychophysiological phenomenon involved.

Existing evidence for dissociations in long-term memory

Advocates of the socio-cognitive model of DID claim that there is no scientific evidence for dissociation. This is not true. In fact, dissociations in long-term memory are one of the most rigorously demonstrated phenomena in cognitive psychology (Cohen and Eichenbaum, 1993). This body of evidence provides a powerful scientific foundation for both traumatic amnesia and polypsychism.

Hundreds of animal experiments involving different species, different sensory modalities, and many different types of experimental tasks, demonstrate conclusively that memory is not a single system. Memory, at a minimum, is composed of two distinct subsystems: declarative and procedural memory. Roughly speaking, declarative corresponds to explicit or conscious memory, and procedural to implicit or unconscious memory.

Declarative memory is rich, flexible and adaptive, while procedural memory is comparatively rigid, rote and inflexible. Procedural memory can persist when the hippocampus is destroyed experimentally, or by disease, surgery or accident and while declarative memory is eliminated. It has to be true that long-term memory is composed of subsystems, otherwise there could be no dissociations in long-term memory, no traumatic amnesia and no DID.

A classical example of intact procedural memory in the complete absence of declarative memory is surgical subject H.M., who had both his hippocampi removed surgically as a treatment for epilepsy. You could meet H.M. fifty times and on the fifty-first meeting you would be a complete stranger to him. H.M. had no conscious long-term memory and forgot everything as soon as it happened. Despite his ongoing amnesia, H.M.'s performance on a complex puzzle improved with practice at the same rate as that of normal college students. He had no memory of ever having seen the puzzle but his procedural memory was learning and directing his behavioral output in a measurable fashion.

A large experimental literature on normal college students demonstrates conclusively that procedural memory can affect verbal and behavioral output in the absence of declarative memory of the information stored in procedural memory (Cohen and Eichenbaum, 1993). A typical example is a *repetition priming* experiment.

In one form of repetition priming, one group of college students is given a list of homophonic word pairs to memorize, such as *reed-read* and *bare-bear*. Later, the students are asked to write down all the word-pairs from the list they remember, and they cannot recall the *reed-read* pair. Next the students are asked to write down the answer to a question which invokes *reed* as the answer, for example: what is a thin, rigid upright plant that grows in marshes? The students misspell *reed* as *read* more often than another group of students who also memorized a list of homophonic word pairs – one that did not include *reed-read*. The repetition priming effect proves that real memories for which one is amnesic can directly affect verbal and behavioral output.

This conclusive body of science proves that the core postulate of the trauma model of DID is a fact of normal human psychology. The research challenge now is to demonstrate that this proven phenomenon exists to a greater degree in DID.

The evidence that memory is composed of subsystems or modules is conclusive. It is a scientific fact that memory modules can be dissociated from each other; specifically, procedural and declarative memory functions can be dissociated. Modularity of mental function is a necessary postulate of polypsychism. Personification or anthropomorphization of dissociated modules is a secondary phenomenon, for both the trauma model of DID and theories of normal polypsychism.

Is dissociative identity disorder an extension of normal or a discrete condition?

If DID is a discrete psychiatric disorder, then by definition it is different from normal. The question then becomes, is DID an extension of normal or is it qualitatively different? What are the implications of each of these two options for polypsychism?

Elsewhere in psychiatry, for other disorders, both the extension-of-normal and qualitatively-distinct perspectives coexist in an unresolved ambiguity. For instance, it is easy to differentiate a teetotaler from an alcoholic who drinks twenty-six ounces of vodka a day. But where does alcoholism begin: after three beers a day, six a day, or ten a day? After one drunken binge a year, one a month, or one a week? Similarly for anxiety and depression, extreme cases are easy to differentiate from normal, but for intermediate cases, the decision about whether to make a psychiatric diagnosis has low reliability. It is absurd to say that one person who scores 19 on an anxiety scale has no psychiatric disorder, while another who scores 20 has a discrete condition. There is no cutoff point at which the distinction loses its absurdity.

The solution to this problem in psychiatry is a version of the wave-particle duality. Certain data fit with the extension-of-normal model, others with the discrete disease state model; neither model accounts for all of the data. Ideological wars between adherents of the two schools of thought about DID continue unabated, however. This is because psychiatry is still dominated by Newtonian logic.

The logic of the wave-particle duality should apply to the relationship between DID and normal dissociation. DID should be both an extension of normal dissociation and a discrete psychiatric disorder. What do the data tell us?

Empirical research

Data from the Dissociative Experiences Scale

A recent review article indicates that the Dissociative Experiences Scale (DES) has been used in over one hundred published research studies involving over eleven thousand subjects (van Ijzendoorn and Schungel, 1996). It is by far the most robust measure of dissociation. DES data from many different languages have been published or presented at conferences (Ross, 1997). The distribution of DES scores in the general population is the same around the world.

The range of possible DES scores is zero to one hundred. The distribution of DES scores in the general population is highly left-skewed, however, with most people scoring in the low teens or lower; a typical general population mean score on the DES is 10.8, with a standard deviation of 10.2 (median score 7.0) (Ross, 1997). By contrast, most series of DID subjects yield mean DES scores in the forties or fifties, which places them in the top tail of the distribution.

The fact that there is no sharp DES cutoff score for DID, combined with the fact that individuals in large samples exhibit all possible DES scores from zero to the mean for DID, supports the continuum model.

However, the picture changes when more sophisticated statistical methods are used. Waller et al. (1996) and Waller and Ross (1997) have demonstrated that when taxometric analytical procedures are applied, 8 DES items out of the total of 28 provide a clear measure of pathological dissociation. Using a statistical procedure called MAXCOV-HITMAX, individuals are either normal or exhibit pathological dissociation – there are few or no intermediate cases.

The appearance of a continuum of increasingly pathological dissociation is an artifact of the inclusion of many non-pathological items in the DES. Subjects with DID report more of these non-pathological experiences than subjects without dissociative disorders. However, it is also true that many people without dissociative disorders experience many of these non-pathological forms of dissociation, such as missing part of a conversation. Pathological dissociative experiences, on the other hand, follow a different pattern and are either present or absent.

The DES items that identify pathological dissociation (called the DES-T) are items 3, 5, 7, 8, 12, 13, 22 and 27 (see Appendix). These DES-T items are obviously abnormal experiences such as not recognizing friends or family members, and finding oneself in a new location and not knowing how one got there.

The best evidence available to date indicates that pathological dissociation including DID is not a variant of normal. Therefore, one might assume that DID has no direct implications for normal polypsychism. Advocates of polypsychism do not consider discrete blocks of missing time lasting for hours or days to be normal. It is hard to see how extremely hostile, accusatory voices commanding self-mutilation could be consequences of normal psychological structure, or normal polypsychism.

There is no literature involving co-administration of measures of pathological dissociation and normal polypsychism. The two constructs could be as independent as dissociation and hypnotizability. Because of the lack of data, everything to be said on the relationship between DID and polypsychism is speculative.

Non-pathologcial elements of dissociative identity disorder

What is pathological about DID and what is not? Based on the DES-T data, other research data (Ross, 1997) and clinical experience, it seems that dysfunction, conflict and highly abnormal experiences such as missing large blocks of time are clearly pathological and characteristic of DID. People with DID do not need treatment simply because they have different identities inside themselves. They require psychiatric care because of symptoms such as self-mutilation, command hallucinations to commit suicide, substance abuse, depression and anxiety.

Patients in treatment for DID are in treatment for a broad range of psycho-pathology and many different comorbid diagnoses, not just for the DID. In theory, one could have many different 'people' inside while experiencing no psychiatric symptoms at all.

It is not the existence of discrete sub-identities as such which causes the problems in DID patients. It is the conflict between the identities, their lack of social skills, their delusions of having separate bodies, and their inability to carry out organized executive planning which require treatment. Clini-cally, DID subjects pass through a phase of more functional, less conflicted multiplicity in the late pre-integration phase of therapy. During this period they still have distinct alter personalities, but have far fewer symptoms, are functioning much better socially, and are consuming far fewer mental health services. Yet they still have DID.

Another paradox is the fact that the DSM-IV criteria for DID, which supposedly define it as a discrete psychiatric disorder, actually emphasize the non-pathological elements of the disorder. These are also the elements that are best accounted for by the socio-cognitive model.

What does clinical experience and reflection tell us about the non-pathological aspects of DID? It is these non-pathological elements that are potentially relevant for understanding normal polypsychism.

Clinical applications

Most psychiatric disorders have subclinical variants. Subclinical cases of depression are the same as major depressive episodes, but less so. One has fewer of the same symptoms from the same symptom list and the individual symptoms are milder, but subclinical depression is the same thing as a full depression, only to a lesser degree. It is also true that a profoundly depressed person has a major problem that puts him or her in a separate category from other people, or from him or herself at different points in time.

Similarly, from one perspective, a person either has or does not have DID. One is either integrated or not. DID is like pregnancy; you cannot have a little of it, according to the DES-T data. On the other hand, DID has milder variants diagnosed as dissociative disorder not otherwise specified (DDNOS) by DSM-IV rules. It appears, by combining DSM-IV rules and the DES-T data, that pathological dissociation is discretely different from normal dissociation. However, within the category of pathological dissociation there is a continuum of severity, with DID being more extreme than DDNOS.

One can have a little bit of DID by DSM-IV rules and receive a diagnosis of DDNOS. Persons with DDNOS will still have positive DES-T scores, however.

Dissociative identity disorder is not directly related to polypsychism

Clinically, the integrated DID patient seems neither more nor less poly-psychic than the average person in our culture. It seems that becoming non-DID is an essential aspect of recovery. The successfully treated DID case involves a remarkable reduction in psychiatric symptoms from many areas of DSM-IV. The fact that one no longer has DID says nothing about one's degree of normal polypsychism, however.

I believe that polypsychism is the normal state of the human mind. However, I believe it is undesirable to have DID. Why? Clinical work with DID patients has convinced me that everyone has DID in one sense, although most people do not have DID. This logic repeats the logic of the wave-particle duality. Everyone has DID in the sense that highly affectively charged ego states do not function or look like single selves to me, in people with no psychiatric disorders. When someone is very angry, or very depressed, he or she does not look, think, move, or talk the same as when in a different extreme mood state.

Working with DID patients has taught me to look at the world through the lens of DID. The highly affectively charged ego states of normal people look as distinct and separate as alter personalities to me. It is part of the pathology of our culture that the average person is not integrated. The ego states of 'normal' people in our culture are not truly integrated into a cohesive yet fluid self. Everyone in our culture could benefit from a DID-like therapy, such as the ego state or subpersonality work described elsewhere in this volume. One might call this usual mode of psychological organization in our culture abnormal polypsychism. It is statistically normal to be pathologically unintegrated in our culture.

What is the difference, then, between abnormal polypsychism and DID? The difference is in the degree of personification of the ego states, the delusion of literal separateness of the personality states, the conflict, and the degree of information blockage in the system. When an ordinarily mild-mannered person bursts into a rage, it is like another person has taken over the body. The thought patterns, body language, gestures, energy level, and animation of the person all change drastically. But this is not DID. The enraged ego state does not have a different name or age, does not fail to recognize friends and family, does not believe it lives in a separate body from the usual mild-mannered self, and does not think it is 1972. DID alter personalities are not uncommonly locked in the traumatic past and literally believe that the current year is 1972, 1981 or some other year from the past. None of these phenomena occur in abnormal polypsychism.

Because of the intensive therapy lasting on average three to five years required for the integration of DID, the integrated DID patient often exhibits less abnormal polypsychism than the average person in our culture. It is as if the DID therapy has included a great deal of ego state therapy for abnormal polypsychism. The integrated DID patient is often healthier than the average person in our culture.

It would appear that there are three categories: pathological dissociation (DID and DDNOS); abnormal polypsychism (the statistical norm in our culture); and normal polypsychism (a degree of healthy, fluid integration of sub-selves which is statistically unusual in Western cultures).

Pathological pseudounity and normal multiplicity

The solution to the conundrum of DID as extension of normal versus DID as discrete condition is to reconfigure the continuum of dissociation. Rather than to posit a continuum of dissociation with normal dissociation at one end and DID at the other, I propose the following. What we call normal in our culture is actually pathological pseudounity (= abnormal polypsychism). The left-hand end of the reconfigured continuum is normal multiplicity (= normal polypsychism), the middle is pathological pseudounity, and the right-hand end is DID, which we might call psychiatric polypsychism.

According to this model, our general cultural problem could be stated in two opposite ways: we are either too polypsychic or not polypsychic enough. On the one hand, we suffer from a lack of fluidity in the psyche, and we abnormally suppress many potentialities of our psyches. We do not exhibit normal multiplicity. On the other hand, we are too rigidly divided internally, with one self usurping executive control and calling itself the only self. We exhibit pathological pseudounity.

From one perspective, DID is an extreme variant of normal psychic organization in our culture. This is so not because it is normal to have DID, but because it is statistically normal to exhibit abnormal polypsychism in our culture. From another perspective, DID is a discretely different condition from normal. This is so because DID is very different from normal multiplicity.

The paradox and the confusion arise from the fact that DID is both like and unlike abnormal polypsychism. Looked at from the vantage point of normal multiplicity, the differences between DID and the usual psychic organization in our culture seem to be only a matter of degree. However, looked at from the vantage point of abnormal polypsychism, DID is a

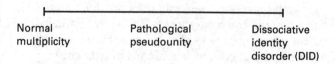

FIGURE 10.1 *The reconfigured dissociative continuum*

discretely different psychiatric disorder. Any account of the relevance of DID to polypsychism must take both these perspectives into account.

According to my vision, many of the most valuable and spiritual elements of the psyche are suppressed developmentally in our culture. One can see the childlike wonder, spontaneity, and beauty of the human soul in children. These qualities of the human spirit are ground under by the time of mid-adolescence in our culture. A fabricated self takes over which is spiritually empty, rootless and has no love of learning. This is the spiritual disease of our culture; it is not a medical problem.

What are the clinical implications of this way of looking at things? DID is a psychiatric disorder, while pathological pseudounity is a cultural sickness. The integrated DID patient is better off having no DID, even though he or she may now exhibit pathological pseudounity. But that is not a fully satisfactory outcome. We need a psychotherapy that can take us from pathological pseudounity to normal multiplicity. As it is, the successfully treated DID patient may be average but still unhealthy. Given that average means spiritually empty, uprooted and unfulfilled in our culture, this is hardly a spiritual victory.

The reason that the integrated DID patient has a good chance of being more healthy than average in our culture is because of the ego-state therapy for abnormal polypsychism that is built into the treatment of the DID.

Polypsychism occurs all along the reconfigured continuum

The human psyche is modular and polypsychic at both ends and the middle of the reconfigured continuum. DID is, therefore, not relevant to any debate about polypsychism. Adherents of the socio-cognitive school of thought do not regard DID as evidence for polypsychism because they do not believe in any form or degree of polypsychism. Therefore proponents of polypsychism can never answer their critics by referring to DID.

There appear to be two schools of thought within the polypsychism movement. One school is dedicated to establishing the modularity of the mind in terms of the cognitive unconscious, parallel processing, memory subsystems and the like. This school and any therapies derived from it could find a comfortable home in academic psychology, once enough data are accumulated and the usual paradigm shift resistances overcome.

The second school of thought, I believe, lies at the heart of the poly-psychism movement. It is more spiritual in nature and is more focused on correcting the general psychopathology of our culture. Our part selves are under the totalitarian rule of a disconnected, atheistic, pseudo-masculine, chauvinist, logic-chopping self: one which cannot appreciate the subtle, fluid logic of the soul and living things, and which can only repress the human spirit, or the spirit in the biosphere.

A measure of truly fluid normal multiplicity would be highly desirable, but it could not become a commonly used measure in experimental psycho-logy without a major paradigm shift in the culture as a whole. The resistance to polypsychism is a covert and unwitting resistance to the spiritual sub-school of polypsychism, I think. Spiritual language is not allowed in academia. The tactical solution to this source of resistance is to emphasize the more mechanistic, modular, researchable aspects of polypsychism. Polypsychic schools of therapy could thereby become grounded in cognitive psychology and gain acceptance.

The theory of polypsychism has clinical implications described in other chapters in this volume. The main points of this chapter are: (a) DID will not convince extreme skeptics of the reality of polypsychism; (b) it is the conflict and dysfunction that are abnormal in DID, not the polypsychism as such; and (c) for polypsychism to be real, it must underlie all points on the reconfigured continuum.

Conclusion

It appears that DID has little to teach us about polypsychism. This is true because the integrated DID patient does not appear to exhibit more or less polypsychism than the average person in our culture. DID is clearly not normal, but polypsychism exists at all points on the reconfigured dissociative continuum (or does not exist anywhere from a socio-cognitive perspective). The integrated DID patient is both too polypsychic and not polypsychic enough, according to the paradoxical wave-particle logic that forms the foundation of this chapter.

References

American Psychiatric Association (1980) *Diagnostic and Statistical Manual of Mental Disorders*. (3rd edn) Washington, DC: American Psychiatric Association.

American Psychiatric Association (1994) *Diagnostic and Statistical Manual of Mental Disorders*. (4th edn) Washington, DC: American Psychiatric Association.

Bernstein, E.M. and Putnam, F.W. (1986) 'Development, reliability and validity of a dissociation scale', *Journal of Nervous and Mental Disease*, 174: 727–35.

Bliss, E.L. (1986) *Multiple Personality, Allied Disorders, and Hypnosis*. New York: Oxford University Press.

Cohen N.J. and Eichenbaum, H. (1993) *Memory, Amnesia and the Hippocampal System*. Cambridge, MA: MIT Press.

Ellason, J. and Ross, C.A. (1997) 'Two-year follow-up of inpatients with dissociative identity disorder', *American Journal of Psychiatry*, 154: 832–9.

Merskey, H. (1995) 'The manufacture of personalities: the production of multiple personality disorder', in L. Cohen, J. Berzoff and M. Elin (eds), *Dissociative Identity Disorder. Theoretical and Treatment Controversies*. Northvale, NJ: Jason Aronson. pp. 3–32.

Ross, C.A. (1997) *Dissociative Identity Disorder. Diagnosis, Clinical Features and Treatment of Multiple Personality*. (2nd edn) New York: John Wiley.

Spanos, N. (1997) *Multiple Identities and False Memories. A Sociocognitive Perspective*. Washington, DC: American Psychological Association.

Steinberg, M. (1995) *Handbook for the Assessment of Dissociation. A Clinical Guide*. Washington, DC: American Psychiatric Press.

Van Ijzendoorn, M.H. and Schungel, C. (1996) 'The measurement of dissociation in normal and clinical populations: Meta-analytic validation of the Dissociative Experiences Scale (DES)', *Clinical Psychology Review*, 16: 365–83.

Waller, N.G. and Ross, C.A. (1997) 'The prevalence and biometric structure of pathological dissociation in the general population: Taxometric and behavior genetic findings', *Journal of Abnormal Psychology*, 106: 499–510.

Waller, N.G., Putnam, F.W. and Carlson E.B. (1996) 'Types of dissociation and dissociative types: As taxometric analysis of dissociative experiences', *Psychological Methods*, 1: 300–21.

Whelan, J.E. and Nash, M.R. (1996) 'Hypnosis and dissociation: theoretical, empirical, and clinical perspectives', in L.K. Michelson and W.J. Ray (eds), *Handbook of Dissociation. Theoretical, Clinical and Empirical Perspectives*. New York: Plenum. pp. 191–206.

Appendix

Dissociative Experiences Scale items that comprise the DES-T are:

3   Some people have the experience of finding themselves in a place and having no idea how they got there.

5   Some people have the experience of finding new things among their belongings that they do not remember buying.

7   Some people sometimes have the experience of feeling as though they are standing next to themselves or watching themselves do something and they actually see themselves as if they were looking at another person.

8   Some people are told that they sometimes do not recognize friends or family members.

12   Some people have the experience of feeling that other people, objects, and the world around them are not real.

13   Some people have the experience of feeling that their body does not seem to belong to them.

22   Some people find that in one situation they may act so differently compared with another situation that they almost feel as if they are two different people.

27   Some people sometimes find that they hear voices inside their head that tell them to do things or comment on things they are doing.

PART III

PRACTICE

---

11   FACILITATING THE EXPRESSION OF SUBPERSONALITIES: A REVIEW AND ANALYSIS OF TECHNIQUES

Mick Cooper and Helen Cruthers

'I feel like I'm living in a war zone', said Lynda[1], during her first session in psychotherapy. 'I'm exhausted,' she continued, 'I can't seem to sit still. I desperately want to rest, but every time I stop I feel terrible and I start shaking so I carry on. Part of me wants to just lie down and cry and cry but then this voice says, "Don't stop, you've got to keep on going . . . don't stop, don't stop, don't stop." ' Lynda is a 45-year-old woman who had been physically, sexually and emotionally abused as a child. She referred herself to therapy with Helen Cruthers because she was experiencing many memories from her childhood, and wanted help with the strong feelings these aroused: disgust, shame, hurt, terror and fury. From the outset, however, it was clear that there was also a powerful struggle going on inside her, and helping her to find ways to express and explore the different sides in this struggle became a major part of the therapeutic work.

In recent years, the notion that an individual encounters their world through a plurality of selves has become increasingly prevalent in psycho-therapeutic theory and practice. These selves have been known by a variety of terms – for example, 'subpersonalities' (Rowan, 1990), 'subselves' (Shapiro, 1976), 'ego-states' (Berne, 1961), 'roles' (Landy, 1993), 'inner children/parents/demons' (Stone and Winkelman, 1989)[2] – and can be generally defined as semi-permanent and semi-autonomous person-like constellations of behavioural, phenomenological, motivational, cognitive, physiological and affective characteristics.

Within all self-pluralistic psychotherapies, open and fluid communication between these different selves – or between the selves and a 'centre'

(Assagioli, 1975) – is considered essential for psychological well-being. As with interpersonal dialogue, if the different aspects of the person can 'talk' to each other and acknowledge and respect each other's needs, then the individual is likely to have an existence which is relatively free of ongoing 'internal' conflict, and in which all the different subpersonalities can work together to ensure that the individual encounters each life-situation in the most effective and actualizing (Rogers, 1961) way. If, on the other hand, the intra-personal dynamic is characterized by discord between the various 'parts' – as seemed to be the case with Lynda – then the individual's existence is likely to be characterized by considerable 'internal' strife, with each of the different parts fighting for supremacy, and with little time or attention paid to what might be most effective and actualizing in encountering the external world. A central component of self-pluralistic psychotherapies, therefore, is to encourage greater dialogue and understanding between the subpersonalities; and for this to happen, the individual must first find a way of expressing the many different sides of themselves – particularly those sides that may be disowned or neglected – in order that these aspects of the person can start to recognize and acknowledge each other, and begin to work together.

Over the years, a number of different techniques have been developed through which this expression of subpersonalities can be facilitated, and this chapter presents a review and analysis of many of these different approaches. In doing so, it classifies these techniques into three broad categories: descriptive, projective and experiential. Some overlap exists between these techniques and few practitioners work with techniques from only one category – even in the same session – yet there is a degree of commonality within each of these categories that makes this discrimination a useful one. The chapter explores each of these categories in turn, describing the techniques and illustrating them with examples and case-studies. The final section then looks at the underlying psychological processes, and compares and contrasts the different techniques.

Descriptive techniques

Descriptive techniques are those approaches in which an individual is encouraged to express her subpersonalities directly through verbal or written description. A descriptive technique may simply involve suggesting to an individual that they may have a number of 'selves', and then asking them to describe these different subpersonalities. Rowan, for instance, suggests: 'Write a list of all your subpersonalities, those you are aware of at a conscious level right now. Give each a name, and write about five lines describing that one' (1993: 12). This can be also done as a table, with rows for the different subpersonalities, and columns for characteristics of the subpersonalities such as: name, appearance, when evoked, need, purpose, and so on. Alternatively, an individual might be asked to view their life as a book, and to write out or imagine their life story (McAdams, 1985). This self-narrative can then be reviewed in terms of the different aspects of self that emerge.

A more time-limited approach is the 'evening review', in which an individual is invited to review the different people they have been throughout a particular day (Ferrucci, 1982). In an early session, Lynda 'reviewed' one day in which she had been constantly rushing around completing tasks, thinking a lot but not particularly aware of any feelings. She named this part of her the 'Busy Coper'. In talking further, Lynda became aware that she felt most comfortable in this mode, and that the busyness seemed to keep more painful and threatening feelings at bay. Her Busy Coper was expressed in therapy by such phrases as, 'You've just got to get on with things haven't you', and by the fast pace and lack of pauses in her speech. On the day under review, however, she noted that she had shifted out of Busy Coper mode while talking to her mother on the phone. During the conversation, she had suddenly become flooded by feelings of hurt, fear and resentment, and had ended up sitting in the corner of the lounge crying and sucking her thumb. Lynda called this her 'Little Lynda' subpersonality. Lynda noted that a third mode of Being had emerged some time after the phone call, when she had been pacing angrily around the flat, cursing her mother and feeling furious. She called this her 'Mrs Angry' subpersonality.

Another widely used descriptive approach to exploring subpersonalities is the 'Who am I?' technique (Rowan, 1993; Shapiro, 1976). Here, the individual is asked to write down on separate pieces of paper as many answers to the question 'Who am I?' as they can: roles, personal qualities, physical characteristics, names and nicknames, etc. The individual can then look through the pieces of paper and try to pile together those answers that 'go together', hence compiling a smaller number of superordinate identities.

Within most self-pluralistic psychotherapies, however, the way in which an individual is encouraged to describe their different selves is relatively unformalized, and develops out of the dialogic interchange between client and therapist. This interactive exploration of an individual's subpersonalities is sometimes termed 'psychic mapping' (Assagioli, 1975; Stone and Winkelman, 1989; Watkins and Watkins, 1979); and in some cases, diagrammatic 'maps' of the client's different selves and their interrelationships may actually be drawn or symbolized (Ryle, 1990; Shapiro, 1976; Stewart and Joines, 1987; Stone and Winkelman, 1989). In those psychotherapies where the practitioner has specific hypotheses regarding the client's different selves – for example, transactional analysis (Berne, 1961) – a descriptive exploration of the client's subpersonalities may also be facilitated through the use of pre-defined diagnostic criteria, such as ego-state-related behaviours (for example, words, tones, gestures, postures and facial expressions) and ego-state-related phenomenological experiences. If, for instance, a client says that he often feels playful, mischievous and young around his girlfriend, it might be suggested that at those times he is expressing his 'free child'.

Projective techniques

Projective techniques are based on the principle of projection: 'the process by which specific impulses, wishes, aspects of the self or internal objects are imagined to be located in some object external to oneself' (Rycroft, 1995: 139). In these techniques, the individual is not asked directly to describe his or her different selves, but is invited to express them indirectly through a variety of non-self mediums.

Perhaps the most frequently used projective mediums for facilitating the expression of subpersonalities is that of imaginal figures. This approach is known as 'creative visualization', 'guided visualization', 'guided imagination', 'active imagination', or 'guided daydreams'. Ferrucci's (1982) guided visualization is typical, and begins by asking individuals to consider one of their prominent traits, attitudes or motives. They are then asked to close their eyes, become aware of this part of them, and then let a representative image spontaneously emerge. Getting in touch with the general feeling emanating from this image, they are then encouraged to let the image talk and express itself, before writing down the characteristics of the subpersonality-image and giving it a name. A similar visualization might begin by asking the individual to consider an animal, someone who is significant to them, a figure coming out of a cave, or a particular subpersonality (for example, their nurturing parent) (Rowan, 1993). Alternatively, they may be asked to imagine their subpersonalities coming through a door (Cullen and Russell, 1989; Shapiro, 1976; Vargiu, 1974), stepping off a bus (Rowan, 1990), performing on, or coming on to, a stage (Rueffler, 1995; Satir, 1978), or meeting as a board of directors/committee (Rowan, 1993; Sliker, 1992).

Once these subpersonality-figures have emerged, the visualization process can then be continued to explore the relationships between the various subpersonalities: what happens once all the subpersonalities emerge?; how will they get on?; which subpersonality will dominate?; and so on. One of Shapiro's clients, for instance, describes what he visualized after his 'whole gang' of subpersonalities came through a door:

> Somehow Father Time seemed annoyed that the others were passing him by, and he began to yell at them. They all kind of made fun of Father Time and formed a ring around him and danced around him, teasing him. Then I think Father Time got into an arm-wrestling contest with the Clown and I could see both of them were enjoying it. I was aware that Father Time was much stronger than he looked. I could only tell by that fierce energy that showed in his eyes that he was anything but fragile. (1976: 76–7)

The client can also be encouraged to ask the subpersonalities different questions, and then to imagine the figures responding. John Rowan lists a number of questions which he believes are of most value in making the subpersonalities concrete and explicit:

> What do you look like?
> How old are you?

What situations bring you out?
What it your approach to the world?
What is your basic motive for being there?
What do you want?
What do you need?
What have you got to offer?
What are your blocks to full functioning?
Where did you come from?
When did you first meet (name of person)? What was going on?
What would happen if you took over permanently?
What helps you to grow?
How do you relate to men/women/children? (1990: 198)

Guided visualizations are frequently used as a first step in exploring an individual's subpersonalities, and they may also be used as an ongoing part of the therapeutic process – as a means, for instance, of further investigating one particular subpersonality. Ferrucci (1982) gives the example of a young doctor, Robert, who felt he was blocked by an inner rigidity which interfered with his relationships and hampered his potential. Robert identified this rigidity as part of a 'critic' subpersonality, which consistently judged and attacked whatever he or anyone else did or said.

> When he deliberately evokes this quality and tries to let an image emerge, Robert sees a bespectacled, old-fashioned priest, grim, stern, and dressed entirely in black. As soon as he can see the image clearly, he also discerns the outlines of the rigidity which has been controlling him. While before he would feel this as a vague discomfort and merely endure it, now for the first time he is able to shake it off. (Ferrucci, 1982: 49)

With Lynda, subpersonality visualizations often began with her current awareness of emotional and physical sensations. In one session, Lynda said she was feeling very alone, and that her body felt rigid. Lynda was asked whether she had an image for how she was feeling, and she visualized a tiny, frightened child, crouched in the corner of an attic of a derelict old house, her body rigid with fear – 'Little Lynda'. Lynda said that Little Lynda desperately wanted to leave the horrible place, but was too frightened to move an inch as the floorboards were rotting away. When asked, 'What does Little Lynda need right now?', Lynda visualized for her frightened little child some toys she could play with and a teddy bear to hug. Through imaging this subpersonality, Lynda started to feel compassion for this hurt and terrified part of herself; and, in doing so, realized that there was also a part of her with the potential to nurture and care for this 'inner child'. She named this mode of her Being, 'Big Lynda'.

Art media are another common means used to facilitate the projective expression of subpersonalities (see, for example, Capacchione, 1991; Shapiro, 1976; Turner, 1988). As Zinker writes: 'painting is a projection of myself, a part of my inner life superimposed on a surface' (1977: 239). Having recognized and named some of her different subpersonalities, Lynda was asked to draw them using only shapes and colours in order to learn as much as possible about these aspects of herself – their feelings, their qualities, their needs, and their interrelationships. Lynda grabbed bottles of red and black paint and squirted them vigorously onto a sheet of paper announcing, 'This is Mrs Angry'. As Lynda surveyed the 'explosion' of painted feeling, she became most aware of how much the paint spilled over the edges of the paper. She related this to her belief that this part of herself knew no limits, and that if she did not keep 'Mrs Angry' on a tight leash then terrible things could happen: like killing one of her parents or going mad. After expressing Mrs Angry, Lynda then became aware of feeling small and vulnerable and moved on to drawing Little Lynda as a blue and black circle in the corner of a page. Immediately she turned the page over, drawing her Busy Coper on the other side – filling the page with orange lines and boxes. When this immediate turning of the page was reflected back to her, she felt that maybe this was something that often happens: that when she feels some of the blue tears and black hurt of her inner child being expressed she quickly shifts into being busy and sensible – effectively pushing these feelings away. She also became aware, however, that the feelings of smallness and vulnerability are not eradicated by this manoeuvre. Rather, they are left constantly waiting, just on the other side of the page, nagging away at her and affecting her ability to concentrate.

Artistic methods of facilitating the expression of subpersonalities can be tailored to particular models of self-plurality. Capacchione, for instance, encourages readers to draw pictures of specific subpersonalities such as their 'vulnerable child' and 'protective parent' using a variety of coloured pens and crayons (1991: 44).[3] Turner's (1988) 'Parent-Adult-Child Projective Drawing Task' (PAC-D) also uses figure drawing as a means of eliciting specific ego states. Clients are given the instructions to draw three figures: one who looks like a parent, one who looks like an adult, and one who looks like a child. 'The essential assumption of the PAC-D is that clients will project into the drawings of each figure the individual character of their own three primary ego states' (Turner, 1988: 61). Rueffler (1995), on the other hand, who comes from a psychosynthesis background, proposes a drawing exercise which incorporates the Assagiolian (1975) notion of an observing, non-subpersonality-like 'centre'. She invites her readers to draw a daisy-like flower with six petals surrounding a middle circle. Readers are then asked to think of six subpersonalities, to draw one into each of the six petals, and then to visualize themselves at the centre, observing and experiencing each of the six surrounding subpersonality-petals.

One particularly effective medium onto which subpersonalities can be projected is that of masks. Because the face plays such an important role in human expression and communication, masks have the potential to symbol-ize extremely powerful and evocative modes of Being. A stern judge's face, for instance, can be used to symbolize an overpowering critical sub-personality; while a terrifying devil mask can be made to symbolize an indi-vidual's 'shadow'. Furthermore, there are a number of interesting parallels between masks and subpersonalities which make them an ideal medium on which to project an individual's different selves. First, like subpersonalities, the mask has the appearance of a person, yet it is not a person – it lacks the multidimensionality of the human face, just as subpersonalities lack the multidimensionality of the human personality. Second, the mask is fixed, and hence parallels the fixidity of the subpersonalities. Like a 'critical parent' subpersonality, for instance, a critical parent mask is scowling whatever the context: it scowls when things go right, it scowls when things go wrong. Third, in those self-pluralistic psychotherapies (for example, psychosynthesis) which advocate the existence of a 'real self' masked by the subpersonalities, then the mask is an excellent representative of that which is worn over the real self (that is, the 'real' face), that which protects the individual, that which can be taken off or swapped around, and that which has the potential to allow the individual to 'be' someone else.

Another projective technique that has been used to facilitate the expression of subpersonalities is that of storytelling (for example, Landy, 1993). This may be augmented through the use of plastic figures, toys or puppets. Twenty-nine-year-old Martin was another of Helen's clients. Asked to choose figures to enact a story, he chose a small pink worm, a muscleman and a good witch. His story went as follows:

> Once upon a time there was a worm who was very unhappy because he felt naked and vulnerable and ugly. He decided to leave home in search of happiness. When he reached the next land he found a muscleman lifting weights. The worm was very impressed by the muscleman's strength and beauty, and wished he could be like that. Suddenly the witch appeared and said: 'I have the power to grant you one wish.' The worm was overjoyed. 'However,' the witch said, 'the rule is that before I grant your wish, you must spend a week with your own kind.' The worm couldn't think of anything worse than spending a week with other ugly, pathetic creatures like himself, but he reluctantly agreed. At first it was horrible, but, he met lots of other worms and realized that what he started to like about them – their wiggly squiggliness, their gentleness and their kindness – he liked about himself too. At the end of the week, the witch returned asking, 'What is your wish?' The worm thought long and hard and said, 'Actually I like being a worm but I would like some friends. I wish that the witch and the muscleman could come and live with me.' . . . and they all lived happily ever after.

Martin felt that the characters in the story symbolized different parts of himself:

> It's like part of me is the worm – all small and pink and weedy – and part of me is the strong and capable muscleman. I like being the muscleman much more, so the worm keeps trying to change and get stronger, but when I really focus on that worm and think about what he's like I can also see his strong points: like his flexibility and sense of compassion. He's not rigid and hard and insensitive like the muscleman. I think the witch is the wise part of me that knows the worm is just as important and just as much part of who I am as the muscleman.

The Jungian technique of 'sandplay' (see, for example, Ryce-Menuhin, 1992) can also be adapted for work with subpersonalities. The sandtray is a shallow box filled with sand, to which water can be added. The sand can then be moulded to make images or represent landscapes, and there is usually a blue base for symbolizing ponds and rivers, etc. The sandtray forms the frame of the picture and can symbolize a miniature world. The individual can then choose sandtray figures – for example, people, animals, monsters, heroes, structures (such as walls, castles, and so on), and various other objects – and place them in the tray to make their image.

As with other projective techniques, a sandtray exploration may start with a particular subpersonality (for example, 'Can you choose a figure to represent this part of yourself?'); or else a client may be invited spontaneously to create an image, choosing figures and objects he or she feels drawn to. These figures may then emerge as subpersonalities. Lynda began one therapy session feeling detached and confused, and was invited to make a sandtray picture. In one corner of the sandtray she put a tiny dinosaur emerging from an egg. When asked what the dinosaur might say, she replied: 'I am a baby but I can grow and I can be strong. I've got sharp teeth but only for eating my food, I don't want to hurt anyone if they don't hurt me. I want to have lots of food and grow and play and feel good. I need this egg for protection 'cos I've been hurt and that feels OK.' After speaking, Lynda was silent for several minutes. She then said, 'I think the dinosaur is Little Lynda too.' Lynda felt that this new image expressed some of the positive qualities and potential of this side of herself – not just the pain and fear of the terrified little girl crouched in the attic.

Experiential techniques

Experiential techniques are those approaches which attempt to help a client express her or his subpersonalities by encouraging the individual actually to enter – behaviourally, cognitively, affectively, physiologically – into that mode of Being. The most direct experiential technique is simply to ask the client to 'become' a particular subpersonality. This approach is used in the 'redecision' and 'cathexis' schools of transactional analysis, where the client is encouraged to regress to their child ego state (Stewart and Joines, 1987). Rueffler adopts a similar approach, inviting clients to close their eyes, deep breathe, and allow themselves to be carried back through time, 'back to the time when you were lying in your mother's breast or in the arms of a primary caretaker' (1995: 106). Rueffler then dialogues with the client in this child-like state, asking them such questions as how they feel, what they sense, whether they are satisfied, and what current subpersonality may be a result of these feelings. Such an immersion into – and dialoguing with – subpersonality modes, can be used with any of the client's aspects of Being. Rueffler, for instance, suggests that the client should think of a situation in the past few days which has kept them preoccupied, imagine themselves in that situation, and then concentrate on how they are thinking, feeling, wanting to act, etc. They can then step back and analyse this mode of Being, thinking about their attitudes and feelings towards it; or else they can respond to further experiential techniques and answer questions such as: 'What is your purpose? Why are you here?'

However, while such an invitation is one way of experientially invoking a subpersonality-complex, numerous other starting points have been proposed: astrological signs, tarot cards, dream characters (Rowan, 1993), roles that emerge from the 'Who am I?' brainstorm (Cullen and Russell, 1989), or subpersonalities elicited through psychic mapping (Shapiro, 1976; Stone and Winkelman, 1989; Watkins and Watkins, 1979). Parts of the body can also be used to elicit subpersonalities (Capacchione, 1991; Landy, 1993; Rowan, 1993). Landy, for instance, encourages his clients to focus on one body part, and then allow a movement to extend from that source: 'for example, a prominent belly may lead to a slow and heavy movement' (1993: 47). Once the movement has extended to the whole body, suggests Landy, the invocation of the subpersonality is complete. Capacchione is even more specific in proposing physiological starting points. She suggests, for instance, that by focusing on areas that are tense, sore or painful, a vulnerable child sub-personality can be evoked.

Aware of Little Lynda's level of terror and need for safety, Lynda reiterated in one session that she still needed to proceed at a slow pace in therapy without any demands being made of her (for example, to talk about her abuse or get more in touch with her feelings). Lynda was expressing much gratitude towards the therapist for having respected this, and for, 'Listening to all this "shit".' While expressing these positive feelings, however, the therapist noted that Lynda was also tapping her foot more and more insistently, and drew Lynda's attention to this. 'What might your foot be saying if it could speak?', Lynda was asked.

> 'Ummm . . . What it would *really* say?' she enquired.
> 'Yes . . . If your foot could say anything it liked.'
> 'Get the fuck on with it you stupid woman!' Lynda shouted.

For Lynda, this statement was an expression of her Mrs Angry sub-personality, who was feeling frustrated with the therapist for the gentle pace of the therapy, and angry with Little Lynda for being so fragile. On reflection, Lynda realized that her Little Lynda subpersonality perhaps was not so powerless after all, but actually had the ability to block out her more aggressive side as a form of self-protection. (It was Little Lynda's strong fear that if she expressed any anger she would be hurt and punished.) Having found a way to express her Mrs Angry subpersonality, however, Lynda saw that it too needed a voice and had positive qualities: strength, protection and self-belief.

Any of the projective techniques can also be used as a starting point for the experiential expression of a subpersonality: for example, 'I'd like you to "be" Father Time.' or, 'I'd like you to "become" the explosion of red and black paint.' Masks, as a wearable projective medium, are perhaps unique in that they allow the wearer actually to inhabit what it is they have projected.

The potentially disinhibiting effect of masked-anonymity may contribute to the fullness of this inhabitation; as may the presence of mirrors, which allow the client to see their face as the 'face' of the subpersonality-mask. Some years ago, we led a workshop in which participants were asked to make a mask of their 'vulnerable child', to put the mask on, to look at themselves in a mirror, and then to speak as their mask. A number of participants described this experience as, 'powerful' and 'surprising', revealing unexpected feelings and responses.

The above techniques allow an individual to immerse themselves in one particular subpersonality, but there are also a number of techniques which are specifically aimed at helping individuals to dialogue between their different selves. One of the most common of these is that of 'chair-work'. Shapiro (1976), for instance, suggests an individual should have a few chairs handy, and then, sitting in one of the chairs, begin with a concern, decision, issue, problem or feeling that they want to deal with. Giving a voice to that situation, they should then let it express itself, before moving to another chair, listening to the message, and then responding in any way that feels appropriate. The individual is then encouraged to continue the dialogue between these two chairs/subpersonalities, or move to new chairs as new subpersonalities emerge. Finally, finding an 'observer'/central chair, the individual is asked to try to hold a 'meeting' of their subpersonalities. This chair-based 'voice dialogue' technique is almost identical to the one outlined by Stone and Winkelman (1989) and Watkins and Watkins (1979). In all these techniques, as the client moves from chair to chair, the individual is encouraged to act out their various subpersonalities, moving at times to an observational position from which she or he can gain a more 'objective', 'central' perspective. This process of moving from subpersonality to subpersonality to centre can also occur with the client physically remaining in one chair (see, for example, Vargiu, 1974; Watkins, 1990).

At the less structured end of the spectrum, in psychodrama and drama therapy (Hawkins, 1988; Landy, 1993; Moreno, 1972; Pitzele, 1991), the process of dialoguing between subpersonalities and centre may be given more dramatic licence. The individual(s) may be encouraged to improvise a scene with their role, act out a story or play, develop monologues (Landy, 1993) or soliloquies (Pitzele, 1991). These soliloquies can then be worked into a group psychodrama, such that there is an ongoing dialogue between the many different parts. Alternatively, the client may be encouraged to act out his or her subpersonality through the medium of different theatrical roles or characters, rather than as a directly personalized aspect of his- or herself (Landy, 1993).

As with an immersion into one particular subpersonality, any of the projective techniques can be used as a starting point for an experiential dialogue between subpersonalities: for example, 'I wonder if you could "become" the orange lines, and tell the blue and black circle on the other side of the page how you feel?' 'Now, can you "become" the circle and reply to the orange lines, telling them how you feel?' With Lynda, sandtray figures were frequently used as the starting point for an experiential expression – and dialogue between – her different sides. In one session, Lynda chose an owl to symbolize her Busy Coper and a monkey to symbolize her Little Lynda. Lynda placed these in the sandtray either side of a big wall. She was then asked to 'be' each of the figures and to enact a conversation between them. She began to enact their communication by banging the monkey's head against the wall. The monkey was trying to get the owl to take notice; but Lynda positioned the owl facing the other way, with its head in a book.

> Monkey: Please let me out I need to play and have fun and I'm hurt and I need a cuddle and I hate it here behind this wall.
>
> Owl: No – there's no room for you in my life, you muck everything up, I don't have time. I don't like you, I don't want you . . . shut up and go away.
>
> Monkey: I'm going to scream and shout and make lots of noise and hammer on the wall and I'm not going to go away.
>
> Owl: Well I'm not going to listen to you, you're trouble.

The dialogue went round and round in circles, and Lynda was beginning to feel decidedly stuck. It was suggested to her, therefore, that she might take on the role of Big Lynda to gain a more 'objective' overview of this conflict. Lynda enjoyed identifying with this empowered, compassionate, wise adult, and was able to talk with both the owl and the monkey about their feelings and needs in a way which they were not able to do for each other.

> Big Lynda: Monkey – I know that you are scared and hurt and I will try to protect you. And it's also really important that the house gets cleaned, the bills get paid, and that the study gets done because it's really important to Lynda that she is achieving something and moving forward in her life. I know you need time to play and that the Owl stops you. The Owl is scared too – she's scared that you're going to take over and not give her any time to get her work done. She needs to know that you'll listen to reason.
>
> Owl – I hope you've heard what I've said to Monkey. She's very important because she's got lots of energy and fun and life can be very dull without her. She's also hurt and she needs time to rest and look after herself or she'll only get worse. I think it's really important that she's not in charge all the time because she's only young, so it's really important that you can be sensible and grown-up and get things done.

As the dialogue between these three subpersonalities continued, the owl (Busy Coper) agreed that the monkey (Little Lynda) could have at least ten minutes every day just to play or be sad. The owl also agreed that she wouldn't ignore the monkey when she needed more attention – she would listen and acknowledge her feelings but explain that right now they needed to work. The Monkey was very pleased to be listened to and felt that ten minutes a day would be just about enough for now. The owl also agreed that the monkey could have more time in therapy. Lynda symbolized this shift by removing the wall and by giving the Monkey toys to play with and bringing her nearer to the owl. She placed a clock in the sand to symbolize their agreement.

An alternative means of experientially facilitating the expression of subpersonalities – particularly appropriate in the absence of a therapist or facilitator – is the use of written dialogue, either between the 'centre' and a subpersonality (Capacchione, 1991), or between two subpersonalities themselves (Rowan, 1993; Shapiro, 1976). Capacchione combines written dialogue with art-work, inviting her readers to talk with and talk *as* the subpersonality-images that they have drawn. Such an approach offers the individual an opportunity to express themselves from a particularly subpersonality, but in a manner less direct and 'total' than if they were acting it out.

Underlying principles

On a manifest level, each of these descriptive, projective and experiential methods of facilitating the expression of subpersonalities would appear somewhat different. And yet, examined more closely, many of them seem to share an underlying premise – a premise that can be developed and applied in an infinite variety of ways. Each method begins with one or more personal characteristics: such as, a role, a prominent trait, character, a name, or a body part. Then, through a variety of mediums – for example, putting pieces of paper into piles, drawing pictures, performing – related characteristics are constellated around the initial one, such that a fully constellated subpersonality emerges. In other words, the assumption is that: 'The entire pattern can be activated by focusing attention on one of its behavioural or experiential elements' (Watkins and Watkins, 1979: 196). For example, in Ferrucci's (1982) guided visualization, the individual is asked to begin with a prominent trait, attitude or motivation, allow an image to emerge representing it, and then let the image talk and express itself. Here, the trait, attitude or motivation is used as the initial starting point, and then, through visualization and verbalizations, the individual is encouraged to constellate related behavioural, phenomenological, motivational, cognitive, physiological and affective components around it until a fully formed subpersonality emerges. The underlying principle behind this seems to be that the subpersonalities, as interdependent gestalt formations, exist as – and act as – unified and inseparable wholes. Hook one element of it, and it will bring up all its related parts.

Despite what seems to be a shared underlying assumption, however, there are a number of dimensions along which each of these techniques varies. First is the amount of the subpersonality-complex which is initially used to attract related elements. In some cases, where the starting point is a sandtray figure, a part of the body, or a prominent attitude, there is little of immediate significance with which to lift out the subpersonality-complex. On the other hand, where the starting point is a role, a term such as 'the vulnerable child', or a previously identified subpersonality, then much of the subpersonality is already known. Both small and large starting points have their advantages. A small starting point, being only a minor part of the total subpersonality-complex, has the advantage that there is much of the subpersonality remaining to elicit. Hence, there is more chance of facilitating the expression of subpersonalities that are deeply hidden or only partially known. Perls, for instance, would put in the empty chair such small starting points as 'your smirk' or 'the old man you saw when you were five and a half'. '[A]ll these things could be talked to and talked back. And as they did so, they turned into subpersonalities – sometimes quite familiar subpersonalities and sometimes new and surprising subpersonalities' (Rowan, 1993: 127). A large starting point, on the other hand, has the advantage that you are more certain that what does emerge is indeed a subpersonality. In other words, a smirk or an old man *might* elicit a subpersonality, but there is no reason to assume that this will always be the case.

Another difference is the degree to which the technique 'distances' the individual from their subpersonality or directly identifies them with it. Projective techniques tend to be the most distancing in that they allow the individual to express an aspect of themselves through an entirely not-self medium. Indeed, in the case of role-play (Landy, 1993), the individual may never actually be asked to identify with the 'subpersonality' they are acting out. This contrasts with those approaches – such as the evening review – where it is clear to the individual from the beginning that what they are expressing is one of *their* subpersonalities. The advantage of the more distancing techniques is that, by allowing the individual to be an 'other' they may feel freer to express parts of themselves that, as them-selves, they would be too inhibited to reveal. Distancing techniques may also provide the individual with more opportunity to 'stand back' from themselves and gain a more 'centred' and 'objective' perspective on their different sides. More direct approaches, on the other hand, may have the advantage of confronting the individual with the fact that what is being expressed really is a side of them – an awareness which may be easier to avoid with the more projective techniques.

A final difference between these techniques is the extent to which the subpersonality is overtly manifested. Whereas in the descriptive and projective techniques, used exclusively, the subpersonality is only talked or drawn *about*; in the experiential techniques, the subpersonality is actually manifested at an overt level. The advantage of this overt manifestation is that the individual can get a sense of their subpersonality from the 'inside', can identify and empathize with it more fully, and can cathart any strong emotions that may be associated with it. The advantage of a more covert expression, however, is that the individual may find it easier to really stand back from the subpersonality and gain a reflective awareness of it.

Given these dimensions, a therapeutic approach which combines elements of descriptive, projective, and experiential techniques may be most effective at facilitating the therapeutic exploration of subpersonalities. Art-work, for instance, might allow the individual to project outwards a relatively un-identified part of themselves. By 'being' the entity they have drawn, they may then have an opportunity fully to understand the phenomenological elements of that mode of Being. Standing back and talking about the sub-personality may then allow them to integrate it at a more reflective level, and to understand how that subpersonality affects their life.

Through a variety of techniques, Lynda learned to express the many different sides of her Being. As a consequence of this process, she began to develop a greater ability to communicate within her-self, and to resolve the self-to-self conflicts that had previously been pulling her apart. When Lynda came into psychotherapy, her Busy Coper had been trying to silence her Little Lynda – albeit unsuccessfully – while her Mrs Angry mode, red with frustration, had been helplessly shouting nearby. Now, having expressed and identified these different sides to herself, Busy Coper had begun to allow some space for Little Lynda who had reciprocated by calling off the ongoing demands for attention, and Mrs Angry was beginning to reveal some of her more positive and constructive qualities. Furthermore, through these tech-niques, a fourth subpersonality had emerged – the centred, wise Big Lynda – who had the potential to understand and bring together the different sub-personalities.

These techniques of expression, then, allow the individual to move from a state of internal distrust and conflict to a state in which the different selves can come to learn about, understand and value each other. This constitutes essential groundwork for the healthy communication between different subpersonalities, enabling them to work together in a more effective and actualizing way.

Notes

1 To ensure complete confidentiality, some details in this case-example have been changed.
2 These terms will be used interchangeably throughout this chapter.
3 L. Capacchione, *Recovery of your Inner Child* (Simon and Schuster, London. 1991) also encourages individuals to draw and write down their subpersonality's words with their non-dominant hand. This, she argues, directly accesses the right brain hemisphere, hence encouraging more creative and less consciously dictated functioning. Capacchione also suggests that the awkwardness and lack of control experienced when writing with the non-dominant hand actually puts individuals into their inner child state.

References

Assagioli, R. (1975) *Psychosynthesis: A Manual of Principles and Techniques.* London: Aquarian/Thorsons.

Berne, E. (1961) *Transactional Analysis in Psychotherapy*. New York: Grove Press.

Capacchione, L. (1991) *Recovery of your Inner Child*. London: Simon and Schuster.

Cullen, J.W. and Russell, D. (1989) *The Self Actualizing Manager*. Thousand Oaks, CA: International Association for Managerial and Organizational Psychosynthesis.

Ferrucci, P. (1982) *What We May Be*. London: Aquarian.

Hawkins, P. (1988) 'A phenomenological psychodrama workshop', in P. Reason (ed.), *Human Inquiry in Action*. London: Sage.

Landy, R. (1993) *Persona and Performance*. London: Jessica Kingsley Publishers.

McAdams, D.P. (1985) 'The "Imago": a key narrative component of identity', in P. Shaver (ed.), *Self, Situations, and Social Behaviour*. Beverly Hills, CA: Sage.

Moreno, J. (1972) *Psychodrama*, vol. 1. Beacon, NY: Beacon House.

Pitzele, P. (1991) 'Adolescents inside out: intrapsychic psychodrama', in P. Holmes and M. Karp (eds), *Psychodrama: Inspiration and Technique*, Tavistock: Routledge.

Rogers, C.R. (1961) *On Becoming a Person: A Therapist's View of Psychotherapy*. London: Constable.

Rowan, J. (1990) *Subpersonalities: The People Inside Us*. London: Routledge.

Rowan, J. (1993) *Discover Your Subpersonalities*. London: Routledge.

Rueffler, M. (1995) *Our Inner Actors: The Theory and Application of Subpersonality Work in Psychosynthesis*. Staefa, Switzerland: PsychoPolitical Peace Institute Press.

Ryce-Menuhin, J. (1992) *Jungian Sandplay: The Wonderful Therapy*. London: Routledge.

Rycroft, C. (1995) *A Critical Dictionary of Psychoanalysis*. (2nd edn) Harmondsworth: Penguin.

Ryle, A. (1990) *Cognitive-analytic Therapy*. Chichester: John Wiley.

Satir, V. (1978) *Your Many Faces*. Berkeley, CA: Celestial Arts.

Shapiro, S.B. (1976) *The Selves Inside You*. Berkeley, CA: Explorations Institute.

Sliker, G. (1992) *Multiple Mind*. Boston, MA: Shambhala.

Stewart, I. and Joines, V. (1987) *TA Today: A New Introduction to Transactional Analysis*. Nottingham: Lifespace Publishing.

Stone, H. and Winkelman, S. (1989) *Embracing Ourselves: The Voice Dialogue Manual*. Mill Valley, CA: Nataraj Publishing.

Turner, R.J. (1988) 'The Parent-Adult-Child projective drawing task: a therapeutic tool in TA', *Transactional Analysis Journal*, 18 (1): 60–7.

Vargiu, J.G. (1974) 'Psychosynthesis workbook: subpersonalities', *Synthesis*, 1: 52–90.

Watkins, J.G. and Watkins, H.H. (1979) 'Theory and practice of ego state therapy: a short-term therapeutic approach', in H. Grayson (ed.), *Short-Term Approaches to Psychotherapy*. London: Human Sciences Press.

Watkins, M. (1990) *Invisible Guests*. Boston, MA: Sigo Press.

Zinker, J. (1977) *Creative Process in Gestalt Therapy*. New York: Vintage Books.

12 THE DOORWAY INTO THE INNER DEEPER WORLD IS THE INSTANT OF PEAK FEELING IN THE SCENE OF STRONG FEELING

Alvin R. Mahrer

Many psychotherapists believe in some kind of inner deeper world. It is made up of all sorts of things like subpersonalities, unconscious impulses and wishes, deep-seated drives and motivations, potentials for experiencing. Whatever the presumed nature of this magical, fascinating, hidden, inner deeper world, one compelling question is how to get into it: how to gain access to this wonderful world. How can we know what lies deep inside this inner world?

The purpose of this chapter is to suggest that a very effective and very useful doorway into this fascinating and magical inner world is the instant or precise moment of peak feeling in the scene of strong feeling. Start with a scene of powerful feeling. Search for the instant of peak feeling. That is the precious doorway down into the deeper world.

The explanation comes from an experiential model of the inner deeper world and how it may be explored. It is fitting, then, to use an experiential justification for why and how the doorway into the inner world is the instant of peak feeling in the scene of strong feeling (Mahrer, 1996). However, it is important to emphasize that this doorway is offered to all therapists who believe in an inner deeper world, and for whom it is valuable to find whatever lies inside this deeper world – whether it is a deeper subpersonality, unconscious wish, potential for experiencing, or anything else.

What is the experiential model of what the insides are like?

The purpose of this section is to provide a picture or model of one way of thinking about the insides.

In this model, a person's insides consist of potentials for experiencing

This model portrays a person as living and being in some kind of external world, some kind of situational context (see Figure 12.1).[1] This situational

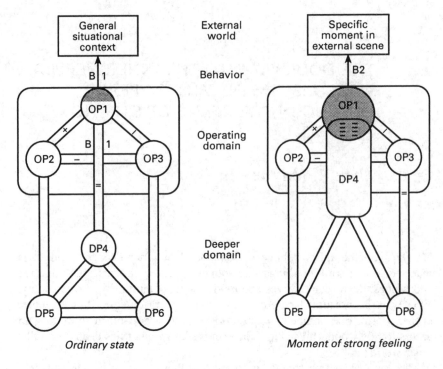

FIGURE 12.1   *The experiential model of a person in an ordinary state and in a moment of strong feeling*

context is 'outside' the person, is the world in which the person is living and being. The person behaves and acts in the context of this external world, and these behaviors are also regarded as being 'outside' the person (Figure 12.1).

What is 'inside' the person is described as ways of being, ways of experiencing, that are available in this particular person, ways this person is capable of being or experiencing. These are called potentials for experiencing. Naming or describing them is mainly providing a short-hand character sketch or picture of this particular way of being or experiencing. Here are some examples: being violent, explosive, destructive; being gentle, loving, soft; being strong, firm, a leader; being independent, autonomous, self-reliant; being mischievous, mean, nasty; being excited, aroused, stimulated; being dominant, controlling, in charge; being drawn toward, attracted to, compelled by; being defiant, refusing, oppositional; being withdrawn, pulled away, distant, removed; being risky, adventurous, daring; being wicked, bad, roguish, irreverent; being docile, compliant, yielding; being close to, at one with, intimate; being the jewel, the precious one, special; being nurturing, succoring, caring for; being honest, straightforward, candid; being playful, silly, whimsical.

According to this model, each potential for experiencing is merely a way of being or experiencing that is available in this person. The more carefully each person's particular potentials for experiencing are described, the clearer it can be that these particular potentials for experiencing are singular to and for this particular person. Furthermore, potentials for experiencing are merely potentials, availabilities, capacities; there is no endowed property of drive, activation, arousal, energy, force or motivation, no endowed property of being satisfied, consummated, fulfilled.

Some potentials for experiencing are more directly connected with behaviors and the external world: operating potentials

Some potentials for experiencing are more directly connected with behaviors; with the way you act, behave, respond, feel, think; the way you construct and are in your daily world. If this is a potential for experiencing being gentle, soft, delicate, then behaviors come from and provide for this kind of experiencing.

In Figure 12.1, this is referred to as OP1 or operating potential 1. It is directly connected with behavior and with the external world. As you softly fondle the baby's face, the ongoing experiencing may be that of gentleness, softness, delicacy. Operating potentials are indicated as OP1, OP2, and OP3 in Figure 12.1.

The sense of 'I-ness' is merely a quality of a relating operating potential; it is not some separate, free-floating entity   In most theories there is an implicit acknowledgement of a sense of 'I-ness', a center of consciousness or awareness, an irreducible core of self. It is the 'I' that says, 'I feel a little . . .; I am gaining understanding of myself . . .; I have a problem controlling my impulses.' In most theories, this is a separated, removed, free-floating entity: an extra component that is consistently implied but seldom acknowledged as a component of personality. Theories may contain cognitions, archetypes, super-egos, egos, learned responses, unconsciousness, and lots more, but rarely do theories explicitly acknowledge an entity called 'I-ness' or its equivalent. Yet most theories implicitly include it as a separate, removed, free-floating entity that is consistently implied as a part of the structure of personality.

Not in the experiential model. In this model, the sense of 'I-ness' – the sense of being conscious and aware, the sense of identity – is merely a property of an operating potential that is related to an operating potential undergoing experiencing. In other words, this sense of I-ness is the expression of a relating neighbor operating potential, rather than coming from some supposedly separated, removed, free-floating, extra added component.

Some potentials for experiencing are deeper, inside, hidden, unknown: deeper potentials

Some potentials for experiencing are deeper inside. They have little or no direct connection with the external world, with the way the person acts, behaves, responds, feels, thinks: the way the person is in moment-to-moment living.

Like the operating potentials, these are simply potentials for experiencing. They may be described as having any kind of content. Either operating or deeper potentials may include, for example, the potential for experiencing gentleness, softness, delicacy; caring, loving, fondness; toughness, hardness, firmness; being better than, superior to, competitive with; being shockingly and openly aggressive, playfully nasty, playfully attacking; being free, liberated, spontaneous; being wicked, nasty, mischievous; flagrant sexuality, sexually open, flaunting and exhibiting sexually; being taken care of, nurtured, succored; standing up to, defiance, refusal.

The deeper potentials are the very foundation of the person. At the base, when you reach rock bottom, there are merely deeper potentials for experiencing. Where some other theories hold that at base there are such things as id impulses or basic needs and drives, in the experiential model there are merely deeper potentials for experiencing, and nothing more (Figure 12.1).

Furthermore, there are no universal basic potentials for experiencing. When we discover the most basic potentials in this person, they will probably have little or nothing to do with the basic potentials in some other person or in most other people.

In experiential psychotherapy, our treasure, our target, our precious aim, is to discover the nature of this person's deeper potentials. We want to see what lies deeper inside.

Potentials for experiencing have good or bad relationships with one another

In this model, potentials for experiencing have some kind of relationship with one another. These relationships may be good or bad, pleasant and harmonious or unpleasant and disjunctive, friendly or unfriendly. They are indicated as the positive or negative signs in the relationships between potentials in Figure 12.1. When relationships are negative, the potentials have a bad relationship toward one another. They hate one another, fear one another, are inclined to seal off and push away one another. Relationships are fractionated, disjunctive, abrasive, opposed. These relationships are called *disintegrative*. When relationships are positive, the potentials bear good relationships toward one another. They love one another, accept, cherish, welcome, appreciate and feel good toward one another. Relationships are harmonious, close, open, friendly. These relationships are called *integrative* relationships.

In the experiential model, all there is to the person are potentials for experiencing that have good or bad – integrative or disintegrative – relationships toward one another.

Operating potentials have bad disintegrative relationships toward deeper potentials
Operating potentials have bad relationships toward their deeper potentials. They are enormously threatened by their deeper potentials and do not want

to have anything to do with them. They are invested in not knowing their deeper potentials. These bad disintegrative relationships are indicated by the two negative signs in the relationships between operating potentials 1–3 and deeper potentials 4–6, on the left in Figure 12.1.

Because of this heightened bad relationship, the person shifts from one operating potential to another, but rarely if ever does the person move from the operating domain down into the deeper domain. The person is almost never being or undergoing the deeper potentials. If we can talk about deeper subpersonalities, this means that the person rarely if ever is being or undergoing a deeper subpersonality.

Ordinary living is being in a personal world that enables experiencing, and undergoing a 'safe' degree of experiencing

What is it that puts the person into motion, that keeps the person being a certain way, that accounts for a person moving from one way of being to another way of being in the course of daily living? As indicated in Figure 12.1, there are two grand principles. One is that the person works to build, construct, organize, a personal external world that is appropriate and helpful in enabling the person to undergo the experiencing of operating potentials. The operating potential works toward fashioning a personal world that provides for its own experiencing.

The other grand principle has to do with the nature of the relationships between potentials, especially the disintegrative relationships between operating and deeper potentials for experiencing. The more an operating potential is experienced, the more its deeper potential is activated, raised up, drawn closer to the person or operating domain. As indicated in Figure 12.1, when there is some experiencing of one operating potential (OP1), its deeper potential (DP4) rises closer to the operating domain. Because of the disintegrative relationships between the operating and deeper potentials, when experiencing of an operating potential goes beyond a relatively safe measure, there is danger – there is real trouble. The operating potential risks being eclipsed, imploded, cracked open, extinguished. Under these conditions, there is usually a safe switch into some other operating potential. The net result is that the imminent, dangerously intrusive deeper potential, is again safely sealed off and lowered.

In this model then, ordinary living is the conjoint interplay of these two principles. All other grand principles, all other grand forces or drives or motivations or missions, are declined.

Deeper potentials for experiencing and 'multiple selves' or 'deeper selves' are somewhat friendly notions, but there may be some notable differences

I am going to speculate that there may be a sensible distinction between multiple selves that may be said to be more on the surface and those that can be described as somewhat deeper, relatively beyond the person's awareness and easy knowledge. If this distinction is allowed, then it seems that there can be a lot in common between what I mean by deeper potentials for experiencing and what may be described as multiple selves.

Deeper potentials for experiencing are a form of multiple selves Both a deeper potential for experiencing and each multiple self are understood as being its own distinctive entity – with its own sense of self, its own sense of I-ness or identity. The ordinary person speaks as one person, and each deeper potential or each multiple self speaks as a qualitatively different person. Both the deeper potential and the deeper self have their own distinctive way of seeing the world, of looking out upon and making sense of the world in which it is being (Ornstein, 1986; Rowan, 1990; Schwartz, 1987). Finally, both each deeper potential and each deeper self may be described as having some kind of relationship with and toward the ordinary person. These are some notable commonalities.

But they differ somewhat in (a) content, (b) degree to which their content can evolve, and (c) degree of universality There are shades of difference in the supposed content of multiple selves as compared with deeper potentials for experiencing. The emphasis, for multiple selves, is on single-word naming of a general role, such as: clown, earth mother, central organizer, gorilla, clinger, professor. Further description generally emphasizes behaviors, so that the clinger wants to be needed, wants women to like him and take the initiative, and the professor is intellectual and interested in everything (Rowan, 1990). In some contrast, the emphasis, in describing deeper potentials, is on a somewhat fuller identification of the experiencing itself. Instead of naming a deeper potential as a gorilla, the description may be the experiencing of sheer power, animal strength, destructiveness, or perhaps the experiencing of being wild, uncivilized, untamed. With potentials for experiencing, the content emphasizes a description of the nature of the experiencing and way of being; with subpersonalities or selves, the emphasis is more on a role and the behaviors that may go with the role.

Whereas the nature and content of a particular self may perhaps change, deeper potentials for experiencing are understood as quite open to gradual but substantial evolution. This evolution occurs as the deeper potential's relationships with other potentials become much more integrative, and as the deeper potential converts into being a genuine part of the operating domain. A deeper potential of hardness, cruelty, uncaringness, coldness, may evolve into an experiencing of self-confidence, self-assuredness, self-certainty. What occurs as a deeper experiencing of being rejected, withdrawn, unwanted, may evolve into the experiencing of independence, autonomy, self-containment. A deeper potential of the experiencing of gentleness, softness, delicateness, may evolve into the experiencing of being close to, intimate with, bondedness, union. With what may be termed integration and actualization, the manifest content of deeper potentials for experiencing may well evolve.

In many approaches, the content of what is presumed to be deeper is understood as just about universal. In the psychoanalytic approach, for example, there is an ego, a superego and an unconscious, and the content of these parts is virtually the same in every person. In a Jungian approach, the personality structure of just about everyone contains a persona, a shadow, animus, anima. In Berne's (1961) approach, virtually every person is to have an inner parent, adult, and child. Some multiple selves are seen as leaning toward perhaps being universal. Not so in regard to deeper potentials for experiencing. The picture of how they come about (Mahrer, 1996) makes it somewhat understandable that any one person's deeper potentials are not likely to be universal. In this model, both the number and nature of deeper and basic potentials for experiencing, when carefully described, are more or less unique to this person alone.

Some common meanings of 'deeper insides'

'Deeper insides' is a rather loose and cloudy phrase. Perhaps something can be described as having three characteristics in order to qualify as a 'deeper inside': (a) it is generally something about the person that is ordinarily outside the person's consciousness or awareness. A person does not ordinarily know what their deeper insides are; (b) it is not generally a part of the surface manifest way the person is, not directly tied to actions and behaviors; (c) deeper insides generally are things that can exert a significant influence on the kind of person the person can be – on who and what the person is capable of becoming.

Although deeper insides seem to share these characteristics, when you get a little closer, there seem to be altogether different kinds of what we call 'deeper insides'. This volume emphasizes such things as deeper multiple selves. But there are plenty of other meanings of 'deeper insides'; the term can refer to:

- deeper potentials for experiencing. For example, it may be a deeper potential for experiencing gentleness, softness, delicateness; wildness, being untamed, undisciplined; control, being in charge, domination.
- hidden, unknown, unconscious ways of thinking about oneself and one's world, general principles for living, life nostrums, short-hand stories about oneself or one's life – I must be loved to be of worth; my parents were mean to me; I am a sensitive person; no matter what I do I end up the loser; people don't properly appreciate me; I am the solid anchor on whom others depend.
- biological needs and drives – a need for survival, a need for sleep, a need for food, a need for sex.
- unconscious impulses and wishes. Here are some examples: a wish to kill the same-sexed parent and have sex with the opposite-sexed parent; a wish to be close to another person, but short of being assimilated into the other person.

- a personality dimension in the form of a polarity, with an outside manifest end and an inside deeper end. Here are some examples: topdog–underdog, extravert–introvert, masculine–feminine, manic–depressive.
- pathologies and mental disorders. Here are some examples: identity diffusion, lack of autonomy, schizophrenia, conduct disorder, post-traumatic stress disorder, bipolar disorder, attention deficit hyperactivity disorder.
- archetypes such as the earth mother, the child-God, the shadow, the animus, the anima.

Many different approaches accept some idea of 'deeper insides'. But they do differ from one another. In the experiential model, what is 'inside' consists of differing potentials for experiencing.

Most ways of trying to get at 'deeper insides' are relatively ineffective

Not all approaches think of 'deeper insides', but if they do, then they almost certainly have ways of trying to see what the deeper insides are: ways of accessing, uncovering, getting at the deeper insides. My impression is that most of these ways are relatively ineffective.

What are some common ways of trying to get at the 'deeper insides'?

A selection of some of the more common ways follows.

- Observe the manifest pole of a polarity, and infer the deeper inside as the unmanifested other end of the polarity. If you think of such grand polarities as topdog–underdog, manic–depressive, masculinity–femininity, weakness–strength, extraversion–introversion, then if what is manifest is extraversion or femininity, the deeper insides are probably introversion or masculinity.
- Know what authorities say are the deeper insides of people who have been through or faced this awful situation, catastrophe, state, stress, trauma, affliction, trouble. Authorities tell you what the hidden deeper insides are of people who were sexually abused as children, whose loved spouse died recently, who have fatal diseases, who are infertile, whose newborn babies are severely handicapped, who have been brutalized, who have been through a near-death experience.
- Figure out the deeper insides from information about the person's infancy and childhood. Experts can tell the deeper insides of people whose infancies and childhoods were characterized by being unwanted babies, by divorces, by controlling parents, by disruptive or dysfunctional family structures, by lack of adequate support, by parents who over-identified with their children, by inconsistent parenting, by lack of adequate role models.

- Know what authorities say the deeper insides are of people with an identified mental illness or disorder. Once you know the person's particular mental disorder, for example, schizophrenia, bulimia, post-traumatic stress disorder, borderline, agoraphobic, then you know what the person's deeper insides are like.
- Determine the manifest pathological symptoms, and know what the symptoms tell about the deeper insides. A headache indicates repressed aggression; delusions indicate a deeper psychotic process; a skin rash is a sign of deeper tabooed sexual impulses.
- Trust what your theory says are universal deeper insides. Then you know that deep inside every person are aggressive impulses or inferiority complexes or social interest or self-preservation or parenting instincts.
- Get the deeper insides by using a system of symbols or a decoding system. When a person does this, it really means that; when a person says this, they really mean that. Use a psychoanalytic decoding system in which a stick or a snake is code for penis. An umbrella is code for penis when the umbrella is closed, and is code for vagina when it is open.
- Give tests that are advertised as telling about the deeper insides. Psychological tests, projective tests and psychometric tests by the hundreds are supposed to tell what the deeper insides are.
- Trust that the deeper insides will emerge when the person is in a state of reduced control and vigilance. Get the person into this state by asking the person to act out dreams, daydreams, fantasies, to let their thoughts and associations run free and loose, to engage in active imagination and guided fantasy (see for example, Ferrucci, 1982; Watkins, 1986). Side-step the person's ordinary controls by putting the person into a hypnotic or hypnogogic state, by having the person take some kind of chemical. Have the person dance, paint, write poems, make music.

These are some ways therapists use to try to get at the person's deeper insides. Are they generally effective? I do not think so.

Most ways of trying to get at deeper insides do not put you directly face-to-face with the deeper insides

Although there are exceptions, most of the common ways of trying to get some idea of the deeper insides keep you far away from any direct contact with the deeper insides. Instead of being eyeball-to-eyeball with the deeper insides, instead of being able to see and touch them, instead of confronting them right before you – alive and real and immediate – you are usually forced to make inferences, intellectual guesses, conceptual deductions. Most of the methods consist of making inferences from what is manifest to what is supposedly deeper.

If this is the case with most methods, one is entitled to consider them to be suspect. If a method has a good chance of being effective in getting at the deeper insides, it probably should put you face-to-face with the deeper insides. Most methods do not do this.

A person in the ordinary state of consciousness is able to know what is deeper inside Versus a person has to get out of the ordinary state of consciousness to be able to know what is deeper inside

Just about the whole field of psychotherapy accepts the idea that a person in the ordinary state of consciousness can come to know what is deeper inside. This is a big puzzlement for clinicians who think of the 'deeper insides' as something of which the person is not especially conscious or aware, something truly inside, rather than something on the surface, more or less observable.

Given this meaning of 'deeper insides', can the ordinary, awake, conscious, functioning person come to know what is there in their deeper insides? The common answer is yes. Almost every way of trying to get at a person's deeper insides is understood as being carried out by the ordinary, conscious, aware person. The idea is that a person can know their deeper insides by putting their mind to it, by carefully observing and reasoning. Nothing inside is really out of bounds if one makes the right effort at trying to find what it is. Of course a person can explore, understand, and know, his or her deeper insides; this is called insight and understanding. Most therapists know that patients can know what is unconscious, what is deeper inside, especially with the help of a fine therapist.

Without many notable exceptions, all of our ways of getting at the deeper insides are based on the idea that a person in the ordinary state of consciousness can come to know what is deeper inside one's self or some other self.

How can the ordinary, conscious person ever come to know the deeper insides? I have puzzled about how a person ever manages to know what might be deeper inside. How do you ever come to know what might be deeper inside, supposedly beyond your consciousness? 'How can we get to know the unconscious? How do we make the unconscious conscious? For, by definition, the unconscious can never become an object for consciousness. I can never be directly aware of my unconscious' (Heaton, 1972: 136). In the experiential mode (Mahrer, 1996), the conscious, aware, operating person has such negative relations with the deeper potentials that the person (OP1, Figure 12.1) can undergo a great deal of pain to ensure that the dreaded deeper potential (DP4, Figure 12.1) is kept down, sealed off, and never comes into conscious awareness.

Yet most therapists cling to the belief that they can penetrate the world of the deeper insides while anchored in a state of conscious awareness. Freud and Jung – and many others who followed in their footsteps – believed that they could come to know their deeper insides by conscious study of themselves. Almost by the sheer force of will and their brilliance, they knew they could reason down into their own unconsciousness and into the deeper insides of their patients. And we maintain this belief today, almost throughout the field of psychotherapy.

In contrast, the alternative perspective is that it makes little or no sense for the ordinary conscious person to attempt to know unconscious deeper insides while remaining in the ordinary conscious state. Nor does it make much sense that one person, in the ordinary conscious state, can ever truly know the deeper insides of some other person. It seems that almost all the common methods somehow require that you just trust that someone, sometime, somehow, actually saw these deeper insides. Then this person, and others, wrote down guidelines, for instance: if a dream contains this element, then your insides are like this. How do you know? Because someone tells us. How do you know that this way of describing an inkblot means that the deeper insides are like this? Where did the rule come from? If you observe a person clasping his hands whenever he talks about his mother, how do you know what this shows about the person's deeper insides? What makes you know that a headache is a sign of repressed aggression, or what is going on inside a woman whose baby just died? How would you truly know? You probably did not see the deeper insides directly, face-to-face. So how do you know? It seems that there are lots of guidelines and rules, yet they are almost all based on the idea that someone once truly saw the deeper insides, and all the guidelines and rules are based on what this person actually witnessed. I have very serious doubts about this.

Some promising ways of coming face-to-face with the deeper insides seem to involve letting go of the ordinary state of consciousness. There are at least two promising ways of enabling a person to come face-to-face with the deeper insides. They seem promising because both suggest that the way to get directly at the deeper insides is to let go of the ordinary state of consciousness.

One way is exemplified by methods like meditation and contemplation where the aim is for the person is to get out of, transcend, or let go of the self: to become free of the ever-present conscious self or I-ness. Whether the person concentrates on a mantra or a gurgling brook, the method aims at allowing the person to disengage from the ordinary sense of self. In the course of losing the sense of ordinary awareness, one may undergo or observe or confront one's deeper insides. Both the method itself, and the working goal or aim, involve getting out of the ordinary state of consciousness.

A second way is to open up the deeper insides directly. Instead of being the ordinary person in the ordinary state of consciousness, the person enters into a particular state of strong feeling that is to lay the deeper insides directly on the table. This method is exemplified in what is called the transference in psychoanalytic therapy. By using particular techniques, the therapist aims at bringing the patient's deeper insides up and onto center stage in the immediate and real patient–therapist situation.

Both of these ways seem eminently promising as ways of coming face-to-face with the deeper insides, and both involve the person's getting out of the ordinary state of consciousness.

We can perhaps be relatively clear on what we mean by deeper insides. But it seems that our ways of trying to get at those deeper insides are relatively ineffective. We seem to be standing on the surface, feet firmly planted on the surface, in frozen indecision between whether to peer down into what we cannot see, or whether to accept the challenge and just jump headlong into our deeper insides.

How and why is the 'moment of strong feeling' such a sensitively precious, but, rarely used, method of discovering the deeper insides?

The moment of strong feeling is a very particular instant – a few seconds or so – when the person is living and being in some scene or situational context and is undergoing strong feeling. It is a loaded instant within the scene or situation. There are some reasons why this precise moment of strong feeling can be, ought to be, a sensitively precious avenue into discovering the deeper insides. Yet it is a rarely used avenue. Thousands and thousands of hours of traditional psychotherapy float by without even coming close to these tiny powerful moments of strong feeling. What may be some of the reasons to account for this?

In order to live and be in the scene of strong feeling, the person and the therapist have to sacrifice attending mainly to one another

Looking for the precise moment of strong feeling means that the person and the therapist have to enter mainly inside the general scene to start searching for the precise moment. It is hard enough for the person and the therapist to live and be inside the scene of strong feeling; it is a far greater sacrifice for the person and the therapist to give up attending mainly to one another. In other words, to find the moment of strong feeling, the person and the therapist have to put most of their attention onto the scene itself, and no longer on one another. This is easy to say, but it is almost unthinkable for most therapists and their clients to sacrifice all the joys of attending mainly to one another (Mahrer, 1996, 1997; Mahrer et al., 1994). This is what therapists call 'having a relationship', and few therapists are willing to give up all the joys of having clients and therapists attending mainly to one another as they talk about all sorts of meaningful things. The net result is that they will almost certainly not enter into, live and be in, the scene of strong feeling; and failing to enter into the scene of strong feeling virtually assures that they will not discover the moment of strong feeling.

In the moment of strong feeling, the deeper insides are close to the accessible surface

The moment of strong feeling refers to a very particular instant or moment – perhaps a few seconds or so – when the person is almost filled or saturated with a feeling that is strong, intense, gripping, powerful. This moment is taking place within some explicit scene or situational context. Furthermore, the scene or situational context may be real or unreal, and it may be from any time in the person's life.

In making a case for how and why the moment of strong feeling is so precious and marvelously useful, I will stay within an experiential model, and will talk about the deeper insides as deeper potentials for experiencing. But I believe that a somewhat similar case can be made within some other models or theories, and for deeper insides other than what I think of as deeper potentials for experiencing.

The answer, in a nutshell, is that the deeper potential comes closest to the accessible surface in the very precious moment of strong feeling. It is in the instant when the feeling is strongest that the person or 'operating domain' (Figure 12.1) and the deeper potential (DP4, Figure 12.1) are touching one another. This is when the deeper potential is so near, so imminent, that the person can sense the deeper potential, can feel its very presence, its breath.

In the moment of strong feeling, the sheer experiencing of the operating potential is at its height. On the left in Figure 12.1 the moderate degree of experiencing is indicated by the bit of shading on operating potential 1; on the right, the powerful degree of experiencing is indicated by shading all over operating potential 1. On the left, deeper potential 4 is well below the operating domain, at a safe enough distance, and the disintegrative relations between the person and the deeper potential are indicated by only two negative signs. Things are ordinary, not threatening. But things are quite different in the moment of strong feeling on the right. The deeper potential has intruded well into the operating domain. In other words, the person is intruded into – is invaded – by the deeper potential. Furthermore, if the invasion continues, it is almost certain that the person – operating potential 1 – will be destroyed, imploded, eradicated. That is the end of the existence of the person. These catastrophic feelings are indicated by the increase to eight negative signs in the overlap between the person, OP1, and the deeper potential, DP4. This is the moment of crisis; this is the moment of very strong feeling.

In the specific moment, the experiencing of the person or operating potential is just about at its height. For example, the person may be undergoing a powerful experiencing of domination, control, being in charge; or a powerful experiencing of being nurturant, caring, succorant; or a powerful experiencing of rebelliousness, defiance, resistance. At the same time, this is the instant when the deeper potential has cracked into the person, threatened to eclipse and destroy the person, and therefore the disintegrative feelings are also at their height. All of this is occurring when the person is in the moment of strong feeling.

The net result is that there is an excruciating moment in which what is going on inside the person is intense: it may be intense good or intense bad or a mixture of both, but it is intense. This is the precious moment when the deeper potential is most accessible. This is one reason how and why the moment of strong feeling is so precious; it can also help to explain how and why the moment of strong feeling is so rarely looked for and used.

It is usually difficult and threatening to go from a scene of strong feeling to the precise moment when the feeling is strong

The very reason why the moment of strong feeling is so very special and precious is also the reason why the moment of strong feeling is so exceedingly threatening. When you come closer to, or when you are actually in, the moment of strong feeling, the deeper potential (DP4 in Figure 12.1) is no longer safely down inside, where it should be. Instead, the deeper potential is now much too close to you, is invading you, is on the verge of eclipsing you, imploding you, ending your very existence. This state of affairs is indicated on the right in Figure 12.1, with the person (OP1) being threateningly intruded into by the deeper potential, and the heightened threat is indicated by the many negative signs in the overlap between the person and the deeper potential. Little wonder that the person may spend a lifetime talking around strong feeling, but never venture into finding and being in the precise moment of strong feeling: it is, simply, too threatening.

Indeed, a person may carry around a scene of strong feeling throughout their whole life, and never ever venture close to the hidden actual moment in which the feeling is strongest. He or she may vividly recall when their beloved mother said goodbye, when he or she was a child, and carry this hurtful scene around throughout their whole life. She or he may have a vivid memory of an older brother drowning or of the uncle forcing her or him to let him put his penis inside her or his mouth. The awful feelings and scenes can remain throughout their lives, yet they never discover what is occurring in the actual moment of strongest feeling. This is too bad. But understandable.

Most therapists stop prematurely as soon as they can call something a problem, and then switch to getting more information about and what to do about the labeled problem

Most therapists hover at the outer surface of incidents, times, situations, and scenes of bad feeling. They hear just enough of the concern, trouble, worry, to label it as some sort of problem. It is as if most therapists listen to what patients say through a schema of ready-made labels and categories of problems and mental disorders, and they are energized to hear just enough to grasp what the patient is saying in terms of some kind of problem label or mental disorder label.

Most therapists stop when they quickly infer that here is a problem of being tense when supervisors are critical, here is an authority problem, here is work stress problem, here is a problem of anxiety. Most therapists stop when they quickly come to the idea that here is a problem of depression, here is a suicidal problem, here is a problem of alcoholism, here is a problem of the client having suicidal thoughts when he or she is drunk and alone in their apartment.

Once the therapist gets the swift notion of some problem, then there is an almost immediate switch to: (a) getting more information about the problem; and (b) seeing what can be done about the problem. Check out all sorts of clinical inferences. See how severe the problem is. What about the patient's support system? How long has the patient had this problem? What are possible causes of the problem? Are there other diagnostic indications? The switch to what can be done about the problem means that the therapist has all sorts of notions about ways out, treatments, problem-reductions: the patient should be able to cope and deal with authorities; criticisms could be handled more adjustively; the goal is for him to deal better with such stress; she should be able to deal with her aloneness, her grief, her suicidal ideation, her depression.

Getting more information about the problem, and seeing what can be done about the problem, take the therapist and patient immediately away from the scene of bad feeling. In sharp contrast, it is at this very point that the alternative therapist is just starting to probe deeper into finding and entering into the scene of strong feeling.

When therapists do a pre-treatment assessment of problems and personality, there is little reason to use subsequent sessions to find scenes of strong feeling

Most therapists do some kind of pre-treatment intake interview, or use the first session to get some idea of the patient's problems and personality. The therapist determines that her problem is binge eating or that she was abused as a child, and the therapist tries to get some picture of the personality, the psychodynamics, the mental disorder, the personality traits, the deeper insides.

Once the therapist gets some idea of the problem and the personality, he or she tends to approach each subsequent session with that picture of the patient, the problem or mental disorder. There is little or no need for the therapist to use subsequent sessions to start all over again, looking for scenes of strong feeling to uncover something of the person's deeper insides. What reason would the therapist have to do that when the therapist knows that the patient has this problem or mental disorder, this kind of personality make-up?

It is the rare therapist whose framework would lead the therapist to use virtually every session to find a fresh scene of strong feeling as a precious entry into the deeper insides that are alive and accessible in this session.

In general, it seems that there can be many reasons why most therapists do not concentrate on finding the precise moment of strong feeling, and why probing inside a scene of strong feeling for the precise moment of strong feeling is so very rare. And yet a case can be made that the moment of strong feeling is a powerful and sensitive method of discovering the deeper insides.

How can you find and use a 'moment of strong feeling' to help discover what is deeper inside the person?

The purpose of this section is to show how to find a moment of strong feeling, and how to use it to discover a deeper potential for experiencing as one kind of 'deeper insides'. *Finding and using a moment of strong feeling requires knowing what to do, how to do it, and the competence to be able to do it.* There is a relatively explicit set of steps that are helpful in finding a moment of strong feeling. If you do not know what steps to follow, and if you are not very good at these steps, you will probably not be able to find a moment of strong feeling. Furthermore, if you are able to find a moment of strong feeling, there are explicit methods to use in discovering the deeper potential for experiencing. If you do not know these methods, or if you are not competent in using them, you almost certainly will be unable to discover the deeper potential for experiencing.

In experiential psychotherapy (Mahrer, 1996), each session opens by enabling the person to focus attention on the strong-feelinged scene that is here for the person in this session. The first landmark in each session consists of uncovering the explicit moment of strong feeling, and using it to discover the underlying deeper potential for experiencing.

1   Show the person how to find a scene of strong feeling

In the very beginning of the session, the therapist starts by seeing if the person is ready and willing to look for a scene of strong feeling. If so, the therapist shows the person how to be in the right posture for the work.

Probably the most helpful posture is for both therapist and person to sit alongside one another rather than face-to-face, and for both to be mainly attending 'out there' – out in front – rather than mainly attending to one another. It is helpful if both of you close your eyes throughout the whole session. It is much easier to see images and scenes if your eyes are closed and if your attention is mainly out there. There is another bonus if both of you have your eyes closed and both are attending mainly out there: this posture minimizes the usual turning of psychotherapy into two face-to-face people, attending mainly to one another, and playing out personal feelings in their interpersonal roles (Mahrer, 1996). If the person is ready, then carefully and slowly say something along the following lines:

> Think of whatever it is that is the main thing on your mind, the thing that bothers you the most. Even just thinking about it makes you have strong feelings . . . Think of the worst feelings that you have . . . Think of the times when you have awful feelings, times when you felt terrible . . . There are times when you have strong feelings, feelings of maybe being happy, feeling just wonderful, exciting

great feelings, or feelings that were terrible, like feeling terrified, lost, hurt, what's the use, frustrated, torn apart, like it's all over, or almost scared to death . . . Think of times when the strong feeling is all inside you, probably didn't show to anyone, or times when the feelings really showed; anyone could see them . . . The time may have been dramatic and special, like it doesn't happen often at all – or the time may have been one that is very ordinary, a little one, nothing much unusual is happening, except that yes the feeling is so strong inside you . . . The time may have been in the last few days or so, maybe in the last week or so, or maybe you're thinking of something that happened some time ago, a few years or more, or maybe very long ago . . . When is it that the feelings in you were so powerful, filled you all over?

The instructions are to help the person come up with a scene of powerful feeling.

2 Find a scene of strong feeling

If the instructions are done well, and if the person is ready and willing to find a scene of strong feeling, it is somewhat common that the instructions will bring forth a scene of strong feeling – some time, incident, occasion when the feeling was very strong.

The older woman listens to the instructions and almost immediately is crying. She says, 'I had tests . . . I don't usually go to hospitals . . . It's been three or four months ago, before Christmas, and the doctor says I had cancer in my lung. Started there. It spread . . . I think I'm going to die.' She says all of this slowly, with tears, and continues: 'The worst time is not then. It's when I wake up in the morning . . . It takes a few seconds . . . (the crying is more intense) and I remember that there is this thing in me . . . That's the worst time . . . I just lay there . . . and I cry.'

She finds a scene of strong feeling almost directly from the opening instructions. This happens sometimes, but it is more common for you to have to search around for some scene of strong feeling.

Often you have to search for a scene of strong feeling Usually the person starts with some feeling, and it takes work on both your parts to find a scene in which the feeling is quite strong. There is a feeling of being very tense, worried, nervous, scared, of being almost out of control, falling apart. It happens anywhere, everywhere. She is close to the feeling, but not to scenes and times when this feeling is strong. You have to look for scenes, times, when this feeling is strong. Sometimes this means searching around, looking here and there. Finally you arrive at a scene. It is when she is in a car, driving, and the car is going relatively fast. This is when the feeling is quite powerful, the particular situation in which she is gripped with this awful strong feeling.

Often you go from a relatively recent scene to some earlier scene of strong feeling. Quite often you start with a relatively current scene and then use this to find an earlier scene where the feeling is exceedingly strong. He starts with times when his father-in-law is curt with him, and he feels numb, tight and put down. Are there earlier times when this feeling is even stronger? We search for earlier times in his life. We arrive at a time, many months ago, when his boss was yelling at him, and he fell into a state of feeling frozen, numb, barely hearing the boss's words, not comprehending what the boss was saying. It was almost terror. If we open up the possibility to include times from years ago – maybe many years ago, when this feeling was even more powerful – what comes to mind was when he was a little boy, some kids were taunting him, and he went into a state he always remembered. He was pulled away, like stone, his whole body rigid, and he stood there for some time, frozen and solid, rigid, even when all the kids seemed to have gone away. The feeling is very powerful.

The scenes are usually ones of strong bad feeling. But they can be ones of strong good feeling.

You have completed this second step when the person seems to regard this as a meaningful scene of strong feeling, when the scene and feeling seem to be quite central and important to the person, when the scene is relatively vivid and real, and when the person's attention is mainly on this particular scene, rather than on talking to you about that scene. You and the person have found a scene of very strong feeling.

The person is portrayed on the left in Figure 12.1. This is the ordinary state of the person. The scene of strong feeling is designated as the 'general situational context'. The person is being operating potential 1 (OP1), and undergoing this experiencing to a mild degree as indicated by the slanted lines. The deeper potential for experiencing (DP4), is far below: hidden, part of the deeper domain. And the person's relationship to the deeper potential is bad, negative, as indicated by the two minus or negative signs in the channel of relationships between the person (OP1) and the deeper potential (DP4).

3   Enter into, live and be in, the scene of strong feeling, and discover the moment of strong feeling

The goal of this step is to discover the precise moment of strong feeling. It is a process of discovery because even when the person finds a scene of strong feeling, he usually has little or no idea what that moment is. Discovering that moment calls for: (a) entering into the scene of strong feeling, living and being in this scene; and then (b) actively searching for the precise moment of strong feeling.

The therapist cannot do this alone. It has to be accomplished by the person. This means that the person has to be ready and willing to enter into the scene of strong feeling, to live and be in this scene, and to search for and find the moment of strong feeling. To be effective in this search, it is helpful if the therapist is ready, willing, and competent in joining with the person in both entering into the scene of strong feeling and in searching for and finding the moment of strong feeling.

If the person is ready and willing, the therapist shows the person how to enter into the scene, how to live and be in the scene of strong feeling. For example, the therapist shows the person how to put virtually all their attention onto the scene itself, how to fill in most of the details of this immediate present scene, how to be and talk in the immediate here-and-now of the ongoing scene, and how to let oneself be filled with the present experiencing and feeling. The therapist helps this to happen by leading the way, and by entering into the scene along with the person. The therapist is in the scene – wholly undergoing the experiencing and in a state of fully being in this scene.

Actual entry into the alive and feelinged scene is a dramatic and qualitative shift. No longer is the person 'taking about' some scene. Virtually all of the person's attention is on what is happening, on actually living and being in the scene in a way that is immediate and present and real, and so that the feelings are immediate and real. The person is virtually no longer here in the office, with a therapist; instead, the person is almost wholly being in this feelinged scene.

Only when you are truly living and being in this feelinged scene can you search around for exactly when and where the precise instant of strong feeling is. This moment is hidden inside the alive and real scene, and can be found by first living and being in this immediate alive scene of strong feeling.

The scene of strong feeling described by the first woman in the example above is when she is driving the car relatively fast. As she details what is happening, hers is the only car on the straight country road. She is looking straight ahead, and she is now actually undergoing tension, worry, fright – almost being out of control. Once she is fully living in this scene of strong feeling, we search for the precise moment when these feelings are strongest. Finally we discover something new, the moment that had been hidden. The awful feelings are strongest when her hands are locked onto the wheel, and she is quite unable to control her arms and hands. In this moment, the road ahead seems to disappear and she doesn't know if it goes down a hill or veers to the left or right. Furthermore, in this precise moment, it is as if she is almost somewhat removed from her body – as if someone else were driving the car! We have discovered the precise moment of strong feeling.

The second woman details and enters into the scene in which she is in bed in the morning, becomes aware that she has cancer, and is crying. With all the tears, with all the horror of lying here and knowing about the lethal cancer inside me, here in my lungs, the scene is intensely real and the feelings are pouring out. We search inside this general scene for the specific moment of strong feeling. Slowly it is uncovered. There are scary glimpses of images of all kinds, and the worst one – the moment when the feelings are strongest – is when she gets a vague and terrifying flash of the cancer itself, inside her lung. This is the discovered moment of strong feeling.

With the man who was frozen and numb when his boss was yelling at him, searching for a scene in which this feeling was especially strong led us to the childhood scene in which the kids were taunting him and he went into a state of being incredibly rigid, like stone, pulled away. Once we entered into this alive and real scene, our search led to a precise moment when this feeling was most powerful. His mother must have been called by someone because in this moment he is seeing mother standing here, in front, and she is staring fixedly at him, a look of disbelief and pity on her face. There are tears in her eyes. He is rigid, eyes glazed, staring straight ahead, body tightly frozen. This is the moment of most powerful feeling.

We have entered into the scene of strong feeling, and have discovered the precise moment of strongest feeling. It is truly a discovery, something utterly new. And it is also real, alive, immediate, present.

4   In the moment of strong feeling, discover the deeper potential for experiencing

You are now in a position to discover the deeper potential for experiencing. Why? The answer is given in Figure 12.1, on the right. You and the person are living and being in the specific moment of strong feeling. Experiencing of the operating potential is now quite full, saturated, alive. This is indicated by the slanted lines filling the operating potential (OP1). The key change is that the deeper potential (DP4) has risen from being far below and outside the boundary of the operating domain – the ordinary functioning person or conscious self – to a point where the deeper potential is now well inside the boundary of the operating domain.

This means that here is a precious opportunity for the person to sense, know, access the deeper potential. It is right here, challengingly close by. However, and this is a powerful however, there are good and proper reasons why the person, located within the operating potential (OP1), is almost unable to sense, know, access the deeper potential. For one thing, the person is fully undergoing the experiencing of the operating potential, in this instant of strong feeling. Perhaps more importantly, the disintegrative relationship between the person (OP1) and the deeper potential (DP4) are now much more disintegrative, as indicated by the increase in negative signs in the channel of relationships between the operating and deeper potentials. What the person has feared is now happening: that is, the deeper potential is now intruded, has broken into the operating domain. What is far worse, the deeper potential is virtually on the brink of imploding the operating potential, invading it, replacing it, destroying it, breaking it to pieces, eradicating it, putting it out of existence. Here is the imminence of death, the cracking apart of one's very existence, identity, self, meaning, life.

How would the therapist know she or he has accessed the deeper potential? There are some very useful signs. One is that you shift out of having such frightening, awful, terrifying, anguished feelings. They are gone, or significantly diminished. Second, you experience something new, something different. This is the sensing of the deeper potential. For a moment, you receive it, you are in its glow, and this is qualitatively different from bathing

and wallowing in the operating potential or the terrible disintegrative feelings of fearing, hating, being terrified by the far too imminent deeper
potential. Third, the immediate situational context will itself change. Its very
meaning and look shift. Fourth, the feeling changes. From fright and terror
and purely awful feeling, there is a breath of lightness, good feeling, a puff
of joy, a lift of buoyant happiness. In other words, you know the deeper
potential is right here when things change; something new happens, and it
feels both different and good.

   You and the person are living and being in the moment of strong feeling.
The deeper potential is close by. How can you receive it, sense it, allow
yourself to be touched by it? There are three ways that seem helpful in
accomplishing this.

Let yourself be in the right location   The person is almost certainly locked
inside the operating potential, pinioned by and filled with the awful feelings.
That location will not especially work to receive the deeper potential; the trick
is that the therapist is usually much freer to be in some other location that has a
much better chance of receiving and sensing the deeper potential. While the
person is filled with the awful feelings, the therapist is in some other place, free
of the awful feelings, and in a place that allows the therapist to have wonderful
feelings that go with accessing the deeper potential. The patient is typically
here, filled with terrible feeling. In exciting contrast, the therapist is over there,
filled with the wonderful feelings of the accessed deeper potential.

   One location is down inside the deeper potential. Unlike the client, the
therapist is free and able to enter into the bowels of the deeper potential
(DP4, right side, Figure 12.1). The therapist can actually be down inside the
very deeper potential from which the person is drawing back. In the moment
of strong feeling, the person is driving the car, all of her attention riveted on
the road straight ahead, her fingers welded to the steering wheel, the car
whizzing faster and faster, and she is almost beyond controlling the car.
While the person is frozen inside the operating potential, the therapist is far
more free and able to slide inside the deeper potential. While the person is
undergoing screechingly awful feelings, the therapist is having the delightful
feelings of undergoing the deeper potential. What is occurring in the
therapist – free of the bad feelings, fully living in this immediate moment,
and being located in the bowels of the deeper potential – is the utterly
wonderful experiencing of sheer unbounded force, open energy, excited
spontaneity. This is the deeper potential for experiencing.

   A second location is inside that thing or person out there, the one on
which the patient's attention is riveted, especially when the patient is almost
drawn toward being inside that other thing or person, as if seemingly
knowing what may be occurring inside the thing or person out there. It is as
if that thing or person actually houses the deeper potential, is the 'agent' or
'carrier' of the deeper potential. In the moment of strong feeling, she is
transfixed on the cancer: the killing machine, the flesh destroyer. The more
she describes the cancer, the more she leans toward entering into the cancer,

the more the therapist is able to enter into actually being that cancer. From within the cancer, free of the bad feeling occurring in the person, the therapist can literally 'be' the experiencing occurring in the cancer. Then it happens. With saturated good feelings, the therapist undergoes the experiencing of absolute destructiveness, viciousness, killing, eradication. This is the deeper potential for experiencing.

A third location is in the near vicinity of the operating and deeper potentials, but just outside the awful feelings. The therapist is close enough to be bathed by the glow of the deeper potential, and is able to receive it while free of the awful feelings. It is as if the therapist is close enough to the person to be in this moment of strong feeling, yet the therapist is like a clone who is removed from the patient's bad feeling. Picture the therapist in the car, right next to the person and the car is hurtling forward, faster and faster, approaching a state of being out of control. While the patient is having agonizing feelings, the therapist is free to undergo the joyous deeper potential of sheer unbounded force, open energy, excited spontaneity.

A final location is inside the very bowels of the awful feelings. Unlike the person who is bathed in intense and awful feeling, the therapist is free to plunge, with innocent naiveté, into the black hole of the worst possible awful feelings. As the therapist plunges deeper and deeper into the absolute worst possible agonizing and catastrophic feelings, wholly open to the worst feeling, he or she will arrive at a point of entry into the vicinity of the deeper potential. When that point is reached, there are no further awful feelings. Dramatically, there is a shift into a good-feelinged state of being touched by the accessed deeper potential. In the moment of strong feeling, the person is a little boy, standing in the cold, his mother looking at him. He is rigid, staring straight ahead, his body frozen, stiff, fixed. The feeling is just awful. Something is wrong with him. Look at the way mother looks at me. I am filled with terrible feelings of being crazy. As the therapist throws him- or herself in the pit of awful feelings, plunging into the increasingly catastrophic terror of becoming crazier and crazier, suddenly there is a new state in the therapist. Here is the newfound deeper potential as the therapist receives the experiencing of being utterly removed, in a new state of being safe, beyond reach, removed, a hard core of being invulnerable: in a state of inviolateness. This is the inner deeper experiencing.

Actively intensify the experiencing until the inner deeper experiencing occurs   The deeper potential is drawn closer because the person is living and being in the moment of strong feeling, and the fuller experiencing of the operating potential lifts up the deeper potential. You can therefore bring the deeper potential even closer, close enough to receive it, to access it, by actively intensifying the sheer experiencing in the person. This means that the person is to go much further in undergoing the sheer experiencing of the operating potential. Pump up the sheer intensity; experience it more: much more fully, with greater power and strength.

In the moment of strong feeling, he is the little boy, standing here rigidly in front of his mother who is watching him, pitiably. The experiencing is that of being the object of pity, utterly passive, withdrawn. As awful as is this state, try to make it far more intense. Make it much more saturated. Let it become much stronger. Take it to a much higher plateau of sheer strength of experiencing. Actively intensify the experiencing of being withdrawn, utterly passive, more and more the pitiable object. As the patient and therapist together spin out into far more actively intensified experiencing, something new happens. The screechingly intensified experiencing gives way to the deeper potential, to something new, and the therapist now has a received experiencing of being safely unreachable: of being a hard inner core of removed untouchability. Here is another way of getting the deeper potential for experiencing.

Include the suddenly added new element As the patient and therapist are living and being in the moment of strong feeling, some altogether new element usually appears. Suddenly the person sees something new in the scene, perhaps something concrete and specific that had been masked, obscured – not there a moment or two before. Or perhaps some new element occurs as the patient blurts out something or is suddenly seized with some new bodily-felt sensation. In any case, some new element is suddenly present, and the deeper potential is received by including this sudden new element in the moment of strong feeling. This moment is now different, and it is this difference that yields the deeper potential.

As he is being the little boy, standing rigidly inflexible in front of his mother, he is full of awful feelings of falling apart, having been wronged, caught up in the frozen state. He sees the look on his mother's face, a look of almost disbelief in what she sees and a look of undiluted pitiable concern. But suddenly he hears something new. 'She says something! . . . Yes . . . Yes . . . She says . . . "My god, who are you!" ' Immediately, with this added new element, the immediate moment changes. The therapist is seized with something new as mother's words are included. Here is the experiencing of the deeper hard core of sheer removability, a safe sense of not being reached, a core of inviolability.

When she is focused on the terrifying cancer, she is filled with the grinding racking feelings of terror, imminent death, helplessness, being the victim. In the midst of this moment, she suddenly blurts out, 'It's a God-damned killing machine!!!' The feelings are suddenly new and different. She is feeling almost a sense of pride in the God-damned killing machine. The therapist, and patient too, are sensing the deeper potential of experiencing absolute destructiveness, viciousness, cold eradication.

She is caught up in the moment of driving the car faster and faster. In the moment, the car is almost spinning out of control and her hands are locked onto the wheel. She is terrified. Then, quite suddenly, she blurts out something as if she has pulled out of the scene of being in the car. She screams: 'If it really went that fast, that car'd *fly!! It'd be a jet!* ' If you envelop this outburst in the immediate moment of strong feeling, screaming these words as you are racing along, the therapist is now experiencing a new sense of sheer unbounded energy, force, spontaneous excitement.

Here are three ways of discovering the deeper insides by being in the moment of strong feeling and then: (a) letting yourself be in the right location in that precious moment; or (b) actively intensifying the experiencing until the inner deeper experiencing occurs; or (c) including the suddenly added new element in the moment of strong feeling. Yet the precious doorway is the moment of strong feeling. I suggest that the moment of strong feeling is probably the best way of discovering the deeper insides.

Conclusions and invitation

Some therapists find it important and helpful to picture patients in terms of deeper potentials for experiencing, deeper inner ways of being, deeper multiple selves or subpersonalities. I find that a very useful way of getting at or discovering this kind of deeper insides is by means of the 'moment of strong feeling'. The first conclusion is that proper use of the moment of strong feeling is a most effective way of discovering inner deeper potentials for experiencing or similar kinds of inner deeper qualities, characteristics, ways of being, deeper selves or subpersonalities.

The second conclusion is more of a friendly challenge. I suggest that proper use of the moment of strong feeling can be the most effective avenue toward getting at deeper insides, however therapists picture the nature and content of whatever is regarded as inner and deeper.

The invitation is for therapists to study, to learn how, and to use the moment of strong feelings to discover, uncover, and get at the person's insides – especially deeper potentials for experiencing, inner deeper ways of being, and similar kinds of deeper insides. Experiential psychotherapy relies on this method. Either follow the experiential method or adapt the method to fit your own approach.

Note

1   Figure 12.1 is referred to throughout the chapter. It is to be found on p. 214, at the beginning of the chapter, for the reader's convenience.

References

Berne, E. (1961) *Transactional Analysis in Psychotherapy*. New York: Grove.
Ferrucci, P. (1982) *What We May Be*. Wellingborough: Turnstone Press.
Heaton, J.M. (1972) 'Insight in phenomenology and psychoanalysis', *Journal of the British Society for Phenomenology*, 3: 135–45.

Mahrer, A.R. (1996) *The Complete Guide to Experiential Psychotherapy*. New York: Wiley.

Mahrer, A.R. (1997) 'Empathy as therapist-client alignment', in A.C. Bohart and L.S. Greenberg (eds), *Empathy Reconsidered: New Directions in Psychotherapy*. Washington, DC: American Psychological Association. pp. 187–213.

Mahrer, A.R., Boulet, D.B. and Fairweather, D.R. (1994) 'Beyond empathy: Advances in the clinical theory and methods of empathy', *Clinical Psychology Review*, 14: 183–98.

Ornstein, R. (1986) *Multiminds: A New Way of Looking at Human Behavior*. Boston, MA: Houghton Mifflin.

Rowan, J. (1990) *Subpersonalities: The People Inside Us*. London: Routledge.

Schwartz, R.C. (1987) 'Our multiple selves: Applying systems thinking to the inner family', *Networker*, March/April: 80–3.

Watkins, M. (1986) *Invisible Guests: The Development of Imaginal Dialogues*. Hillsdale, NJ: Analytic Press.

13   THE INTERNAL FAMILY SYSTEMS MODEL

Richard C. Schwartz

This chapter provides some practical ways to understand and work clinically with subpersonalities by highlighting conceptual and clinical aspects of the internal family systems (IFS) model, an approach to psychotherapy that has evolved over the past fifteen years (Schwartz, 1987, 1988, 1992, 1995; Breunlin et al. 1992; Goulding and Schwartz, 1995). Because the IFS model respects and works with the multiplicity of the mind, it contains elements in common with other approaches in this book. Its unique elements derive from the influence of systems thinking and its beliefs about, and use of, what it calls the Self.

While designing this model, my colleagues and I tried to presuppose as little as possible so as to build it in collaboration with clients and their subpersonalities (what IFS calls 'parts'). We tried to listen carefully to people's (and our own) parts and learn from them how to help them transform. With embarrassing frequency, the presuppositions we did have were destroyed in this process and replaced by the ideas and techniques described below.

The internal family systems model

The IFS model represents a new synthesis of two already existing para-digms: systems thinking and the multiplicity of the mind. It brings concepts and methods from various schools of family therapy to the world of subpersonalities. This synthesis was the natural outcome when I, as a young, fervent family therapist, began hearing from clients about their inner lives. After I was able to set aside my preconceived notions about therapy and the mind, and began really to listen to what my 72 clients were saying, what I heard over and over were descriptions of what they often called their parts – the conflicted subpersonalities that resided within them. This was not a new discovery. Many other theorists have described a similar inner phenomenon, beginning with Freud's id, ego, and superego; Jung's archetypes and com-plexes; and more recently the object relations conceptions of internal objects, as well as being at the core of less mainstream approaches like transactional analysis (ego states), psychosynthesis (subpersonalities), and now manifesting in cognitive-behavioral approaches under the term 'schemata'.

As I listened to my clients, my understanding of the nature of sub-personalities shifted from a unidimensional position akin to a schema – that is, that there was an angry part, a sad part, a self-critic, etc. – to the multidimensional view that each part has a full range of feelings and beliefs, but displays only a portion of those because of its role in the system.

This multidimensional view of subpersonalities situates the IFS model within the tradition of Jung (1956, 1962, 1969a, 1969b) and his younger contemporary, Roberto Assagioli (1973, 1975; see Ferrucci, 1982) who developed psychosynthesis. Since Jung and Assagioli, a number of theorists have recognized our natural multiplicity and, in exploring this territory, have made observations that are remarkably similar to one another. They share a belief that these internal entities are more than clusters of thought or feeling, more than mere states of mind. Instead they are seen as distinct personalities, each with a full range of emotion and desire, and of different ages, temperaments, talents and even genders. These inner personalities have a large degree of autonomy in the sense that they think, say and feel things independent of the person in which they exist. Jung's later writing describes archetypes and complexes in ways that approach autonomous multiplicity, as does a Jungian derivative called Voice Dialogue (Stone and Winkelman, 1985; Stone and Stone, 1993). In addition, ego state therapy developed by hypnotherapists John and Helen Watkins (Watkins, 1978; Watkins and Johnson, 1982; Watkins and Watkins, 1979) approaches, and Assagioli's psychosynthesis subscribes to, full-personality multiplicity (see Rowan, 1990; and Schwartz, 1995, for more on multiplicity).

A systemic view

Most of these groundbreaking approaches focused on individual aspects of different subpersonalities, giving less attention to how these inner entities functioned together, as a system. Since my training steeped me in systems thinking, it was second nature to begin tracking sequences of internal inter-action in the same way I had tracked interactions among family members as a structural/strategic family therapist (for information on tracking sequences, see Haley, 1976; Breunlin et al., 1992). As I did, I learned that, across people, parts take on common roles and common inner relationships. I also learned that these inner roles and relationships were not static and could be changed if one intervened carefully and respectfully. I began conceiving of the mind as an inner family and experimenting with techniques I had used as a family therapist.

Boundaries

The structural family therapy techniques called enactment and boundary-making, for example, involve improving the boundaries around subsystems within a family (Minuchin, 1974; Minuchin and Fishman, 1981). For instance, when two polarized family members are discussing issues, the therapist prevents others from interrupting and keeps the two engaged until some new resolution is achieved. In working with internal families, it quickly became clear that parts were as highly polarized as the external families in which they developed. Many parts had never related directly to one another and maintained extreme views of what the others were like. They formed alliances and coalitions, and would interrupt one another with impunity.

As I began trying to improve inner boundaries by asking parts to step back and not interfere when other parts were interacting, I found that – as is true in external families – long-standing polarizations often melted once two parts communicated directly and without the influence of other parts. It also became clear that parts have boundaries in the sense that they can separate their indiosyncratic emotions and beliefs from one another, and that helping them do this not only allows them to resolve their conflicts more easily but also helps them each identify what their feelings and beliefs really are – separate from the role they are forced into or from the general inner tumult.

Good parts in bad roles

The IFS, then, sees a person as containing an ecology of relatively discrete and autonomous minds, each of which has valuable qualities and each of which is designed to and wants to play a valuable role within. These parts are forced out of their valuable roles, however, by life experiences that can reorganize the system in unhealthy ways. A good analogy is an alcoholic family in which the children are forced into protective and stereotypical roles by the extreme dynamics of their family. While one finds similar sibling roles across alcoholic families (for example, the scapegoat, mascot, lost child, etc.), one does not conclude that those roles represent the essence of those children. Instead, each child is unique and, once released from his or her role by therapeutic intervention, can find interests and talents separate from the demands of their chaotic family. The same process seems to hold for internal families – parts are forced into extreme roles by external circumstances and, once it seems safe, they gladly transform into valuable inner family members.

What are the circumstances that force parts into extreme and sometimes destructive roles? Trauma is one factor and the effects of childhood sexual abuse on internal families has been discussed at length (Goulding and Schwartz, 1995). But it is also a person's family values and interaction patterns that create internal polarizations which escalate over time and are played out in other relationships. This, also, is not a novel observation; indeed it is a central tenet of object relations and self psychology. What is novel to IFS is the attempt to understand all levels of human organization – intrapsychic, family and culture – with the same systemic principles, and to intervene at each level with the same techniques.

Joining respectfully

Structural family therapy helped me view this inner family as a delicate ecology that one must enter carefully and with respect for the gatekeepers (Minuchin, 1974; Minuchin and Fishman, 1981). Structural family therapists are taught the technique of joining – as soon as possible, showing respect to and earning the trust of the people (often the parents) who are responsible for protecting the system. Similarly, I quickly learned that if I tried to bypass the parts who protected a person's inner system, I would encounter a great deal of resistance; however, if I joined with those parts by learning about and addressing their fears, not only would they not resist but they would provide assistance and direction. These manager parts want the system to heal, but they want to know that it can be done safely and that the therapist is competent. It is their duty to resist until that has been demonstrated.

Patterns of parts' roles

Are there common roles for parts across people? Family therapists look for patterns of interaction that indicate how family systems are structured. After working with a large number of clients, some patterns began to appear. As described above, most clients had parts that tried to keep them functional and safe – tried to maintain control of their inner and outer environments by, for example, keeping them from getting too close or dependent on others; criticizing their appearance or performance to make them look or act in ways that would avoid rejection; focusing on taking care of others rather than on their own needs. These parts seemed to be in protective, managerial roles so they are called the *managers*.

Where a person has been hurt, humiliated, frightened or shamed in their past, they will have parts that carry the emotions, memories and sensations from those experiences. Managers often want to keep those feelings out of consciousness and, consequently, try to keep these vulnerable and needy parts locked in inner closets. Those incarcerated parts are known as the *exiles*.

The third and final group of parts goes into action whenever one of the exiles is upset to the point that it may flood the person with its extreme feelings or make the person vulnerable to being hurt again. When that is the case, this third group tries to put out the inner flames of feeling as quickly as possible, so they are called the *firefighters*. They tend to be highly impulsive and they are driven to find stimulation that will override or dissociate from the exile's feelings. Bingeing on drugs, alcohol, food, sex or work, are common firefighter activities.

The Self

There is one other key aspect of the IFS model. This is the belief that, in addition to these parts, everyone has at their core a Self that contains many crucial leadership qualities like perspective, confidence, compassion and acceptance. Working with hundreds of clients for more than a decade, some of whom were severely abused and showed severe symptoms, has convinced me that everyone has this untarnished, healing Self despite the fact that many people have very little access to it initially. When working with an individual, the goal of IFS is to differentiate this Self from the parts, thereby releasing its resources; and then in the state of Self, to help parts out of their extreme roles.

Self = Soul

The Self in the IFS is less analogous to an executive or observing ego as it is to the spiritual concept of a soul. Virtually all the world's spiritual practices are designed to help people get in touch with their soul, a transcendent state of compassion and calm from which emanates wise, healing energy. In contrast, based on assumptions from developmental psychology that such a healthy inner leader can only develop if a person received adequate parenting during a crucial early period, many psychotherapies view clients as lacking anything resembling this healthy inner state. Consequently, therapists try to build ego strength where it is believed that little previously resided.

The IFS model not only recognizes the existence of this soul-like state of Self at everyone's core, but has developed ways to help people access and release it. Once in this state of Self-leadership, people can harmonize and heal their inner systems of subpersonalities or 'parts' that they experience as extreme thoughts and emotions.

The client's Self as healer

With certainty in the existence of a healing, loving Self within clients, a therapist's task is transformed. Rather than dealing directly with a client's parts – which leads to a parent-like relationship with the client – the IFS therapist works as a partner to the client's Self, and the client's Self becomes a compassionate therapist or leader with his or her parts. Thus it is the client's Self, rather than the therapist, that takes the lead in helping parts transform and harmonize. The therapist's job shifts from providing key interpretations or reparenting experiences to helping clients maintain a state of Self-leadership so they can heal themselves.

This shift is a difficult one for most therapists because it requires trusting that inherent healing wisdom exists in clients, even those with severe symptoms and whose behavior suggests the absence of wisdom of any kind. Often therapists only learn this kind of trust after repeatedly witnessing the power of Self-leadership in their clients. Much of the IFS technique is designed to help clients release their Selves so both client and therapist can learn to trust it.

Releasing the Self

Suppose a client, Joe, enters your office complaining that he is having trouble at work because he's quick to explode at co-workers in anger, even when they make small mistakes. If you're oriented toward subpersonalities you would want to know more about this angry part of him – how he feels toward it, how he tries to handle it, how often it takes over. You may even ask him to focus on it and see if an image comes to him for it. He says he sees a monster who looks enraged. He says he's afraid of it and tries to avoid situations where it might be provoked.

Separating parts from the Self

From the IFS perspective, *Joe* (as his Self) is not afraid of it because, by definition, his Self would not be. Therefore, Joe's Self must be blended with the feelings and beliefs of another part of him that is afraid. So, you ask him to find the scared part by focusing internally on those fears, and ask that scared part if it is willing to separate from him for a minute. If his scared part has some trust in his Self, he will feel an immediate shift of demeanor, away from fear and toward some other emotion.

In response to your enquiry, Joe says that after the fear left, he now feels angry at the angry part because it's screwing up his life. You ask him to find the subpersonality that's angry at the angry part and ask it to separate too. He makes that internal request and reports that suddenly he feels sorry for the angry part because it looks like a frightened young boy who's trying to act tough. He wants to find out why that boy is so upset. In his mind, he approaches the boy but the boy clearly doesn't trust him and threatens him. After several sessions of remaining compassionately present with the boy, the boy shows scenes from Joe's past when he was humiliated by his stepfather.

The scenario described above is a common one in my caseload. I present it to illustrate how quickly, in some cases, a person can differentiate his or her Self. Often by simply asking parts that have blended to separate and trust the Self, a person will shift immediately, and will shift in the direction of qualities like perpective, compassion, curiosity, confidence – qualities that make working with the target part much easier. Often their perception of parts or of people will shift also. The threatening monster suddenly became a frightened boy. It was this discovery – that when extreme parts agree to separate, the person that is left always displays those qualities spontaneously – that convinced me of the existence of the Self at everyone's core. This discovery was a serendipidous by-product of applying the boundary-making technique from family therapy, described earlier, to inner systems.

Once the Self has been released in this way, therapy is less effortful because it is like working with a very competent co-therapist that lives with the person. The client's Self sees or senses his or her parts and comforts, educates or listens to them. The therapist tries to detect when extreme parts are influencing the client's Self and helps the Self convince them to separate.

When parts fear separating

The problem is that some clients' parts are reluctant to allow their Selves to lead in this way. Sometimes manager parts have been in charge for years and do not trust that it is safe to relinquish control. This is particularly true for people who have been hurt severely in their lives. An example of this would be if, when you asked Joe's scared part to separate, it wouldn't and so he remained afraid of the angry part. Where that is the case, rather than trying to force the part out or proceeding even though he's frightened, you would ask to work with Joe's scared part and try to help Joe understand and address its fears. Joe's scared part tells him it is afraid that if it steps back, the angry part will take over even more often than it already does. Joe negotiates with it by agreeing to put the angry part in a locked room in his mind before he talks to it and not getting close to it until the scared part feels secure that the angry one has agreed not to take over.

Thus, the differentiation of the Self may take time and require many such negotiations. People's internal systems are full of polarizations like the one between Joe's fear and his anger. When you try to approach one part, inevitably those that are polarized with it become upset and interfere – just like in family therapy. When a person's Self is not accessible initially, IFS therapists work with the parts that are afraid to permit access, until those parts are reassured enough to permit some Self-leadership.

The other advantage of having a client's Self (rather than the therapist) being the primary healer is that clients feel that they healed themselves. Many are able to do the work on their own outside of sessions and, consequently, sometimes the therapy can be relatively brief. They leave therapy feeling empowered: knowing what to do when something upsets them.

Releasing and working with a client's Self in this way is a key difference between the IFS and many other models that work with subpersonalities. Many models are not aware of the existence of this Self, so they work with subpersonalities directly. In a sense, they try to become the Self to the system. Some other models (for example, psychosynthesis and Jungian psychology) share the concept of a transpersonal or higher self, but either see it as a passive, non-judgemental witness state, or are less systematic in accessing it. The releasing of the Self and letting it heal the system has become the central practice of the IFS model.

Unburdening

Once a client's Self is able to show compassion to a part and form a trusting relationship with it, there are steps one can take to help the part transform. As the frightened boy (formerly the angry monster) comes to trust that Joe cares for him, the boy becomes less frightened. But after years of helping people get to that point, I concluded that for many parts, comforting them in the present was not enough. Often a part would calm down in one session only to be terrified when we found it again in the next session. Parts carry extreme beliefs and emotions, derived from events in the past, that do not vanish simply because the Self cares for them.

Compassionate witnessing

I began getting clients to ask their parts where their extreme beliefs or feelings had come from, and the parts began showing the person scenes from their pasts. Once a client's Self was able compassionately to witness the scenes that a part wanted to show such that the part felt understood – felt that the Self appreciated how bad those events were – the part was able to shed the beliefs and emotions it took from the past events, and I mean literally shed them. That is, if you ask a part where in or on its body (that is, the image's body) it carries a troublesome belief or emotion, it will be able to pinpoint an object that it is carrying.

You ask Joe to ask the boy where he carries his fear in or on his (the boy's) body and the boy says it is a knife in his (the boy's) heart; Joe asks where he carries the rage and it is a black, tar-like substance in his stomach. In response to asking the boy where he got the knife and the tar, the boy shows Joe scenes from his childhood in which he was beaten by his stepfather. These are scenes that Joe remembered but had tried to forget. After the boy believes that Joe appreciates how bad that was for him, you get Joe to ask the boy if he's willing to take those burdens out of his body. In the imagery, the boy takes the knife out of his heart but is reluctant to release the tar. He says he's afraid he might still need it to protect himself. Joe respects his fear and decides to let him keep the tar until Joe has demonstrated to the boy that he can trust Joe for protection and no longer needs to hold the rage.

Burdens

What are we to make of the knife and the tar – these burdens that parts can identify. (If the reader is skeptical about the existence of such burdens, I recommend simply asking clients' parts.) I have been taught by parts that burdens are beliefs or emotions (energies) that enter the person from the outside world – from intense interactions or events – and become implanted in or attached to certain parts who become the bearers of those burdens. The burdens then govern a part's existence, coloring its perceptions and organizing its behavior – much as an implanted computer program might.

While its burdens are attached, a part cannot help but react automatically in rigid and extreme ways. Once burdens are released, parts are able to transform. They often literally change image and are free to take whatever role they may prefer – invariably a role that is valuable to the person. Once he trusted that it was safe to unburden his fear, Joe's little boy became a playful imp who liked to have fun with other people. The outcome of this transformation cannot be predicted. The new role is often far removed from the original role – who would have guessed that the treatening monster would become a playful imp?

The nature of parts

There are several different theories regarding the nature and origin of subpersonalities. The most popular theory portrays them as internalizations of significant people. Another common formulation is that they were created to cope with trauma; that they are fragments of the originally unitary personality.

The unburdening phenomenon strengthens the argument that subpersonalities are the natural state of the mind. If parts are, indeed, inherently valuable resources that exist to help us survive and thrive, then their often immediate transformation after unburdening from an extreme or destructive state to a valuable one makes sense. If instead they were mere internalizations or fragments, one would not expect such transformations. They would either disappear or slightly modify their original role.

The IFS position is that they are full-bodied personalities which, if a person were raised in an ideal environment, would find their natural, valuable, and harmonious role within the person's inner tribe of parts. Since the environment in which most of us are raised is far from ideal, our parts often have moved far from this pristine state and, instead, are forced into bothersome and destructive roles that they do not want but feel afraid to relinquish.

It is burdens that keep parts constrained to rigid roles: freezing them in the past as if what happened then is happening now, clouding their perceptions with anachronistic ideas, and loading them with destructive or desperate impulses. But these burdens are not always so easy to unload. They often become embedded in the system's overall set of defenses, so that unburdening may threaten other parts and they will resist.

For example, sexual abuse survivors always have parts that carry the burden of worthlessness. While these parts may want to unload their shame, other parts may – correctly – fear that if the survivor did not feel so worthless, she would become enraged at the abuser rather than at herself. They fear that if her rage was aimed at the appropriate target, the abuser would hurt her again, would abandon her, or would follow through on some other threat made when she was a child. As a result, she won't be able to unburden her worthlessness until she has worked with the rageful part to the point that the others are not so afraid of it.

A systemic approach to firefighters

It is the recognition of these kinds of interconnections among parts or burdens that makes systems thinking so valuable in working with intra-psychic process. Therapists who do not appreciate that each part is em-bedded in a network of internal relationships are likely to encounter much more 'resistance' than therapists who are willing to find out about these networks before intervening forcefully. For example, I used to waste hours of therapy in futile power struggles with firefighters (those impulsive, frantic parts that made clients binge on food or alcohol, or made them cut them-selves or feel suicidal) as I tried to coerce or convince them out of behavior that I thought to be self-destructive. It was not until I gave up the pushing and instead encouraged clients' Selves to respectfully ask such parts what they were afraid would happen if they did stop their behavior that I learned how constrained in their roles they were. The following is a typical dialogue with a firefighter.

> *Therapist* (to bulimic client): Susan, could you ask this part that makes you binge why it does that?
> *Susan*: It says it just likes to feel good – it likes the rush of a sugar high.
> *Therapist*: Ask what it's afraid would happen if it didn't make you binge?
> *Susan*: It says that I would feel sad.
> *Therapist*: And ask it what's so bad about feeling sad . . . what's it afraid will happen if you felt sad?
> *Susan*: It says that if I felt sad I might die.
> *Therapist*: What makes it think that you might die if you got sad?
> *Susan*: It's reminding me of the time when I almost killed myself with pills.

So the part of Susan that makes her binge has good reason to be afraid of her sad, exiled parts – they might trigger the suicidal firefighter who tries to take her out of misery once and for all. Until the binge part can be convinced that this will not happen, it cannot – indeed, it should not – give up its role.

Self-destructive or Self-protective?

Much apparently self-destructive behavior is done by firefighters who are struggling to protect the system. If a therapist does not recognize the some-times large and complicated web of constraints in which a part is embedded, the therapist will conclude that it is irrational and will increase a client's inner polarization by encouraging him or her to fight the part. If, instead, the therapist respectfully explores the network of inner relationships that keep the part in its role, and then asks permission to begin releasing these constraints, 'destructive' parts will often gladly (although skeptically) co-operate.

> *Therapist*: Okay, could you show the binge part you appreciate its protecting you from another of those suicidal episodes?

Susan: I'm afraid to because I don't want to encourage its bingeing.

When Susan says she is afraid to do this, the therapist suspects that another part, not her Self, is doing the talking. This is because, in the IFS model, the Self is never extreme and, consequently, would not be afraid.

Therapist: Could you find the part that's afraid of that happenning and ask that part if it's willing to step back and not interfere right now and trust you and me with this binge part?

Susan: Okay, it stepped back.

Therapist: How do you feel toward the binge part now?

Susan: I just thanked it for protecting me and it has softened considerably. I think it liked being appreciated.

Therapist: Ask the binge part: If we were able to help the parts it reacts to – the sad and suicidal parts – so they weren't so sad or suicidal any more, would it have to keep making you binge as much?

Susan: It says no, but it doesn't think they can be helped. It thinks they're hopeless.

Therapist: I understand that, but if that was possible, the binge part would like that?

Susan: It says yes, it's tired of doing this to me.

Therapist: Ask it what it might like to do if it didn't have to do this to you and instead could do anything it wanted to.

Susan: It has no idea – it's done this for so long it didn't know anything else was possible.

Therapist: Ask it to just think about it for a second.

Susan: It says it might like to help me have fun and not be so afraid of being with people.

Therapist: How does that sound to you?

Susan: That sounds great.

Therapist: Tell it that we'll try to help it into that role but first we'll have to help the suicidal part and then the sad parts that it protects. Do we have its permission to approach the suicidal part?

Susan: It's worried about me wanting to kill myself if I get near it.

Therapist: I totally understand that concern and I wouldn't want that either. But let the binge part know that it's possible to get close to the suicidal without being overwhelmed by it. We'll start with it in a totally enclosed room and, before we have you enter the room and get anywhere near it, we'll ask it not to overwhelm you and won't have you get close until that's in place. The suicidal part can control that process, and if it thinks that by not overwhelming, it will get help, it'll cooperate. Does the binge part believe what I'm saying?

Susan: It says it's willing to give it a try, but it wants to come along and watch to see that we don't screw up.

Therapist: That's fine. It can be there and stop the action at any time it thinks we're doing anything dangerous, or that you'll be overwhelmed. I value its help in monitoring the process.

Fear of being overwhelmed

This fear, that if one part steps back the person will be overwhelmed by another part resulting in dangerous consequences, is a common constraint. It took years before my colleagues and I discovered a way to address this very realistic fear. It turns out that the parts themselves, not the Self, can control whether or not parts overwhelm. By convincing them that it's in their best interest not to take over, clients' Selves can get next to parts that are brimming with extreme emotions or impulses and, while they will feel some of that, will not lose control.

> *Therapist*: Ask the binge part if it knows which part tried to commit suicide.
> *Susan*: It says yes.
> *Therapist*: Will it point that suicide part out to you?
> *Susan*: I see a hooded figure in the dark. It's hard to see it clearly.
> *Therapist*: Let's put it in an enclosed room and you're outside the room. Can you see it in the room?
> *Susan*: Yes, but it's not happy being locked up.
> *Therapist*: How do you feel toward it?
> *Susan*: I'm relieved to be away from it, but I'm still frightened of it.
> *Therapist*: Find the parts that are afraid of it and ask them to trust you and me to just get to know it a little so we can relieve it of this dangerous role.

Ultimately, enough parts separate so that Susan wants to get to know the suicidal part and is no longer frightened by it. She enters the room and listens to its story and asks if it would like another role if she could find another way to get out of her misery. Thus, this conversation is very similar to the one she had earlier with the bingeing firefighter. The suicidal part gives her permission to work with the sad parts that it reacts to and, once she has formed a trusting relationship with those hurt exiles, they show her scenes from her past where they accumulated their burdens of pain and then remove those burdens – much as Joe's little boy did earlier in this chapter. After that unburdening, Susan returned to the suicidal and binge parts and found them both quite relieved and willing to show their own stories and unburden.

My colleagues and I have worked this way with a wide range of apparently destructive, addictive and irrational behaviors and always find that the part involved in those behaviors would like to change, but feels it cannot until the parts it protects or is polarized with also change. Thus, family therapy's big epiphany – that people cannot change in isolation because they are embedded in systems that constrain change – also applies to subpersonalities. No matter how many agreements Susan's binge part made to stop bingeing, it would still give her that impulse whenever the sad parts were triggered. Coercing or attacking it just makes it more fightened that she'll become suicidal and more determined to prevent that.

Nonetheless, therapists continue creating models designed to wrestle firefighters into submission and teach clients to cope with the fact that they'll always have these impulses. I believe that much of the mounting burnout among therapists is related to the frustration and disappointment inherent in misguided attempts to suppress firefighters. Therapists are always relieved and grateful when they are able to step out of those power struggles and remain compassionate – even with parts that, at first glance, seem intractably destructive.

Self-leadership of the therapist

It is this ability of the therapist to remain compassionate, confident, curious and respectful – what IFS calls Self-leadership – that creates the climate in which clients' parts can transform. Over the years, the Self and the concept of Self-leadership have become increasingly central to the IFS model. Effective therapists learn to maintain Self-leadership in the face of provocation from their clients' parts. In addition, the more one's life is Self-led, the more one is able to relax and enjoy it, and the more harmony one has in internal and external relationships. Self-leadership is similar to what the Buddhists call mindfulness and, like mindfulness, it requires practice.

As therapists we are fortunate to have a set of daily Self-leadership opportunities to practice, otherwise known as therapy sessions. Sessions are times deliberately to concentrate on practicing Self-leadership, and clients' parts provide a variety of challenges and provocations. Before a client arrives, a therapist can try to feel the energy of the Self in his or her body and then try to hold that energy flowing through the whole session. During the session, he or she is asking parts to step back and trust the Self – trust that energy. With particular clients, this is especially difficult.

Maintaining Self-leadership

To maintain Self-leadership in the face of provocation, a therapist's parts must be able to trust his or her Self enough quickly to step back and let his or her Self handle the situation, even while the parts are upset. When this works, a therapist will feel inner turmoil, but will not be overwhelmed by the upset parts and will remain the 'I' in the storm – dealing calmly, confidently, and even compassionately with the situation, while sensing parts that are seething or cowering inside.

The Self may want to speak for some of those parts so they feel acknowledged, but not have the parts take the driver's seat. When a part overtakes the therapist's Self, it often has the effect of distorting the therapist's perceptions and triggering parts of the client. In contrast, the Self can say the same words that a part would say and yet clients do not resist because they hear the caring behind the words. Their connection to the therapist is not broken, whereas it often is broken when parts take over.

Some therapists think that Self-leadership means always being warm, open and nurturing so they are reluctant to trust their Self in situations that call for assertiveness. This is a misconception. The Self can be forcefully protective or assertive. The energy of the Self is both nurturing and strong – yin and yang. Thus, it is possible and preferable to let the Self handle occasions where the therapist has to set boundaries as well as times when he or she is in a healing role. Much of the martial arts is about the practice of Self-leadership.

When parts take over

This is not to say that parts should never take over, just that Self-leadership means that when they do it is by choice rather than an automatic reaction. There are times when it's fun or necessary to allow a part to take over – for example, at a party, or when a person will not hear you any other way. But that should be temporary and by conscious choice.

Self-leadership is disarming: it melts the other's protectors and nurtures the other's exiles – it strengthens the Self-to-Self connection with other people. As hard as it is to maintain at first, Self-leadership ultimately saves energy because one does not go away from interactions still stewing about them. Parts have all kinds of arguments about why it is crucial for them to remain in control, but they really wish they did not have all that responsibility and want the Self to prove it can handle life for them.

Thus, like mindfulness, Self-leadership is a kind of spiritual practice in which we can engage continuously. For the therapist, this turns therapy into a spiritual practice rather than merely a job or a career.

External family constraints

Therapists who use the IFS model sometimes become so fascinated with their own or their clients' inner worlds that they forget that external relationships are also part of the web of constraints holding parts in their extreme roles. When discussing constraints with a client, it is important to include their family, work, or peer situations. IFS therapists will often work with a client's family before, or simultaneous to, going with the client on inner journeys. In many cases, the inner work will not be possible or will not go well until the client is no longer constantly bombarded by external provocation.

Thus, therapists must be adept at shifting back and forth between a client's inner and outer worlds. This shifting is made easier because the therapist can use the same principles and techniques to work with both levels (Schwartz, 1995). From this perspective then, a client's Self is embedded in a complex system that has two levels – internal and external – each of which can exert a powerful constraining force. Fortunately, however, improvements at one level often create improvements at the other so therapists do not have to work constantly at both. Instead, many IFS therapists shift rhythmically from one level to the other, creating an integration of intra-psychic and family therapies.

Conclusion

In this chapter I focused on the unique elements of the IFS model, which derive from its systemic base and the way in which it accesses and uses the Self. It is but one of many approaches that enter the labyrinth of the mind with sensitivity, and respect the personhood of those who dwell there. The more we continue to do this, the more we will learn from our Selves how to heal ourselves.

References

Assagioli, R. (1973) *The Act of Will*. New York: Penguin Books.

Assagioli, R. (1975) *Psychosynthesis: A Manual of Principles and Techniques*. London: Turnstone Press.

Breunlin, D., Schwartz, R. and Mac Kune-Karrer, B. (1992) *Metaframeworks*. San Francisco: Jossey-Bass.

Ferrucci, P. (1982) *What We May Be*. Los Angeles: J.P. Tarcher.

Freud, S. (1923/1961) 'The ego and the id', in J. Strachey (ed.), *The Standard Edition of the Complete Psychological Works of Sigmund Freud*, vol. 21. London: Hogarth Press.

Goulding, R. and Schwartz, R. (1995) *Mosaic Mind: Empowering the Tormented Selves of Childhood Sexual Abuse Survivors*. New York: Norton.

Haley, J. (1976) *Problem-Solving Therapy*. San Francisco: Jossey-Bass.

Jung, C.G. (1956) *Two Essays on Analytical Psychology*. Cleveland, OH: Meridian.

Jung, C.G. (1962) *Memories, Dreams, Reflections*. New York: Pantheon Books.

Jung, C.G. (1969a) *The Collected Works of C.G. Jung: The Archetypes and the Collective Unconscious*. (2nd edn, vol. 9) Princeton, NJ: Princeton University Press.

Jung, C.G. (1969b) *The Collected Works of C.G. Jung: The Structure and Dynamics of the Psyche*. (2nd edn, vol. 8) Princeton, NJ: Princeton University Press.

Minuchin, S. (1974) *Families and Family Therapy*. Cambridge, MA: Harvard University Press.

Minuchin, S. and Fishman, H.C. (1981) *Techniques of Family Therapy*. Cambridge, MA: Harvard University Press.

Rowan, J. (1990) *Subpersonalities: The People Inside Us*. London: Routledge.

Schwartz, R. (1987) 'Our multiple selves', *Family Therapy Networker*, 11: 25–31, 80–3.

Schwartz, R. (1988) 'Know thy selves', *Family Therapy Networker*, 12: 21–29.

Schwartz, R.C. (1992) 'Rescuing the exiles', *Family Therapy Networker*, 16: 33–7, 75.

Schwartz, R. (1995) *Internal Family Systems Therapy*. New York: Guilford Publications.

Stone, H. and Stone, S. (1993) *Embracing Your Inner Critic*. San Francisco: HarperCollins.

Stone, H. and Winkelman, S. (1985) *Embracing Ourselves*. Marina del Rey, CA: Devross and Co.

Watkins, J. (1978) *The Therapeutic Self*. New York: Human Sciences Press.

Watkins, J. and Johnson, R.J. (1982) *We, the Divided Self*. New York: Irvington.

Watkins, J. and Watkins, H. (1979) 'Ego states and hidden observers', *Journal of Altered States of Consciousness*, 5: 3–18.

14 PATHWAYS BETWEEN THE MULTIPLICITIES OF THE PSYCHE AND CULTURE: THE DEVELOPMENT OF DIALOGICAL CAPACITIES

Mary Watkins

Buber teaches us that in the Hasidic apprehension of reality 'a divine spark lives in every thing and being, but each such spark is enclosed by an isolating shell. Only man can liberate it and re-join it with the Origin: by holding holy converse with the thing and using it in a holy manner' (1970: 5–6). What does such 'holy converse' look and sound like, and where do we encounter it? I would like to draw attention to those qualities of dialogical presence that open up the possibility of such holy converse. Further, I want to explore the way that such dialogue echoes from one level of human experience to another: between the intrapsychic, the interpersonal and the cultural, the imaginal, the ecological, and the spiritual.

Unfortunately, it has become necessary to stress the relationship between intrapsychic dialogue and dialogue on these other levels. Often interior life has become used as part of a veil of privatism: a buffer against cultural, economic, and ecological realities and sufferings. In recent Western culture and its psychology we have lauded the development of the autonomous, highly rationalistic individual, bounded from others and nature, presumably responsible for his or her own fate. The threads of interrelationship between self and other, self and community, self and nature, self and spiritual reality have increasingly been neglected by the enactment of such a paradigm of selfhood. Correspondingly, the 'inner' world has been more and more looked to for meaning, relationship, ritual, and spirituality. It is imagined by some as though an untouched wilderness, a rich preserve to which one can turn for entertainment, mystery, and nurture.

Yet in the most private of the dialogues in our dreams and fantasies, in the most intimate portions of our conversations with ourselves, we come upon the metabolization of culture, economics, and politics. In the structure of power between ourselves and the other voices of thought, we can see the bounty of democratic form, the inbalances issuing from such things as racism and sexism, the struggle between the single voice of monotheism and the multiple voices of a more ancient polytheism, the efforts of a heroic ego attempting to assert control. While the dialogues of dreams and thought seem able to transcend culture in moments, their dramatic personae and the relations between them more frequently conserve it, reflect it. Few of us have had a dialogue with the upper-soul of a banana plant – a vision and dream not uncommon to the Temiar in Malaysia.

As we listen in our thought to the critiques of ourselves and of others, we hear not only the voice of the mother or the father, but the teacher, the style of pedagogy we were schooled in, the structure of the workplaces and their values that we have given credence to. The intrapsychic, the interior or the imaginal is not an isolated preserve; it is a distillation of history, culture, religion, and nature. We may be most able to recognize the voice of the mother – that major protagonist of interior life since industrialism's attack on the extended family and its removal of the father from the home – but there are many others, disguised by the quickness of their elliptical form of speech in our thoughts.

If we can hear how the intimate – so-called interior – dialogues of thought and dream body forth the public, the cultural and the economic, then can we continue to believe that these dialogues can deeply transform without attention to interpersonal, cultural, ecological and economic life? For instance, if racism in the culture affects the intrapsychic dialogue of a black child, causing one voice within her to derogate the color of her skin, should we attend to this through a psychotherapy that elicits and modifies self-talk? Or should there also be opportunities for dialogue at home, in the classroom, in the neighborhood, and in the larger culture which invite the voices that inhabit this child to speak, and which contribute toward an inner alternate voice of valuing, respecting, and cherishing the differences among us? Such an alternate voice could engage the voice of derision, question it, see through to its origins, insight its functions for the dominant culture, as well its functions for the child herself – trying as she is to assume a popular position, even to her own detriment.

In my work *Invisible Guests: The Development of Imaginal Dialogues* (Watkins, 1986), I have described the dialogical nature of thought, how thought is a mosaic of voices in conversation. The complexity of thought can begin to be grasped as we discern the nature of the various voices who are speaking, and become aware of the manner of relation between them and between our 'observing ego' and each of them. I argued there that the promoting of dialogue among the multiplicity was crucial to psychological awareness and well-being.

Let me be more specific about the kind of dialogical capacities I am referring to: the allowing of the other and the self freely to arise and to be given a chance for expression; to allow the other to exist autonomously from myself; patiently to wait for relations to occur in this open horizon; to move toward difference not with denial or rejection but with tolerance, curiosity, and a clear sense that it is in the encounter with otherness and multiplicity that deeper meanings can emerge. Such dialogue presupposes the capacity to grant the other an interiority different from our own – one that is not diminished or dehumanized in any way. Such dialogue assumes the capacity to de-center and to attempt to take the perspective of the other, to attempt to 'feel' the feelings of the other. It presupposes a capacity to take a third-person perspective on the self, so that one can reflect on how one's actions and attitudes have affected the other and the situation.

As these capacities develop, the self moves from being an unreflective center that finds the other to be either like oneself or as needed to be to serve the self's ends, to a self who is able to step to the side, who is aware of the co-creating nature of the interaction with the other, who knows that the other's experience departs from the self's – often in radical ways. In this chasm, where such departures differentiate self and other, there is a choice available to penetrate it through attempts at dialogue and understanding. This penetration is never only an opening toward the other's experience and reality. It signals a willingness to see and question as assumptions one's most cherished attitudes: the core of our own beliefs, approaches, and commitments. To be able deeply to entertain the difference that the other poses we must, as well, be able to disidentify from our passionately held beliefs, and be able to see what ideologies they are based on and to be able to interrogate the function and effects of these beliefs (Bohm, 1996). Through the grasping of the other's difference from us – be it intrapsychic other or interpersonal other – we come to see more clearly who we are. Jung puts clearly the interpenetration of inner dialogue and outer objectivity:

> The present day shows with appalling clarity how little able people are to let the other man's argument count, although this capacity is a fundamental and indispensable condition for any human community. Everyone who proposes to come to terms with himself must reckon with this basic problem. For, to the degree that he does not admit the validity of the other person, he denies the 'other' within himself the right to exist – and vice versa. The capacity for inner dialogue is a touchstone for outer objectivity. (Jung, 1969: para. 187)

It is through such dialogue with the other, the stranger, that the liberation and re-joining that Buber (1970) speaks of can occur.

This manner of holy converse can describe equally well relations with others as our relations with ourselves, imaginal others, the beings of nature and earth, and that which we take to be divine. As such dialogue occurs there is a shift from the ego as a monolithic, heroic center – one which struggles to maintain power – to an 'ego' which seeks to mediate the multiplicity of any given situation. Elsewhere I have contrasted the individualistic self of modern Western cultures with the paradigm of the interdependent self (Watkins, 1992) or what Sampson (1988) has called the ensembled self. The ensembled self is aware of multiplicity at all levels. It locates power and control in a field of forces that includes but goes beyond the person (Sampson, 1988). Dialogue is a way of working amid this field, this multiplicity.

In our Cartesian psychologies we have carefully sorted self from other, body from mind, the imaginal from the perceptual, the spiritual from the material, the so-called 'inner' from the so-called 'outer'. Experientially these separations are not as neat as our modern categories would suggest. Once made discrete, theoreticians approach how they are related in opposing, often lopsided ways. For instance, either imaginal dialogues are seen to subserve interpersonal dialogues allowing us to rehearse for more of the 'real' thing, or interpersonal dialogue is viewed more as a diversion from the 'more important' unfolding of subjective experience. Which side of the Cartesian see-saw is seen as more valuable, more originative of the other? Do experiences with imaginary playmates harm children – as claimed in the 1950s – because they defend children from 'actual' friendship; or does social interaction obscure our listening to the 'springs of the self'? Here my hope is to shine some light on the subtle – yet strong – threads that hold these domains together in a more interdependent web. I will do this through a close look at dialogue, as I see I–Thou dialogue as a necessary capacity when we understand the multiplicity we are homed in on – on the levels of both psyche and culture.

Dialogue is both a fact of our givenness and a deep potentiality of our being. We are thrown from our beginning into a multiplicity – ancestors, family, trees, rivers, earth, animals, neighbors. As Jung said, 'The self comprises infinitely more than the mere ego, as symbols have shown since time immemorial. It is just as much another or others as it is the ego. Individuation does not exclude the world but includes it' (1947: 477). We are always selves-in-relation or selves-in-dialogue. What is at stake is the kind of relationship we are in, and the paths from it to a manner of dialogical relationship that liberates being.

When we emphasize this frame, there are a number of developmental theorists whose work speaks to the interpenetration of imaginal, social, cultural, natural, and spiritual domains in terms of the development of dialogical capacity: for example, the research on the coordination of inter-personal perspectives and resulting pair therapy of Robert Selman; the work on adolescent girls' loss of voice of Brown and Gilligan; and the work with women's ways of knowing that affect both their internal dialogue and their relations to others of Mary Belenky and her colleagues; the large group dialogue work of David Bohm and Patrick de Mare; and, finally, the liberational pedagogy of Paulo Freire. I will turn to these as exemplars to help us see some of the developmental threads that criss-cross between dialogical domains, and to establish signposts beyond this text for those who wish to pursue the cultivation of dialogue.

The capacity to play and the capacity to be a friend: differentiating and coordinating the perspectives of self and other

Klein and Winnicott noted that some disturbed children have an incapacity to play, which psychotherapy must address. In Winnicott's words: 'where playing is not possible then the work done by the therapist is directed towards bringing the patient from a state of not being able to play into a state of being able to play' (1971: 38). Selman and Schultz (1990), working with the interpersonal relations of emotionally disturbed children, have noted that interactive fantasy play is markedly absent in the history of children whose interpersonal understanding is at primitive levels. These children do not understand that self and other can interpret the same event differently; that is, the other is not understood to have an interiority different from my own. They are unable to differentiate between an unintentional act of another and an intentional one (the action is equated with the intent). Neither do they differentiate physical from psychological characteristics of the person (that is, if the person is deemed pretty then she is a good person). In short, they are unable to 'differentiate and integrate the self's and other's points of view through an understanding of the relation between the thoughts, feelings, and wishes of each person' (Selman and Schultz, 1990: 6).

This capacity to differentiate and integrate the self's and other's points of view is at the core of dialogical capacity. As Selman and Schultz (1990) point out, a deficit in this ability shows both in problematic interpersonal relating and in an absence of the dialogues of pretend play. Further, however, they describe how the seeds for interpersonal dialogue can be planted in the dialogues of play. In their pair therapy work with children who are isolated by their own patterns of withdrawal or aggression, they pair a submissive, withdrawn child (self-transforming style) with a child who is over-controlling, sometimes downright bullying (other-transforming style). Initially, they each cling to his or her own style, making impossible a deepening of relationship. Selman and Schultz share an image from a session with two such boys where one traps the other in the up position on the see-saw. There is no movement! In pretend play these two boys initially replicate their roles on the see-saw:

> Andy initiated a fantasy in which he was the television/comic book character 'The Hulk,' a large, powerful, fearsome mutant who is good inside, but who cannot control his feelings to let the good direct him. Paul then took a part as 'Mini-Man,' a being of his own creation who is smaller than anything else in the world and can hide in flowers. . . . The play was a fantasy in which one boy had the power to control the thoughts and will of the other by virtue of a psychological 'force field.' (Selman and Shultz, 1990: 169–70)

With these roles personified, however, each boy seems as though seduced into wanting to embody each of the available roles. Paul experiments with putting up his force field and then with 'zapping' his partner, just as Andy relaxes his grip on power and enjoys the submissive position of 'mini-Man'.

> Theoretically speaking we believe that this switching of roles in play is a key therapeutic process, in effect a way to *share experience*. Andy was able to relax his defenses and express the message that part of him was happy to be or even had a need to be controlled, taken care of, told what to do. He could abandon for the

moment the tenderly held goals for which he generally fought so fiercely. . . . And Paul, often too frightened to take the initiative in actual interactions, was able to take steps toward assuming the control that felt too risky in real life, despite its practical and emotional attractions. . . . When it is just play, children can dress rehearse for changing roles on the stage of real-life interaction. (Selman and Shultz, 1990: 171)

Here we see the interrelation between the dialogues of play and those of peer relationship. Now, rather than 'inner speech' being the internalization of actual social discourse, as in Vygotsky's theory, we see the dialogues of play as the seed that travels up into the soil of potential friendship. Indeed, in Selman and Schultz's (1990) third year of work with these boys, we see them able to withstand the storm of each other's emotions, to venture into different roles with one other, and to begin to share around the deepest areas of each boy's concern: missing their absent parents, and the fear of one boy that his mother does not miss or love him.

Andy's tone is low. 'That's the problem – my mother doesn't miss me' . . . Andy relates an incident from the past weekend, when he and his parents were going to go out together. As Andy tells it, he rode off on his bike telling his mother where he'd be, but his mother forgot to call him. 'And when I came back my mom had gone to bed, and my dad had gone to sleep. And I was left alone' . . . Paul says softly, 'I'm sorry.' After a brief pause, he adds, 'By the way Andy, if you see any raffle tickets around, I've lost mine.' Rather than being put off and hurt by this sudden change of subject on Paul's part, Andy immediately picks up on the new topic. 'Let's go look for them in the afterschool room,' he says.

Are not such moments of friendship creative of our capacity to receive and hear our own pain, to be with it, and yet capable of engaging beyond it?

Sustaining one's voice among others

For authentic dialogue to occur it is not enough for one to be able to differentiate one's perspective from the other and to allow the other a voice. One must also be able to maintain one's own voice amid the fray of relationship. For instance, the most disturbing auditory hallucinations are not due to a confusion of perception with image, but because the ego's point of view becomes swamped by the voice(s) of the other. The other's command often becomes the self's action without benefit of reflection. Dialogical space collapses as the self becomes the instrument of the voice (Watkins, 1986). In less severe experience we witness similar imbalances in power between 'inner' voices that criticize, berate, predict doom, and the often more fragile self who is the victim of these critiques and disparagements. Indeed, the psychotherapy of depression can be seen as addressing such inner abuses of power that leave other voices silenced or rendered impotent. The inner sustaining of voice in situations where the culture (family, school, wider culture) one is in has systematically discouraged it, is particularly difficult – often impossible. Carol Gilligan and her colleagues' work with adolescent girls exemplifies this (Brown and Gilligan, 1992).

In turning their attention to normative development in pre-adolescent and adolescent American girls, they unfortunately found that not all the changes they witnessed in girls were ideal. On the one hand:

> As these girls grow older they become less dependent on external authorities, less egocentric or locked into their own experience or point of view, more differentiated from others in the sense of being able to distinguish their feelings and thoughts from those of other people, more autonomous in the sense of being able to rely on or to take responsibility for themselves, more appreciative of the complex interplay of voices and perspectives in any relationship, more aware of the diversity of human experience and the differences between societal and cultural groups.

On the other hand, they found

> that this developmental progress goes hand in hand with evidence of a loss of voice, a struggle to authorize or take seriously their own experience – to listen to their own voices in conversation and respond to their feelings and thoughts – increased confusion, sometimes defensiveness, as well as evidence for the replacement of real with inauthentic or idealized relationships. If we consider responding to oneself, knowing one's feelings and thoughts, clarity, courage, openness, and free-flowing connections with others and the world as signs of psychological health, as we do, then these girls are in fact not developing, but are showing evidence of loss and struggle and signs of an impasse in their ability to act in the face of conflict. (Brown and Gilligan, 1992: 6)

In order to maintain the semblance of relationship these girls were struggling with 'a series of disconnections that seem at once adaptive and psychologically wounding, between psyche and body, voice and desire, thoughts and feelings, self and relationship' (Brown and Gilligan, 1992: 7). Too often girls were found stepping away from articulating their thoughts and feelings if these would bring them into conflict with others. What was initially conscious public disavowal of thoughts and feelings, over time became unconscious disclaiming. Girls then expressed that they felt confused about what they thought and felt – that they were unsure. Over time, many took themselves out of authentic relationship – with others and with themselves. They became unable to identify relational violations, and were thus more susceptible to abuse. Brown and Gilligan began to wonder if they were 'witnessing the beginning of psychological splits and relational struggles well documented in the psychology of women' (1992: 106).

To encourage girls' resistance and resilience, Gilligan and her colleagues realized that it was not enough to help girls put into words for others their thoughts and feelings. For many, the fear of how their thoughts and feelings would be received had already metamorphosed into the girls' not listening to themselves. And so the women working with these girls tried to find ways to help to prevent the inner ear going deaf and to revive a capacity to listen to one's selves, *while at the same time* building a group where the girls could experience that others can survive their voice(s): that authentic dialogue is possible, not just false or idealized relations. Without such an experience of being received – to counter the culture's messages – the ear cannot reawaken and the voice cannot speak; be it in 'internal' dialogue or 'external' dialogue.

Akin to Selman and Schultz's (1990) move toward play, Gilligan's team moved toward supporting the girls' diary and journal writing, their dramatic and poetic writing, and their literally claiming their voices in voice work.

Dialogue – in the ideal sense – necessitates both the capacity deeply to receive the other *and* the capacity to receive oneself; to allow the other a voice *and* to allow the self voice. Dialogue requires the experience of being listened into words.

Being silenced vs opportunities for dialogue: voice, mind, relationship and social action

Belenky et al. (1986), in *Women's Ways of Knowing: The Development of Self, Voice, and Mind*, vividly describe the interpenetration of dialogical domains I am addressing, as they study different ways of women's knowing. In one group of women they studied, women's silence in adulthood was linked to family experiences of neglect and abuse. These women were passive, subdued, and subordinate in adulthood. 'The ever-present fear of volcanic eruptions and catastrophic events leaves children speechless and numbed, unwilling to develop their capacities for hearing and knowing' (1986: 159). These women experienced themselves as mindless and voiceless. Their childhoods were not only lived in isolation from their family members and others outside the family, but most often were lived *without play*. The intersection of an absence of dialogue with an absence of play turned out to be particularly damaging for these children as they grew to womanhood.

> In the ordinary course of development, the use of play metaphors gives way to language – a consensually validated symbol system – allowing for more precise communication of meanings between persons. Outer speech becomes increasingly internalized as it is transformed into inner speech. Impulsive behavior gives way to behavior that is guided by the actor's own symbolic representations of hopes, plans, and meanings. Without playing, conversing, listening to others, and drawing out their own voice, people fail to develop a sense that they can talk and think things through. (1986: 33)

Moreover, the world becomes a place of simple dichotomies – good/bad, big/little, win/lose – losing all subtlety and texture.

Without the imaginal dialogues of play and substantive interpersonal dialogues the child is constrained within a narrow band of reality. Both play and dialogue allow the child to visit the perspectives of others, as well as to dream of that which has not yet come into reality. 'What is' and 'who one is' become radically widened as one decenters from the ego's perspective and the given. Through the metaphorizing of play one leaps past the given confines of 'self' and 'reality'. The dialogues of play and the dialogues of social interaction are both creative of the self and liberatory of the self. Through each empathic leap, through each re-embodiment of ourselves in play, we pass beyond our usual borders and exceed what has been. What 'is' is surpassed by what might be, and 'who' I am is replaced by my transit beyond myself – either through projection of the self or through the reception of the other. Working an issue through play – expressing it, addressing it from several perspectives, taking the role of the others in play – is translated into the dialogues of thought and those of our everyday interactions. It should come as no surprise that the complexity and subtlety of a child's play, his or her flexibility in moving between the dramatis personae, can be seen in their participation in interpersonal dialogue, and in their capacities for reflection.

The childhoods that do not give opportunity for pretend play – that movement between dramatis personae – whose families discourage interpersonal dialogue and whose schools limit the classroom experience to verbal exchanges that are unilateral and teacher-initiated, make it highly unlikely that children will learn the 'give and take of dialogue' (Belenky et al., 1986: 34), giving them access to what lies beyond a narrow self which has been schooled for silence. For such children, and the adults that are generated from them, words have force only when uttered violently. Thus they

> tend to be action-oriented, with little insight into their own behaviours or motivations. Since they do not expect to be heard they expect no response, the volume of their voices is more important than the content. They lack verbal negotiating skills and do not expect conflicts to be resolved through non-violent means. (Belenky et al., 1986: 160)

Those who do not escape silence pass the legacy of their early homes on to their children:

> Mothers who have so little sense of their own minds and voices are unable to imagine such capacities in their children. Not being fully aware of the power of words for communicating meaning, they expect their children to know what is on their minds without the benefit of words. These parents do not tell their children what they mean by 'good' – much less why. Nor do they ask their children to explain themselves. . . .
>   We observed these mothers 'backhanding' their children whenever the child asked questions, even when the questions stemmed from genuine curiosity and desire for knowledge. It was as if the questions themselves were another example of the child's 'talking back' and 'disrespect.' Such a mother finds the curious, thinking child's questions stressful, since she does not yet see herself as an authority who has anything to say or teach. (1986: 163–4)

Interestingly, these women were not aware of any experience within themselves of dialogue with a self or of having an inner voice; nor did their words express a familiarity with introspection or a sense of their own consciousness.

Those women in Belenky's study who were able to emerge from silence into adulthood had the benefit of a school which encouraged the cultivation of mind and an interaction with the arts, had been able to forge significant relationships outside the home despite the prohibition not to do so, or had 'created such relationships for themselves through the sheer power of their imaginations, by endowing their pets and imaginary playmates with those attributes that nourish the human potential' (1986: 163).

In the other ways of knowing that Belenky et al. describe – received knowing, subjective knowing, procedural knowing and constructed knowing – intrapsychic and interpersonal dialogue are intimately related to each other, together forming a sense of the flatness or complexity and fullness of reality. For instance, in received knowing women experience others as the authority, silencing their own voices to be better able to imbibe the wisdom of others. It is not surprising that they seek to eliminate ambiguity from their worlds, and can be described themselves as literal-minded. On the other hand, subjective knowers conceive of all truth arising internally, stilling their public voice, and often turning a 'deaf ear to other voices'. Often distrusting words, they cover disagreement with conformity, and live in the isolation of their own thoughts and inner voices.

In what is clearly their preferred developmental telos, Belenky and her colleagues describe those who experience constructed knowing. In this way of knowing, knowledge is contextual. There are multiple viewpoints to be had, but not all are equally adequate to revealing what one is trying to understand. These knowers are familiar with listening to the inner voice or voices. Yet they know that even an inner voice may be wrong at times, for it is but one part of a whole. They are, as well, adept at patient listening to the voices of others. They have a high tolerance for internal contradiction and ambiguity.

Just as the child breaks the confines of the given through the dialogue of play, so too may the adult who can move between perspectives and systems of knowing. Liberated from subservience to external authority, to any one system of thought, and from slavish devotion to their own internal voices, these knowers have the dialogical tools to break the oppressive aspects of 'reality'. Strikingly, their nurture, care, and engagement with their own voices, the voices of others, and ideas broaden out to their nurture and care of aspects of the world. They understand that cultural dialogue itself can be intervened in, affected, and transformed. Such a work, however, cannot be undertaken when there is little or no awareness of the multiplicity of thought, little or no experience of being listened into speech, or of practice being an active participant in the give and take of dialogue – revealing as it does the perspectival nature of truth.

From cultures of silence to liberatory dialogue: the work of Paulo Freire

This connection between coming to see the context one is in, gaining voice in relation to this context, and being able creatively to engage in efforts to affect culture is beautifully articulated in the work of Paulo Freire. Here silence and lack of dialogical capacity is understood to arise through oppression, which purposely creates voicelessness and obscures context in order to maintain power. Paulo Freire, the founder of the literacy movement in Brazil and radical pedagogist, argues that − for the disenfranchised − learning to read should involve a process of becoming able to decode the cultural and socio-economic circumstances that shape your life and your thinking. Once able to decode these conditions, one is then able to participate in the shaping of those circumstances. He called the first step in this empowering process 'conscientization', a group process which allows one actively to engage with the structures one has previously identified with and been blind to.

In Freire's model, an 'animator' helps group participants to question their day-to-day experience, their concerns and suffering: exploring the relation between daily life and the cultural dictates that suffuse it. Here words, much like play for the child, begin to open up the realm of the possible, liberating 'reality' from the bonds of the given. Efforts at change are not directed foremost to the individual level, but to wider cultural change that will, in the end, affect the participants. This change becomes possible through the second step of Freire's method: 'annunciation'. Once a group knows how to decode the dominant paradigm and its effects − through having spoken together − they can begin to conceive of social arrangements which are more just through the process of dialogue.

Why is this process necessary? Freire says that the dominant class attempts 'by means of the power of its ideology, to make everyone believe that its ideas are the ideas of the nation' (Freire and Faundez, 1989: 74). A dominant paradigm operates by way of the monologue, not dialogue. It requires voicelessness on the part of the other to sustain itself. 'The power of an ideology to rule', says Freire, 'lies basically in the fact that it is embedded in the activities of the everyday life' (Ibid.: 26–7).

It is through dialogue that one breaks out of the 'bureaucratization' of mind, where there can be a rupture from previously established patterns. 'In fact, there is no creativity without *ruptura*, without a break from the old, without conflict in which you have to make a decision' (Freire, in Horton and Freire, 1990: 38). For Freire, true education is not the accumulation of information, placed in the student by the teacher. True education must encourage this rupture through dialogue. Teacher and student must each be able to affect, to communicate with, and to challenge each other, rather than perpetuate domination through monological teaching methods that further disempower.

Freire is well aware of the internalization of oppression. Through the animator's questioning, a participant begins to claim what she or he knows about the situation under discussion. Instead of being a passive recipient of the situation, the words of writing and speaking usher a transformation from object to subject. It is such a subject who can then dream a different reality than that which is given. The animator is careful not to indoctrinate, to announce the problem and the solution; to do so would intensify the internalized oppression the participant is subject to, encouraging inner and outer silence and subservience. It is the radical listening, hosting, of the animator that opens a space for the voice to occur – both internally and externally. As the other group members, who are similar to the first one, are able to speak and take hold of their situation in words, this empowering of voice is felt by those who listen, as if it were their own.

With brilliant clarity Freire connects dialogue with love:

> Dialogue cannot exist, however, in the absence of profound love for the world and for women and men. The naming of the world, which is an act of creation and re-creation, is not possible if it is not infused with love. Love is at the same time the foundation of dialogue and dialogue itself. It is thus necessarily the task of responsible subjects and cannot exist in a relation of domination. Domination reveals the pathology of love: sadism in the dominator and masochism in the dominated. Because love is an act of courage, not of fear, love is commitment to others. No matter where the oppressed are found, the act of love is commitment to their cause – the cause of liberation. And this commitment, because it is loving, is dialogical . . . (Freire, 1970: 77)

Dialogue across difference: Bohm's large group dialogue

In Freire and Faundez's work the concept of culture is not linked to ideas of unity, but to diversity and tolerance. This shift toward the acknowledgment of diversity, invites voices to speak that have been marginalized by the dominant culture and its paradigms. This movement from center to margin requires a process of dialogue that assumes difference and seeks to articulate it. Truth is not located in a particular perspective, it 'is to be found in the "becoming" of dialogue' (Faundez, in Freire and Faundez, 1989: 32).

David Bohm, physicist and colleague of Krishnamurti, describes a kind of large group dialogue where it is through the difference that is present that one can begin to hear one's own assumptions. Bohm asks that once we hear these assumptions we try to suspend them, rather than using our character-istic defensive moves of overpowering the other voices – defending our assumptions as the truth. This acknowledgment and suspension of assump-tions is done in the service of begininning to see what it is one means. It is through the diversity of the group that the partialness of a single mind can be grasped. The opportunity for this kind of large group dialogue begins to release the self from such partiality, and makes possible a more complex and subtle form of thinking. De Mare, a colleague of Bohm's, says that:

[d]ialogue has a tremendous thought potential: it is from dialogue that ideas spring to transform the mindlessness and massification that accompany social oppression, replacing it with higher levels of cultural sensitivity, intelligence, and humanity. (de Mare et al. 1991: 17).

When we defend an assumption, says Bohm, we are at the same time 'pushing out whatever is new. . . . There is a great deal of violence in the opinions we are defending' (1996: 15). Through coming to see our own and others' assumptions we arrive at a place where we can begin to think together, seeing more of the totality that comprises our situation. Sampson (1993: 1220, 1223) is careful to remind us that allowing others to speak is not enough, however, if they cannot be 'heard in their own way, on their own terms', rather than constrained to 'use the voice of those who have constructed them'.

Here, one is required to take a third-person point of view toward oneself, reflecting on how one's actions, attitudes, and assumptions arise from particular ideologies. And, further, how the ideologies we are identified with have affected the other – the stranger.

As is the case in imaginal dialogues, such dialogue in a large group requires the suspension of usual egoic modes of operation: judging, condemning, deeming oneself superior (or inferior). These interfere with listening deeply, with the radical entertaining of the other, which at the same moment can awaken us to where we each stand. Bohm releases thought from the confines of an individual person. To adequately think, we need to invite and witness the multiplicity within the group. Without this reflective, conscious practice, mind remains partial – blinded by the assumptions it has identified with.

Coda

In the end, I am urging us not to focus only on inner multiplicity and inner dialogue. Imaginal dialogues do not exist separately from the other domains of our lives. The present hierarchies of our culture, schools, and family – and thus of mind – do not deeply invite dialogue; neither does the voicelessness directly resulting from such hierarchies of power. Here I am trying to underscore the interpenetration of dialogues with imaginal others, with dialogues with oneself, one's neighbors, within one's community, between communities, and with the earth and its creatures. The effort to section off the imaginal from this larger fabric is, at best, defensive; at its worst, it is wasteful of the energies needed to work at much-needed reconciliations. Depth psychology – if it is not to become a Euro-American relic from the nineteenth and twentieth centuries – must use its energy to penetrate the depths of difference. Dialogue is the method for this hosting, penetration, and holding of difference.

These examples show the deep reciprocity between what I have called dialogical domains. The liberation of a potential voice through play, for instance, can be a harbinger of a substantial shift in the range of how one can be with another, interpersonally. Likewise, the experience of deep inter-personal receptivity in a group can call into voice someone who has been silenced; this establishment of dialogical space is then more available in internal conversation. Such a focus on dialogue moves psychological focus from the self and its interiority to the 'between', across domains.

The implications of this for those interested in the recognition of poly-psychism and the promotion of imaginal dialogue are profound. We are pointed not only toward an illumination of psychic structures and their personified voices but toward the creation of childcare contexts where the dramatic fray of play can be delighted in; to elementary schools where the leap between self and others in a small group can be practiced; to spiritual education and practice where the voices within silence can be discerned and addressed. It points us toward high schools and colleges where previously marginalized voices can be admitted to the mosaic, changing the underlying structure of education from the conveyance of dominant paradigms to one of dialogue across difference. It turns us toward the processes of non-violent communication and often of reconciliation that are needed to nurture the neighborhoods and communities – and ultimately nations – that we are homed in. And, finally, it turns us toward the dialogue beyond words required between nature and humans if our actions are, finally, to preserve this earth.

References

Belenky, M., Clinchy, B., Goldberger, N. and Tarule, J. (1986) *Women's Ways of Knowing*. New York: Basic Books.

Bohm, D. (1996) *On Dialogue*. London: Routledge.

Brown, L. and Gilligan, C. (1992) *Meeting at the Crossroads*. New York: Ballantine Books.

Buber, M. (1970) *The Way of Man*. New York: Citadel Press.

de Mare, P., Piper, R. and Thompson, S. (1991) *Koinonia: From Hate, Through Dialogue, to Culture in the Large Group*. London: Karnac Books.

Freire, P. (1970) *Pedagogy of the Oppressed*. New York: Seabury.

Freire, P. and Faundez, A. (1989) *Learning to Question: A Pedagogy of Liberation*. New York: Continuum.

Horton, M. and Freire, P. (1990) *We Make the Road by Walking: Conversations on Education and Social Change*. Philadelphia: Temple University Press.

Jung, C.G. (1947) 'Der Geist der Psychologie', *Eranos-Jahrbuch* 1946: 385–490.

Jung, C.G. (1969) 'The structure and dynamics of the psyche', *Collected Works*, vol. 8. Princeton, NJ: Princeton University Press.

Sampson, E. (1988) 'The debate on individualism: Indigenous psychologies of the individual and their role in personal and societal functioning', *American Psychologist*, 43 (1): 15–22.

Sampson, E. (1993) 'Identity politics: Challenges to psychology's understanding', *American Psychologist*, 48 (12): 1219–30.

Selman, R. and Schultz, L. (1990) *Making a Friend in Youth*. Chicago, IL: University of Chicago Press.

Watkins, M. (1986) *Invisible Guests: The Development of Imaginal Dialogues*, Hillsdale, NJ: Analytic Press.

Watkins, M. (1992) 'From individualism to the interdependent self: changing paradigms in psychotherapy', *Psychological Perspectives*, 27: 52–69.

Winnicott, D.W. (1971) *Playing and Reality*. New York: Penguin Books.

NAME INDEX

SUBJECT INDEX

Entries are arranged in word-by-word alphabetical order. Page numbers in italics refer to figures.